JESUS
& THE RESTORATION
OF ISRAEL

A Critical Assessment of N. T. Wright's

JESUS AND THE VICTORY OF GOD

Edited by Carey C. Newman

InterVarsity Press	Paternoster Press
Downers Grove, Illinois, USA	Carlisle, UK

InterVarsity Press
P.O. Box 1400, Downers Grove IL 60515, USA
World Wide Web: www.ivpress.com
E-mail: mail@ivpress.com

Paternoster Press
P.O. Box 300, Carlisle, Cumbria, CA3 0QS, UK
World Wide Web: www.paternoster-publishing.com

InterVarsity Press® is the book-publishing division of InterVarsity Christian Fellowship/USA®, a student movement active on campus at hundreds of universities, colleges and schools of nursing in the United States of America, and a member movement of the International Fellowship of Evangelical Students. For information about local and regional activities, write Public Relations Dept., InterVarsity Christian Fellowship/USA, 6400 Schroeder Rd., P.O. Box 7895, Madison, WI 53707-7895.

Paternoster Press is an imprint of Paternoster Publishing.

Cover photograph: Erich Lessing/Art Resource: New York

USA ISBN 0-8308-1587-2
UK ISBN 0-85364-986-3

Printed in the United States of America ∞

Library of Congress Cataloging-in-Publication Data

Jesus & the restoration of Israel : a critical assessment of N. T.
  Wright's Jesus and the victory of God / edited by Carey C. Newman.
      p.   cm.
    Includes bibliographical references.
    ISBN 0-8308-1587-2 (pbk. : alk. paper)
    1.   Wright, N. T. (Nicholas Thomas).   Jesus and the victory of God.
  2. Jesus Christ—Historicity.   I. Newman, Carey C.   II. Title:
  Jesus and the restoration of Israel.
  BT303.2.J45   1999
  232—dc21   99-36483
                                                                              CIP

British Library Cataloguing in Publication Data

A catalogue record for this book is available from the British Library.

20	19	18	17	16	15	14	13	12	11	10	9	8	7	6	5	4	3	2	1
15	14	13	12	11	10	09	08	07	06	05	04	03	02	01	00	99			

To Alan and Larry
Scholars, Mentors, Friends

Contents

Preface

I FIRST NEED TO RECOGNIZE THE GOOD SENSE OF DAN REID AT INTERVARSITY PRESS FOR suggesting this project. My initial reaction to his invitation was suspicion: not only did I question his choosing me as the editor, but I also openly wondered abut the wisdom of producing yet another book on the historical Jesus. Although full justification must await the considered judgment of readers, several features of this volume have convinced me (at least) that this project is worthwhile—even imperative.

Part of this book's importance is purely derivative. It rides the crest of the wave created by N. T. Wright's audacity. He has proposed a six-volume series, Christian Origins and the Question of God, that treats (1) method and background, (2) the historical Jesus, (3) the resurrection, (4) the Gospels, (5) Paul and (6) the early church. Not since Rudolf Bultmann has anyone attempted the full hermeneutical, historical, literary and theological task. Wright's *Jesus and the Victory of God* thus merits a sustained evaluation not afforded by normal reviews or review essays simply because of the potential importance of the series and the crucial role that Jesus plays in the series. Simply stated, if Wright fails in his reconstruction of the historical Jesus, then the whole series is in serious jeopardy.

While compiling a list of issues to be treated was fairly straightforward, selecting contributors was a bit trickier. Most of the time scholarly conversations are rather insular, taking place within (and not among) different disciplines and theological perspectives. Since Wright willingly takes on all parties in *Jesus and the Victory of God,* regardless of discipline or theological stripe, it seemed best to be as inclusive in providing critique. Therefore, in what follows readers will find essays by historians of Second Temple Judaism, Scripture scholars, systematic theologians and philosophers. This volume intentionally widens the scholarly conversation about the historical Jesus beyond the normal confines of discipline and perspective.

Consequently, this volume pulls no punches. Readers will find contributors who deem Wright's overall approach preferable to other options, even if they feel compelled to identify major and serious problems Wright has yet to resolve. Other contributors finally reject Wright's agenda, even if they find large parts of his argument quite convincing. Thus, ironically, many of the endorsements of Wright's work are given begrudgingly, while most of the criticisms are levied with reluctance. This too makes for a very interesting read.

Finally, I find it a great privilege to acknowledge the contributions of two scholars, Alan F. Segal and Larry W. Hurtado. Although these two had very little formal involvement in the production of this book, they have had a good bit of influence in helping shape who I am. To them I offer my sincere thanks.

Carey C. Newman
Ash Wednesday
Louisville, Kentucky

Part One

Introduction

One

Right Reading, Reading Wright

CAREY C. NEWMAN

*J*ESUS JUST WON'T GO AWAY. THE RECENT FLURRY OF ARTICLES AND BOOKS DEVOTED to the study of the historical Jesus, and not just to Jesus as some disembodied theological idea, stands as a literary monument to his enduring power to attract and fascinate, inspire and command. He won't go away because we won't let him, and he won't go away because, finally, he won't let us let him.[1]

The debate about the historical Jesus taking place today, however, is quite different from that of just two or three decades ago. The question that drove research throughout the middle years of the twentieth century and was fiercely argued and typically answered in either minimalist or maximalist ways is this: What can be assuredly known about the historical Jesus? Today, however, the question has been reformulated: Which Jesus should be remembered?[2]

This new question does not reflect a more sanguine opinion on the nature of historical reconstruction (in general) or of the canonical Gospels (in particular). Quite the contrary. The profiles of Jesus spawned by Q, Thomas or some combination of other real (or reconstructed) documents are now regularly pitted against—and most often preferred over—those generated by the canonical Gospels. Suspicion (of the canonical Gospels) has found a new best friend in openly revisionist historiography.[3] The debate remains as intense as ever, if not more so.

Ignoring proverbial wisdom, N. T. Wright willingly takes on all parties in his *Jesus and the Victory of God* (often abbreviated as *JVG*).[4] With those who wish to lay claim to the mantel of Enlightenment historiography (but against those who think that the theological concerns associated with Jesus somehow insulate them from serious, historical study), Wright concurs that the question of the historical Jesus cannot be avoided. With those who believe something can be known about Jesus (and against those who hide behind a skeptical, Enlightenment epistemology), Wright avers that investigations of Jesus are no different from historical studies of other figures of antiquity and, thus, that the major historical questions (who was Jesus? what were his aims? why did he die?) not only are fair game but are, in principle, answerable. And with those whose first line of appeal is to the canonical Gospels (and against those who privilege later or nonextant sources), Wright seeks a reconstruction of Jesus that, on the one hand, is grounded in first-century Judaism and that, on the other, can explain the nature and shape of Christianity. Wright's *Jesus* charts a third way.

Wright divides the almost seven hundred pages of substantive text that compose *Jesus and the Victory of God* into fourteen chapters, arranged in four parts. Part one clears the deck. After a whirlwind tour of the last one hundred years of Jesus research (chapter one), Wright focuses his attention on the last twenty years. Here Wright strategically deploys the figures of William Wrede and Albert Schweitzer to highlight the two dominant approaches in the study of the historical Jesus—the wide and oft traveled road of Wrede's "consistent skepticism" (chapter two) and the narrow gate of Schweitzer's "consistent eschatology" (chapter three). Having decided to go the way of Schweitzer, Wright then previews his own hypothesis and its associated problems (chapter four).

Part two profiles the mindset of Jesus against the worldview of Second Temple Judaism. This entails an investigation of the prophetic praxis characteristic of Jesus (chapter five), the story (or stories) of the kingdom that Jesus implicitly invoked and explicitly told (chapters six through eight) and the way in which his words and deeds challenged and ultimately undermined the cherished symbols of Judaism, a subversive posture that consequently placed Jesus on a collision course with the temple authorities (chapter nine). To conclude part two, Wright examines the way in which Jesus' prophetic deeds and kingdom preaching provide coherent answers to the major questions of any worldview (chapter ten).

Part three concentrates on discovering the aims and beliefs of Jesus. According to Wright, Jesus believed himself to be the Messiah, a vocational calling that included prophetically enacting in himself Israel's long-awaited return from exile (chapter eleven), intentionally dying to achieve the defeat of Israel's true enemy (chapter twelve) and announcing, symbolizing and embodying Yahweh's return to Zion (chapter thirteen). Finally, in part four (chapter fourteen), Wright briefly draws together the major strands of his research.

Jesus and the Victory of God can only be understood as the second installment in Wright's planned six-volume series devoted to Christian origins and the question of God. The first volume, *The New Testament and the People of God* (often abbreviated as *NTPG*),[5] heralds the way for this one. (The extensive cross-referencing in *JVG* to *NTPG* proves the connectedness.) There Wright described and defended the methodology for his entire project. By blending the epistemology of critical realism, the narratology of A. J. Greimas and a sophisticated notion of worldviews, Wright articulated an approach that symphoniously unites the polyphonic and many times discordant disciplines of literature, history and theology. Wright also applied the critical realist epistemology and narrative analysis to an extensive study of Second Temple Judaism and thereby painted the religious and cultural backdrop for his full scale portrait of Jesus in *Jesus and the Victory of God*. While these two books enable readers to anticipate where Wright will ultimately go, four volumes remain to be written—full studies of the resurrection, Paul and the Gospels, and a concluding volume. The six volumes, when taken together, seek to chart the ways in which Christians began to understand their role in the unfolding purposes of Israel's God (and thereby to redefine Israel's God).

The sheer audacity of the projected six volumes is only exceeded by the copious, sophisticated and nuanced arguments contained within the first two already in print. The sovereignty with which Wright moves through both primary and secondary sources is breathtaking. The reader senses that Wright has read and dissected absolutely everything relevant to the subject and most everything that is tangential. Wright's prose is lively, metaphorical and clever. More often than not, his critique of others is as winsome as it is devastating.

But it is Wright's apologetic and prophetic tenor that is most striking. Apologetically, he proposes and defends a completely new historiographic paradigm— an educated, coherent and consistent framework for reconstructing a historical portrait of Jesus. Prophetically, he boldly announces the presence of this new hypothesis, challenging and inviting others to adopt it and all the while warning of the dire philosophical and theological consequences of languishing in the mire of other historical explanations.

The essays in this volume assess whether or not we should heed Wright's prophetic call to repentance. Craig Blomberg's opening essay not only provides an overview of Wright's eclectic methodology but also serves as an excellent road map for finding a way through *Jesus and the Victory of God*. Paul R. Eddy examines in detail the three categories that, in Wright's reconstruction, work together to constitute the vocational aims of Jesus. Klyne Snodgrass probes Wright's strategic use of parables as windows into the message and mission of Jesus. Since the return-from-exile theme figures so prominently in the pages of *Jesus and the Victory of God,* Craig A. Evans compiles the most complete inventory of evidence that a restoration eschatology was indeed a significant feature of first-century Judaism. The essays by Darrell L. Bock (on the death of Jesus) and Dale C. Allison Jr. (on Jesus' eschatology) can be read in tandem. Jesus' death cannot be separated from his talk of vindication, and vindication cannot be separated from his use of apocalyptic language to invest history with its full theological significance. Richard B. Hays investigates the ethical implications inherent in Wright's understanding of Jesus' preaching—it was a call for Israel to be Israel and not some timeless ethic. The essays by Alister E. McGrath, C. Stephen Evans and Luke Timothy Johnson should be read together, for they reflect different takes on the relationship between historiography and theology in *Jesus and the Victory of God.* The two responses by Marcus Borg and Wright himself point up disagreements and issues that need clarification. Finally, my concluding remarks point the way toward the church's Christology.

If, according to Schweitzer, at the beginning of the century Jesus came to us as one yet unknown, then, according to Wright, the situation has changed little by the end of the century. Jesus is still largely misunderstood, and herein lies the justification for *Jesus and the Victory of God.* Despite all the effort that has gone into the study of Jesus, Wright can say,

> I have come to believe that these questions are vital, central, *and as yet not fully answered;* and that a clearly worked out historical method, and a fresh reading of first-century Judaism and Christianity, will point us in the right direction. (*JVG* xiii, emphasis original)

Jesus and the Victory of God proposes to take us in the (W)right direction.

Part Two

Assessment

Two

The Wright Stuff

A Critical Overview of
Jesus and the Victory of God

CRAIG BLOMBERG

O NE OF THE MOST EXCITING AND SIGNIFICANT WRITERS IN THE CROWDED FIELD
of contemporary historical Jesus research is N. T. Wright. Having
already established himself in this field by updating Stephen C. Neill's
classic history of New Testament interpretation[1] and by composing a short
book on Jesus, particularly in response to several recent aberrant approaches,[2]
Wright has now penned what may be the most important contribution to the
topic in this generation. The book, *Jesus and the Victory of God,* appears as volume two of a projected six-volume series entitled Christian Origins and the
Question of God. Volume one, *The New Testament and the People of God,* pre-
viewed the entire series, dealt with New Testament backgrounds and laid out in
much greater detail the methodology on which Wright now builds in volume
two. In short, Wright defends a philosophical and historiographical approach
known as critical realism.[3] Eschewing a naive objectivism, Wright nevertheless
rejects the currently more popular postmodern subjectivism, believing that
truth exists, that events which happened can in principle be reconstructed by

historians and that the ideological significance of those events can be determined at least in considerable measure. Much like the scientists who devise successive experiments to test the formulas they are positing, the historian and theologian also have sufficient data and adequate criteria to make statements that are at least probably true by repeatedly interacting with the evidence and revising their initial presuppositions as they go (*NTPG* 32-37).

The hypothesis Wright wishes to test and ultimately defend is that Jesus came announcing the "end of the exile," for which almost all Jews longed, in his own person and work, yet without producing most of the characteristic signs that were expected to accompany that end (most notably, ridding the land of the Romans). To do this, Wright begins by surveying the past and present landscape of historical Jesus research, setting the stage for how his method will differ from almost everyone else's (*JVG* 3-144). Then he examines the worldview, or mindset, of Jesus by considering in sequence his praxis, stories and symbols and the questions generated by his ministry (*JVG* 145-474). The conclusions of part two enable Wright to address the vexed question of Jesus' intentions (*JVG* 475-653), while part four (*JVG* 655-62) briefly summarizes the results of Wright's research. An appendix surveys references in early Christian literature to the theme of the kingdom of God (*JVG* 663-70), and a comprehensive bibliography reflects the breadth of Wright's reading (*JVG* 671-704).

Wright's "Introduction"

In chapter one (*JVG* 3-27) Wright insists that rigorous history and theology belong together, especially when dealing with Jesus (*JVG* 8). He recognizes the false dichotomy, perpetuated by so many, that pretends committed theologians cannot also function as serious and careful historians. In *The New Testament and the People of God* (14), Wright adds a third dimension into the mix, namely, literary criticism. Here again he insists on holding together what many rend asunder, especially those who are calling for literary-critical models to supplant historical-critical ones.[4] The rest of chapter one quickly but masterfully surveys the last two hundred years of quests for the historical Jesus. To understand Wright's own location on this landscape, one must recognize that Wright is at least as much opposed to the *method* of conservative fideism as he is to the *results* of liberal historiography. Thus, for example, he agrees with Marcus Borg and J. Dominic Crossan that historical research is crucial in determining who Jesus was[5] and strongly dissents from Luke Timothy Johnson's repeated, simplistic appeals to church tradition and canonical authority to bypass the historical process. But he agrees with Johnson and sharply opposes Borg and Crossan in criticizing their actual use of historical methods and the inappropriately skewed and skeptical results they produce.[6]

Chapters two (*JVG* 28-82) and three (*JVG* 83-124) contrast the legacy of William Wrede's thoroughgoing skepticism in the post-World War II New Quest of the historical Jesus with the heritage of Albert Schweitzer's thoroughgoing apocalyptic in the more recent Third Quest.[7] With Schweitzer (and more recently E. P. Sanders and Ben F. Meyer),[8] Wright agrees that Jesus needs to be fitted securely into the context of the Judaism of his day and that the resulting portrait of Jesus is consistently eschatological, although he recognizes that Schweitzer did not have the tools to understand the nature of first-century Judaism adequately. This approach drastically differs from that of the more atomistic New Quest that focused on individual sayings of Jesus, evaluating them by discrete "criteria of authenticity" and in many instances producing an innocuous Jesus who dispensed wisdom but eschewed apocalyptic.[9]

Wright's survey of past and present historical-Jesus research proves incisive. Wright correctly diagnoses the failure of the New Quest (and its current heirs, such as the Jesus Seminar, Crossan and Burton L. Mack)[10] to fit Jesus' overall life and ministry into sufficiently historical contexts and the broader theological narratives of his day. Wright helpfully observes that the uniquely North American work of the Jesus Seminar members is so idiosyncratic that it is often not even taken seriously in other parts of the world (*JVG* 35 n. 23). Nevertheless, their work demands a response, not least due to the amount of attention it has received in North America, and Wright offers a devastating critique of both the Jesus Seminar and Mack (*JVG* 29-44). Crossan, too, whose work is far more learned and lucid, nevertheless ultimately falls under this same critique (*JVG* 44-65),[11] while Borg's historical Jesus work forms a bridge of sorts between the New and Third Quests (*JVG* 75-78).[12] If one wishes to defend a Cynic Jesus, à la Mack and Crossan, the less well known work of the British scholar F. G. Downing is actually more important and substantial,[13] but ultimately it too fails to convince Wright (*JVG* 66-74). Among the problems with all of these works are their lack of adequately Jewish portraits of Jesus, their uncritical appeal to the *Gospel of Thomas* as a putatively early source independent of the canonical Gospels and their implausible hypotheses of several editions of Q, the earliest of which supposedly contained wisdom material rather than apocalyptic as the foundation of Christian theology.[14]

In turning to his discussion of the Third Quest, Wright observes how the criterion of authenticity known as "dissimilarity"—or, more correctly, "double dissimilarity"[15]—has determined the results of much twentieth-century Jesus study. According to this criterion, only those sayings or actions of Jesus in which he differed both from the conventional Jewish world around him and from the early church that followed him may be accepted as authentic. Various writers acknowledge to varying degrees that other material may be authentic but then allege that, as a historian, the scholar has no way of identifying this material. The possibility always remains that data attributed to Jesus that do not pass both halves of this dissimilarity test may have been invented, either by early Jewish Christians who were trying to domesticate the Jesus tradition and turn him into a more conventional figure than he actually was or by other (presumably more Hellenistic) Christians who were reading their more developed theology back onto the lips of Jesus. All along, this dissimilarity criterion has stood in tension with another widely accepted criterion of historical authenticity, that of coherence with an early first-century Palestinian environment. But Wright advances the discussion substantially by proposing a criterion of double similarity and double dissimilarity (*JVG* 86). In other words, no truly human figures in history can ever differ too radically from their immediate contexts (for if they do, they are locked up as mad!).[16] At the same time, one must expect a substantial amount of continuity between the founders of movements and their first followers. On the other hand, a mark of distinctive new leaders (the religious or philosophical genius) is that they do consistently differ in striking and challenging ways from their environments and are usually never fully imitated by their disciples. Thus when we come to the main body of Wright's work, we see him repeatedly sketching out ways in which each of the major facets of Jesus' ministry actually satisfies this double similarity and dissimilarity criterion, suggesting that we can recover with confidence the primary outlines of who Jesus was and what he did and said. But this criterion is not applied atomistically to individual sayings but as part and parcel of Wright's larger agenda of testing and interpreting the Gospels' story line about Jesus in the light of other prevailing Jewish narratives concerning the end of the exile.

Wright also correctly recognizes that one's only hope in making progress with supposedly historical literature from antiquity is not to approach it "in a spirit of resistant scepticism" (*JVG* 87 n. 17).[17] This brief quotation in a footnote would have been worth expanding into a full-fledged subsection in one of these introductory, methodological chapters. One wonders if Wright is identifying himself with the minority of scholars who believe that the burden of proof in historical Jesus research rests squarely on the shoulders of the skeptic.[18] Wright also correctly observes that historians of antiquity in general regularly admit "harmonization" as one legitimate solution to evidence that at first glance appears contradictory. Individual points of view of the respective historians or biographers must be carefully taken into account, "but the object of the exercise is to produce a coherent synthesis which functions as a hypothesis and must be treated as such" (*JVG* 88).[19] But discussions about both the burden of proof and harmonization usually unfold within parameters of the New Quest. It would be enlightening to see how Wright recasts them within his methodology of hypothesis verification.

With this prolegomena out of the way, Wright is ready to begin outlining a sequence of questions frequently raised elsewhere in the Third Quest, the answers to which will form the heart of his study. First, "how does Jesus fit into Judaism," particularly recognizing that he announced the arrival of the climactic moment in Israel's history (*JVG* 91-98)? This question will of necessity require addressing the issue of Jesus' self-understanding (or, at least, the ways his contemporaries understand him). Following Sanders, Wright agrees that the temple cleansing is a solid historical datum with which to begin,[20] but if temple and king interlock, then the question of whether or not Jesus intended messianic claims by this action cannot be avoided (*JVG* 94). So, too, one finds oneself addressing the ways in which Jesus was political, since in his world to be nonpolitical was to be irrelevant (*JVG* 98). Second, "what were Jesus' aims?" (*JVG* 99-105). Here Wright closely follows and elaborates on the important work of Ben Meyer.[21] Wright is not raising the question that some literary critics declare involves the "intentional fallacy."[22] He is seeking to recover not the psychological states of Jesus' mind but rather the larger intentions that governed his life, intentions that are determinable from his actions, in ways that reveal a combination of the worldview of the culture and the mindset of the individual (*JVG* 100-101). Three subordinate issues emerge here (*JVG* 102):

1. Did Jesus' aims remain consistent throughout his life?
2. Did Jesus go to Jerusalem to die?
3. Did he intend to found the church?

The third, broader question, which only recent historical Jesus work, recapturing the interest of Schweitzer, has begun adequately to consider, is "why did Jesus die?" (*JVG* 106-9). This issue must be addressed first of all at the historical level but then also at the theological level, namely, why did the early church see Jesus' death as having atoning significance? Fourth, "how and why did the early church begin," especially with respect to its proclamation of Jesus as alive after his death, a component of the kerygma unparalleled in the earliest stages of the movements of the founders of other world religions and philosophies (*JVG* 109-12)? Particularly crucial here is an explanation of the early church's worship of Jesus, especially because it arose out of the staunch monotheism of Judaism.[23] Fifth—and Wright recognizes that space constraints require this question to be deferred until a later book in his series—"why are the Gospels what they are?" (*JVG* 112-13). A sixth and final question to which Wright will respond later still is that of how the answers to the first five questions impact or relate to the contemporary church and world (*JVG* 117-21).

More so than with any other contributor to the recent quests for the historical Jesus, Wright has clearly thought out and laid out all the correct issues in advance and proposed a compelling sequence in which they must be analyzed. He also properly observes that all of these questions are interlocking, and it is refreshing to see him not retreat from resolutely facing the theological significance of the results. Wright helpfully summarizes his task as how to explain the diverse and vigorous movement of the early second century (i.e., post-New Testament) church as "a story about one Jesus of Nazareth, a figure of the recent past" (*JVG* 90).[24] What other writers have sometimes called the criterion of "necessary explanation"[25] remains implicit in all of this introductory discussion and will loom large in Wright's study. Many other scholars, even those in the Third Quest, fail to give a suitably convincing explanation both for why Jesus was perceived as such a threat that he had to be crucified and for the rise of widespread worship of Jesus (rather than merely Yahweh) in an undeniably Jewish-Christian milieu with religious convictions that would normally have prevented this overly close association between Jesus and God.

The final chapter of Wright's introductory part one (*JVG* 125-44) introduces his central thesis about Jesus' message: Jesus was announcing that the Jewish exile was ending and that he himself was the agent of Israel's peculiar return from exile (*JVG* 126-27). Here Wright begins with the well-known story of the prodigal son (Lk 15:11-32). But, flying in the face of almost the entire history of the interpretation of this parable, he sees it not as primarily about the return of wayward individuals (cf. Lk 15:1-2) but as primarily about Israel's homecoming as a nation (*JVG* 125-31). This restoration takes place in surprising fashion, as the prodigal depicts the outcast within Israel (symbolic, too, of the later, more overt inclusion of Gentiles in God's kingdom) as the remnant who return. Wright does not defend the legitimacy of this interpretation in any detail against the variety of previous approaches that have dominated the history of exegesis but, in keeping with his overall strategy, puts it forward as a hypothesis to test in light of the major questions enunciated above (*JVG* 131-33). He suggests, as we continue to study the Synoptic data, that this interpretation of the core of Jesus' message will recur again and again in ways that make sense of passages otherwise less clearly related to the larger whole (or center of the kerygma).

Wright does later insist that his corporate interpretation of Jesus' stories does not exclude (but actually enhances) the "personal meaning" for every listener (*JVG* 246). Indeed, the only way Israel can corporately be restored is as numerous individuals within the country themselves return from exile. Wright also supports his interpretation of the prodigal by appealing to the double similarity and dissimilarity criterion (*JVG* 132) and argues for the authenticity of the parable via the very balanced analysis of Jewish oral tradition recently described by Kenneth E. Bailey as both "informal" and yet "controlled" (*JVG* 134-36).[26] How much of the rest of the actions and teachings of Jesus make similar sense as announcing the end of the Jewish exile? Wright is ready to examine Jesus' praxis, stories and symbols more generally, in that order.[27]

Wright's "Profile of a Prophet"

The largest part of *Jesus and the Victory of God* begins with the contention that a central category for understanding the praxis of Jesus emerging from the undeniably authentic Synoptic material is that of prophet. Here is a title that has recently been rehabilitated in the work of other Third Questers as well,[28] but Wright elaborates it further and more convincingly. Chapter five (*JVG* 147-97) begins with a list of fundamental items accepted as authentic by just about everybody as summarizing Jesus' life and public activity (*JVG* 147-48).[29] Most of this list was established by the New Quest, with its older criteria of authenticity,[30] but the items equally merit inclusion via Wright's double similarity and dissimilarity criterion (*JVG* 149-50). Especially crucial here is his argument that Jesus' prophetic praxis creates continuity with John the Baptist's ministry, which was even more clearly prophetic, and yet Jesus did not simply repeat John's message or mimic his style. So, too, the early church would never have invented Jesus as prophet because its Christology quickly and consistently became much "higher," but neither did the church attempt to suppress or deny that whatever else Jesus was he was also a prophet. So we have the necessary combination of distinctives from and similarities with both Jesus' predecessors and his followers to declare the material authentic (*JVG* 160-62).

As for what kind of prophet Jesus was, he falls into the oracular and leadership categories (*JVG* 162-68). Particularly important here are Jesus' teachings about John the Baptist in Matthew 11:7-19 and Luke 7:24-35, in addition to parallels with various Old Testament prophecies. Not only John but Jesus himself is portrayed as a prophet like Elijah (see esp. Lk 7:11-17; 9:51-55), which among other things means that he would have been perceived as a troublemaker in Israel, particularly as he claimed to reconstitute Israel apart from the normal channels of religion and power (*JVG* 169, 172). One could quibble and ask whether Ben Witherington's language of "freeing" rather than merely "reconstituting" Israel might fit the evidence slightly better,[31] but it seems likely that Wright means to subsume both of these concepts under the same heading.

Wright's use of the label of "prophet" as his starting point for understanding Jesus' praxis suggests an important part of any response to the charge that Jesus or the Gospels were anti-Semitic. The Old Testament prophets unleash some of the harshest invective in all of Scripture against Jews,[32] and yet clearly, as members of the community of Israel themselves, they were not in any meaningful sense of the term anti-Semitic.[33] On more than one occasion in biblical history, God has had to speak harsh and painful words to his people, even in trying to remake them into what he intended them to be. On the other hand, Wright may slightly exaggerate the continuity between John the Baptist and Jesus. Only briefly (*JVG* 167) does he mention the dramatic distinction between Jesus' bringing a message of joy and salvation and John's predominantly emphasizing austerity and judgment (see esp. Mt 11:16-19 par. Lk 7:31-35). In part three, however, he will clearly defend substantial additions to the database of authentic material impinging on the Christology of Jesus.

The category of prophet does make good sense of Jesus' itinerant ministry; his central call to repentance of sin, which echoes John's message; his speaking in extensive discourses; and his use of parabolic speech—not merely to provide information via catchy illustrations but as performative language (or what the new hermeneutic used to call "language events")—as the actual means of bringing the kingdom to birth (*JVG* 170-76). All of this also places Jesus squarely in the context of early Jewish apocalyptic, as Schweitzer correctly observed, and against the Borg/Crossan/Mack/Jesus-Seminar trajectory of a noneschatological mission and message of Jesus (*JVG* 177-82).[34] But Jesus the apocalypticist remains every bit as subversive as the cryptic epigrammatist of Crossan and company (*JVG* 179-80). In this context, Wright properly rejects the false dichotomies between allegory and parable, steno-symbols and tensive symbols that have dominated so much of the twentieth century's parable research (*JVG* 178).[35]

Wright proceeds to furnish a helpful and detailed catalog of the amount of Jesus' teaching that falls into the category of oracles of judgment, furthering his case for Jesus the prophet (*JVG* 183-84). Jesus' mighty deeds fit in here as well (*JVG* 186-96). Although Wright discusses the subject only briefly, he helpfully stresses that we must bracket our modern tendency to presuppose a post-Enlightenment worldview, complete with its sharp dichotomy between natural and supernatural (*JVG* 187-88). When we do so, the historical evidence for what traditionally have been called Jesus' miracles appears strong.[36] Jesus' healing ministry, like the message of his parables, targets the outcasts of his society. His exorcisms elicit the charge of being possessed by Beelzebul (Mk 3:20-30 and par.), a claim that his loyal followers would never have fabricated. More generally, the miracles present the same troubling ambiguities as do his parables, proverbs and other cryptic speech, a further testimony to their authenticity. With the majority of recent critics, but again contra Crossan et al., Wright concludes that Jesus' prophetic message may be summarized as the inauguration of the kingdom of God (*JVG* 192-93).[37] He is now ready to move from Jesus' praxis to a detailed exploration of Jesus' stories that flesh out this distinctive teaching about God's dynamic reign or rule.

Jesus' prophetic praxis needs to be placed into the context of the prevailing, open-ended narrative in first-century Judaism of Israel and its destiny. This forms the agenda of chapter six (*JVG* 198-243). God had promised Israel the land in peace, prosperity and freedom from her enemies, but the Jews were not experiencing the fulfillment of this promise. In *The New Testament and the People of God* (167-243) Wright helpfully sketches how each of the major Jewish sects and movements would have explained the nation's plight and advocated a solution. Jesus offers his own unique but still very Jewish answer: the solution to Israel's plight is that she must be the people of God in Jesus' new way and that there will be a great, climactic end to the story with judgment on the impenitent and vindication for his followers. The greatest enemy of God's people is not the Romans but Satan; and the greatest battle, not victory over the physical oppressors but liberation from sin (*JVG* 200).[38] Once again, numerous pieces of the Gospels' puzzle fall into place on this hypothesis, and the criterion of double similarity and dissimilarity is repeatedly satisfied. In chapter six, Wright also reviews his understanding of apocalyptic, already presented in some detail in his previous volume (*NTPG* 280-338). He argues that no Jew was looking forward to the dissolution of the current space-time universe by the cosmic intervention of God; rather, the colorful and vivid apocalyptic language of both Old Testament prophets and

Jesus is consistently metaphorical, depicting the great sociopolitical changes that God's spokespersons anticipate (*JVG* 202-9). Thus Wright denies that the so-called parousia passages in the Gospels refer to a literal public, visible return of Christ to this earth at the end of the age, as is more clearly depicted in the rest of the New Testament.

Wright's hypothesis about how Jesus' agenda resembles and differs from other Jewish analyses of Israel's first-century plight proves extremely helpful. His reconstruction of the major open-ended narrative that was variously concluded seems nothing short of brilliant, even if one wonders whether he at times tries to fit too much material into the "return from exile" mold. Wright appropriately distances himself from the increasingly fashionable trend, particularly in North America, of understanding Jesus' message and ministry in entirely nonapocalyptic and even noneschatological categories (*JVG* 210-14).[39] He also strikes a crucial balance between those Third Questers who seem to be reviving the picture of a politically radical, or even revolutionary, Jesus[40] and those whose Jesus is merely politically correct by contemporary American standards.[41] As Wright has stressed even more in other recent works, the kerygma that remains still announces a kingdom with sociopolitical implications, even if these are subordinate to more overarching spiritual categories.[42]

The most problematic portion of this section of part two involves the seemingly complete rejection of any concrete parousia. Wright offers seven possible options in a spectrum of definitions of eschatology ranging from "the end of the space-time universe" at one end of the list to "critique of the present socio-political scene, perhaps with proposals for adjustments" at the other end (*JVG* 208). While admitting that his seven options are not the only possible ones, Wright would appear to have omitted from his list the option that seems most likely to reflect prevailing Jewish beliefs. Granted that no Jew looked for the simple end of the current space-time universe,[43] it nevertheless seems that there is an intermediate position between Wright's second definition, "eschatology as the climax of Israel's history, involving the end of the space-time universe," and his third definition, "eschatology as the climax of Israel's history, involving events for which end-of-the-world language is the only set of metaphors adequate to express the significance of what will happen, but resulting in a new and quite different phase within space-time history." Such an intermediate option would agree that in a coming millennium this current space-time universe continues without having yet experienced the dissolution that will immediately precede the total re-creation of heavens and earth (2 Pet 3:10; cf. the sequence of Rev 20; 21—22). But it also allows for this millennial period to be established by Christ's concrete, bodily return from heaven to earth, while at the same time admitting that much, though not necessarily all, of the apocalyptic language depicting this event is metaphorical rather than literal.[44] This view may or may not be the correct one, but it is an option that Wright does not even address. As a result, he has not made his case for his third definition's being the best possible explanation of New Testament apocalyptic. Also left unaddressed is the question of how the early church, including the remaining New Testament writings, developed the concept of a concrete parousia (esp. Acts 1:11; 1 Cor 15:51-57; 1 Thess 4:13-18; 2 Thess 2:1-8; Rev 19:11-21). Wright does not disclose whether he would deny a literal referent to all New Testament apocalyptic or, if not, how writers like Paul, whose apocalyptic language is filled with allusions to Jesus' teaching, so quickly misunderstood and misrepresented him.[45]

As Wright continues to present Jesus' redefinition of the conventional Jewish narrative concerning Israel's plight and solution, he stresses how the traditional Jewish symbols are completely missing. The story is no longer limited to one nation, race or piece of geography. The praxis of the kingdom (holiness) proceeds largely without reference to Torah (*JVG* 218). Only an origin in a figure as charismatic and influential as Jesus, emerging out of a Jewish milieu, can account for all of these redefinitions (*JVG* 220). Elsewhere Wright stresses even more clearly how the subsequent Christian mission to the Gentiles is the logical outcome of belief in the end of exile, not merely a later response to widespread Jewish rejection of the Gospel.[46] Here he proves particularly incisive with his analysis of Mark 4:11-12 and parallels and the reason for Jesus' teaching in parables. The hardening process described does indeed lead to judgment but, as in the broader context of Isaiah 6, which Jesus cites, "there will be mercy beyond the judgment" (*JVG* 236).[47] Wright concludes that, as with the message of the Old Testament prophets, Jesus' announcement of the kingdom can be summarized under the headings of welcome and warning. So, too, both Jesus and the prophets aimed their message first of all at Israel itself (*JVG* 243). Unpacked, this announcement leads to Jesus' invitation to repentance and belief, his welcome to all who will come, his challenge to live as renewed Israel personally and corporately and his summons to go with him to Jerusalem to die (*JVG* 245-46). These four topics occupy the successive sections of chapter seven (*JVG* 244-319).

At this juncture, Wright introduces for the first time in *Jesus and the Victory of God* a scheme he will draw on later and one on which he relied extensively in

The New Testament and the People of God. He adopts the actantial analysis of A. J. Greimas, which reduces narratives to six key "actants" that fill the slots in a chart demonstrating how "a sender" tries to send an "object" to a "receiver" by means of an "agent" who is alternately aided by a "helper" or obstructed by an "opponent."[48] The basic narrative that sums up Jesus' message thus becomes one in which Yahweh wants to confer upon Israel a return from exile by means of Jesus. Disciples and enemies alternately help or oppose this mission (*JVG* 244-45; cf. 310).

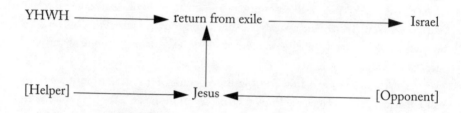

It is not clear how much of Greimasian philosophy Wright presupposes by his use of these diagrams. In *The New Testament and the People of God* (57 n. 23, 70-73) his seeming explicit rejection of "deep" structural analysis would suggest the answer, not much. But then one wonders why he appeals to this model at all, given the questions it raises about possible alignment with Greimas's reductionist, determinist and even Marxist presuppositions.[49] Apparently the diagrams are just a helpful visualization of the various Jewish story lines Wright perceives and do not imply anything beyond their straightforward translation into normal prose. In addition, they demonstrate graphically the irreducible narratives that worldviews contain (*NTPG* 38). We may thus proceed to comment on other elements of "invitation, welcome, challenge and summons."

In a Jewish milieu, the crucial feature of repentance as defined by Jesus is that it does not imply the use of animal sacrifices or participation in the temple cult (*JVG* 257). Here Wright helpfully critiques Sanders's well-known views on repentance according to Jesus.[50] Sanders correctly observed "that Jesus did not ask for repentance in the normal sense," but he was "wrong to deny that he asked for it at all" (*JVG* 248). What was both central and radical was that Jesus offered membership in God's renewed people on his own authority and by his own method—that of abandoning revolutionary zeal (*JVG* 249-50). Throughout this chapter, high christological implications emerge, which Wright could have stressed even more, though he will later collect a number of these together.

Repentance is not the only term Jesus redefines. *Faith*, according to Jesus, refers to loyalty or trust in a leader (*JVG* 250-51). In this specific case, it requires believing that Israel's God was "acting climactically in the career of Jesus himself" (*JVG* 262). This action leads to the forgiveness of even the worst of sinners and discloses yet another slant on Jesus' understanding of the return from exile (*JVG* 264-74). Wright correctly follows Sanders against Joachim Jeremias; the sinners are the notoriously wicked not merely the *'Am ha-aretz*, to which Jesus and most of his followers already belonged anyway.[51] But Wright broadens Sanders's understanding of the scandal Jesus caused by his offer of forgiveness for these sinners. Not only does Jesus welcome those who have not yet proved themselves by the practice of penance, he actually redefines the kingdom by "replacing adherence or allegiance to Temple and Torah with allegiance to himself" (*JVG* 274).

Does all of this imply that Jesus intended to found a church? Wright resonates with Gerhard Lohfink, who argued that Jesus could not have wanted to establish a church because there already was one, namely Israel itself (*JVG* 275).[52] Rather, he wanted to reform Israel. Here again, with Witherington, it seems slightly preferable to speak of freeing Israel, but the point is a minor one. Clearly, Jesus is not going to impact the entire nation but will ultimately focus on one small subgroup or sect (*JVG* 276). The renewal of the covenant ultimately implies a renewal of the heart (*JVG* 282-87), as in Jeremiah's famous prophecy (Jer 31:31-34). By this point in Wright's study, it is clear that in general, in contrast to many works of the recent historical Jesus quests,[53] Wright is not attempting to defend the authenticity of each passage that fits his larger synthesis, although periodic appeals to double similarity and dissimilarity continue to punctuate his narrative. Instead, he is demonstrating the coherence of the overall picture created by beginning with his core of undeniably authentic texts and supplemented by a larger collection of Synoptic material filtered through his particular interpretive grid. A both/and approach that combined both the application of valid criteria of authenticity to each passage with an appeal to the overall coherence of the resulting narrative could prove even more convincing. But this may be too much to ask of any scholar; one may simply need to read Witherington's *Christology of Jesus* or John P. Meier's *A Marginal Jew* alongside Wright![54]

The "challenge" of the gospel message perhaps reaches its zenith with the Sermon on the Mount. For Wright, the sermon stands as "a challenge to Israel to be Israel" (*JVG* 288). On the one hand, this interpretive grid offers an excellent reminder that Jesus' ethical teachings were never intended either to be legislated by civil governments or to be used merely as personal guidelines for individual lifestyles. Rather, Jesus is mandating how God's people should behave in community.[55] On the other hand, one wonders if too organized a form of social action is being read into the text, as, for example, when the commands to turn the other cheek, go the extra mile and not exact revenge (Mt 5:38-47) are taken as "creative non-violent resistance" (*JVG* 291).[56] But Wright certainly seems to have captured a crucial balance between those who read the sermon as supporting full-fledged pacifism and those who find ways to claim Jesus as an advocate of armed resistance, even despite the antitheses of Matthew 5:21-48 (*JVG* 296).[57] Perhaps one needs to recognize multiple lessons and multiple layers of meaning from many forms of Jesus' teaching, not only from the parables.[58]

Where is this central narrative of Jesus' teaching ultimately headed? Wright concludes in chapter eight (*JVG* 320-68) that it leads to both judgment and vindication. Here he helpfully sets Jesus' narrative in the context of the Psalms, the Dead Sea Scrolls, the Maccabean literature and Josephus, though interestingly there are hints of an afterlife in a different world in all of these books, of a kind that Wright apparently denies to Jesus' own teaching. In fact, he even admits that Jesus' teachings on hell may have "wider implications" than just for this life; but he then alleges that those implications remain "outside the scope" of this book (*JVG* 323), though it is not at all clear why. The double similarity and dissimilarity criterion would seem to work well for conventional views of the parousia, heaven and hell:

1. There are clear hints of all of these concepts in Jewish literature, but no one ever develops them as fully as does Jesus.

2. The early church rightly picked up on these basic elements of Christian eschatology, but it often added speculative detail and alternately exaggerated or underestimated their significance in proportion to the rest of Jesus' teaching.[59]

Wright's statement that the Olivet Discourse (Mk 13 and par.) cannot be divided into two halves (contra R. T. France) on the basis of the double introductory question—the former dealing with Jerusalem and the latter with the second coming—is an example of a rare instance in which Wright offers mere assertion, when detailed argument is needed instead (*JVG* 346 n. 105).[60]

Particularly problematic in this context is Wright's treatment of the coming of the Son of Man in Mark 13:26 and 14:62. Wright correctly recognizes that Daniel 7:13 lies in the background—the coming of the Son of Man on the clouds to heaven into the presence of the Ancient of Days (*JVG* 361).[61] But this cannot be the meaning of Mark 14:62, in which Christ's coming takes place after he has been seated at right hand of the Father.[62] Rather, the direction of his coming on the clouds there must be from heaven to earth.[63] Yet neither can this coming be equated in its totality with the destruction of Jerusalem and the temple by the Romans in 70 C.E. When Wright declares that Jesus was teaching that "this generation will see the end" (*JVG* 364), this is precisely what the text does not say. As several recent commentators have stressed, the "these things" of Mark 13:30, which will take place in the lifetime of Jesus' disciples, must refer back to the "these things" of verse 29. But in verse 29, whatever "things" are in view are happening so that observers know that the end (or parousia) "is near, right at the door" (NIV). It makes no sense for "these things" to include the parousia because then "it" would have come rather than simply being near, close at hand. But this means that Jesus must be envisaging "the day or hour" of the parousia, which even he in his incarnate limitations did not know (Mk 13:32), as a separate later event, not necessarily occurring within "this generation" and therefore not coterminous with the destruction of the temple in 70 C.E.[64]

The next step in Wright's program (*JVG* 369-442) is to discuss the major symbols of Jesus' ministry. Here Jesus' strategy is largely to attack and undermine the traditional Jewish badges of national righteousness—sabbath, food laws, land, temple, family and material possessions. Here Wright draws on the strengths of the "new look" on first-century Judaism, associated especially with Sanders and James D. G. Dunn,[65] while avoiding some of its pitfalls.[66] Jesus' distinctive eschatological beliefs and expectations clearly generated distinctive political agendas (*JVG* 390). While his challenges to the Pharisaic ideology were often implicit, they were present and perceived. Jesus did at least hint "cryptically" at radical changes in the Jewish law; his ambiguities "avoided an outcry, but provoked alarm among those who suspected that there might be disloyalty lurking beneath the surface" (*JVG* 398 n. 92). The strength of Wright's view is that it explains why Jesus' controversy stories generated the level of hostility that they did and why ultimately he was crucified. It is precisely Wright's focus on the symbols of Israel's national identity, rather than on just Jesus' individual sayings, that enables him to undermine Sanders's very negative conclusions about the historicity of the controversy material.

Wright then moves to Jesus' temple clearing (Mk 11:15-19 and par.) as the focal event that ensured his demise (*JVG* 405-28). Again with Sanders, Wright seems correct in taking Jesus' demonstration as a parable of judgment; but against Sanders, and also apparently correctly, Wright argues that Jesus did not merely desire to replace the temple but was critiquing the entire system (*JVG* 417).[67] But who has the right to come to the temple and pontificate on it in word and deed except one who has links with royalty (*JVG* 411)? So the messianic question comes in through the back door here as well. "Jesus saw himself, and perhaps his followers with him, as the new Temple" (*JVG* 426). An important methodological point that emerges in this context is Wright's insistence that the Gospel writers consistently did not invent material to fit later needs of the church but instead suppressed material that did not fit or seem relevant to the churches to which they were addressed (*JVG* 436). This point could have been pressed in numerous other instances as well.[68] But what proves crucial here is that the very verse that Sanders excludes from the temple incident as inauthentic—Mark 11:17[69]—is precisely what Wright sees via the criterion of double similarity and dissimilarity as at its heart (*JVG* 418-20). It is the prevention of the Gentiles from worshiping in the temple in the way God had ordained for them that both fits the Old Testament (Is 56:7 and Jer 7:11 are explicitly quoted), while contrasting with current Jewish practice, and accounts for the later Christian mission to the Gentiles, but without the requirements of worshiping in one fixed locale. Throughout, Wright captures the core of Jesus' relationship with Torah as one of neither abolition nor preservation but fulfillment (cf. Mt 5:17). Little wonder, then, that the charge of Jesus' leading the people astray permeates anti-Christian Jewish critique from the Gospels to the Talmud. In the former, Jesus' mighty deeds, particularly his exorcisms, elicit the charge of being demon-possessed (Mk 3:22-30 and par.). Even his family thinks he is mad (Mk 3:21). These two perspectives are almost certainly authentic, because no Christian would ever have invented such charges (*JVG* 439-42). But there are other options for understanding Jesus.[70]

As Wright turns to the final stage in analyzing the profile of Jesus the prophet (*JVG* 443-74), he discusses Jesus' implied answers to six key worldview questions that sum up all of part two: Who are we? We are the true Israel. Where are we? We are we in the process of being freed from exile. What is wrong? We have been duped into thinking that Rome rather than Satan is the real enemy. What's the solution? We must follow the road to the cross rather than revolt. What time is it? It is a time of opportunity to be seized (the present dimension of the kingdom) before the coming judgment (the future dimension of the kingdom). In short, "Jesus intended to bring the story of Israel to its god-ordained climax, in and through his own work" (*JVG* 473).[71]

Wright's "Aims and Beliefs of Jesus"

At last we arrive at part three—on Jesus' aims and beliefs. Here appear some of the most exciting and significant findings of the entire book, as Wright mounts a

step-by-step argument, with a fresh reading of dozens of key texts in their original Jewish context, for saying that

1. Jesus thought of himself as Messiah;
2. he believed it was his vocation to die vicariously for Israel and the world;
3. he believed himself to be the embodiment of Israel's God.

In other words, in successive chapters Jesus' messiahship, atonement and incarnation are each grounded not in theological a prioris but in careful historical
argument of a type largely unknown in critical biblical scholarship.

Chapter eleven (*JVG* 477-539) is entitled "Jesus and Israel: The Meaning of
Messiahship." Here Wright employs perhaps the most helpful methodology of
the entire book, as he surveys in some detail much of the data in the Gospels that
point toward Jesus' own belief in his messiahship. Wright is quite clear that we
must distinguish between what was entailed even in Jesus' redefinition of Jewish
messianism and the later Christian development of understanding Jesus as the
second person of the Trinity (*JVG* 478). Nevertheless, Wright argues that Jesus
quite self-consciously came not merely to announce the kingdom but to enact
and embody the return from exile, the defeat of evil and the coming of Yahweh to
Zion (*JVG* 481). As evidence, he highlights how the Synoptic Gospels are full of
implicit Christology (riddles and symbols that point to a messianic self-understanding) in both sayings and deeds (*JVG* 489-538), all of which is too muted to
be the later creation of the early church with its more explicit worship of Christ,
but all of which is sufficiently suggestive to conclude that Jesus had some sort of
messianic consciousness (see esp. *JVG* 489).[72] In this section, Wright reasons
convincingly from the clearest messianic actions and statements of Jesus at the
end of his life (esp. his temple action and teaching and his confession before
Caiaphas) backwards, one step at a time, to show precedents for such messianic
self-understanding at every phase of his ministry from his baptism onward—his
discussion with the disciples on the road to Caesarea Phillipi, his enacting the
messianic ministry of the kingdom-proclaimer of Isaiah 52 and 61, his feasting
with his followers, his choosing twelve disciples, his contrasting himself with
David and Solomon and so on (*JVG* 482-538).

Here, too, is where a discussion of the resurrection narratives finds its rightful place. Only a bodily resurrection from the dead can adequately account for the
later church's move beyond the cryptic, implicit hints of messiahship to its much
more explicit Christology. Conversely, while resurrection is a necessary criterion
of early Christian faith, it is not a sufficient one. There is nothing in Old Testament or Jewish expectation about resurrection in and of itself, much less about

the resurrection of a messianic claimant, to explain why the early church viewed Jesus as the Christ. Rather, the disciples must have recognized that Jesus had taught and demonstrated his convictions on this topic, however ambiguously at times, while he was yet alive, so that the resurrection then becomes a vindication of those claims (*JVG* 488).[73] Wright does discuss some of the more explicit titles of Gospel Christology briefly here and there throughout this chapter, although this is not his major focus. Perhaps his most helpful contribution to titular Christianity is to insist, again with several recent scholars, that "Son of Man" is more than just an Aramaic circumlocution for "I" or "a man like me,"[74] not least because of its use in a more exalted sense in the early Aramaic-speaking Jewish Christian church (*JVG* 513-19). A rather obvious yet oft-neglected point of method is well captured by his quotation of George B. Caird: "What was linguistically possible for the early Aramaic-speaking church cannot have been linguistically impossible for the Aramaic-speaking Jesus" (*JVG* 518 n. 144).[75]

Chapter twelve (*JVG* 540-611) moves to a discussion of how the historian proceeds from Jesus' messianic acts and words to his death. Wright insists that both Jewish and Roman leaders were involved, much as the Gospels claim they were, in bringing about Christ's crucifixion (*JVG* 543-52).[76] Jesus was perceived as making messianic claims that sufficiently threatened Jewish religious scruples and Roman political insecurities so as to make him dangerous to leaders of both groups.[77] The Last Supper forms the key symbolic action, especially on the heels of Jesus' demonstration in the temple, inasmuch as it clarified his claim that his own person, now to be given over in death, formed the locus of God's saving activity (*JVG* 555-59). Paul's use of this early tradition in 1 Corinthians 11:23-26 attests to its authenticity (*JVG* 558 n. 81), and numerous teachings of Jesus leading up to this climactic meal cohere with its import but again in a sufficiently enigmatic fashion that is not likely the product of early Christian creation (*JVG* 559-76). Schweitzer was right to see Jesus' self-understanding as he went to the cross in the context of the messianic woes that would set in motion the climax of the old age and the arrival of the new (*JVG* 577-79).[78] There are more disturbing echoes of Schweitzer later on when Wright insists that Jesus "must have known that he might have been deeply mistaken" (see esp. *JVG* 609; cf. 653). Again the reader who is not yet convinced looks for an argument but finds merely robust affirmation.

Nevertheless, Wright well defends the messianic implications of Jesus' death as part of his larger discussion of suffering and redemption within Judaism. Instead of beginning with the Suffering Servant passage of Isaiah 52—53, with all of its exegetical conundrums, Wright surveys a wide variety of biblical and intertestamental texts on suffering individuals in Israel (Is 40—55 included) to demonstrate yet another fulfillment of the double similarity and dissimilarity criterion: Jesus could very easily have found redemptive suffering in his Jewish and scriptural tradition, but the combination of servant, Messiah, suffering and vicarious sin-bearing was unique to himself, though less explicit than in later Christian theologizing (*JVG* 579-92).[79] The permeation of scriptural texts and themes in the passion narratives are better explained as Jesus' own appropriation of his Bible than, with Crossan, as later Christian fabrication based on scriptural meditation (*JVG* 584-91).[80] It is credible, then, to suggest that Jesus, as a first-century Jew, could come to believe that Yahweh would act through the suffering of an individual like himself to defeat Satan and redeem both Israel and the world (*JVG* 592-611).

In chapter thirteen (*JVG* 612-53) Wright begins by surveying pre-Christian Jewish hopes for the coming of Yahweh to Zion (*JVG* 615-31). Of particular relevance are those traditions, building on the two thrones of Daniel 7:9, that find Yahweh sharing exalted status with various angels, martyrs, pious individuals and, arguably, even Messiah (*JVG* 624-29). Combine these traditions with Jewish language of Shekinah, Torah, Wisdom, Logos and Spirit as "ways of affirming YHWH's intimate involvement with his people and his world" along with "his sovereignty and transcendence over the whole cosmos" (*JVG* 630), and one can understand Jesus' "riddles of return and exaltation" (*JVG* 631-44). The double similarity and dissimilarity criterion again comes into play. Astonishing as it seemed, Jesus' own sense of vocation could have involved the notion that loyalty to God would now take the form of loyalty to himself (*JVG* 645-51). Here are the seeds of the notion of incarnation or of the divinity of Jesus, yet without the elaborate superstructure that later Christian theology would erect on top of it.

But unanswered questions emerge from this chapter, too. How does Jesus' going to die in Jerusalem to bring about the turn of the ages fit in with Wright's insistence that the really crucial terminus of the exile is the destruction of Jerusalem in 70 C.E. (see esp. *JVG* 631-45)? Does Wright's theology of the crucifixion in fact call into question his interpretation of Jesus' parousia passages? Generally left unaddressed, too, is the relationship between Jesus' resurrection and Wright's interpretation of the events of 70 C.E.[81] But these questions must not be allowed to overshadow Wright's largely new and convincing approach to arguing, as a historian, for what must surely count as a kind of divine self-understanding on Jesus' part.

Wright's "Conclusion"—and Ours

As one assesses Wright's summary of his "results" (*JVG* 655-62), it is worth stressing again how impressive both his method and his product are. Wright has succeeded in staying relatively rigorously within the historical constraints of Jesus' lifetime and within the limits of what can plausibly be defended as historical or authentic by reasonable critical criteria. Even if one begins by affirming that one can know little else than Jesus' crucifixion, one must explain why he died. Only a relatively high Christology, however implicit it was during his lifetime, can fully account for the conflicts Jesus generated and the threats he elicited. This high Christology is not the result of some late Hellenizing distortion of the once simple message of a Galilean Jewish peasant. The Jesus of the Gospels remains thoroughly intelligible as a product, and perhaps a mutation, of Jewish hopes and forms of thought. Nor is this Jesus identical with the philosophically sophisticated dogma of Nicaean or Chalcedonian Christology, even while he remains in recognizable continuity with it. And the resurrection is a necessary condition for explaining why people continued to talk about Jesus as more than just "a remarkable but tragic memory," especially inasmuch as "the category of failed but still revered Messiah . . . did not exist" (*JVG* 658).[82]

Wright cannot fairly be accused of setting out to fashion a cleverly disguised apologetic for historic Christian orthodoxy, even as his work may function as powerful support for the historicity of the major contours of the canonical Jesus.[83] One may still debate which is more probable: whether the unique combination of teachings, actions, stories, symbols and beliefs reflected in the Synoptic Gospels reflects individual genius or community invention. But Wright has surely placed the burden of proof back into the camp of those who would doubt that we can know much about the historical Jesus, who would question that he makes sense within early first-century Judaism or who would insist that he dramatically diverged from the most central tenets of later historic Christian faith. Wright ends his volume by standing Schweitzer's famous words on their head: "We come to him [Jesus] as ones unknown, crawling back from the far country, where we wasted our substance on riotous but ruinous historicism. But the swinehusks—the 'assured results of modern criticism'—reminded us of that knowledge which arrogance had all but obliterated, and we began the journey home." When we arrive, "we shall discover again and again not only who he is but who we ourselves are: as unknown and yet well known, as dying and behold we live" (*JVG* 662). With these closing words, Wright's prose reaches the heights of rhapsody and the depths of profundity.

Early on in *Jesus and the Victory of God*, Wright insists the picture of Jesus that has emerged from this study makes him very uncomfortable. It was not created in Wright's own image, either as a scholar or a churchman (*JVG* xv). This may be true vocationally, but the broadly orthodox Jesus that emerges from Wright's study matches closely the broadly evangelical Wright in overall theological convictions.[84] But surely this is not a weakness. Schweitzer's famous critique of the Old Questers having remade Jesus into their own image was unnecessarily condemning. After all, who would want a scholar or believer who professes to follow Jesus at some level to have beliefs and a lifestyle that did not match his or her understanding of the life of Christ?[85] We may need to remind ourselves that the process of setting aside our biases is more difficult than is admitted by even the well-nuanced form of critical realism that Wright espouses.[86] But unless one is prepared to abandon all attempts to write history according to any traditional definition—that is, of things that really happened in the past—or, for that matter, to give up meaningful communication of any kind in the present, we must insist that there are limits on what words, sentences and actions in various contexts can mean and that there are ways of approximating an understanding of what speakers and actors intend by their sayings and actions.[87] Wright has moved us a long way, indeed perhaps just about as far as we can go, in our quest to reconstruct these meanings in the case of the historical Jesus. For that, scholars and laypersons alike owe him their deepest gratitude.[88]

Three

The (W)Right Jesus

Eschatological Prophet, Israel's Messiah, Yahweh Embodied

PAUL R. EDDY

O NE OF THE MOST INSIGHTFUL AND PROMISING MODELS TO EMERGE FROMT HE
recent ferment within historical Jesus research is that of N. T. Wright,
as presented in his landmark study *Jesus and the Victory of God*. In short,
he argues that Jesus was an eschatological prophet who understood himself to be
simultaneously both Israel's Messiah and, in some sense, the very embodiment of
Yahweh. It is the purpose of this essay to reflect upon both the historical foundations and theological implications of this model.

Initial assessments of Wright's proposal have tended to share a number of
common characteristics. Regardless of his or her final estimations, virtually every
reviewer to date has expressed deep admiration for the scholarship, clarity, boldness and sheer magnitude of *Jesus and the Victory of God*. One can only concur
with such assessments. This is a breathtaking work within an extraordinarily
ambitious multivolume project. Also noteworthy is the type of project it represents. The modern history of Jesus studies has tended toward a polarization
between radical skepticism and confessional fideism, between H. S. Reimarus

and Martin Kähler.[1] With the arrival of the Third Quest, we are witness to a distinctive stream of scholarship that serves to break this trend. Within this segment of the Third Quest, one can find conservative scholars presenting concrete models of Jesus that are both rooted in and open to serious historical investigation. It is within this refreshing stream of scholarship that Wright's project is to be located as a particularly brilliant example.[2]

In light of the scope of Wright's thesis and the fact that his wider project is still in process, most of the initial responses have come in the form of probing questions that will need to be addressed by Wright as he seeks to clarify, develop and defend his proposal. This essay is meant as an appreciative supplement to this endeavor. The following reflections will center on two general questions: First, does the historical evidence support Wright's model of Jesus? And, finally, granting his model, what theological implications of import follow from it?

Initial Considerations

While the focus of this essay is not singularly upon Wright's methodology, one cannot legitimately embark upon an assessment of a particular model of Jesus apart from some consideration of method. Religio-philosophical presuppositions shape one's historical methodology, which, in turn, significantly influences decisions regarding crucial "data" questions—questions such as which texts (or portions thereof) of the Gospel tradition are recognized as historically reliable and, ultimately, which models of Jesus could ever be entertained as historical possibilities. Unfortunately, throughout the history of the Jesus Quest, such considerations have often been ignored. Wright is correct when he asserts that much of what goes on in the name of Jesus research today is "largely the projection of an undiscussed metaphysic" (*NTPG* 31).[3] In many quarters of the contemporary Quest, unstated and unargued religio-philosophical presuppositions (generally rooted in some variation of a deistic or naturalistic worldview) serve to bracket from serious consideration any historical methodology that deviates from the one Wright and others have come to recognize and unmask as the unproven remains of a naive historical positivism whose day has come and gone.[4]

Wright offers a concrete and well-developed alternative, complete with an explicit epistemology (*NTPG* 29-144). To this reviewer's mind, Wright's moves here are to be congratulated. Whether or not one agrees with every detail of his approach, he is to be recognized as one of a growing number of Jesus scholars today who are tracing out a new and fruitful methodological trajectory, which is able to integrate serious historical investigation with a worldview that is not held captive to minimalism. It is a trajectory that calls for a revised form-critical approach, one specifically *Jewish* in nature (*NTPG* 418-35; *JVG* 86-88, 372-83). It is open to the role that "*informal* and *controlled*" oral traditions (i.e., a position between Rudolf Bultmann's and Birger Gerhardsson's) played in the formation of the Gospel tradition and to the implications this holds for questions of reliability (*JVG* 134, emphasis original).[5] This approach asks the question, Why not suppose that Jesus himself was at least as theologically creative as the standard form- and redaction-critical approaches assume the evangelists and early church were (*JVG* 478-79)? Thus, it recognizes that the multiple oral performances that would naturally have arisen during the course of Jesus' itinerant ministry are probably as important in explaining the variations within the tradition as are the creative energies of the early church (*JVG* 170-71, 632-33). Finally, it recognizes that only those models of Jesus that firmly situate him within the complex socio-historical context of Second Temple Palestinian Judaisms have any claims to real historical plausibility.[6] It is one of Wright's greatest accomplishments that he has mastered a wealth of material on the Second Temple period and has gone on to make good historical sense of Jesus within this context.[7]

Wright's approach begins with and concentrates on large-scale historical hypotheses and their verification, as opposed to narrowly focused debates regarding isolated logia (*NTPG* 98-109; *JVG* 86-91). He recognizes that an analysis of a person's words apart from the context of the symbolic acts and explanatory events in which they were originally embedded is artificial and generally unfruitful (*JVG* 79, 131-37, 171, 543, 554). He has largely exchanged the overly stringent and narrowly focused "authenticity criteria" of the New Quest for a broader set of tests designed to assess hypotheses as wholes, including comprehensiveness, simplicity, explanatory power, fit within historical constraints, and a refined "double criterion of similarity and dissimilarity"—that is, both dissimilarity and similarity to Judaism and early Christianity (*JVG* 338). With such moves, Wright's historiographical method is able to shift a good amount of the burden of proof to those who would approach the texts of the tradition with an a priori historical skepticism.[8] One of the important ramifications of this methodological trajectory is that it allows for a positive reassessment of the historical value of the canonical Gospels (*JVG* 89).[9] Thus, it is clear that whether or not one shares this methodological trajectory with Wright will seriously affect one's assessment of his model of Jesus.[10] It should be stated up front that this reviewer, for one, finds Wright's general methodological approach to be historically sane and refreshing.[11]

Jesus as Eschatological Prophet

Increasingly, one finds that scholarly reconstructions of Jesus deal not in single-faceted, monochromatic silhouettes but rather in complex, multidimensional models. Wright's is a prime example of this trend. When assessing models of this nature, two primary questions should steer the course:

1. Is each individual element of the model supported by the historical data?

2. If so, can the individual elements be held together to form a coherent, historically plausible model of Jesus?

These two questions shall always linger in the background of the following reflections on Wright's proposal.

Wright proposes that the primary paradigm arising most naturally in the study of Jesus is that of prophet. More specifically, Wright reads Jesus as a popular Jewish prophet who combined elements of both "oracular" (i.e., he spoke judgment to rebellious Israel) and "leadership" (i.e., he founded a liberation movement) types within the context of an itinerant ministry (*JVG* 152-54, 162-86).[12] Finally, his message was characterized by an eschatological urgency.

This basic claim has strong historical plausibility to it. That Jesus fit the mold of a popular Jewish prophet is a widely held view within the Quest today—the dissenting voices of many within the Jesus Seminar notwithstanding.[13] Even among those who argue for a contrasting primary rubric, often there is the acknowledgment that a prophetic element is central to an accurate vision of Jesus.[14] That Jesus was an itinerant prophet is beyond serious doubt.[15] Wright also accurately highlights both the oracular and leadership/action characteristics of Jesus' prophetic persona.[16] Again, Wright wisely refuses to pit "religious" against "social" prophet (*JVG* 296-97). As Lester Grabbe has demonstrated, the notion of "prophet" in ancient Judaism allowed for a wide range of possible instantiations.[17] Wright is to be commended for allowing the novel combination of elements of Jesus' own prophetic aims to emerge unfettered by the bounds of rigidly conceived heuristic categories.

Finally, there is the issue of Jesus as an eschatological prophet. Wright locates himself, along with Albert Schweitzer and others, within that time-honored tradition that most fundamentally understands Jesus as an eschatological prophet (*JVG* 150). However, Wright has a distinctive and controversial reading of Jewish apocalyptic thought that is integral to his interpretation of Jesus. Taking an interpretive cue from his Oxford mentor, George B. Caird, Wright argues for a strongly historicized view of first-century Jewish apocalyptic thought.[18] Wright summarizes this as follows:

> *There is virtually no evidence that Jews were expecting the end of the space-time universe.*
> There is abundant evidence that they . . . knew a good metaphor when they saw
> one, and used cosmic imagery to bring out the full theological significance of
> cataclysmic socio-political events. . . . What, then, did they believe was going to
> happen? They believed that *the present world order* would come to an end—the
> world order in which pagans held power, and Jews, the covenant people of the
> creator god, did not. (*NTPG* 333, emphasis original; cf. *JVG* 208)

This present work is not the place for anything like a thorough evaluation
of Wright's understanding of Jewish apocalyptic thought. However, since his
views here have direct bearing upon his vision of Jesus, I will pose several issues
that, left unresolved, could present problems for Wright's model. First, one
wonders if Wright has built too monolithic a model of Jewish apocalyptic
thought. Has Wright prematurely collapsed into one conceptual mold the
diversity of eschatological thought that one would expect to find in the various
"Judaisms" of the day?[19] It may be true that no ancient Jews were expecting the
"end of the space-time universe." (What exactly this expectation could mean in
a pre-Einsteinian conceptual world is not quite clear.) Nonetheless, it would
seem that passages such as John 3:13 do suggest that some of them could read
Daniel 7 as pointing to a literal "coming on the cloud" event for a Son of Man
figure.[20]

This leads to a second issue. It appears that there is something of a false
dichotomy at work in Wright's thesis. His discussion focuses upon the two
options: the proposed historical interpretation on one hand and the disappear-
ance of the entire space-time universe on the other. Why not something of a
middle-ground between these extreme alternatives? Why not a "non-natural"
in-breaking of God, a divine intervention of such *cosmic* qualities and proportions that—although the cosmos itself would remain—to call it purely "historical" in Wright's sense would be woefully inadequate? It seems there is an
important qualitative difference between, for example, the end of the space-
time universe and the coming of a transcendent figure in the clouds, both of
which, however, are events beyond the ken of the merely "historical" (as Wright
seems to use the term).[21] Again, a purely historical solution (i.e., one that leaves
fundamentally unchanged the very nature and structure of the cosmos) would
appear to miss the expectations of Jewish apocalyptic thought. From the
moment this purely historical event occurs, there would exist the imminent
threat that, due to the vicissitudes of history, this event might be reversed in the
next turn of events.[22]

The final issue concerning Wright's view of Jewish apocalypticism is connected to two other elements that he sees at the heart of Jesus' prophetic mindset. Thus, it will be fruitful first to sketch the contours of Wright's vision of Jesus' prophetic message and to then return to the apocalyptic connection.

According to Wright, Jesus proclaimed a message about the coming reign/kingdom of Israel's God. Wright claims that most first-century Jews would have associated three primary expectations with the kingdom of God: Israel's return from exile, the defeat of evil (especially Israel's enemies) and the return of Yahweh to Zion (*NTPG* 206). In short, the kingdom of God represented the long-awaited hope that Yahweh, the sovereign Creator of all the earth, would one day save his people by fulfilling his covenant promises toward them, bringing both vindication to Israel and the defeat of her enemies. Here Wright correctly emphasizes an important aspect of the biblical vision of the kingdom of God that too often suffers a low profile, particularly in conservative circles: the fact that God's kingship consistently is manifested within the context of a battle with powerful opponents.[23]

Here arises a central tenet of his thesis: namely, that in the first-century Palestinian world, "many, if not most, Jews regarded the exile as still continuing. The people had returned in a geographical sense, but the great prophecies of restoration had not yet come true" (*JVG* 126; cf. *NTPG* 268-72, 299-301). Wright's still-in-exile thesis has come under fire by more than one reviewer.[24] Broadly understood, however, this proposal can make sense of much historical data.[25] It correlates nicely with the "two ages" temporal/eschatological dualism characteristic of Jewish apocalyptic thought.[26] Thus, Wright's still-in-exile thesis is one way of expressing the sentiments of a significant segment of Second Temple Judaism.[27]

According to Wright, Jesus' prophetic proclamation of the kingdom of God involved a radically subversive retelling of this basic Jewish hope. Central to his thesis is the conviction that Jesus was an adamant antirevolutionary (in the militaristic sense) who strongly denounced Israel's nationalistically driven movements of violence (*JVG* 159, 290-91, 296, 420-21, 447-50, 462-65, 506-7, 549). In his announcement of the arrival of the kingdom, Jesus challenged the strong anti-Gentile sentiments and violent political aspirations, and he radically redefined the concepts of "Israel" and "the reign of god" by suggesting that, in his own words and ministry, the story of Israel was finding both its recapitulation and climax (*JVG* 235). Thus, Jesus' message was "*doubly* revolutionary": It rejected the political programs of both Rome and nationalistic Judaism, and it replaced them with Jesus' own (*JVG* 465, emphasis original).

With Wright, most will agree that Jesus consciously turned away from revolutionary aspirations. But the importance Wright places upon this thesis leads him, at times, to press for exegetical conclusions that seem forced. For instance, it is not clear that with the phrase "den of robbers" (*lēstēs*) in Mark 11:17 Jesus was suggesting that the temple had become the seat of national resistance (*JVG* 418-24). There is good evidence that the term *robbers*, or *bandits*, would have described the general sentiments of many first-century Jews toward (what was at least perceived as) the corrupt temple system and its officials.[28] Beyond this, given the centrality of an antirevolutionary program for Wright's Jesus, can dullness and perpetual misunderstanding (*JVG* 301) really account for the presence and use of Peter's sword on the final night of Jesus' life (Mk 14:47 and par.)? And if so, what does Wright do with Jesus' statement that "the one who has no sword must sell his cloak and buy one" (Lk 22:36)? That Jesus was not a revolutionary is clear. That an antirevolutionary agenda played the kind of dominant role in Jesus' prophetic mindset demanded by Wright's thesis is less certain.

Wright fleshes out his profile of Jesus the prophet by suggesting the answers that Jesus would have given to some basic worldview questions (*JVG* 443-74).

1. Question: Who are we? Answer: "We are the real, the true, Israel" (*JVG* 443).

2. Question: What's wrong? Answer: "The satan," a cosmic enemy, had deceived historic Israel into blindly adopting a demonic worldview, a central pillar of which is a self-destructive policy of idolatrous nationalism and violent militarism (*JVG* 446-63).

3. Question: What's the solution? Answer: The kingdom of God, which had decisively arrived in Jesus' own life and work. Thus, Israel's real enemy was neither Roman powers nor corrupt Jewish leaders, neither Pilate nor Caiaphas, but rather the personal, cosmic, satanic force that stood above and behind both of these historical entities. And it was through Jesus that the satanic adversary would be defeated, not by a nationalistic holy war (itself a satanically inspired scheme designed to distract Israel from its true vocation) but, paradoxically, via the cross (*JVG* 463-67).

Wright's proposal does a remarkable job of explaining much of the data within the context of Jewish apocalyptic thought. Many apocalyptic texts of the day recognized that evil spiritual forces were aligned with, and ultimately held sway over, the enemies of Israel and that their demise would coincide with the anticipated "age to come."[29] It is also clear that an apocalyptic "spiritual warfare" worldview dominated the thought of Jesus.[30] As such, Satan, not Rome, was the ultimate enemy in need of address.[31] In fact, this theme could be significantly developed by Wright to show the wide and varied dimensions in which Jesus' ministry would have been understood in many first-century Jewish apocalyptic circles as direct attacks upon Satan's kingdom and powers (*JVG* 191-96).[32] One point at which Wright's exegesis does appear strained is his contention that Jesus' words concerning "whom to fear" (Lk 12:5 par. Mt 10:28) refers to the satan, rather than God (*JVG* 454-55). While this offers a supportive apologetic for his "Rome and Satan" thesis, it is less than convincing. Both the long-standing "fear of Yahweh" tradition and the common apocalyptic theme that pictured God, not Satan, as the judge who would finally destroy his adversaries in the eschatological flames—themes the Gospels suggest were not foreign to Jesus (e.g., Mk 9:45-47; Lk 18:1-4)—count against Wright's interpretation.[33]

With this, it is time to return to the final question regarding Wright's view of Jesus' prophetic eschatology. There is an important sense in which it appears that his "historical" reading of apocalypticism is in tension with the view that the satan, a cosmic spiritual entity, is Israel's true enemy. If the real enemy is not a merely historical entity (Rome, Caiaphas), but rather a nefarious, cosmic, personal power, how can one expect a purely historical solution to sufficiently address the real problem? Put more broadly, how could ancient Jews have expected an event to have anything like "cosmic significance" (Wright's phrase, *NTPG* 283) apart from an expectation that it would significantly affect the real cosmic problem on a cosmic level? As Wright has demonstrated, the use of metaphorical language to describe the theological significance within and behind sociopolitical events is a significant part of Jewish apocalyptic thought. However, if all apocalyptic language is metaphor for purely historical realities, then the satan becomes mere metaphor for Rome (or whomever), and Wright is back to a Jesus who really does see the enemy as a particular political entity. Conversely, to allow that Jesus took talk of "the satan" literally is to admit that apocalyptic language—for all of its strangeness to our ears and even the ears of other first-century Jews—can and does refer literally to referents that are trans-historical in nature. It would appear that Wright can't have it both ways. If Jesus and other Jews could swallow a literal cosmic personal enemy called "the satan," which Wright's thesis requires them to do, where is the problem with a literal cosmic Son of Man coming on a cloud? Cosmic problems, it would seem, demand cosmic solutions, wherein the very structure of the world and its history, as it has hitherto been known, must be done away with, and a new cosmic-structural (not merely historical-political) order set in its place. Relieved of its false dichotomy (either historical or end of the space-time universe), Wright's view of apocalyptic eschatology could be modified to solve this problem.

A final prophetic aspect to consider is that of Jesus' symbolic actions. With the dawning of the kingdom of God in Jesus' ministry came a sense of eschatological urgency. This new state of affairs left the traditional Jewish symbols (sabbath, purity, nation, land, temple)—tarnished as they were through the abandonment of the vocation that, alone, unlocked their intended meaning—out-dated and "redundant" (*JVG* 400; see also 402). Instead, Jesus offered a new variation of these symbols, which, like his message, highlighted and clarified the renewed Israel that was presently being reconstituted around himself. In his healings, Jesus was symbolically enacting that which was expected to accompany Israel's long-awaited return from exile (*JVG* 428). With his practice of open-table fellowship, Jesus dramatized the eschatological messianic banquet, thus replacing the old symbol of purity via food laws. In the process, Jesus offered another powerful symbol as he created a new fictive kinship group: those who had given themselves to his vision and agenda had become a new family; more specifically, they were the restored Israel, with Jesus at the center (*JVG* 430-32). With his proclamation of the arrival of the eschatological forgiveness of sins came a fresh covenant marker, one that would serve both to redefine the old covenant badge, the Torah, and to mark out his followers as the new-covenant people. Most importantly, the essence of Jesus' prophetic and eschatological agenda was clearly demonstrated in two paradigmatic symbolic acts: the temple action and the Last Supper.

In Wright's analysis of Jesus' symbolic actions, one finds the kind of fruit born from the new turn in Jesus studies toward a focus upon acts and events over isolated sayings. It is clear that the acting out of dramas, either memorialized in or anticipated by the Old Testament, was not uncommon fare among popular leadership prophets in early Judaism.[34] Josephus connects Theudas, the Samaritan, the Egyptian and other unnamed prophet-types with just such symbolic enactments.[35] John the Baptist was remembered not so much for what he said but for what he did. Likewise, Jesus often performed meaning-laden actions that, in themselves, symbolize, reveal and even embody the kingdom of God.[36] Thus, Wright is correct to identify certain key events in Jesus' life as important symbolic actions that help unlock the mysteries of his intentions.[37] Wright eventually concludes that Jesus himself "was the greatest symbol of his own career" (*JVG* 438).

To raise the next issue—whether or not Wright has correctly interpreted Jesus' central symbolic actions—is to begin to explore the second element of his model.

Jesus as Messiah

It is as Wright moves to a historical analysis of Jesus' aims and intentions—his sense of vocation—that the next element of his complex model emerges: Jesus was not only a prophet with a prophetic message for Israel; Jesus believed himself to be Israel's Messiah.[38] His claim is straightforward:

> Jesus applied to himself the three central aspects of his own prophetic kingdom-announcement: the return from exile, the defeat of evil, and the return of YHWH to Zion. . . .
>
> He regarded himself as the one who summed up Israel's vocation and destiny in himself. He was the one in and through whom the real "return from exile" would come about, indeed, was already coming about. He was the Messiah. (*JVG* 477, 517)

Wright uncovers hints of messianic aims early on in Jesus' ministry. There was the explanation of his ministry in messianic terms (Lk 4:18-21; cf. Is 61), the healings and the table fellowship that could be construed as a symbolic enactment of the messianic banquet. There was the self-designation of "the shepherd" (Mt 10:16; 12:11-12; 18:12-14; cf. Ezek 34) and the comparison of himself with David (Mk 2:25-28) and Solomon (Mt 12:42). Finally, the baptismal inauguration of Jesus' ministry suggests either the call to or the confirmation of his messianic vocation (*JVG* 537).

Wright builds his main case for Jesus' messianic aims around the temple action and the Last Supper. In the temple incident, Wright sees "the most obvious act of messianic praxis within the gospel narratives" (*JVG* 490). In a precedent set by Solomon, it is the king, the anointed one—that is, the Messiah—who has ultimate authority over the temple. Both the triumphal entry, which was itself "clearly messianic," and the temple action invoked the Maccabean paradigm of victorious entry into Jerusalem and cleansing of the temple (*JVG* 491-93). Wright argues that no fewer than six "royal riddles" found in the Gospel tradition offer historical signals of Jesus' messianic aims, and, taken together, they provide Jesus' own necessarily cryptic interpretation of his act in the temple (*JVG* 493-510). In this event, Wright also sees a symbolic enactment of the future destruction of the temple. As a prophet, Jesus routed the traders in order briefly to suspend the sacrificial process (this was not permanent cleansing or reform but a momentary symbolic dramatization), an element of the event that Wright takes as a key to his intention; thus Jesus announced the future judgment and destruction of the temple at the hands of Rome (*JVG* 423). This judgment was Yahweh's response to Israel's sin, specifically the refusal of their vocational calling (i.e., to be ambassadors of Yahweh and a light to the world) and the (countervocational) adoption of a program of nationalistic violence. As Messiah, Jesus had already demonstrated the redundancy of the temple in light of his own presence by forgiving sins outside of its sacrificial system. Therefore, the future destruction would be followed not by a rebuilding of a physical temple (contra E. P. Sanders), but rather by the establishment of its replacement: the messianic community, with Jesus at its center (*JVG* 426, 432-37). Thus, both Jesus' prophetic reputation and his messianic authority hinged upon his announcement of the temple's coming destruction, the fulfillment of which would mean his vindication on both counts (*JVG* 362).

In the Last Supper, Wright finds a second symbolic action that elucidates Jesus' sense of messianic vocation. As with the temple action, Wright identifies a series of riddles—"riddles of the cross"—that, along with the more explicit passion predictions (which Wright judges as authentic), illuminate Jesus' Last Supper symbolism by marking out the course that he consciously followed to Jerusalem and his death (*JVG* 565-76). For Jesus, the Last Supper was "a deliberate double drama," in which the history of Israel (symbolized by the Passover meal) and the climactic moment of his own ministry were fused together (*JVG* 554). By celebrating the ritual meal a day early, Jesus set up an alternative Passover of sorts, one in which he himself—and particularly his impending sacrificial death—became the centerpiece of a new exodus (*JVG* 555-59).[39] In the bread, Jesus symbolized his life-giving death for his followers. In the cup, Jesus symbolized the blood, his blood, of the new covenant (*JVG* 560-61). Thus, for Wright, the temple action and the Last Supper are "mutually interpretative" (*JVG* 438): in both instances, Jesus' symbolic action serves to displace the present temple system and to replace it, in no uncertain terms, with himself (*JVG* 553-63).

Wright argues that first-century Jewish eschatological thought provided the narrative, conceptual and textual contexts within which Jesus' self-consciously messianic vocation of vicarious suffering for Israel was quite understandable (*JVG* 576-92). By "standing on the shoulders of Schweitzer and Caird," Wright reaches a view of Jesus' understanding of his own death that he judges to be "substantially new" in the field today (*JVG* 594 n. 203).

Jesus conceived of his messianic vocation in terms broadly familiar to many

Jews of his day: he was called to liberate Israel from exilic bondage by defeating its enemies. However, his vocation also contained several novel twists. First, his global vision burst the nationalistic boundaries of common Jewish messianisms. Second, as part of his messianic task, he sensed a calling to take upon himself the wrath incurred by Israel for rejecting Yahweh's program of a peaceful, antimilitaristic kingdom. In one stroke, Jesus saw his death both as a one-time vicarious sacrifice (one that would replace the temple cult) and as the paradoxically victorious battle that would finally undo the satanic enemy of Israel. As an eschatological prophet, he announced Israel's judgment precipitated by the rejection of his kingdom agenda. As Messiah—that is, as "Israel-in-person, Israel's representative" (*JVG* 538)—he would take upon himself that same judgment. In this single act, read through the interpretive lens of the Last Supper, one witnesses the arrival of "the new exodus, the renewal of the covenant, the forgiveness of sins, the end of the exile. It would do for Israel what Israel could not do for herself. It would thereby fulfil Israel's vocation, that she should be the servant people, the light of the world" (*JVG* 596-97). Thus, Jesus, the self-giving, forgiving martyr-messiah, would defeat evil and, in so doing, would become the very means of "the victory of God" (*JVG* 610).

It should be noted that there is no inherent tension between Wright's two elements thus far: Jesus as prophet and as Messiah.[40] Given Wright's methodological approach, one is not surprised to see this second dimension of his model appear. He joins the ranks of those contemporary "Questers" who share a generally optimistic assessment of the canonical-Gospel tradition's reliability and, thus, the historical conclusion that Jesus demonstrated messianic aims.[41] Given the historicity of the three key symbolic enactments during Jesus' last week—the entry into Jerusalem, the temple action and the Last Supper—such a conclusion is difficult to avoid.[42] With Zechariah (among others) supplying the prophetic script, Jesus' entry into the city on a donkey and his subsequent temple action (whatever else it signifies) would have consciously evoked messianic expectations.[43]

In turning to Wright's interpretation of Jesus' temple action, one enters an area of complexity and controversy within the field of Jesus research today. That the event is historical is clear to most scholars.[44] What the event means is far less certain. Wright has pointedly identified the problem: "the Temple-action is clearly underdetermined" (*JVG* 414). Apart from the wider visions of Jesus they support and the roles they play therein, the evaluation of competing interpretations is difficult.

Wright's view has several qualities that suggest its viability. First, it fits with the growing recognition that Jesus engaged in symbolic enactments. Second, it offers something of a synthesis of the commonly polarized "reform"/"cleansing" and "symbolic destruction" interpretations.[45] Wright's own view is heavily invested in the latter perspective. He is correct in noting the unavoidable evidence in the tradition of the connection between Jesus' words and actions regarding the temple and the theme of destruction. The destruction view also comports better with the symbolic-enactment thesis than does the reform/cleansing interpretation.[46] However, Wright also acknowledges an element of corruption in the first-century temple system and thus the need for prophetic critique and judgment. Relatedly, Wright is to be commended for taking the much needed correctives of the so-called new view of Judaism and the law to heart while, at the same time, not falling to the opposite extreme of categorizing as retrojections the points at which Jesus critiqued the Judaism of his day.[47] Finally, in tandem with certain nuances of his Jesus-as-Messiah thesis, it offers an intriguing temple-restoration schema—messianic community as functional temple replacement—that has historical parallels (Qumran) and makes good sense of much of the data.

Wright's proposal, however, does raise some questions. To begin with, there is an apparent tension within his overall interpretation of the event. As a prophet, Jesus announced in word and deed that the temple "was under divine threat, and, unless Israel repented, it would fall to the pagans" (*JVG* 417). Here, Wright seems to present Jesus' message as a warning of judgment that is conditional upon Israel's repentance. As Messiah, however, Jesus, according to Wright, is taking authority over the temple and, in light of the fact that he saw "himself, and perhaps his followers with him, as the new Temple," declaring its eschatological redundancy (*JVG* 426). In the first strand of thought, repentance on Israel's part would seem to reverse the warning of covenant judgment upon the temple; the anticipated curses of destruction are potentially avoidable. In the second strand, however, the destruction of the temple is inevitable. Its necessity is not linked to the covenant behavior of Israel at all but rather to the fact that the dawning of the messianic age has rendered the temple obsolete, having given birth to its intended replacement—the messianic community. How these two strands are to be reconciled is not immediately apparent.

Beyond this, questions involving specific exegetical matters emerge. First, it is not at all clear that Jesus' primary concern with the temple was the sin of nationalistic violence. Second, the claim that "this mountain" (Mk 11:23) referred to the temple mount is at least highly debatable. Here one faces an inevitable problem in intertextual matters, one that Wright himself explicitly raises: "When is an allusion not an allusion?" (*JVG* 584). Does Zechariah unlock the mystery of Jesus' referent, or does the more immediate context of the event point us toward the Mount of Olives?[48] Third, how does the claim that Jesus saw the temple as redundant and himself and his followers as its replacement square with the strand in the tradition that presents Jesus as supportive of the temple system (e.g., Mk 1:40-44; Mt 5:23-24)? In the testing of large-scale historical hypotheses, one must be cognizant that today's admirable attempt to "fit" the various data (an attempt that should initially characterize any such venture) may well become tomorrow's Procrustean bed. This is not to call the messianic element of Wright's model into question but rather to suggest that, at certain exegetical defense points, a more tentative tone and further exploration are called for.

Let us turn next to the Last Supper, the historicity of which can be convincingly supported.[49] Key to Wright's thesis is a connection between the Last Supper and the Passover. His argument for going with John's chronology (which gives the Last Supper on the day before the Passover) is intriguing, but in either case the events of Passover would have offered the necessary connection. Of course, each assessment here will depend on one's sense of what, exactly, the particular acts of the Supper—set in the context of Jesus' prior symbolic deeds and sayings—would have elicited in the minds of Jesus and his followers. In any case, read as a prophetic action and within the wider context of Jewish apocalyptic thought in general and Jesus' ministry in particular, the "messianic" elements required of Wright's thesis are there to be found, from messianic banquet to Jesus as salvific focus.[50]

As Wright indicates, the various elements of the tradition force the question of how to account for and reconcile the apparently conflicted data of Jesus' self-identity, namely,

1. messianic aims and the attendant expectation of victory over Israel's enemies
2. the expectation of impending death

Wright's thesis offers a brilliant resolution that fits (though with a distinctive twist) within the conceptual categories of first-century apocalyptic Judaism and that accounts for the data. Once Jesus' own creative theological abilities are allowed into the equation, the solution presents itself as an innovative synthesis—Jesus' synthesis—of themes available in Judaism at large and within his prior ministry. This solution finally comes together in the symbolism of the Last Supper: messianic victory and forgiveness of sins through covenant *peirasmos* in the form of an Isaianic servant's death; a new Passover celebrating a new exodus (end of exile) that gives birth to a new (renewed) covenant community.[51] The genesis of a new community is hard to miss here. From the selection of the Twelve and their mission, to what appears to be something of a (renewed) covenant ratification ceremony or meal in the Last Supper—broken and shared bread,[52] shared cup of the "blood of the (new) covenant" (cf. Ex 24:8)[53]—Jesus' symbolic reconstitution of Israel is apparent.[54]

With Wright's Jesus-as-Messiah thesis comes the claim that Jesus saw himself as "Israel-in-person, Israel's representative, the one in whom Israel's destiny was reaching its climax" (*JVG* 538). Thus, for Wright's Jesus, the end of the exile and the reconstitution of Israel as well as the judgment of Israel and the defeat of the satan were all taking place within himself. Such a claim raises the issue of just what conceptual world could fuel such notions. Ben Witherington III has posed the question of whether this view is rooted in "a rather dubious idea of corporate personality."[55] He goes on to suggest that Wright's thesis would be better served by presenting Jesus as "Israel's representative" as opposed to as "Israel itself."[56] Wright has rejected this critique as a false dichotomy, but without much discussion (*JVG* 532 n. 191). Here, Wright's thesis would benefit from the support of a revamped model of corporate solidarity.

Unfortunately, it is as common to find the wholesale rejection of corporate personality (solidarity) today as it was to find its equally uncritical acceptance fifty years ago. Recently, however, there have appeared signs that a middle ground between H. Wheeler Robinson, on one hand, and his critics (e.g., John Rogerson), on the other, is opening up for fruitful exploration.[57] Suffice to say that Robinson's original conception has been reworked by detaching it from questionable psychological theories (e.g., "primitive mentality"), clarifying some of its ambiguities and taming its excessive claims. The result is a model that, while allowing for individual awareness, recognizes the primacy of the role of the covenant community—as epitomized in its leader—in self-definition. Such a notion would provide the conceptual foundations required to support Wright's understanding of Jesus' messianic self-consciousness.

So supported, Wright's Jesus-as-Israel thesis can find further supplemental evidence within the historical data. For example, one possibility arises with Wright's willingness to grant a historical core to the temptation narratives ("stylized and polished" as they may be [*JVG* 457]) and countenance the possibility of tracing the essential points of the struggle back to the life of Jesus (*JVG* 457-59).[58] Whereas Wright traces the kernel of the temptation back to a messianic identity

crisis, one might complement and clarify this by following the equally compelling strand back to the "Israel as son of God" tradition and, specifically, to the
wilderness-testing tradition (e.g., Deut 8:2-3). Whereas Israel failed their covenant testing, Jesus the Messiah—the new Israel in person—remained the faithful
Son of God.

The general thrust of Wright's proposal appears to pass his proposed historical criteria, not least the double similarity and dissimilarity test. Once again,
however, questions arise regarding internal coherence and exegetical details.
First, while the messianic model and the textual data allow for a Jesus-as-Israel
view, the claim that Jesus also saw himself as the "new Temple" is less defensible
(*JVG* 426). To claim that Jesus' words at the Last Supper suggest he saw his
impending death as functionally replacing the temple's sacrificial system is one
thing. To make the broader claim that he would replace the temple per se requires
further substantiation. Second, the tension previously noted between Wright's
historical view of apocalyptic eschatology and his recognition of a (literal) cosmic
enemy, the satan, returns again. What, exactly, did Jesus' disciples' "return from
exile" and victory over evil consist in if they (the redeemed New Israel) continued
to live, as they did, under Roman domination and persecution? Any response that
would spiritualize the restoration would seem to conflict with Wright's purely
historical reading of Jewish eschatology.[59] Finally, if Jesus thought he was taking
Israel's judgment upon himself at the cross, why would he then prophesy that
Israel would (again?) be judged and destroyed within a generation?

Jesus as Yahweh Embodied

The final element of Wright's model comes to the fore as he identifies Jesus'
treatment of the third element of Jewish expectation regarding the kingdom of
God—the long anticipated return of Yahweh to Zion. Here, Wright enters a field
of discussion rarely traversed today in historical Jesus studies: "the christology of
Jesus" (*JVG* 612). Wright clearly asserts that he is not asking the metaphysical
question of whether or not Jesus was divine. Rather, he is exploring a historical
question, one forced upon us by the data, including the fact that Jesus was worshiped early on by his followers within a monotheistic Jewish context.

Again, Wright begins by exploring the fertile terrain of "symbolic action."
His conclusions center on Jesus' final, fateful journey to Jerusalem and prove,
once again, to be both unique and provocative: "Jesus went to Jerusalem in order
to embody the third and last element of the coming of the kingdom. He was not
content to *announce* that YHWH was returning to Zion. He intended to enact,

symbolize and personify that climactic event" (*JVG* 615, emphasis original).

Wright's thesis is based on several conclusions regarding the thought world of Second Temple Judaism. He argues that there was a general sense that, although the Jews had returned to their land after the exile, the promise of Yahweh's return to the temple/Zion remained unfulfilled (*JVG* 615-24). He also claims that some Jews held that "when YHWH acted in history, the agent through whom he acted [i.e., the Messiah] would be vindicated, exalted, and honoured in a quite unprecedented manner" (*JVG* 624). In this context, Wright claims Jesus believed that he was the very embodiment of Yahweh's return to Zion and that, as the messianic agent of eschatological liberation, he would finally be vindicated, even exalted to a position of enthronement with Yahweh himself. Wright offers three primary lines of evidence for this claim.

First, Wright argues—against a long history of Christian interpretive tradition—that Jesus' riddles and parables of a "return" refer not to a distant future second coming but rather to the return of Yahweh, symbolized and embodied in his own mission (*JVG* 631-42). Specifically, Wright argues that Jesus' parable of the talents/pounds, concerning the departure and return of a king or master (Mt 25:14-30 par. Lk 19:11-27), should be viewed as the "key explanatory riddle" for his symbolic journey to Jerusalem (*JVG* 639-42). Second, Wright detects in Jesus' "riddles of exaltation" (e.g., Mk 12:35-37; 14:61-2) the claim that "as true king, he not only had authority over the Temple, but would share the very throne of Israel's god" (*JVG* 643-44). Finally, he locates various foreshadowings of this sense of ultimate vocation throughout Jesus' ministry, instances where Jesus virtually assumes the role of Yahweh: his calling the Twelve into being, self-designations such as "the bridegroom" and "the shepherd" (designations for Yahweh in the Old Testament), claims of authority over Torah and the ability to forgive sins—actions that suggest he was the embodiment of divine Wisdom, with the unique sense of a special connection with Yahweh as Father (*JVG* 645-51).

With many other Jews of his day, Jesus was committed to the fundamental beliefs of monotheism, election and eschatology. The difference was this: he also believed that the kingdom of God was finally taking place in and through his own person (*JVG* 652). In this final piece of his model, Wright recognizes "the deepest keys and clues to gospel christology" (*JVG* 653). He concludes that Jesus' sense of vocation called him to "enact in himself what, in Israel's scriptures, God had promised to do all by himself. . . . He would embody in himself the returning and redeeming action of the covenant God" (*JVG* 653).

This last element of Wright's model is as intriguing as it is controversial. His setting of the conceptual stage is compelling. The textual evidence substantiates that, at least in some Jewish minds, Yahweh's postexilic return to Zion was still outstanding (see *JVG* 616-22 for a collection of texts). His claim regarding a strand of Jewish speculation that looked toward the vindication and exaltation or enthronement of Yahweh's agent is also historically well-situated. Here, Wright's thought is tied to the new stream of scholarship exploring the connections between Second Temple Jewish speculations on intermediary beings and the Christology of the early church.[60] Jewish monotheism is being seen in new light today, and fruitful possibilities are now available by which to make historical sense of the rise and development of Christian reflection on Jesus.[61] Thus, it may well be that Caiaphas was reacting to a minority-view speculation that the Messiah would actually share the very throne of Yahweh. If so, then "Blasphemy!" would be a natural response to Jesus' provocative linkage of two texts (Ps 110 and Dan 7) that, together, could generate this sort of "dangerous" theology.[62]

The general thrust of Wright's argument for Jesus' seeing himself, in some sense, as the embodiment of Yahweh's saving presence is compelling. Much of the data (e.g., actions, riddles, etc.) Wright identifies within the ministry of Jesus would have been heard by Jewish ears as allusions to various Old Testament texts featuring Yahweh and his future salvation of Israel. Several recent studies on New Testament christological exegesis of Old Testament texts corroborate these kind of connections.[63] Again, under Wright's methodological approach, one can take the conclusions of such studies (which tend to make few historical claims beyond the Evangelists' redactional intentions) and begin the project of tracing certain generative moments back toward the life of Jesus.[64] Isaianic texts figure prominently here. The connections between the long-anticipated new exodus (end of exile) and Jesus are many and wide ranging. One theme that has emerged in several recent studies, and one that would serve to bolster Wright's model, involves the clear and early allusions in the tradition that identify Jesus as the embodiment of the Yahweh-as-warrior motif.[65]

Again, it is in turning to the specific exegetical arguments that questions surface. The first involves the incredible weight placed on Jesus' symbolic journey to Jerusalem as the enactment of Yahweh's to Zion. It is true that a fairly strong case can be made that Jesus would have been conscious of the parallels here, and Wright is not alone in making it.[66] However, that the parable of the talents/pounds was meant to be read as an allusion to Yahweh's return in Jesus' final symbolic journey is highly debatable.[67] Other questions concern the coherence of the thesis, both internally and in regard to further data. First, did Jesus see himself as embodying both Israel and Yahweh? Was Second Temple Judaism in possession of the conceptual resources that would allow both notions to cohere without conflict?[68] Second, if Jesus held that Yahweh had not yet returned to Zion, what does one do with the saying "whoever swears by the sanctuary, swears by it and by the one who dwells in it" (Mt 23:20)? Finally, while a sense of corporate solidarity may account for conceptual fluidity between Jesus-as-Israel versus Jesus-as-Israel's-representative, it is not clear that it can do the same when it comes to Jesus and Yahweh. For Messiah to be a "vicegerent" (*JVG* 630) of Yahweh is to be as distinct as a vassal is from his suzerain. While relational ties of this sort allowed for the virtual identification of a vassal's (or ambassador's) authority with that of the superior, it nonetheless constituted a relationship of representation as opposed to personal identity. There were any number of models of relationship and identity available in Jesus' day. Further clarity regarding just which ones Wright is detecting within Jesus' aims and intentions, and especially in what sense, would be helpful.

There is much to learn from Wright's well-informed and ambitious proposal about Jesus. In the final analysis, he has produced a tripartite model of Jesus that appears able to fit much of the historical data and to cohere conceptually (a few issues calling for further clarification notwithstanding), particularly within the context of Second Temple prophetic activity. As one would expect with regard to any project of this magnitude, certain questions remain to be answered. Some may simply be matters for further elucidation and development (e.g., Jesus as Israel and Yahweh). Others seem to go to the very heart of the thesis itself (e.g., Wright's interpretation of apocalyptic eschatology) and may eventually call for moments of reassessment and adjustment. In any case, Wright's model deserves to be recognized as one of the primary contenders within historical Jesus discussions today.

Concluding Reflections

Wright has indicated that, theologically speaking, his historical conclusions about Jesus have been anything but anticipated or settling. Rather, they have turned him "inside out and upside down" and have led him to a reevaluation of his understanding of Christianity itself.[69] This essay will conclude with a brief consideration of the question, Granting Wright's model of Jesus, what important theological implications follow from it?

Wright's model of Jesus, particularly the "Yahweh embodied" element, points toward the presence of a high Christology historically rooted in Jesus' own self-consciousness. Such a conclusion has not been a common deliverance within the history of the Quest. Wright himself has articulated the implications well: "Those who have desired to explore and understand the incarnation itself have regularly missed what is arguably the most central, shocking and dramatic source material on the subject, which if taken seriously would ensure that the meaning of the word 'god' be again and again rethought around the actual history of Jesus himself" (*JVG* 661).

If Wright is correct, then the later christological formulas of the orthodox creeds can be recognized as legitimate developments of a basic theological intuition that traces back to Jesus. For it is not a long stretch from Jesus as both Israel and Yahweh embodied to Jesus as "fully God and fully human." At the same time, Wright's model would remind twentieth-century Christians that Jesus' own christological self-consciousness was embedded within a distinctly Jewish mindset, one that must be understood on its own historical and cultural grounds lest decontextualized distortions rob it of its own profound and novel revelation.

Wright's distinctive reading of apocalyptic eschatology offers both theological resources and problems. First, if his views are correct, then he has found a way to take Jesus seriously as an apocalyptic prophet without having to say that he failed in his prophetic predictions: A.D. 70 vindicated Jesus. Second, it is true that apocalyptic eschatology has often been misread in far too literalistic and genre-ignorant terms throughout church history, not least in the twentieth-century. One of the unfortunate effects of this has been a sense of apathy toward God's creation in general and social and political injustice in particular. After all, if God is coming any day to incinerate this planet literally (2 Pet 3:10-13; Rev 21:1), why bother spending much time worrying about it? If anything like Wright's more historicized view is correct, it might cause much of the evangelical church to rethink its eschatology in far more concrete and this-worldly terms. In the process, it could serve to awaken an often sleepy evangelical consciousness with regard to ecological, social and political concerns.[70]

Wright's view of eschatology also brings theological problems. Despite Jesus' expectations and claims of the final defeat of evil in and through his kingdom mission, evil apparently remains as firmly ensconced in the very fabric of the cosmos as it ever was. The satan seems to remain the "ruler of this world" (Jn 12:31).[71] At one point, Wright appeals to an "inaugurated" (or "already-but-not-yet") view of eschatology (*JVG* 468-72).[72] However, on Wright's thesis, it seems that the "not yet" aspects of Jesus' own vision would have been entirely encompassed by the combination of the return of Yahweh to Zion in his final journey to

Jerusalem and his postmortem "vindication" as Yahweh's prophet (i.e., fulfillment of his prophetic word regarding the temple's destruction) and Messiah (i.e., exaltation to Yahweh's throne).[73] He suggests that any idea of a second coming beyond this "looks much more like a post-Easter innovation than a feature of Jesus' own teaching" (*JVG* 635). Apparently then, the A.D. 70 destruction of Jerusalem spelled the vindication of Jesus and thus the full realization of his eschatological vision.

But the theological problem remains: evil is not overcome. The questions force themselves upon us: Will evil really ever be defeated? Why do Jesus' followers (the "true Israel") continue to live historical lives that look for all the world as if they are still in exile? Has Wright's view of eschatology saved Jesus from the charge of false prophet at one juncture only to fall victim to it in another? How relevant (a criterion that even Wright acknowledges has a role to play, for better or worse) is his Jesus when in fact evil remains alive and well in this world (*NTPG* 101-2; *JVG* 657)? Again, one wonders why, if ancient Jews had a multi-dimensional view of the world as Wright recognizes, Jesus could not have anticipated both a historical and a cosmic eschatology, both a near (judgment upon "this generation") and a not-so-near (the parousia as classically understood) element of future expectation.[74] These problems are clear. One looks forward to responses to these types of questions in future volumes of this provocative project.

Four

Reading & Overreading the Parables in *Jesus and the Victory of God*

KLYNE R. SNODGRASS

IRST, CREDIT SHOULD BE GIVEN WHERE CREDIT IS DUE. TOM WRIGHT'S *JESUS and the Victory of God* is one of the most comprehensive, consistent and perceptive works on Jesus to appear in several decades. He has provided a coherent explanation of Jesus' intent and mission and has brought back to the fore questions that deserve ongoing discussion. In particular, he has focused attention rightfully on Jesus' Jewish context and on Jesus' relation to the task of Israel. He has also emphasized again the question of eschatology, which should promote serious reconsideration of the content of Jesus' teaching about the kingdom and God's future plan. The New Testament guild and Christians in general owe Wright a rather large debt.

My assessment of Wright's treatment of Jesus' parables cannot be separated from the context of an evaluation of his whole agenda. Therefore, some indication of my response to his approach and the framework from which I make my assessment is necessary. There are several areas in which I think Wright is directly on target. He is correct in his assessment of various historical quests for

Jesus, even if the paradigm "Old Quest, No Quest, New Quest, Third Quest" is a bit overdrawn.[1] His critiques of people like H. S. Reimarus, the members of the Jesus seminar, John Dominic Crossan and Burton L. Mack are all justified and telling. With regard to method he is also correct to bypass the critical attempt to find a strata of authentic sayings. As Wright points out, all such attempts proceed from a presupposed picture of what the historical Jesus was really like and accept as authentic only what fits with the presupposed picture.[2] Furthermore, he is correct to emphasize the necessity of a historical approach and to focus on Jesus' place in Israel's story. His emphasis on Jesus' intent to reconstitute Israel under his own leadership is an essential foundational element in understanding Jesus' mission, as people like E. P. Sanders and Ben F. Meyer have also argued.[3] His placing of Jesus within a Jewish apocalyptic context is not to be questioned, and he is certainly correct to argue that Jesus presented himself as a prophet. He is correct to emphasize the political overtones of Jesus' ministry and to see Jesus' conflict as a confrontation with the temple authorities. Also correct is the further emphasis on the cross as an identification with the sufferings of Israel and a taking on of the task and fate of Israel (*JVG* 592-93). Integral to these elements are Jesus' message of judgment on the nation and his expectation of vindication.[4] In my estimation, without these foundational ideas one will never arrive at a proper understanding of Jesus.

At a second level several positions Wright has taken are more open to discussion or are questionable. Some will argue he has placed too much emphasis on the belief that Jews still felt themselves to be in exile.[5] Many Jews—not all—had returned to Palestine, the temple sacrifices were being performed, and the Hasmonean leaders had been partially successful. Did Jews still think they were in exile? Before discounting this aspect of Wright's argument, one should at least note that sufficient evidence can be marshaled to make such a belief plausible. A recent collection of essays investigates attitudes toward the exile and underscores that a variety of views was held and that some texts view the exile as a permanent state for Jews.[6] One may argue Wright has overstated this theme, but the issue whether Jews believed they were still in exile (or half-exile) is almost irrelevant, for Wright is correct to emphasize that Jews knew the promises that God would return to comfort his people, destroy evil and establish righteousness had not been fulfilled. Even if the exile was over, its effects were not, and the acts of God terminating those effects had not occurred. As Nehemiah 9:36 puts it, the Jews who returned from exile were slaves in the land God gave their forefathers (see also Ezra 9:8-9).

Probably the most questionable area of Wright's work is his explanation of Jesus' eschatological expectations. Wright rejects that Jesus expected the end of the world, and he is probably correct in doing so, even though the idea of a new heaven and a new earth has precedent (e.g., Is 65:17). Israel's hope focused primarily on God's setting things right for Israel and the nations in this world. Wright correctly focuses on the kingdom as present, but he reduces Jesus' message of judgment and his emphasis on the coming of the Son of Man in glory almost exclusively to references to the destruction of Jerusalem in 70 C.E. It would be easy to read *Jesus and the Victory of God* and conclude that Wright sees no expectation in the message of Jesus beyond 70 C.E., but that would be wrong. Wright indeed points to a future element in the teaching of Jesus, one that anticipates final judgment and resurrection (*JVG* 217-18, 305, 322-23). Granted, these themes do not receive sufficient attention, and Wright certainly needs to explain more how these subjects fit with Jesus' teaching about the future, but Wright's Jesus can see beyond 70 C.E. At the same time, it seems to me that the destruction of Jerusalem—as important as it is—has been overemphasized. Is the wrath of God limited to Roman swords (*JVG* 317)? If the subjects of Jesus' eschatology are the present kingdom, the fall of Jerusalem and God's future victory and kingdom, then Wright gives very little attention to the last. In my estimation the coming of the Son of Man in glory or the vindication of Jesus cannot be limited to the destruction of Jerusalem. This reduces Jesus' victory to a relatively small-scale destructive act, which coheres very little with any idea of the revelation of God's glory. Further, to focus so much on the destruction of Jerusalem creates additional problems. What is so important about the destruction of Jerusalem in 70 C.E. that qualifies it as the vindication of the Son of Man as opposed to the destruction in 586 B.C.E. or 135 C.E.? What shows Jesus to be embodying the return of God more so than Jeremiah did at the earlier destruction? In connection with this same theme, how does Wright move from seeing Jesus as embodying God's return like a prophet to seeing Jesus as more than a prophet? This is a movement that does need to occur, but the transition is not clear in this volume.

I do indeed think that Jesus pointed to the destruction of Jerusalem and grant that part of the trouble in understanding Jesus' eschatological teaching results from the uncertainty in sorting out what refers to Jerusalem and what refers to future eschatology. But in my estimation there is not enough "victory" in the destruction of Jerusalem to place all the focus there. A good deal of Jesus' message focuses on *end* judgment, as Wright admits but does not explain. Texts focusing on the messianic meal with Abraham, Isaac and Jacob (Mt 8:11-13), on eating and drinking at Jesus' table in his kingdom and the disciples' sitting on thrones judging the twelve tribes of Israel (Lk 22:29-30; cf. Mt 19:28-29), on woes to cities like Chorazin and Bethsaida (Mt 11:21), on the Ninevites and the queen of the South arising to condemn at judgment (Mt 12:41-42) or on discussions about who should sit on Jesus' right or left in his kingdom (Mt 20:20-28) all presuppose a focus on end-time eschatology that is not given sufficient treatment in Wright's work. This lack of focus on end-time eschatology creates a large gulf between the teaching of Jesus and the teaching of the early church. No doubt the next volume in Wright's portrayal of Christian origins will explain the movement to the church's position, but the gulf is not as large as he has made it.

One further issue should be raised at this point. Wright effectively counters Sanders's de-emphasis of repentance in the message of Jesus, but he views the sin from which people need to repent as revolutionary zeal or violent nationalism (*JVG* 250, 317). The Gospel accounts seem to have a much broader understanding of sin and place little emphasis on nationalism as the sin preventing people from following God.

Operative Assumptions About Parables

Before analyzing Wright's treatments of specific parables, attention should be given to the assumptions he makes about parables in general and the way they are to be interpreted. The foundation that Wright builds in his general treatment of parables is sound. He shows that parables are particularly fitting for one who presents himself as a prophet and that Jesus' parables are modeled on Old Testament examples. From the standpoint of literary criticism he understands well how parables function as lenses and as creating new worlds. Somewhat surprisingly, he suggests that narrative analysis of the parables is still in its infancy. As to purpose, says Wright, the parables do not merely teach but are part of the means by which the kingdom is brought into being. Parables are performative utterances. He correctly rejects Adolf Jülicher's false distinction between allegory and parable and Norman Perrin's false dichotomy between steno- and tensive symbols; consequently he is willing to find multiple correspondences or resonances between the parables and the realities they represent. He correctly sees the parables as a reworking of Israel's prophetic and apocalyptic traditions. Because of their use of traditional material in a conflict setting to create a new understanding of the people of God, he views parables as essentially secretive and necessarily cryptic. This secretive function worked by analogy with other Jewish hermeneutical models evidenced at Qumran and in apocalyptic literature. He argues that the parables do not properly belong in any other context than the ministry of Jesus. That is, they do not stem from the early church. By the time the church is on the scene, the secret is an open one and parables are not the appropriate form. He correctly views the parables in the Gospel of Thomas as later versions stripped of their historical and Jewish specificity. He takes seriously, as he should, that Jesus used similar parables on different occasions and that some of these different versions appear in our sources. He views the parables then primarily as subversive stories—"most of them juridical in nature"[7]—which were told to bring to birth a new way of being the people of God (*JVG* 174-82).

Wright is to be commended for his general description of parables and for avoiding the excesses of much modern parable interpretation. Although I might qualify certain statements, with regard to the general approach the only caution I would raise applies to most other explanations of parables. Scholars tend to form understandings of parables from a select few and then assume that all the parables have this same pattern; but parables can be quite varied and used for quite different purposes. For example, not all parables lead to judgment on oneself—for example, the parables of the seed growing secretly, the mustard seed, the leaven, the pearl and the treasure. Many parables are didactic or persuasive, rather than juridical.

The place where Wright has generalized from some of the parables to almost all of the parables is in his belief that the parables are stories about Israel. They are "Israel's-story-in-miniature" (*JVG* 179). This decision is one of the most determinative for Wright and will be among the most debated by his readers. Virtually all the parables are understood as parables of Israel, including those of the prodigal son, the rich fool and the unjust steward. In some cases, as we will see, parables are indeed a mirror held up to the nation or society as a whole, and Wright has read them correctly. With other parables, however, I suggest that the parables have been overread and conformed to a larger hypothesis, even if I am in broad agreement with that larger hypothesis.

One issue behind this discussion is the degree to which the message of Jesus is a call and challenge to each person and the degree to which it is about Israel. How does one category relate to the other? Did Jesus only tell national stories, or are some parables stories about the life of the individual before God? Were all the parables told to the nation and Jews in general, or were some of them directed to disciples—not just the twelve but people who had become members of the community of those following Jesus? The more the latter is a reality, the more we might expect some parables to address such people and the way they should live.

We may grant quickly that Jesus did not come to teach timeless ethics (*JVG* 228); his coming was tied explicitly to Israel's particular history. At the same time, Jesus did teach what the will of the Father is for all who would obey. For example, does the parable of the wise and foolish builders, which tells of one man who built a house on the rock and of one who built a house on the sand (Mt 7:24-27), really refer to the temple and its coming destruction, as Wright argues (*JVG* 292, 334, 436-37)? Every occurrence of *oikos* (house) cannot be assumed to be a reference to the temple, and *petra* (rock) is unlikely to be a reference to the foundation stone of the temple.[8] The parable refers to obedience to Jesus' ethical teaching; certainly that is Matthew's intent. We may grant that it is not always easy to separate teaching about Israel from teaching about discipleship—which Wright certainly would not want to do—but I see nothing in this parable that suggests we are dealing with Israel and the temple. Rather, Wright has taken imagery and a theology of building one's life on obedience to Jesus and applied them to the temple. Such an *application* is as legitimate as any movement from the general to the particular, but the referent of the parable is not the temple. Similarly I would argue Jesus' teaching that one should remove the plank in one's own eye before removing the speck in a neighbor's is ethical instruction about the will of God to counter the human tendency to ignore one's own faults while needling others about theirs (Mt 7:1-5). This passage is not questioning why Israel looked at the speck in her neighbor's eye when there is a plank in her own, as Wright suggests (*JVG* 329). The theology may again be applied to Israel, but the referent is elsewhere.

Part of the difficulty in assessing Wright's adaptation of the parables is evidenced in these examples. He often makes quick reference to a parable or uses its language without giving a longer explanation, and sometimes one is uncertain whether a parable has been interpreted of Israel or only adapted to Israel. Many of the parables receive comment, and space does not allow assessment of each one. Attention will be focused on parables receiving more extended treatment and on those places where Wright—in my estimation—is reading the parables correctly and those where he is overreading them by forcing them to mirror Israel's coming judgment.

Reading the Parables: Some Parables Do Retell Israel's Story

Certainly the parable that most convincingly demonstrates Wright's case that Jesus told stories as Israel's-story-in-miniature is that of the wicked tenants (Mt 21:33-46 par. Mk 12:1-12 par. Lk 20:9-19).[9] Wright justifiably describes this parable as the key parable for understanding Jesus' temple action. The story is an allegorical reworking of themes from Isaiah 5 (and Ps 80) and functions as an urgent summons that seeks to break open the world-view of the present tenants and replace it with a new one. The parable tells the story of Israel, explains Jesus' temple action (which suggests the temple invited prophetic denunciation and divine demolition), presents Jesus as the final messenger (the Messiah) and culminates in judgment. The stone quotation of Psalm 118:22-23 functions like a riddle and links closely with the idea of the new temple (see *JVG* 178-79, 497-501, 565-66).

Wright convincingly shows how this parable fits in the context of Jesus' life and his prophetic warning of judgment on Israel. The parable is most likely directed at the temple authorities. I am more inclined to think Psalm 118:22-23 connects to the new temple builder than the new temple, but as Wright is careful to point out, we do not possess sufficient information as to how Psalm 118 was read in first-century Judaism.

Other parables that Wright correctly sees as parables mirroring Israel are those of the fig tree (Lk 13:6-9) and of the wedding feast and banquet (Mt 22:1-14 par. Lk 14:15-24).[10] These parables are not discussed in detail, which maybe should not be expected in such a book, but a fuller treatment of these parables would strengthen the argument. The parable of the fig tree is an obvious warning to Israel, and Wright uses it to illustrate the warning and judgment motif in Jesus' message (*JVG* 253, 331, 421, 641). The treatment of the parables of the wedding feast and of the banquet is especially brief in view of both the way these parables mirror Israel's failure and coming judgment and the importance each parable has in its Gospel. Wright does draw attention to the eschatological importance of the feast imagery and to Jesus' banquets as symbolic evocations of the coming messianic banquet. He underscores the judgment theme conveyed by the message that some expecting to be at the messianic banquet will not be. In Matthew the parable is viewed as part of the explanation of Jesus' temple action (*JVG* 328, 502, 532). Although more needs to be said, Wright has correctly read Jesus' intent with these stories.

Surprisingly, however, another parable that could have buttressed Wright's case receives only slight mention. The parable of the two sons (Mt 21:28-32) mirrors both the disobedience of the temple authorities and the obedience of those who repented in response to the messages of Jesus and John the Baptist. It does not depict Israel's history, however. Wright does use the parable to show Jesus was redrawing the boundaries of Israel (*JVG* 329).

The reading given the parables of the mustard seed (Mt 13:31-32 par. Mk 4:30-32 par. Lk 13:18-19) and the leaven (Mt 13:33 par. Lk 13:20-21) is fairly standard. These parables provide redefinition of the kingdom and point to its inauguration within Israel, although what God was doing was veiled and cryptic (*JVG* 241-42). The parable of the seed growing secretly (Mk 4:26-29) also expresses the hidden character of God's work, but it includes the expectation of judgment (*JVG* 241-42).[11]

The most important part of Wright's rereading of the parables is his treatment of the parable of the sower, although I confess that I was not convinced on my initial reading of his treatment. At points he is guilty of overstatement: for example, his claim that the parable shows "*particularly* the return from exile" (*JVG* 230, emphasis original) or that the parable is "a retelling of Israel's controlling narrative about the *kingdoms of the world* and the *kingdom of god*" (*JVG* 232, emphasis added).[12] In his basic argument, however, Wright is correct in saying this parable evokes Isaiah 6 as a way of telling the story of Israel and the story of Jesus' ministry. How much the story mirrors Israel's past in distinction from her present is not obvious, but the use of Isaiah 6 suggests both are included. Wright argues the parable exhibits an apocalyptic narrative mode such as in Daniel 2 and that Mark 4:1-20 resembles an apocalypse: cryptic story, transition passage about mysteries and point-by-point interpretation. The seed is a shorthand for the remnant, a metaphor for true Israel, which is understandable from Isaiah 55:10-13, where the seed is a picture of Yahweh's sowing his word and the result is the return from exile. The sower is understood to be Yahweh himself, and the unfruitful sowings depict the rejected prophets in a way similar to the depiction in the parable of the wicked tenants. The parable describes Jesus' own ministry as the encapsulation of that prophetic heritage (*JVG* 230-39).

If correct—and I believe essentially it is—this argument is of major significance, for it sets aside usual scholarly understandings (and difficulties) with this text. The parable and its interpretation belong together, and the coherence of Isaiah 6 with the parable and its interpretation alleviates the need for a so-called Marcan parable theory of hardening, which was always less than satisfactory anyway. The parable is not merely a nice picture of response to preaching but a warning and an enactment of the kingdom's presence and a promise about its future.

The convincing factor is the role of Isaiah 6:9-13, which describes the judgment conveyed by Isaiah's preaching and uses "holy seed" (Is 6:13) to describe the promised remnant. Within Judaism (and, later, Christianity) this text is a classic text on hardening and is reused often. This midrashic treatment of Isaiah 6 shows a correspondence between the ministry of Isaiah and that of Jesus but, with the seed being sown and the certainty of harvest, makes a statement about what is happening in Jesus' ministry to fulfill the promises of God. The message may be cryptic, but it is unavoidable. As Jesus sows the word, the remnant is being established among those who receive it. Nuancing may be necessary, for the sower, rather than pointing to Yahweh, points to Jesus as God's agent,[13] but Wright has correctly understood the background and significance of this parable.

Overreading the Parables: Making Them Conform

For Wright most of Jesus' parables are "Israel's-story-in-miniature" (*JVG* 179); but in my opinion a number of parables have been pushed beyond their purpose and made to conform to this emphasis. The focus of Jesus' ministry on Israel, on his appeal for Israel to repent and avert the coming judgment and on the reconstitution of Israel under his leadership does not depend on the overreading of these parables. In fact, Wright's case would have been stronger without the distraction these overreadings cause.

Most obvious of the overreadings is his treatment of the parable of the prodigal son. Equally obvious is the fact that Wright does not think his interpretation is an overreading, for this parable is the starting point for his explanation of Jesus' message as an announcement of the return from exile. He grants that no one else has seen his reading of this parable, which is reason enough for caution,[14] but he is convinced that this is the story of Israel, in particular the story of exile and restoration. The exodus story is the ultimate backdrop, but the Babylonian captivity is also in mind. Those who stand in the way of Israel's return are the mixed multitude, not least the Samaritans, so that those who grumble at what is happening in Jesus' ministry are cast in the role of the Jews who did not go into exile. They are virtually Samaritans (even though, as Wright notes, this nuance does not fit Luke's view of the Samaritans). Jeremiah 31:18-20, a text about exile and repentance that refers to Israel as God's dear son, provides the background for the understanding of the parable. The references to resurrection at Luke 15:24, 32 are metaphors for return from exile. The parable is an enactment of the return from exile and, whatever else it is, a classic account of repentance (*JVG* 125-31, 242, 254-55).

Several difficulties emerge on this reading. Wright accepts the setting Luke has given the parable (*JVG* 129), but I do not see how Luke's context fits with Wright's reading. If the parable is a defense of the rightful place of tax collectors and sinners who have returned to the Father, how is it also a depiction of Israel's return from exile? Nothing points either to the exodus or to the Babylonian captivity unless one accepts that Jeremiah 31:18-20 is the basis of the parable. But not every mention of a son necessarily refers to Israel, and I see nothing that points to Jeremiah as the intended background. The two sons represent the response of two kinds of people to Jesus' message (much like the parable of the two sons in Mt 21:28-32), but they do not depict Israel's story of exile and restoration. Most difficult of all—and impossible to me—is that the elder brother in the story depicts the Samaritans who did not want Israel to return from exile. I see no reason to interpret the parable as pointing to anything other than abandonment of (disobedience to) the Father, repentance, rejoicing and the disdain that some scrupulous Jews felt toward those deemed less pious, a theme evidenced elsewhere, especially in the parable of the Pharisee and the toll collector (Lk 18:9-14).

In my estimation what Wright has done here and with other parables is distill the theology inherent in the parable and apply it to Israel. One should note at the beginning and end of the book (*JVG* 9, 15, 17, 662) that Wright creatively and legitimately applies the theology and imagery of the parable of the prodigal son to modern Christians and to modern scholarship. Just as surely as he has redirected the parable to apply it to us, he has redirected it to apply it to Israel. The theology of repentance and return operative in the parable is valid for Israel and was already in evidence in various writers such as Jeremiah. The parable of the prodigal, however, is not about us or Israel's return from exile. It is about two kinds of response to the kingdom forgiveness Jesus embodied: a repentance that leads to reconciliation and celebration, and irrational disdain, the result of which this parable leaves undetermined.

Other treatments also are overreadings of the parables—several of them in brief comments more than extended discussions. The field with wheat and weeds mixed (Mt 13:24-30, 36-43) and the good and bad fish caught in a net (Mt 13:47-50) are both taken to be pictures of Israel (*JVG* 183, 328, 460). First-century Jews were the initial hearers, but these are parables of the kingdom. And the vision of these parables is not limited to Israel, especially when in Matthew the field is interpreted as the world and both parables are interpreted with regard to the *consummation* of the age, which in Matthew certainly does not point to the destruction of Jerusalem (cf. Mt 28:20). If the argument is that Matthew has altered the original intent, that must be demonstrated.

We are told with regard to the parables of the treasure in the field and the pearl of great price (Mt 13:44-46) that people must abandon their cherished assumptions concerning the restoration of the national fortunes of Israel. What must be given up includes an attachment to the ancestral inheritance of the land. The pearl of great price was available for those who sold everything else, including the traditional symbol of the sacred land itself (*JVG* 242, 299, 429). Similarly, the parables of the tower builder and warring king (Lk 14:28-32) are understood as saying Israel must stop clinging to family identity or it will be like someone who is building a tower and is unable to finish or like a king with a small army who is going up against a king with a large army (*JVG* 332). One could understand the appropriation of these biblical metaphors as ways of speaking about Israel, but that does not seem to be Wright's point. Surely, however, the intent of these parables is not to depict Israel but to depict humanity preoccupied with mundane pursuits, as is evidenced in a variety of discipleship sayings demanding total allegiance (e.g., Mt 6:33; 10:37-39; 16:24-26; 19:16-22 and par.).[15] It is especially difficult to see how the treasure in the field should be interpreted as the abandonment of attachment to the ancestral land when the finder in the parable sells all to buy land!

Parables about money are also narrowed to be descriptions of Israel. Unless the language is intended to be merely metaphorical, the parable of the rich fool (Lk 12:13-21) is cryptically interpreted of Israel. Israel is like the rich fool, storing up land and property when the world is about to collapse (*JVG* 291, 331). The parable of the unjust steward (Lk 16:1-9) reflects the judgment hanging over Israel's head (*JVG* 332).[16]

For Wright, the parable of the rich man and Lazarus (Lk 16:19-31) is not a description of the afterlife but the story of what is happening to the rich and poor *in the present time*. Similar to the parable of the prodigal, Jesus' welcome of the poor is understood as a sign that the return from exile, the resurrection, was happening. The five brothers correspond to the elder brother in the parable of the prodigal: the resurrection is occurring, but they cannot see it. The rich man is like those who seek a national or personal agenda for the restoration of land and property or ancestral rights (*JVG* 255-56, 291).

Part of the assumption behind these interpretations of the money parables is the conviction that the kingdom had nothing much to do with what happened to humans after they died (*JVG* 202, 255). Granted, the subject of Jesus' teaching is not how to get to heaven, and the parable of the rich man and Lazarus should not be taken as a picture of the afterlife. But Jesus' teaching and the evidence in the Gospels about the interests of his contemporaries do reveal significant concern with the afterlife. When the lawyer in Luke 10:25 and the rich young ruler in

Matthew 19:16 (and par.) asked about eternal life, they were not asking about the restoration of Israel, which, no doubt, they took for granted. They were asking about their own destiny in the age to come, as Wright also affirms.[17] Nor is Israel's restoration in mind in the instructions to cut off an offending part of the body to ensure entrance into life rather than being whole to go to Gehenna (Mk 9:43-48 and par.).[18] People are not to accumulate treasures on earth but in heaven (Mt 6:19-21 and par.). A number of the texts that teach about judgment have end judgment in view (e.g., Mt 12:36; 13:41-43, 47-50; 16:27; 19:28-29 and par.).[19] The more Jesus and his contemporaries concern themselves with eternal life, the more difficult it is to focus all the attention on Israel and the coming judgment.

Consequently, I would argue that the three money parables—those of the rich fool, the unjust steward, and the rich man and Lazarus—are not about Israel. All three of them in one way or another provide a warning about the right use of wealth and teach that God's judgment *after death* or *at the end* is directly connected to whether wealth was used appropriately. The context of the parable of the rich fool certainly points in this direction, as does the implication of the rich man's death in Luke 12:20. Assuming that Luke 16:9 belongs with the parable of the unjust steward, the concern is about being received into eternal dwellings. And it is difficult to see how the parable of the rich man and Lazarus can point to what is happening in Israel's *present* when the story states that both men died. Even if Jesus' parable has echoes of well-known folktales, I see nothing to suggest a reader should know that Lazarus' reception in Abraham's bosom parallels the welcome of the prodigal by the father nor that the five brothers of the rich man parallel the elder brother. The five brothers do not grumble like the elder brother; their problem, which is expressed only by implication, is that they pay no attention to the law and the prophets as to how they should treat their neighbor.

Two other parables about judgment—the wise and the foolish virgins (Mt 25:1-13) and the sheep and the goats (Mt 25:31-46)—receive only brief comment from Wright. However, both are important in an assessment of his approach, for neither fits easily into a view that sees the "great day which was coming, the day of vindication and judgment" as referring to Jesus' entrance into Jerusalem or to the city's destruction. Wright uses these two parables to point to the coming judgment, to the use of the shepherd imagery as a messianic motif and to the return of Yahweh to Zion in the ministry of Jesus (*JVG* 315, 533, 640), but he takes both parables as Jesus' announcement of judgment on Jerusalem and its current leaders. An understanding of the referent of the parable of the virgins depends on how one understands "the kingdom of heaven," but I have the greatest difficulty thinking that the celebration of the coming of the bridegroom points to Jesus' entrance to Jerusalem or to the destruction of the city. Rather, this parable points to the ultimate victory of God, the future kingdom that Wright knows is an essential part of Jesus' message.

Even more, the parable of the sheep and the goats—which barely qualifies to be called a parable—must be taken as referring to the final judgment. Also difficult for Wright's approach is that the setting of this parable is the time when the Son of Man comes in glory to judge the nations. If it is granted that this parable is about end judgment, then Wright must reassess his approach to other eschatological parables and sayings that have been limited to a focus on Israel and the destruction of Jerusalem.

Another parable that has been slighted in Wright's approach is that of the widow and the unjust judge (Lk 18:1-8). His brief comments indicate the parable is part of Jesus' announcement of judgment on his generation (*JVG* 332, 366). He is right to emphasize the apocalyptic context of the parable; it is not merely a parable about prayer. He is also aware that the parable's context refers to the time when the disciples would long to see one of the days of the Son of Man. He could point to the fact that the only occurrence of *ekdikēsis* ("vindication" or "judgment") in Luke outside this parable is in 21:22, referring to the destruction of Jerusalem.[20] But it seems to me that the language of the parable and its context, even though enigmatic enough, point both to an interval during which people long for vindication and to an event that far exceeds Jesus' entrance to Jerusalem or the destruction of Jerusalem. The Son of Man's coming is like lightening from one horizon to the other (Lk 17:24), and no one after 70 C.E. could have felt the elect were vindicated. John Nolland may be correct that for Luke the time of one's death, the time of the destruction of Jerusalem and the time of the end judgment and vindication are closely related,[21] which could account for the difficulties. But in any case, in its call for faithfulness this parable implies an interval and a focus on a future vindication and victory worth celebrating.

A Tantalizing Reading of the Parable of the Talents

One last parable must be considered—the parable of the talents (Mt 25:14-30 par. Lk 19:11-27). Wright's treatment of this parable is intriguing, but in the end I think this reading too—though tantalizing—is an overreading.

Wright thinks neither Matthew's nor Luke's version is derived from the other; nor does he think that the two came from a single source. Since Jesus used such stories on numerous occasions, this is a justifiable conclusion. Wright accepts that Luke's account alludes to the events surrounding Archelaus's petition to be king. He views Jesus' final journey to Jerusalem as the symbolic enacting of Yahweh's return to Zion to judge and to save, and he places the parable in this context. While most scholars read parables about a returning king or master as referring to the return of Jesus, Wright points out that the Son of Man in Daniel 7 does not come to earth from heaven but goes to heaven to get a kingdom. Stories in Judaism and in Jesus' teaching about kings most often refer to God. Consequently, the king's return in the parable does not refer to the second coming of Jesus but to the return of Yahweh to Zion as embodied by Jesus' journey to Jerusalem.[22] The other parables in Matthew 25 (those of the virgins and of the sheep and the goats) are taken as referring to the judgment that is coming very soon on Jerusalem and its leaders, so in Wright's view the parable of the talents is best read in light of Malachi 3:1-3. Yahweh is returning as king to Zion, but he comes as much for judgment as for salvation.

Wright points out that the interpretation of this parable depends on where, within the story, the hearer is supposed to be located. It has been assumed the story is told from the perspective of the beginning of the process when the master is leaving. But Wright—reminiscent of C. H. Dodd's shifting the time of harvest in agricultural parables from the eschaton to the ministry of Jesus[23]—argues it is more likely that the ideal hearer is located near the end of the story when the master is about to return. The parable is not about the delay of the parousia but the imminence of judgment. In keeping with his interpretation of other parables, Wright believes Jesus intended the servant who buried his master's money to refer to the Jewish nation and its leaders, particularly the temple regime. This parable then is understood as a key explanatory riddle for Jesus' action in journeying to Jerusalem (*JVG* 631-39).

This is not an easy parable, particularly since it has two movements—a rejected king and servants who are given responsibility[24]—but I do not find Wright's explanation convincing. That some parables with a king associate that king with God does not mean all parables do, as is obvious with the parable of the warring king (Lk 14:31-32).[25] Parables are not to be made to "stand on all fours," but the idea of Yahweh's being represented by a nobleman going to a far country to receive a kingdom is difficult to conceive. From whom would Yahweh obtain a kingdom? The idea of Jesus' receiving a kingdom as Son of Man, however, makes good sense and fits with Daniel 7. Wright draws a parallel between the rejection of the owner's son in the parable of the wicked tenants and the rejection of the king (Yahweh) in the parable of the pounds (*JVG* 638). Is the parallel between the rejected king (Yahweh) and the rejected son, or do not both parables point to the rejection of Jesus? The point of this section of the parable is that many Jews were treating Jesus, who was in fact the Messiah, as their fathers had treated Archelaus. The rejection of the owner's son implies a rejection of the owner, but the intertwining of God and God's agent sometimes leaves the picture confusing, even in Wright's explanation. Even though he interprets the parable of Yahweh's return to Zion, he says the judgment will occur when the Son of Man comes—using Roman armies—to crush rebel Jerusalem (*JVG* 638). That Jesus expected the glory of the Son of Man to be revealed through Roman armies is difficult to accept.

I also think Wright objects too strongly to the idea of Jesus' returning. (Wright does nevertheless believe in a future coming.) He is correct that Daniel speaks of the Son of Man's going to the Ancient of Days to receive a kingdom, but what happens then? The purpose of receiving a kingdom in Daniel is that the nations might serve the Son of Man in an everlasting kingdom. The parable of the sheep and the goats is not about the destruction of Jerusalem but about the time when the Son of Man comes with his angels to judge the nations (note especially Mt 25:31-32, 46). Other texts also point to an interval (Mt 9:15 and par.; 23:38-39 and par.;[26] 26:29 and par.; Lk 17:22), a time when Jesus is not present.[27] The more this is true, the more the idea of a return and instruction for this time are legitimate. If Wright accepts that Jesus anticipated his own death and pointed to vindication and resurrection (*JVG* 304, 554-611), why is the idea of return so far-fetched?

The parable gives no clues to indicate that it warns of the imminence of judgment or that Israel is mirrored in the inactive servant. On such a reading who is mirrored by the two successful servants? Rather than showing Yahweh's return to Zion, the parable portrays the rejection of Jesus by the nation and the faithful service expected of his followers during a time of absence. Certainly Luke has understood the parable in this way, or he could not have introduced it as Jesus' attempt to slow down eschatological excitement.[28] The theme of faithful adherence even in difficult times is a focus for Luke, especially from 17:1 on.

Concluding Remarks

Jesus and the Victory of God is not a book on the parables, and an assessment of one segment of a work is to some degree artificial. For many parables one could wish for more extended treatment, but that would require a different kind of book. My disagreements with many of Wright's interpretations do not mean I do not value his work. Quite the contrary. Anyone working on parables must pay serious attention to this volume.

The accomplishment of Wright with regard to the parables is significant, once the overreadings are set aside. His general approach to the parables and his keeping them in the context of first-century Judaism are both welcome relief in comparison with several recent idiosyncratic books on the parables of Jesus. He is to be commended especially for showing how thoroughly the Hebrew Scriptures pervade Jesus' mindset and teaching. He has given helpful and constructive readings to show how the parables proclaim the presence of the kingdom and depict the crisis in which Israel finds itself.

Possibly one of the most significant results of Wright's effort will be the renewed focus given to eschatology. The dual focus on the present and future kingdom is a commonplace both for Wright and most of New Testament scholarship. Incidentally this dual focus is glaring in Luke 19:9-11: salvation has come today, but the kingdom of God is not yet. Despite its being a commonplace, it is by no means clear how this dual eschatology sorts out in detail. The future and near future are so interlaced that sorting them out is not an easy task, but it is one that New Testament scholarship needs to give more attention. Further, regardless of how one answers the eschatological questions, Wright has put his finger on a devastating problem that most seek to ignore: the real problem is the presence of evil after the resurrection of Jesus (*JVG* 659). Possibly more focus on future eschatology would help address the issue, but the parables teach repeatedly about a victory over evil that impacts the present world, as Wright is correct to emphasize and to challenge readers to live out the victory Jesus achieved.

Five

Jesus & the Continuing Exile of Israel

CRAIG A. EVANS

N T. WRIGHT HAS ARGUED THAT FOR MANY JEWS, ISRAEL'S EXILE HAD NOT ended and would not end until God redeemed his people. According to Wright,

Most Jews of this period, it seems, would have answered the question "where are we?" in language which, reduced to its simplest form, meant: we are still in exile. They believed that, in all the senses which mattered, Israel's exile was still in progress. Although she had come back from Babylon, the glorious message of the prophets remained unfulfilled. Israel still remained in thrall to foreigners; worse, Israel's god had not returned to Zion. (*NTPG* 268-69)

Wright defends this claim in the context of the passage just cited and repeats it in *Jesus and the Victory of God* (*NTPG* 268-72; *JVG* 126-27, 203-4).

Wright is not alone in his view. A similar position has been argued by several contributors to a recently published collection concerned with the theme of exile.[1] But Wright's view has not gone unchallenged. In an issue of the *Journal for the*

Study of the New Testament, Wright's *Jesus and the Victory of God* was reviewed by Clive Marsh and Maurice Casey.[2] Each author raised several issues, but Casey directly challenged the notion that many Jews viewed Israel as in a state of exile. After touching on suspected deficiencies having to do with Aramaic, Casey averred,

> The next serious problem is almost a leitmotiv of the whole book: the notion that Jews believed that they were in exile. At the time of Jesus, many Jews lived in Israel. Some lived permanently in Jerusalem. Jews came to Jerusalem from all over Israel and the diaspora for the major feasts. In the Temple, the *Tamid* was sacrificed twice a day, a special symbol of God's presence with Israel. As Jesus put it, "And he who swears by the sanctuary swears by it and by Him who lives in it" (Mt. 23.21). We would need stunningly strong arguments to convince us that these Jews really believed they were in exile when they were in Israel. All Wright's arguments for this view, however, seem to me to be quite spurious.[3]

Casey challenged Wright's understanding of the significance of Jesus' forgiving sin, denying that this has anything to do with Israel's being in exile (whether in a literal sense or a spiritual sense). Wright is vulnerable here because he focuses on covenant and offers little direct evidence that could support the notion that many Jews did view Israel as in a state of exile and bondage. Perhaps Wright felt the point was obvious, only requiring interpretation of its significance (especially for Jesus' theology) rather than a vigorous defense.[4] In any event, Casey's criticisms call for further assessment of Wright's claims. In the balance of this study I shall attempt to show that many Jews did indeed believe Israel to be in a state of bondage, if not exile, and therefore in need of redemption.

First-Century Restoration Hopes and the Idea of Exile

According to Josephus, two Jewish men in the first century promised fellow Israelites signs of salvation; one by parting the Jordan River, the other by bringing down the walls of Jerusalem. These men and their provocative claims offer features of interest for the present study.

We begin with Theudas (*Antiquities of the Jews* 20.5.1. §97-98). Louis H. Feldman renders the passage as follows:

> During the period when Fadus was procurator of Judaea, a certain impostor named Theudas persuaded the majority of the masses to take up their possessions and to follow him to the Jordan River. He stated that he was a prophet and that at his command the river would be parted and would provide them an easy passage. With

this talk he deceived many. Fadus, however, did not permit them to reap the fruit of their folly, but sent against them a squadron of cavalry. These fell upon them unexpectedly, slew many of them and took many prisoners. Theudas himself was captured, whereupon they cut off his head and brought it to Jerusalem.[5]

Next we may consider the episode of the Jew from Egypt (Josephus *Jewish Wars* 2.13.4-5. §§258-63; *Antiquities of the Jews* 20.8.6. §§167-72). H. St. J. Thackeray and Feldman render the passages as follows:

Besides these there arose another body of villains, with purer hands but more impious intentions, who no less than the assassins ruined the peace of the city. Deceivers and impostors, under the pretense of divine inspiration fostering revolutionary changes, they persuaded the multitude to act like madmen, and led them out in to the desert under the belief that God would there give them signs of freedom. Against them Felix, regarding this as but the preliminary to insurrection, sent a body of cavalry and heavy-armed infantry, and put a large number to the sword.

A still worse blow was dealt at the Jews by the Egyptian false prophet. A charlatan, who had gained for himself the reputation of a prophet, this man appeared in the country, collected a following of about thirty thousand dupes, and led them by a circuitous route from the desert to the mount called the Mount of Olives. From there he proposed to force an entrance into Jerusalem and, after overpowering the Roman garrison, to set himself up as tyrant of the people, employing those who poured in with him as his bodyguard. His attack was anticipated by Felix, who went to meet him with the Roman heavy infantry, the whole population joining him in the defense. The outcome of the ensuing engagement was that the Egyptian escaped with a few of his followers; most of his force were killed or taken prisoners; the remainder dispersed and stealthily escaped to their several homes.[6]

With such pollution did the deeds of the brigands infect the city. Moreover, impostors and deceivers called upon the mob to follow them into the desert. For they said that they would show them unmistakable signs that would be wrought in harmony with God's design. Many were, in fact, persuaded and paid the penalty of their folly; for they were brought before Felix and he punished them. At this time there came to Jerusalem from Egypt a man who declared that he was a prophet and advised the masses of the common people to go out with him to the mountain called the Mount of Olives, which lies opposite the city at a distance of five furlongs. For he asserted that he wished to demonstrate from there that at his command Jerusalem's walls would fall down, through which he promised to provide them an entrance into the city. When Felix heard of this he ordered his soldiers to take up their arms. Setting out from Jerusalem with a large force of cavalry and infantry, he fell upon the Egyptian and his followers, slaying four hundred of them and taking two hundred prisoners. The Egyptian himself escaped from the battle and disappeared. And now the brigands once more incited the populace to war with Rome, telling them not to obey them. They also fired and pillaged the villages of those who refused to comply.[7]

Theudas and the Egyptian Jew were offering their contemporaries confirming signs, in keeping with the traditions of the exodus. The word *signs (sēmeia)* is very common in the exodus story (some three dozen occurrences). The combination *terata kai (sēmeia)* ("wonders and signs"; cf. *Antiquities of the Jews* 20.8.6. §168) is common in the exodus story, especially as retold in Deuteronomy (LXX Ex 7:3, 9; 11:9-10; Deut 4:34; 6:22; 7:19; 11:3; 13:3 [in reference to false "signs and wonders"]; 26:8; 28:46; 29:2; 34:11), while reference to "signs" taking place "in the wilderness" is also attested in the exodus tradition (Num 14:22).

It is probable that Theudas and the Egyptian Jew were laying claim to the Deuteronomistic promise that someday God would "raise up a prophet like Moses." Such a prophet would have to be confirmed by the fulfillment of a prediction. The relevant portion of Deuteronomy 18 reads as follows:

> The LORD your God will raise up for you a prophet like me from among your own people; you shall heed such a prophet. This is what you requested of the LORD your God at Horeb on the day of the assembly when you said: "If I hear the voice of the LORD my God any more, or ever again see this great fire, I will die." Then the LORD replied to me: "They are right in what they have said. I will raise up for them a prophet like you from among their own people; I will put my words in the mouth of the prophet, who shall speak to them everything that I command. Anyone who does not heed the words that the prophet shall speak in my name, I myself will hold accountable. But any prophet who speaks in the name of other gods, or who presumes to speak in my name a word that I have not commanded the prophet to speak—that prophet shall die." You may say to yourself, "How can we recognize a word that the LORD has not spoken?" If a prophet speaks in the name of the LORD but the thing does not take place or prove true, it is a word that the LORD has not spoken. The prophet has spoken it presumptuously; do not be frightened by it. (Deut 18:15-22)

There are several details that slip through the biased report of Josephus that suggest Theudas and the Egyptian Jew did indeed view themselves as the promised Mosaic successor. The actions of Theudas are reminiscent of Joshua, the successor to Moses. According to Josephus, this man "persuaded the majority

of the masses to take up their possessions and to follow him to the Jordan River."
Theudas claimed to be a "prophet" *(prophētēs)* at whose "command the river
would be parted," allowing for "an easy passage" (*Antiquities of the Jews* 20.5.1.
§97). Calling himself a prophet coheres with the Mosaic promise of Deuteronomy 18:15, 18-19. Persuading people to gather at the Jordan River, whose waters
will be divided and which will then be crossed with ease, is surely patterned after
the example of the generation of Israelites who crossed the Jordan, following
Joshua (Josh 1-4). Taking up possessions heightens the parallel, for the ancient
Israelites carried their possessions across the Jordan to the Promised Land. It is
intriguing that the word for "possessions" used by Josephus *(hai ktēseis)* is found
in Leviticus 25 in the passage concerned with the jubilee (cf. LXX Lev 25:10, 13,
16). The choice of word may be coincidental, but it may reflect a jubilee promise
in the preaching of Theudas.

In the case of the Egyptian Jew the details are somewhat different, but the
Joshua-successor-to-Moses pattern is just as obvious. Josephus speaks of people
being led out into the desert (*Jewish Wars* 2.13.4. §259). As already mentioned,
this theme is common to the exodus story, but it also is a feature in the story of
the great Joshua, conqueror of the Promised Land (Josh 1:4; 5:6; 24:7).

The Egyptian Jew offered his followers "signs of freedom" *(sēmeia eleutheria)*.
Although "freedom" is not used this way in the older part of the Old Testament,
it is in 1 Maccabees 14:26: "For he and his brothers and the house of his father
have stood firm; they have fought and repulsed Israel's enemies and established
its freedom *[eleutheria]*." The Hebrew equivalent of the word appears on the coins
struck during the great revolt of 66-70 C.E. (e.g., *hrwt ṣiwn*, "freedom of Zion")
and on those struck during the Bar Kokhba revolt of 132-135 C.E. (e.g., *lhrwt
isra'l*, "for the freedom of Isra'l"; *lhrwt irwslm*, "for the freedom of Jerusalem").[8]
Also very revealing is Josephus's reference to the "circuitous route" (*periagō*, "led
around"). This word occurs in an important passage in LXX Amos 2:10 ("And I
led you up from the land of Egypt and led you around *[periagō]* in the desert *[en
tē erēmō]* forty years"). As the usage of the word in Amos shows, what Josephus
seems to be describing is a reenactment of the exodus. Finally, in the later
account in *Antiquities,* Josephus says that this man "wished to demonstrate from
there that at his command Jerusalem's walls would fall down, through which he
promised to provide them an entrance into the city" (*Antiquities of the Jews*
20.8.6. §170). Here we have an unmistakable reference to Joshua's first major
conquest in the Promised Land—the collapse of the walls surrounding the city of
Jericho.

Thus, although Josephus did not discuss the biblical precedents and goals of men like Theudas and the Egyptian Jew, we are able, nevertheless, to catch glimpses of their true purposes. It is very probable that both of these men promised a new conquest of the land, perhaps reflecting hopes of an eschatological jubilee in which the dispossessed could reclaim their lost patrimony.

What may be inferred from such movements of restoration is that many Jews regarded Israel as in a state of bondage, even exile. A new conquest of the Promised Land presupposes the assumption that the people really do not possess the land. They have been dispossessed of their land—by foreigners, such as the Greeks and later the Romans, and by their own leaders who collaborate with the foreigners—and now they hope to repossess it.

To ask what meaning Jesus and the evangelists found in Israel's exile of the biblical period (Egyptian, as well as Babylonian) and the exile of the later periods (Greek and Roman), and therefore to ask how it may have shaped their respective understandings of Israel's plight and what solution is required, is to pose a question that is tantalizing and probably impossible to answer in any definitive manner. To explore it, nonetheless, is necessary and important. We must begin with the evidence that suggests many Jews believed Israel had never truly escaped exile.

Israel Still in Exile

The actions of men like Theudas and the Egyptian Jew are clarified by several Second Temple texts that appear to assume that Israel is still in exile, notwithstanding the century of freedom secured by the Hasmoneans or the semiautonomy enjoyed during the reign of Herod the Great.

In the view of Yeshua ben Sira (ca. 180 B.C.E.) Israel remains in a state of oppression and, at least for those Jews scattered abroad, in a state of exile. Sirach 36 pleads for God's mercy, yearning for the appearance of "signs" and "wonders" (Greek text, v. 5) and "wondrous deeds" (v. 14) and for the fulfillment of prophecies (vv. 15-16). The sage petitions God: "Gather all the tribes of Jacob, and give them their inheritance, as in the beginning" (v. 10; cf. 48:10). Taken in context, the signs and wonders for which ben Sira longed are those God performed in liberating Israel from Egypt, protecting Israel in the wilderness and enabling Israel to take possession of the Promised Land.[9] The respective agenda of Theudas and the Egyptian Jew were in answer to this kind of longing.

When righteous Tobit laments, "He has scattered you among them" (Tob 13:3),[10] we should not assume that the reference is simply historical, that is, a reference to the Assyrian exile of the northern tribes of Israel (the ostensible setting of this pseudepigraphon). The book of Tobit was written in the second century B.C.E.; chapter 13 (Tobit's prayer) may have been written later.[11] The reference to the scattering of the Jewish people probably reflects a contemporary concern.[12] The whole of the prayer is addressed to Israel's Second Temple malaise. Its futuristic hope is in places tinged with apocalyptic (cf. Tob 13:16-18).

The same should probably be assumed with respect to Baruch, a work composed sometime between 150 and 60 B.C.E.

> All those calamities with which the Lord threatened us have come upon us. Yet we have not entreated the favor of the Lord by turning away, each of us, from the thoughts of our wicked hearts. And the Lord has kept the calamities ready, and the LORD has brought them upon us, for the Lord is just in all the works that he has commanded us to do. Yet we have not obeyed his voice, to walk in the statutes of the LORD that he set before us." (Bar 2:7-10 NRSV)

The disobedience and the resulting calamities over which the prophet's secretary laments reflect the late intertestamental period and not simply what the author imagined the exiles of the sixth century to have thought.[13] O. H. Steck has concluded that according to the author of Baruch, the "present Israel should see itself still in a condition of exile."[14] I believe he is correct.

The author of 2 Maccabees leaves us with a similar impression. According to him, Jeremiah rebuked those trying to find the cave where the prophet had hidden the "tent and the ark and altar of incense" (2 Macc 2:5). The prophet is said to have told the people: "The place shall remain unknown until God gathers his people together again and shows his mercy" (2 Macc 2:7). From the perspective of this author, who composed his epitome of Jason's history sometime in the first century B.C.E., the period of exile is not over. The "tent and the ark and altar of incense" have not yet been recovered, nor can they be recovered "until God gathers his people together again." The point is made once more a little later, when the author affirms: "We have hope in God that he will soon have mercy on us and will gather us from everywhere under heaven into his holy place" (2 Macc 2:18). Jonathan A. Goldstein rightly concludes that the author of the second epistle (contained in 2 Macc 1:10—2:18) believed that the Jewish people were still experiencing the age of wrath, with many Jews still in exile.[15]

Exilic imagery is also found in the Dead Sea Scrolls. The language used to describe the events that lead up to the long-awaited eschatological battle draws upon exilic imagery: "when the exiles of the Sons of Light return from the wilderness of the peoples to camp in the wilderness of Jerusalem" (1QM 1:3). This expectation coheres with the idea elsewhere expressed that the Teacher of Righteousness went into exile and was pursued by the Wicked Priest (1QpHab 11:4-6, commenting on Hab 2:15). It applies also to the Qumran covenanters as a whole: "The Well is the Law, and its 'diggers' are the captives of Israel who went out of the land of Judah and dwelt in the land of Damascus" (CD 6:4-5, commenting on Num 21:18).[16]

The "Words of the Heavenly Lights" (4Q504-506) contains several expressions that strongly suggest the author viewed Israel (second century B.C.E.) as enduring a period of exile and God's wrath. Almost the entire document could be cited, but only a few excerpts can be offered here:

> Please, Lord, act as is your character, by the measure of your great power. Fo[r] you [for]gave our fathers when they rebelled against your command, though you were so angry at them that you might have destroyed them. Still, you had pity on them because of your love, and because of your covenant (indeed, Moses had atoned for their sin), and also so that your great power and abundant compassion might be known to generations to come, forever.
>
> May your anger and fury at all [their] sin[s] turn back from your people Israel. Remember the wonders that you performed while the nations looked on—surely we have been called by your name. [These things were done] that we might [repe]nt with all our heart and all our soul, to plant your law in our hearts [that we turn not from it, straying] either to the right or the left. Surely you will heal us from such madness, blindness and confusion. . . . [Behold,] we were sold [as the price] of our [in]iquity, yet despite our rebellion you have called us. [. . .] Deliver us from sinning against you, [. . .] give us to understand the seasons [of your compassion]. (4Q504 2:7-17)

> You have raised us through the years of our generations, [disciplining us] with terrible disease, famine, thirst, even plague and the sword—[every reproa]ch of your covenant. For you have chosen us as your own, [as your people from all] the earth. That is why you have poured out your fury upon us, [your ze]al, the full wrath of your anger. That is why you have caused [the scourge] [of your plagues] to cleave to us, that of which Moses and your servants the prophets wrote: You [wou]ld send evil ag[ain]st us in the Last Days. (4Q504 3:7-14)

> Nevertheless, you did not reject the seed of Jacob nor spew Israel out, making an end of them and voiding your covenant with them. Surely you alone are the living God; beside you is none other. You have remembered your covenant whereby you

brought us forth from Egypt while the nations looked on. You have not abandoned us among the nations; rather, you have shown covenant mercies to your people Israel in all [the] lands to which you have exiled them. You have again placed it on their hearts to return to you, to obey your voice [according] to all that you have commanded through your servant Moses. [In]deed, you have poured out your holy spirit upon us, [br]inging your blessings to us. You have caused us to seek you in our time of tribulation, [that we might po]ur out a prayer when your chastening was upon us. We have entered into tribulation, [cha]stisement and trials because of the wrath of the oppressor.

Surely we ourselves [have tr]ied God by our iniquities, wearying the Rock through [our] si[ns.] [Yet] you have [not] compelled us to serve you, to take a [pa]th more profitable [than that] in which [we have walked, though] we have not harkened t[o your commandments]. (4Q504 5:7-21)[17]

Commenting on this text, as well as several others from Qumran, Paul Garnet finds the vocabulary of exile, often drawn from the prophetic tradition, liberally sprinkled throughout. He has concluded that an exile theology plays an important role in Qumran's understanding of salvation: Israel remains in a state of exile, awaiting redemption.[18]

There are also texts that attest to the incompleteness of Israel's restoration, following the return from Babylon and the rebuilding of the temple and the walls of Jerusalem. The earliest witness to this understanding is found in Hebrew Scripture. Ezra the scribe confesses (Ezra 9:8-9 RSV; emphasis added),

But now for a brief moment favor has been shown by the LORD our God, to leave us a remnant, and to give us a secure hold within his holy place, that our God may brighten our eyes and grant us *a little reviving in our bondage. For we are bondmen; yet our God has not forsaken us in our bondage,* but has extended to us his steadfast love before the kings of Persia, to grant us *some reviving* to set up the house of our God, to repair its ruins, and to give us protection in Judea and Jerusalem.[19]

Elsewhere Ezra is even more explicit when he says, "Here we are, slaves to this day—slaves in the land that you gave to our ancestors to enjoy its fruit and its good gifts" (Neh 9:36).

The fourth book of *1 Enoch* (the "Dream Visions"; chaps. 83—90) contains some relevant material. After the Babylonian-Persian exile the people of Israel

again began to build as before; and they raised up that tower which is called the high tower [i.e., the temple]. But they started to place a table before the tower, with all the food which is upon it being polluted and impure. Regarding all these matters, the eyes

of the sheep became so dim-sighted that they could not see—and likewise in respect
to their shepherds—and they were delivered to their shepherds for an excessive
destruction, so that the sheep were trampled upon and eaten. The Lord of the sheep
remained silent until all the sheep were dispersed into the woods and got mixed
among the wild beasts—and could not be rescued from the hands of the beasts. (*1
Enoch* 89:73-75)[20]

This reflects the Greek period, prior to the Maccabean revolt, which people
believed would lead to the messianic kingdom (cf. *1 Enoch* 90:20-42). The significance of the passage lies in its assumption that oppression would continue until
the messianic era dawned.

The *Testament of Moses* also attests the idea that restoration is yet to be realized: "Now, the two tribes will remain steadfast in their former faith, sorrowful
and sighing because they will not be able to offer their sacrifices to the Lord of
their fathers. But the ten tribes will grow and spread out among the nations during the time of their captivity" (*T. Mos.* 4:8-9).[21] Israel's oppression and travail
continue until the appearance of God's kingdom (see comments below).

The author of Tobit has the righteous exile prophesy: "But [after the exile]
God will again have mercy on them, and God will bring them back into the
land of Israel; and they will rebuild the temple of God, but not like the first one
until the period when the times of fulfillment shall come" (Tob 14:5). The infe-
riority of the second temple symbolizes the incompleteness of Israel's partial
postexilic recovery. Restoration will not finally be realized "until the times of
the age are completed."

The same idea is expressed in *2 Baruch*, which was composed near the end of
the first century or the beginning of the second century C.E.: "And at that time,
after a short time, Zion will be rebuilt again, and the offerings will be restored,
and the priests will again return to their ministry. And the nations will again
come to honor it. *But not as fully as before*" (*2 Bar* 68:5-7, emphasis added).[22]

We also find a very revealing statement in Josephus: "Whence did our slavery begin? Was it not from party strife among our forefathers, when the mad-
ness of Aristobulus and Hyrcanus and their mutual dissensions brought Pompey
against the city, and God subjected to the Romans those who were unworthy of
liberty?" (Josephus *Jewish Wars* 5.9.4. §395-96). Even when we allow for his bit-
terness and cynicism, we may have here a hint of the idea that many Jews considered Israel to be in a state of slavery *(douleia)*. According to Josephus, this slavery
was brought on by "party strife," not sin. Most of the writers already considered

would sharply disagree with this assessment. But it is interesting nonetheless that even Josephus regarded the Roman period as slavery.

Finally, there are texts that look for another disaster (comparable to the one of 586 B.C.E.) to precede final restoration: The sixth and seventh weeks in Enoch's "Apocalypse of Weeks" (*1 Enoch* 93) speak of spiritual decline, destruction and apostasy (*1 Enoch* 93:8-9). At the end of the seventh week "there shall be elected the elect ones of righteousness from the eternal plant of righteousness" (*1 Enoch* 93:10). The author of the *Testament of Moses* foresees nothing but gloom and doom until the appearance of the kingdom of God. But just before the appearance of the kingdom, a great catastrophe is predicted: "See, sons, behold a second punishment has befallen the people; cruel, impure, going beyond all bounds of mercy—even exceeding the former one" (9:2); "Then his kingdom will appear throughout his whole creation" (10:1). The "second punishment" *(ultio altera)* probably refers to the Babylonian destruction of Jerusalem, described in *Testament of Moses* 3:1-3.[23] In a certain sense, then, these Babylonian destructions bracket Israel's exile. The first one inaugurates Israel's exile; the second terminates it.[24]

The expectations of redemption also imply that Israel remains in a state of exile. To these expectations we now turn.

Expectations of Redemption

Most of the texts that in various ways speak of Israel's continuing exile and oppression also express hopes of redemption and restoration. They foresee the day when the scattered tribes will be regathered, the city of Jerusalem rebuilt and the temple either rebuilt, refurbished or purified.

As already noted, Tobit's prayer and prophecy ostensibly anticipate the end of the Babylonian-Persian exile. But in all probability they express intertestamental hopes that Israel's degraded condition will some day finally and completely come to an end:

> He will afflict you for your iniquities,
> but he will again show mercy on all of you.
> He will gather you from all the nations
> among whom you have been scattered. . . .
> for they will be gathered together
> and will praise the Lord of the ages. (Tob 13:5, 13)

> But God will again have mercy on them, and God will bring them back into the land of Israel; and they will rebuild the temple of God. . . . After this they all will return from their exile." (Tob 14:5)[25]

Similar expectations are expressed in Baruch: "Look toward the east, O Jerusalem, and see the joy that is coming to you from God! Behold, your sons are coming, whom you sent away; they are coming, gathered from east and west, at the word of the Holy One, rejoicing in the glory of God" (Bar 4:36-37; cf. 5:5). Jonathan's prayer expresses the same hope: "Gather together our scattered people, set free those who are slaves among the Gentiles. . . . Plant your people in your holy place, as Moses promised" (2 Macc 1:27, 29). The epitomist in his second epistle goes on to say, "God, who saved his entire people and restored the heritage to us all, will also restore *[apodōsei]* the kingdom and priesthood and the sanctification" (2 Macc 2:17).[26]

The author of Enoch's Dream Visions also anticipates the end of the exile: "All those [sheep] which had been destroyed and dispersed, and all the beasts of the field and the birds of the sky were gathered together in that house; and the LORD of the sheep rejoiced with great joy because they had all become gentle and returned to his house" *(1 Enoch 90:33).*[27]

The author of the *Psalms of Solomon* (first century B.C.E.) looks forward to the regathering of the twelve tribes of Israel, part of the messianic task:

Bring together the dispersed of Israel with mercy and goodness, for your faithfulness is with us. (*Pss. Sol.* 8:28)

Sound in Zion the signal trumpet of the sanctuary; announce in Jerusalem the voice of one bringing good news *[phōnēn euangelizomenou]*, for God has been merciful to Israel in watching over them. Stand on a high place, Jerusalem, and look at your children, from the east and the west assembled together by the Lord. From the north they come in the joy of their God; from far distant islands God has assembled them. He flattened high mountains into level ground for them. (*Pss. Sol.* 11:1-4; cf. Is 40)

Lord, you chose David to be king over Israel, and swore to him about his descendants forever, that his kingdom should not fail before you. . . . See, Lord, and raise up for them their king, the son of David, to rule over your servant Israel in the time known to you, O God. . . . He will gather a holy people whom he will lead in righteousness. . . . He will distribute them upon the land according to their tribes. (*Pss. Sol.* 17:4, 21, 26-28)

Blessed are those born in those days to see the good fortune of Israel which God will bring to pass in the assembly of the tribes. (*Pss. Sol.* 17:44)[28]

In the aftermath of the tragedy of the Roman destruction of the city and the temple, the author of *2 Baruch* clings to the hope that the dispersed of Israel will someday be regathered: "For if you do these things in this way, he shall continually remember you. He is the one who always promised on our behalf to those who are more excellent than we that he will not forever forget or forsake our offspring, but with much mercy assemble all those again who were dispersed" (*2 Bar* 78:7).[29]

We find in the *Isaiah Targum*, whose exegetical roots have been traced to the first century,[30] great interest in the gathering of the exiles of Israel (*Targum of Isaiah* 6:13; 8:18; 27:6; 28:2, 6, 13, 19, 25; 35:6, 10; 42:7; 43:6, 14; 46:11; 51:11; 54:7, 15; 66:9; cf. *Targum Neofiti I* Num 24:7; *Targum of Jeremiah* 30:18; *Targum of Hosea* 2:2; 14:8; *Targum of Micah* 5:3). The Aramaic paraphrase of Isaiah 28:1-6 is especially suggestive. The priesthood is criticized in the first four verses. Because of their sin and folly, "Gentiles will come upon them and exile them from their land to another land" (v. 2). Exile ends with the appearance of the Messiah: "In that time the Messiah of the LORD of hosts will be a diadem of joy and a crown of praise, to the remnant of his people; and a command of true judgment to those who sit in the house of judgment, to judge true judgment and to give the victory to those who go forth in the battle, to return them in peace to their houses" (vv. 5-6).[31] The exile of Israel will come to an end when the Messiah appears, judges truly, enjoys victory in battle and returns the Jews "in peace to their houses." This paraphrase reflects the early Roman period, and its ideas may reach back to the time of Jesus.

Of special interest also is the paraphrase of *Targum of Isaiah* 53:8: "From chastisements and punishment he will bring our exiles near." It is important to remember that in the Isaiah Targum the servant is understood as the Messiah (*Targum of Isaiah* 52:13; 53:10: "they will see the kingdom of their Messiah"; cf. *Targum of Hosea* 14:8: "They shall be gathered from among their exiles, they shall dwell in the shade of their Messiah"; *Targum of Micah* 5:1-3: "from you shall come forth before me the Messiah, to exercise dominion over Israel. . . . He shall arise and rule with might . . . and they shall be gathered in from among their exiles"). Bruce D. Chilton believes this servant song received its distinctive shape in the period between the two major wars with Rome (i.e., 70-135 C.E.).[32] New Testament usage of Isaiah 52:13–53:12, in that the song is associated with Jesus (e.g., Mt 8:17; 12:18-21; Lk 22:37; Acts 8:32-33; Heb 9:28; 1 Pet 1:24-25),[33] suggests that messianic interpretation was probably pre-70 C.E. The messianic hopes expressed in the *Psalms of Solomon* further suggest that the idea of the

Messiah's gathering Israel's exiles and distributing them according to traditional patrimony was an ancient one.[34]

Some traditions articulate requirements or conditions as prerequisites for restoration and the end of the exile. According to Tobit, God will regather his people if they repent: "If you turn to him with all your heart and with all your soul, to do what is true before him, then he will turn to you and will no longer hide his face from you" (Tob 13:6). According to *Jubilees*, restoration cannot take place until the law is interpreted properly and obeyed faithfully (*Jub.* 23:18-31). Hardship and persecution will be Israel's lot, according to the *Testament of Judah*, until there is repentance: "Then the LORD will be concerned for you in mercy and will free you from captivity under your enemies" (*T. Jud.* 23:5).

Finally, we should take into account Philo of Alexandria, who makes a very revealing statement about Israel's condition. Philo warns against armed rebellion, based on empty boasting (Philo *De Praemiis et Poenis* 16.94-97). He believes that liberty will come when his fellow Jews obey God's word wholeheartedly (*De Praemiis et Poenis* 28.162-63):

> For even though they dwell in the uttermost parts of the earth, in slavery to those who led them away captive, one signal, as it were, one day will bring liberty to all. This conversion in a body to virtue will strike awe into their masters, who will set them free, ashamed to rule over men better than themselves. When they have gained this unexpected liberty, those who but now were scattered in Greece and the outside world over islands and continents will arise and post from every side with one impulse to the one appointed place, guided in their pilgrimage by a vision divine and superhuman unseen by others but manifest to them as they pass from exile to their home. (Philo *De Praemiis et Poenis* 28-29.164-65)

> Everything will suddenly be reversed, God will turn the curses against the enemies of these penitents, the enemies who rejoiced in the misfortunes of the nation and mocked and railed at them. . . . Then those of them who have not come to utter destruction, in tears and groans lamenting their own lapse, will make their way back with course reversed to the prosperity of the ancestral past. (Philo *De Praemiis et Poenis* 29.169-70)[35]

Although one encounters differences in detail, a fairly consistent pattern emerges. Many Jews during the Second Temple period believed that the exile perdured. Most obviously, the exile was evident in the dispersion of the Jewish people and in the continuing foreign domination of Israel. Less obviously, the exile was evident in the failure on the part of many Jews to obey the law. Just exactly what was entailed in obedience to the law was itself a matter of dispute; and many groups and individuals were eager to make their views known. The activities of men like Theudas and the Egyptian Jew, as well as many others of whom we now know little or nothing, were driven by the hope that Israel's liberation from exile was finally at hand. Calls to repentance (such as we have from John the Baptizer; Mt 3:2, 8, 11; Mk 1:4; Lk 3:3, 8; Josephus *Antiquities of the Jews* 18.5.2. §§116-17), promises of signs (as in Theudas and others) or demands for signs (in the case of Jesus' critics) are symptomatic of a society in which many of its members hoped for and anticipated national deliverance. Against this backdrop Jesus must surely be interpreted; but in what sense Jesus proffered deliverance is a difficult question. To it we now turn.

Exile and Redemption in Jesus and the Gospels

Exile theology underlies Jesus' teaching and actions at several points.[36] In a general way, therefore, his conception of Israel's plight and of his own calling runs parallel to that of such men as Theudas. There are, however, important points of difference between Jesus and these other would-be deliverers. There are at least six significant features in Jesus' teaching and activities that justify the claim that exile theology played an important role:

1. Jesus' appointment of twelve apostles
2. the request for a sign
3. Jesus' appeal to Isaiah 56:7 while demonstrating in the temple precincts
4. Jesus' allusion to Zechariah 2:6, a passage that envisions the gathering of Israel's exiles
5. Jesus' prophetic threats against Israel's rulers, which threaten exile
6. traces of exile theology and motifs in the New Testament and early Christian writings

We shall consider these six points in turn.

1. Jesus' appointment of twelve apostles. The single most important datum that attests to the presence of exile theology in Jesus' thinking is his appointment of the Twelve. They are called the "twelve apostles" (Mt 10:2 par. Lk 6:13), the "twelve disciples" (a Matthean favorite—Mt 10:1; 11:1; 20:17; 26:20) and simply "the twelve" (Mt 10:5; 26:14, 47; Mk 3:14; 4:10; 6:7; 9:35; 10:32; 11:11; 14:10, 17, 20, 43; Lk 8:1; 9:1, 12; 18:31; 22:3, 47; Jn 6:67, 70-71; 20:24; Acts 6:2). The latter, simpler designation has the strongest claim to originality because of its widespread attestation and because the fuller epithets are probably secondary.

The authenticity of the tradition of the Twelve is supported by the criteria of embarrassment and of dissimilarity. The first criterion may be invoked because it is not easy to explain why the early church would invent a tradition of twelve disciples, one of whom betrayed Jesus. That the name of Judas Iscariot stubbornly clings to the various lists of twelve apostolic names confirms that the appointment of the Twelve derives from Jesus, who attached significance to this number. The phrase "the twelve" was entrenched too early and too deeply in the early community's memory of Jesus to be discarded, despite having been tainted by Judas's defection and betrayal. The second criterion also lends a measure of support to the authenticity of the tradition of the Twelve simply because the number twelve proved to be of little theological consequence for the church. To be sure, it plays a symbolic role in Revelation (see Rev 7:5-8; 12:1; 21:12, 14, 16, 21; 22:2) and may have played a role in the church's early mission to Israel (see Acts 26:7), but it does not seem to play any role whatsoever in the development of early Christian ecclesiology (with the possible, minor exception of Jas 1:1). Had it been otherwise, then suspicion that the tradition of the Twelve had been read back into the life and teaching of Jesus would be justified. But such is not the case.[37]

It is probable that Jesus' appointment of the Twelve was intended to symbolize the reconstitution of the twelve tribes of Israel. With reference to Jewish eschatological hopes in late antiquity, E. P. Sanders comments, rightly in my judgment, that " 'twelve' would necessarily mean 'restoration.' "[38] Wright agrees with Sanders, asserting that Jesus' summons to become part of his family was "remnant-theology, return-from-exile theology," and that the "call of the twelve said . . . this is where YHWH was at last restoring his people Israel" (*JVG* 430-31). Jesus' assertion, moreover, that his mission is to the "lost sheep of the house of Israel" (Mt 15:24; cf. 10:6) implies an interest in regathering Israel.[39] The lost (i.e., leaderless) sheep probably do not refer to the lost ten tribes (which would make no sense in Mt 10:5-15) but to the nation as a whole.[40] But tending to the lostness of Israel carries with it the implication that the scattered Jews of the Diaspora would be gathered.

Another important feature of the symbolism of the number twelve in Jesus' theology is seen in the saying that the twelve disciples will "sit on twelve thrones, judging the twelve tribes of Israel" (Mt 19:28 par. Lk 22:30). The Twelve are to rule over Israel, judging the nation much as the judges of old judged the twelve tribes (see Judg 3:10; 4:4; 10:2-3; 12:7-9, 11, 13-14; 15:20; 16:31; 1 Sam 4:18; 7:6, 15). That is, the disciples are to protect and provide the nation with new and just leadership. Israel's current leadership will itself be judged and removed from its stewardship (see Mk 12:1-12). The restoration of the twelve tribes, as implied by the symbolism of the twelve disciples, coheres with the promise that the disciples will someday sit on thrones, judging the tribes. What we may have here is a fragment of the idea that restored Israel will be similar to the idealized pre-exilic period when Israel's king was God.[41]

2. The request for a sign. The request for a "sign from heaven" (Mk 8:11-13) is a piece of tradition, however contextualized by the evangelists, in which the nature and validity of Jesus' ministry were questioned. Given the promise of signs proffered by men like Theudas, the Egyptian Jew and others, it is probably right to assume that Jesus' ministry was interpreted by some of his contemporaries in a similar light.[42] The request itself conforms to biblical precedent (1 Sam 2:34; 10:1-8; 2 Kings 19:29; 20:8-9; Ps 74:9; Is 7:10-14; Jer 44:29 par. LXX Jer 51:29) and is even regulated by biblical tradition (Deut 13:1-3; 18:21-22). The idea in Jesus' day that signs would presage the approach of the eschaton is attested in the Dead Sea Scrolls:

> This shall be the sign [*ha'ot*] that this shall come to pass: when the sources of evil are shut up and wickedness is banished in the presence of righteousness, as darkness in the presence of light, or as smoke vanishes and is no more, in the same way wickedness will vanish forever and righteousness will be manifest like the sun. The world will be made firm and all the adherents of the secrets of [??] <sin> (MS: wonder) shall be no more. True knowledge shall fill the world and there will never be any more folly. This is all ready to happen, it is a true oracle, and by this it shall be known to you that it cannot be averted. (1Q27 frag. 1, 1:5-8)[43]

Josephus provides significant evidence of the importance that his contemporaries attached to signs (for references to signs, see *Jewish Wars* 1.1.11. §28; 1.19.4. §377; 2.13.4. §259; 3.8.9. §405; 4.10.7. §623; 6.5.2. §285; 6.5.3. §§296-97; 6.5.4. §315; 7.11.1. §438; *Antiquities of the Jews* 20.8.6. §168). Josephus does not doubt the validity of signs, but he does dispute their meaning with his fellow Jews (for example, the signs augured the coming Jewish defeat and destruction of the temple; for the Romans they augured the accession of Vespasian). His description of the star is particularly significant (*Jewish Wars* 6.5.3. §§288-91):

> Thus it was that the wretched people were deluded at that time by charlatans and false messengers of God; while they neither heeded nor believed in the manifest portents that foretold [*prosēmainein*] the coming desolation, but, as if thunderstruck

and bereft of eyes and mind, disregarded the plain warnings of God. So it was when a star *[astron]*, resembling a sword, stood over the city, and a comet which continued for a year. So again when, before the revolt and the commotion that led to war, at the time when the people were assembling for the feast of unleavened bread, on the eighth of the month Xanthicus, at the ninth hour of the night, so brilliant a light shone round the altar and the sanctuary that it seemed to be broad daylight; and this continued for half an hour. By the inexperienced this was regarded as a good omen.[44]

The appearance of the star and comet probably called to mind the prophecy of Numbers 24:17 (LXX: "a star *[astron]* from Jacob will arise, and a man from Israel will stand up") and would have whipped up eschatological expectations in the minds of many. It is probably to this prophetic passage that Josephus alludes when he refers to the "ambiguous oracle," which more than anything else incited his countrymen to rebellion (*Jewish Wars* 6.5.4. §§312-13). However, Josephus applied it not to a Jewish ruler but to the Roman general Vespasian, "who was proclaimed Emperor on Jewish soil" (*Jewish Wars* 6.5.4. §313).

Josephus goes on to describe other signs and portents: the cow that gave birth to a lamb; the eastern gate of the inner court of the temple precincts that opened by itself; the appearance in the sky of chariots and armies "hurtling through the clouds"; the voice, heard by priests, that cried, "We are departing from here" (*Jewish Wars* 6.5.3. §§292-300). Josephus tells us that the "uninitiated" interpreted these signs as good omens, while the "learned" saw them as portending coming desolation.

The point of all of this is to underscore how important signs were to Jews, even to a sophisticated and skeptical person like Josephus. Paul is not guilty of an unfair generalization when he asserts that "Jews demand signs" (1 Cor 1:22). It is also important to underscore the fact that the only signs described by Josephus, those of men who proclaimed salvation, have to do with the exodus and the conquest of the Promised Land. I refer, of course, to Theudas and the Egyptian Jew. Both of these men promised signs that recalled Israel's conquest of the land. Jesus' wilderness wanderings, feeding of the multitude and various other activities and teachings reminiscent of Moses, the exodus and Israel's wilderness sojourn may have led some of his contemporaries to interpret his ministry in a light somewhat similar to the claims and promises of men like Theudas. It is against this backdrop that the demand for a sign from heaven should probably be interpreted. Jesus' ministry was viewed as a prelude to Israel's redemption; a confirming sign was required.

3. Jesus' appeal to Isaiah 56:7 while demonstrating in the temple precincts. During the temple incident (Mt 21:12-13 par. Mk 11:15-18 par. Lk 19:45-46) Jesus is said to have alluded to Isaiah 56:7 and Jeremiah 7:11. Mark's version, which is longer and probably more original,[45] reads,

> He was teaching and saying, "Is it not written, 'My house shall be called a house of prayer for all the nations'? But you have made it 'a den of robbers.'" (Mk 11:17)

The Midrashic juxtaposition of these texts from Isaiah and Jeremiah is intriguing. If Jesus has in mind the wider contexts of these respective oracles, then we may infer that he has criticized the temple establishment for failing to live up to the eschatological expectations enunciated in Isaiah 56:1-8 and so now stands under the judgment uttered by Jeremiah (esp. in Jer 7) against the temple establishment of his day.[46]

What is of particular interest for the present concerns is that the oracle in Isaiah 56 comes to be understood as a time of ingathering of Israel's exiles. The Hebrew text according to the Masoretic tradition reads:

> Thus says the Lord, "Safeguard justice, and do righteousness; for my salvation is about to come, and my righteousness to be revealed." Blessed is the man that does this, and the son of man that holds it fast; that observes sabbath, not profaning it, and keeps his hand from doing any evil. Neither let the son of a foreigner, that has joined himself to the Lord, speak, saying, "The Lord will surely separate me from his people"; neither let the eunuch say, "Behold, I am a dry tree." For thus says the Lord to the eunuchs that keep my sabbaths, and choose the things that please me, and hold fast my covenant: "To them will I give in my house and within my walls a memorial and a name better than of sons and of daughters; I will give them an everlasting name, that shall not be cut off. Also the sons of a foreigner that join themselves to the Lord, to minister to him, and to love the name of the Lord, to be his servants; every one that keeps sabbath from profaning it, and holds fast my covenant; even them will I bring to my holy mountain, and make them joyful in my house of prayer. Their burnt-offerings and their sacrifices shall be accepted upon my altar; for my house shall be called a house of prayer for all peoples." The Lord God, who gathers the outcasts of Israel, says, "Yet will I gather others to him, besides his own that are gathered."

The LXX represents a fairly literal translation of the Hebrew, with only a few minor variants. Verses 7-8 read:

"I will bring them to my holy mountain, and make them rejoice in the house of my prayer. Their whole-burnt offerings and their sacrifices shall be acceptable upon my altar; for my house shall be called a house of prayer for all the Gentiles," said the Lord that gathers the dispersed of Israel. "For I will gather to him a congregation."

The only noteworthy variant in this portion is in verse 7, where the Hebrew's "peoples" *(ha'amim)* becomes "Gentiles" *(ta ethnē)*.[47] The Aramaic paraphrase also offers us something of interest. Verses 6-8 read as follows (with departures from the Masoretic text italicized in the English):[48]

> And the sons of *Gentiles* who *have been added* to *the people of* the Lord, to minister to him, to love the name of the Lord, and to be his servants, every one who *will* keep *the* sabbath from profaning it, and hold fast my covenants—these I will bring to *the* holy mountain, and make them joyful in my house of prayer; their burnt offerings and their *holy* sacrifices will *even go up* for *my pleasure* on my altar; for my *sanctuary will be* a house of prayer for all the peoples. Thus says the Lord God who *is about to* gather the outcasts of Israel, yet will I *bring near their exiles, to gather them.*

The Aramaic paraphrase offers a few interesting contributions of its own. The rephrasing found in verses 3 and 6 ("Gentiles who have been added to the people of the Lord") is probably intended to make it clear that these foreigners, who "minister" to the Lord, are in fact proselytes and not simply Gentile visitors. Understood in this sense, the translator does not object to their ministering to the Lord (as apparently did the scribe of the Great Isaiah Scroll, which reads: "Also the sons of a foreigner that join themselves to the Lord, to be his servants, and to bless the name of the Lord"). Probably the most important interpretive element is in verse 8, where the meturgeman renders the Hebrew's "yet will I gather others to him, besides his own that are gathered" with "yet will I bring near their exiles, to gather them." The hope of the eschatological gathering of Israel's dispersed and exiled people finds expression in the liturgy of the ancient synagogue (cf. *Amida* §10; Sir 51:12-13 [in the Hebrew version]), a liturgy that also longs for the appearance of the Davidic Messiah (cf. *Amida* §14; Sir 51:12h [in the Hebrew version]). Later midrashim state, "They should not attempt to go up from the diaspora by force. For if they do, why should the King Messiah come to gather the exiles *[glywtyhn]* of Israel?" (*Song Rabbah* 2:7 §1); "For what purpose will the royal Messiah come, and what will he do? He will come to assemble the exiles *[glywtyhn]* of Israel" (*Genesis Rabbah* 98.9 [on Gen 49:11]).

If the utterance in Mark 11:17 is authentic and if the whole of the oracle of Isaiah 56:1-8 is in view, then an important aspect of Jesus' exile theology lies before us. As the Davidic Messiah—and as such invested with the authority to appraise the temple and its activities—Jesus has complained of the failure of the ruling priests. Instead of becoming a place of prayer for Gentiles and a place for the regathering of Israel's exiles, the temple fosters oppression and neglects the needy (as seen in many of the pericopes that make up Mk 12).[49] Temple polity is out of step with Jesus' proclamation of the kingdom.

4. Jesus' allusion to Zechariah 2:6, a passage that envisions the gathering of Israel's exiles. Mark 13:27, which alludes to Zechariah 2:6 (Hebrew v. 10), envisions a gathering of the exiles: "And then he will send forth the angels and he will gather his elect from the four winds, from the ends of the earth to the ends of heaven." Zechariah 2:6-12 (Hebrew vv. 10-16) envisions the regathering and restoration of Israel: "The LORD will inherit Judah as his portion in the holy land, and will again choose Jerusalem" (v. 12; Hebrew v. 15). The passage from Zechariah speaks of Gentiles who join the Jewish people in this era of reconciliation to God. This feature coheres with the early church's interest in the Gentile mission (note also the Great Commission in Mt 28:18-20).

The exilic orientation of Zechariah 2 is rendered explicit in the Targum: "These are the kingdoms which scattered the people of Judah and did not permit anyone to walk with erect stature; and these have come to frighten them, to destroy the kingdoms of the nations which took up arms against the land of the house of Judah and to drive it into exile" (*Targum Zechariah* 2:4; English 1:21).[50] But even without the phrase "to drive it into exile," the Hebrew's "to scatter it" is a reminiscence of the Babylonian exile.

Did Jesus utter these words, or do we have here the theology of the early church or possibly that of the evangelist Mark? It is not easy to decide. However, in favor of authenticity is the possibility that the elect who are to be gathered include the exiles of Israel. If this is correct, and it is admittedly uncertain, it is probable that the saying derives from Jesus. The early church would probably not invent a saying having to do with the regathering of Jewish exiles. What we may have here is an authentic saying of Jesus, which originally had to do with the regathering of exiles and which the early church later understood as referring to those who believe in Jesus (i.e., Christians). The wider context of Zechariah 2, in that it anticipates Gentiles' joining Israel, coheres with Isaiah 56:1-8, which lends further support to the possibility of authenticity.

Elsewhere in Jesus' teaching, the theme of return from exile seems to be presupposed. One immediately thinks of the return of the prodigal son from a foreign land to his father's house (Lk 15:11-32). Wright, in reference to this parable, says, "Jesus and the people around him, his motley group of followers, either constitute the real Israel or they are nothing. They are the returned-from-exile people, the people who at last know YHWH and are known by him, the new-covenant people whose sins are forgiven, at whose coming into existence the angels sing for joy" (*JVG* 444, cf. 129). The parable of the prodigal son, as well as other parables, enjoins Israel to welcome those who repent. Jesus' proclamation of repentance, moreover, coheres with the Jewish belief that repentance was a prerequisite for ending the exile.[51] Jesus' allusion to Isaiah 35:5-6 in his reply to the Baptist (Mt 11:5 par. Lk 7:22), given the wider context (cf. Is 35:1-10), may have implied that Jesus' healing ministry signaled the end of the exile (*JVG* 428-30).

5. Jesus' prophetic threats against Israel's rulers, which threaten exile. Some of Jesus' critical statements appear to threaten exile. Two texts enjoying reasonable claim to authenticity predict disaster: "Woe to you, Chorazin! Woe to you, Bethsaida!. . . . At the judgment it will be more tolerable for Tyre and Sidon than for you. And you, Capernaum, will you be exalted to heaven? No, you will be brought down to Hades" (Lk 10:13-15 par. Mt 11:21-23). Joseph A. Fitzmyer leans in favor of the authenticity of this Q saying.[52] But is Jesus threatening eschatological judgment or temporal destruction and exile? Being "brought down to Hades" favors the former alternative. But how are cities judged in this manner? Threats made against cities in the Old Testament anticipate temporal judgment and exile of the inhabitants (cf. Is 14:2-20; 16:1-7; 17:1-3; 60:11; Nahum 2:7; 3:10). Jesus' language may be metaphorical (compare the highly colorful oracles of doom pronounced against Babylon and Tyre in Is 14 and Ezek 28).

More promising is another Q saying: "Jerusalem, Jerusalem, the city that kills the prophets and stones those who are sent to it! How often have I desired to gather your children together as a hen gathers her brood under her wings, and you were not willing! See, your house is left to you" (Lk 13:34-35 par. Mt 23:37-38). Arguments against the authenticity of this saying are not compelling.[53] Jesus' desire to gather the children of Jerusalem could imply hopes of gathering the exiles of Israel. Because of the city's refusal to repent, the gathering will not take place. Indeed, Jerusalem's lot will become worse: its house is forsaken. If "your house" refers to the temple, then we again have an important point of coherence with Jesus' demonstration in the temple precincts and his employment of Jeremiah 7:11.

Threats of exile are found elsewhere. Luke 19:41-44 and 23:27-31 may contain authentic utterances of Jesus, but their lack of multiple attestation and the distinct possibility of Lukan composition (from words and phrases taken from the LXX) make appeal to them hazardous. Nevertheless, Fitzmyer thinks they may ultimately derive from Jesus, even if edited and recontextualized by the evangelist.[54] Luke 21:20-24 is another oracle that appears to have been heavily edited by the Lukan evangelist (cf. Mt 24:15-19 par. Mk 13:14-17). This text explicitly threatens exile: "they will fall by the edge of the sword and be taken away as captives among all nations" (Lk 21:24; cf. Deut 28:64).

Perhaps we may infer from these threats a foil against which the earlier positive message of the kingdom of God should be read. I see no reason why we should suppose that Jesus could not have revised his message. Following his entry into Jerusalem he has been rejected by the religious leaders (the High Priest and his ruling priestly colleagues) and evidently has been ignored, perhaps even shunned, by most of the inhabitants of Jerusalem. Jesus may very well have revised his message and begun speaking of judgment.

6. Traces of exile theology and motifs in the New Testament and early Christian writings. The word *exile* appears twice in Matthew 1:11-12, 17 as a pivotal point in the messianic genealogy. Fourteen generations lead up to the Babylonian exile; fourteen follow it leading up to the birth of the Messiah. The Matthean genealogy may have been intended to suggest that the exile did not really come to an end until the appearance of Jesus, the Davidic Messiah. Although it is a post-Easter reflection, it may be rooted in a pre-Easter belief that as the Davidic Messiah, Jesus would deliver Israel from its exile. If so, then we have further evidence of exilic ideas in the theology of Jesus and his followers.

Finally, this essay concludes with a general observation that may have relevance for our concerns. It is interesting to reflect on Jesus' use of traditions from Daniel,[55] Zechariah[56] and Isaiah.[57] All three of these books play a major role in Jesus' theology; and all three reflect periods of exile in the life and history of Israel. Daniel reflected an exilic perspective, ostensibly the Babylonian exile but in reality the Seleucid period of oppression and terror. Zechariah stems from the exilic period and entertains hopes that Israel's kingdom will be restored under the leadership of the "two sons of oil" (Zech 4:14)—Zerubbabel of Davidic descent and Joshua the High Priest. Second Isaiah calls for a new exodus and a new Israel, which he dubs the "servant" of the LORD. Jesus' use of these books, indeed his being informed and shaped by them, is very revealing. It strongly suggests that Jesus identified himself and his mission with an oppressed Israel in need of redemption and that he himself was the agent of redemption. He was the Danielic "Son of Man" to whom kingdom and authority were entrusted. He was the humble Davidic king of Zechariah's vision who entered the temple precincts and offered himself to the High Priest and took umbrage at temple polity. And, of course, he was the eschatological herald of Second Isaiah who proclaimed the "gospel" of God's reign and the new exodus.[58] All of this suggests that, among other things, Jesus understood his message and ministry as the beginning of the end of Israel's exile. In my opinion the evidence fully justifies N. T. Wright's emphasis on exile theology in Jesus and his contemporaries. In short, Wright is correct, and Casey is wrong.

Six

The Trial & Death of Jesus in N. T. Wright's *Jesus and the Victory of God*

Darrell L. Bock

*T*HOUGH THIS ESSAY'S TITLE HIGHLIGHTS THE TRIAL AND DEATH OF JESUS, OUR real topic is to evaluate the last three chapters of N. T. Wright's *Jesus and the Victory of God* and to consider his approach to the last week of Jesus' life and ministry. In part, this is because the last week of Jesus' career brings the story of his life and ministry together. The confrontations of the final week of his earthly life and the subsequent religious-political examinations of Jesus led to his eventual death. The entire sequence gave rise to the week's surprising sequel, an empty tomb and the claims of divine vindication from those who only two days before were in the throes of despair because of their leader's execution. In other words, there is no satisfactory way to examine Jesus' trial and death without some consideration of the events in the last week that led up to these final decisive moments.

Our study proceeds in two steps. First, I survey Wright's presentation of this climactic section of Jesus' life. Second, I assess his synthesis, noting what I believe to be its strengths and the questions I have about his approach. The final portion of my study will concentrate on the points of disagreement. However, let it be said at the start that I find much of Wright's work on the mark and all of it worthy of careful reflection. It represents a proper example of how the pursuit of the historical Jesus should be conducted.[1]

Wright's View of Jesus' Challenge in His Last Week

Wright considers the events of the last week from three angles: those involving the Jewish authorities, those involving Pilate and those involving Jesus. Wright's assessment of the perspective of the leaders and Pilate is relatively simple compared to his explanation of Jesus' own contribution to these events. An extended quotation from *Jesus and the Victory of God* (551-52) summarizes how he sees the Jewish and Roman view of the matter:

> In terms of the Jewish authorities, then, the question, "Why did Jesus die?" evokes a fivefold answer. He was sent to the Roman governor on a capital charge
>
> (i) because many (not least many Pharisees, but also, probably, the chief priests) saw him as "a false prophet, leading Israel astray";
>
> (ii) because, as one aspect of this, they saw his Temple-action as a blow against the central symbol not only of national life but also of YHWH's presence with his people;
>
> (iii) because, though he was clearly not leading a real or organized military revolt, he saw himself as in some sense Messiah, and could thus become a focus of serious revolutionary activity;
>
> (iv) because, as the pragmatic focus of these three points, they saw him as a dangerous political nuisance, whose actions might well call down the wrath of Rome upon Temple and nation alike;
>
> (v) because, at the crucial moment in the hearing, he not only (as far as they were concerned) pleaded guilty to the above charges, but also did so in such a way as to place himself, blasphemously, alongside the god of Israel.
>
> The leaders of the Jewish people were thus able to present Jesus to Pilate as a seditious trouble-maker; to their Jewish contemporaries (and later generations of rabbinic Judaism) as a false prophet and a blasphemer, leading Israel astray; and to themselves as a dangerous political nuisance. On all counts, he had to die.
>
> Their verdict was not, of course, a *sufficient* cause of Jesus' death. They needed Pilate to ratify and carry out the sentence. It was, however, a *necessary* cause of Jesus' crucifixion: Pilate himself would not have brought charges against Jesus, or, if he had, they would most likely have only resulted in a flogging. Pilate's decision was both a necessary and a sufficient cause of Jesus' crucifixion. If he had refused to

comply, Jesus would have been flogged and released; once he had agreed, the matter was concluded.

It does not take long to see that both political and religious factors weigh into the cause of Jesus' death from the Jewish and Roman points of view. But what was Jesus' intention? Assembling a synthesis of this question is more complicated. It involves a consideration of Wright's treatment in chapters eleven through thirteen, a full discussion of the controversies of the last week as well as the Last Supper and the various judicial examinations of Jesus. Wright's case is assembled by a meticulous study of a sequence of symbolic actions and sayings, which he calls "riddles," that reveal Jesus' intent to retell Israel's story with Jesus as the climactic key to its realization, the embodiment of the presence of Israel's God. For Wright, Jesus plays a unique and exalted role in the plan of God. Though it is expressed in somewhat different terms than in more traditionally oriented, theologically framed summaries, there is much here worthy of careful reflection.

Two examples must suffice. First, Wright argues in great detail that the parable of the talents/pounds is not about a distant return but rather focuses on YHWH's impending return to Zion (*JVG* 632-39). He presents a full defense of his fresh reading, arguing both for his reading and against the more traditional approach. This reading shows how Wright's fresh paradigm for Jesus' eschatology works. I will assess the treatment of this text and what it represents below.

Second, Wright argues for Jesus' seeing his death in terms of scriptural prophecy (*JVG* 597-604). Here Wright highlights Isaiah 53 as determinative for Jesus' vocation. Jesus in his death shares in Israel's sufferings and does so "as the key action in the divinely appointed plan of redemption for Israel and the world" (*JVG* 603). Here his argument takes on two other approaches from either end of the critical spectrum. On one end, there is a denial that Jesus had any redemptive intention or that Isaiah 53 really tells us very much about how Jesus saw his death as redeeming. On the other end, usually a more traditional approach, the handling of sin is abstracted almost to the point where one loses sight of the role of Israel's story in that redemption. Wright does not argue that the portrait he defends is the dominant one in Jesus' sense of vocation but only that it is one key element in a complex whole. Once one grasps Wright's point here, there is a corrective to each of the existing alternatives that is worth seriously considering. It is one of the values of his work that he grounds the presentation so thoroughly in its original setting (a point I shall make below more forcibly in my assessment).

The center of Wright's assessment of Jesus' prophetic kingdom announcement involves three claims that emanate from Jesus' self-identification with the task of Israel: the return from exile, the defeat of evil and the return of YHWH to Zion. For Wright, Jesus saw himself as the "leader and focal point of the true, returning-from-exile Israel"; this meant that he was the Messiah, "the king through whose work YHWH was at last restoring his people" (*JVG* 477). The events of Jesus' last week reveal the symbolism of this understanding in Jesus' actions. Jesus' temple action, the various royal riddles in his teaching[2] and his prediction of the temple's destruction in his Jerusalem discourse show "the vocation and destiny to embody in himself that great 'return from exile' which was one of the three main meanings of his announcement of the kingdom" (*JVG* 519).

The extent of authority typified in these events (some of which were public, while others were private) contributed to making the authorities nervous. It also discloses a consistent pattern of symbolic action that reveals Jesus' real intention.

Jesus' examination before the Jewish authorities reveals a similar view. The movement in the trial from questions about the temple to Messiah is perfectly natural in a first-century Jewish setting, since the Messiah was associated with the temple in Jewish eschatological hope. In Jesus' answer, with its combination of Psalm 110 and Daniel 7, comes the indication of how Jesus fulfills kingdom restoration and return from exile. Once again it is best to let Wright speak for himself at length (*JVG* 524-25):

> Both texts, taken together with their previous resonances still audible, provide an answer not only to the question about Messiahship but also to the question about the Temple: one aspect of Jesus' vindication would be the destruction of the Temple, and, by implication, of its present ruling regime. And both texts, taken together, imply that when all this happens the composite event will constitute the restoration of the kingdom to Israel, the liberation of the people of YHWH from the power of the beasts, the real return from exile.
>
> Jesus' response, then, resonates with ironic power. Now at last, when it can no longer be misunderstood, he can retell the story of Daniel 7 in his own revised version. He is claiming to be the representative of the true people of God. Like the martyrs on trial before pagan tyrants, he is refusing to abandon the ancestral faith and hope, even if it costs him his life. Like Susannah on trial before Jewish judges who turned out to be no better than pagans, he stands before a court who, in his eyes, represent cynical compromise rather than loyalty to YHWH. He therefore declares that Israel's god will vindicate him; and that vindication will include the destruction of the Temple which has come to symbolize and embody the rebellion

of Israel against God, her determination to maintain her national exclusivism at the cost of her vocation.

Jesus is not, then, suggesting that Caiaphas will witness the end of the space-time order. Nor will he look out of the window one day and observe a human figure flying downwards on a cloud. It is absurd to imagine either Jesus, or Mark, or anyone in between, supposing the words to mean that. Caiaphas will witness the strange events which follow Jesus' crucifixion: the rise of a group of disciples claiming that he has been raised from the dead, and the events which accelerate towards the final clash with Rome, in which, judged according to the time-honoured test, Jesus will be vindicated as a true prophet. In and through it all, Caiaphas will witness events which show that Jesus was not, after all, mistaken in his claim, hitherto implicit, now at last explicit: he is the Messiah, the anointed one, the true representative of the people of Israel, the one in and through whom the covenant god is acting to set up his kingdom.

The result is a trial in which the claim is thoroughly messianic. Here also is a clear indication of how Wright deals with the cosmic, eschatological language surrounding Jesus. This position represents one of the more controversial aspects of Wright's model that requires careful analysis. For Wright, metaphors often traditionally seen as relating to the return of Jesus or to cosmic activity of one degree or another refer to events within the period closely contemporary to Jesus and his opponents.

The "blasphemy" of Jesus before the Jewish leadership involved four elements (*JVG* 520-28, 624-29). First, Jesus has set himself against the temple and the anointed High Priest. Second, Jesus' seating at the right hand of God involves fundamentally a royal status in which he has the status of God's "right-hand man." It may also suggest an understanding that he possesses, in some sense, the divine glory in that role, without explicitly being a claim to a transcendent role.[3] Jesus would be "one of the central figures in a theophany" (*JVG* 643). Jewish precedent in figures like Joseph and Daniel, the "two powers" dispute, Jewish speculation about Moses, Metatron, and Akiba's view of David show that such categories existed in Judaism. Third, Jesus' exaltation "on the clouds" represents a theophany in which he shares a role with God. Fourth, this strong set of claims led to Jesus' being perceived by Caiaphas as a false prophet (Deut 13), who, in leading Israel astray, was subject to death as a blasphemer.

The entire portrait is enhanced when one considers some of the earlier scenes in Jesus' ministry. The confession at Caesarea Philippi, the Isaianic character of his speech in Luke 4, the reply to John the Baptist in Luke 7 about the eschatological significance of his healings, and his use of shepherd and Solomonic imagery—these all point to Jesus as the eschatological-messianic representative of true Israel.

Jesus' intention to portray the defeat of enemies and represent YHWH's return surfaces in several other elements that show up in the last week of Jesus' ministry. Restoration emerges in the Last Supper, where Jesus redefines a traditional meal of Judaism, pointing to the arrival of the new covenant and a new exodus in and through himself. A series of sayings, parables and events points to the same end and suggests that he knew he would suffer in the process. This significance may be observed in the rejected son in the parable of the wicked tenants, the authority represented in the reply about the great commandment, the symbolism of Jesus' being anointed for burial, the remarks about the judgment coming on the dry wood, Jesus' picturing himself as desiring to gather the nation like a hen would her chicks and his saying about the cup he must drink and the baptism he faces. Here is where the passion predictions earlier in Jesus' ministry fit. Messianic woes and individual suffering all point to the reenactment of Israel's story.

However, the suffering had a strange twist. Jesus' suffering was a way of showing Israel the way to redemption—by providing for it. He would establish a reality that would supersede the temple (*JVG* 604-5). God would also bring vindication both through and after the suffering. The task of Israel would be fulfilled in him. His death would be the new exodus, the new covenant, the forgiveness of sins and the end of exile. Behind this expectation stands scriptural hope from texts like the book of Daniel, Zechariah 9—14, the Psalms of the suffering righteous and Isaiah 40—55 (including the servant image).

In the process, Jesus reveals how the victory comes in his superseding the temple and defeating the enemies of Israel. Those enemies included forces of darkness, which also stood behind the visible opponents present in Rome and among the Jewish leadership. In this vocation of suffering, offered as an expression of love, he provides the way of redemption. Jesus opens up an alternative to the temple, but he does so in a way that was intended "in some sense . . . sacrificially" for that which was previously associated with activity "in and through the Temple itself" (*JVG* 604). The messianic victory not only took on Rome and its paganism, but it also addressed the attempt by Israel to be like the world in the way she attempted to defeat her foes. Acting on behalf of Israel, he would be what she failed to be. Vindication would come not only in God's exalting him but also in the judgment on the symbol of Israel's uniqueness, her temple.

YHWH's return to Zion emerges in the shared throne the vindicated one occupies on behalf of his true people, but it was anticipated and represented in the journey to Jerusalem as Jesus' actions indicated that God had returned to them through him. To reject his coming was to risk judgment—judgment that would be another coming not to deliver but to judge and vindicate Jesus and those who had stood with him. This return and the "coming of the Son of Man" fit within this history. The judgment of the temple and the vindication it completes is the coming of God that Jesus anticipated. Texts that traditionally are associated with a second coming really fit here. They show that in Jesus' coming, YHWH also comes.

It is best to let Wright himself summarize. First, as he discusses the trial and then Jesus' vocation as a whole.

> The trial scene, which we have already studied from several angles, now comes into complete focus. At stake was the whole career of Jesus, climaxing in his journey to Jerusalem, which itself exploded in his action in the Temple, and was further explained by his Last Supper. The trial opened, as it was bound to do, with the question about the Temple. Jesus had claimed authority over it, authority indeed to declare its destruction. This could only be because he believed himself to be the Messiah? Yes, answered Jesus: and you will see me vindicated, enthroned at the right hand of Power. The whole sequence belongs together precisely *as* a whole. The final answer drew into one statement the significance of the journey to Jerusalem, the Temple-action, and the implicit messianic claim. Together they said that Jesus, not the Temple, was the clue to, and the location of, the presence of Israel's god with his people. Sociologically, this represented a highly radical Galilean protest against Jerusalem. Politically, it constituted a direct challenge to Caiaphas' power-base and his whole position—and, of course, to those of Caesar and Pilate. Theologically, it was either true or it was blasphemous. Caiaphas wasted no time considering the former possibility. (*JVG* 644)

> I have argued that Jesus' underlying aim was based on a faith-awareness of vocation. He believed himself called, by Israel's god, to *evoke* the tradition which promised YHWH's return to Zion, and the somewhat more nebulous but still important traditions which spoke of a human figure sharing the divine throne; to *enact* those traditions in his own journey to Jerusalem, his messianic act in the Temple, and his death at the hands of pagans (in the hope of subsequent vindication); and thereby to embody YHWH's return. (*JVG* 651)

> I propose, as a matter of history, that Jesus of Nazareth was conscious of a vocation: a vocation, given him by the one he knew as "father," to enact in himself what, in Israel's scriptures, God had promised to accomplish all by himself. He would be the pillar of cloud and fire for the people of the new exodus. He would embody in himself the returning and redeeming action of the covenant God. (*JVG* 653)

Wright's summary of Jesus' last week is both clear and complex. Jesus did indeed believe his death would be the one-off act of redemption, for Israel and the world, and Jesus interpreted this vocation through scriptural meditation and interpretation. He was the unique provider and enabler of God's redemption. His death was the result of a combination of religious, political and social forces that collided at his trial with the Jewish leadership's claim that his affirmation of authority to sit at God's right hand constituted blasphemy. Roman leadership allowed that judgment to stand by seeing it in political terms and sending Jesus to his death, a death God would vindicate through resurrection and judgment on Israel for refusing his message. What are we to make of it?

The following assessment of Wright keeps two points in mind. First, Wright is discussing the self-understanding of Jesus as gleaned through the Gospel portraits. In other words, the portrait of Jesus that emerges must be sorted out in the midst of the evangelists' own interests and emphases. Wright's study desires to get at this Jesus from within the teacher's own setting. The book is a study of Jesus' own actions and aims. This probably explains, in part, the omission of the birth narratives from his account. To make an assessment of the ministry of Jesus requires that we look at what he did and said. That is how we get at his sense of vocation.

Within this first point another consideration is key. What the evangelists often present with clarity may only develop what was merely an implicit piece in the original setting. The more historical context one has, the better one can see the whole of the story. In other words, it took time for the whole of Jesus' story to emerge as the symbols were piled on top of one another and worked together to interpret one another. One of the strengths of Wright's study is that it pays serious attention to the momentum of the story and its sequencing. But Wright's reader should never forget that the questions being pursued in this book have to do with Jesus and his own actions and not the intentions of the authors of the Gospels or even of other authors of the New Testament. My guess is that these other sources will come into the story in the subsequent volumes. Thus I believe that it would be a mistake to argue that Wright denies the presence of certain doctrines on the basis of this volume. They may well show up in his later treatments, further on down the line of early church development. Wright has carefully disciplined himself on this question.

Second, Wright's study is not completed. This is but the second of five projected volumes. Questions raised here in my critique may be treated in part in subsequent volumes. The concern of my assessment is not to treat how themes Jesus taught were handled in the rest of the New Testament but to keep its focus on the issue of the historical Jesus. It is a focused concern attempting to match that of this volume. It may be that the questions I raise Wright believes are better treated, or more explicitly present, in this broader sphere, but I believe I raise them to address the same context his volume is treating.

Strengths

I see five basic strengths in this work. The first four can be treated briefly, as they relate to method. They will be stated in principal form and not elaborated with illustration. The fifth requires elaboration, since it treats the fundamental structure and details of the actual portrait of the events of this last crucial week of Jesus' ministry.

1. Wright is unashamedly committed to the connection between history and Christianity in an era when some wish to sever the two. Wright is clear that Christianity is neither an ideology nor an ethic grounded in some idealized story of origins; it is a faith making claims about divine activity in the affairs of humanity. This means that those events, their significance and their connections matter very much. However, historicity and the interpretation of historical events is a complex matter, since its results depend on the nature of the slice of history analyzed and the perspective chosen from which to look at the events.

Many interpreters treat events poorly. They err in a variety of ways. Some treat them as if the events had a once-for-all quality to them. Others act as if the sequel to the events should have no impact in appreciating what originally took place. Still others believe that the sequel disqualifies one from seeing roots in an earlier moment. Finally, whether expressed out of the piety of the pristine claim of faith or from a profound skepticism, others argue that a careful sorting out of the events really does not matter for the story. But history is inherently about sequence. Historical events cannot be chopped up into independent pieces like this. The flow is a crucial part of the story. What happens subsequently can be historical commentary on what happened originally as well. Criticism in its frequent divide-and-conquer approach to historicity often causes us to lose sight of the whole and its sequence, which is where the fundamental claims of the story reside.

Wright understands this. His constant pursuit of double similarity and dissimilarity attempts to honor the flow of history and yet be sensitive to the differences between Jesus and the early church. It honors the fact that Jesus was Jewish but that he was so in his own way, while looking for the seed that often flowered in a more fully developed way in the church or for a scaffolding that disappeared once the larger structure was built.

2. This stress on the whole story leads to what may be called coherent historicity. Here is another strength. Wright seeks to make the whole of the story and its many parts cohere into a unified explanation—no bits-and-pieces patchwork here. If we have a portrait of Jesus, then one should be able to see a coherent story line. Ben F. Meyer, in defending "critical realism," makes the same point by speaking of the inner quality of events. He expresses the goal of this quest this way:

> The result, inevitably, is to discover something of the "inside" of the event under investigation; that is, to grasp it as motivated in some way, moving in some direction, significant in some context. This internal factor, which gives the event its human and historical density, can only be described in terms of meaning. The meaning of the event—the meaning intrinsic to and constitutive of it has two sources: the intention of its author(s) and the context of its actualization.[4]

This is one of the reasons that Wright's study shows us how historical Jesus study should be done. He is constantly trying to make sense out of the story as a whole as well as considering how each piece works. His view of Jesus makes sense at several key points:

☐ The result of this pursuit is a correct recognition that Jesus is not just a sage. He claims to be the central, even pivotal, figure in God's plan. On this point I think Wright brings us fundamentally closer to the real Jesus than have others who tried to pit one Jesus portrait against another in a claim that there is a plurality of Jesuses in the Gospels.

☐ Wright is correct to reject the acceptance of a "wisdom" Jesus over and against a kingdom/apocalyptic Jesus (see *JVG* 316). This kind of disjunction, so common in critical study of the Gospels, represents a fundamental logical fallacy of the excluded middle, as well as being historically problematic.

☐ Wright is also clearer on the Jewish involvement behind Jesus' death than some who wish to shift responsibility largely to Rome (in part to attempt to allay fears of anti-Semitic readings of these texts).[5]

☐ He is also quite correct in highlighting the messianic self-understanding of Jesus as the way into appreciating the development of Jesus' self-presentation to Israel, something many critics have disregarded.

☐ Finally, he is on the mark in explaining how Jesus saw his approaching suffering and defined it through existing scriptural texts, showing that Jesus' seeming innovation of a suffering redemptive figure was not without potential roots in the Hebrew Scripture. These fundamental points of coherence show the depth of strength in Wright's model.

3. *The result of this commitment is that Wright constantly and carefully considers the primary setting of these events, the first* **Sitz im Leben.** Granted this is something that has to be sifted out from the sources; but the more coherent the story, the more credible the reading. The proof is in the pattern. The result for method is that one takes seriously the Jewish backdrop to these events, one of the hallmarks of the Third Quest. The question is, how would this event have been heard, seen and understood in its original context? Rather than seeing a message for the early church, the possibility is entertained that the point also had relevance in the setting of Jesus' ministry or that the text as we have it can be read in a way that reveals how it was originally presented and appreciated. With a few exceptions, this kind of approach has sadly been missing in much critical scholarship. The common critical practice is another example where history is read in one-dimensional ways.

4. *Wright's linguistic sensitivity also surfaces in his treatment of metaphors being connected to this world and this history.* This point was made, as Wright acknowledges, by George B. Caird.[6] I shall raise questions about the particularity of certain readings making this point. Nevertheless, the point is an important element of reading many of these texts. Jesus' eschatology was not escapist. God was acting in history through Jesus now and would do so as well in the future. The renewing and victory that comes is a part of the redemption of this creation. Whatever heavenly or otherworldly dimensions it possesses, it does so while having a connection to this world and its history.

5. *Wright's general portrait of the last week is fundamentally sound.* Now we come to a careful consideration of the actual, key elements of the final week. Though I shall suggest a different reading of some of the details below, including one of Wright's major points, I find much of his overall description compelling. Wright's work on the last week represents a significant advance on most portraits of the close of Jesus' ministry. Much of my evaluation concentrates on the sociopolitical aspects of Jesus' death, since these elements in particular are often the

most ignored aspects of the history. In saying this, it is important to remember that political and social issues are not as distinct from religious matters as they often are in Western culture. To challenge the political structure of Judaism was to make a religious claim, especially about authority.

a. The leadership sought Jesus' removal because they believed that his claims were dangerous for Judaism and for the leaders' role within the faith. They represented a threat to Israel's already shaky relationship to Rome. They probably did see him as a "false prophet" of the Deuteronomy 13 mold, whose activity jeopardized the nation. A text Wright does not note supports his point here. The evidence of the Temple Scroll (11QTemple 64:6-10) at Qumran has potential relevance.[7] This text reads:

> If a man slanders his [i.e., God's] people and delivers his people up to a foreign nation and does evil to his people, you shall hang him on the tree [note the allusion to Deut 21:22-23], and he shall die. According to the testimony of two witnesses and the testimony of three witnesses he shall be put to death, and they shall hang him on a tree.

This passage shows that a challenge to God's people, especially when it could be perceived as placing the nation at political risk, was viewed as a serious situation. Better for one threatening figure to die than that a nation should perish.

Jesus' actions in the temple, whether conceived of as a call to reform or a prediction of destruction or both (something which could be debated), raised serious questions of authority and inherently challenged the leadership. There was in Judaism a strong association between Jerusalem's coming greatness, the temple and the messianic hope. Only a genuine messianic figure could possess the authority to challenge the leadership as Jesus did. This is seen in the ancient prayers of Judaism like the Eighteen Benedictions, a national prayer whose roots on this topic may well go back to the time of Jesus.[8] It is another piece of evidence to include in Wright's portrait. In the traditional version, benedictions 14 and 15 read as follows:

> And to Jerusalem, thy city, return with mercy and dwell in its midst as thou hast spoken; and build it soon in our days to be an everlasting building; and raise up quickly in its midst the throne of David. Blessed art thou, Lord, who causest the horn of salvation to shoot forth.
>
> Cause the shoot of David to shoot forth quickly, and raise up his horn by thy salvation. For we wait on thy salvation all the day. Blessed art thou, Lord, who causest the horn of salvation to shoot forth.

The Palestinian version of the prayer combines these benedictions into

> Be merciful, Lord our God, with thy great mercies, to Israel thy people and to Jerusalem thy city; and to Zion, the dwelling place of the glory, and to thy Temple and thy habitation; and to the kingship of the house of David, thy righteous Messiah. Blessed art thou, Lord, God of David, who buildest Jerusalem.

If there is a question as to the antiquity of such an expectation, one need only read *Psalms of Solomon* 17:32-33: "He [Messiah] shall glorify the Lord in a place to be seen of all the earth; and he shall purge Jerusalem, making it holy as of old."[9]

What is immediately evident from these prayers and the hope expressed in the *Psalms of Solomon* is the close association in expectation between the presence of Messiah and the wholeness of the temple. Jesus' actions invoke these kinds of issues.

Thus it comes as no surprise that the first question Jesus is asked after the cleansing is where he gets the authority to do what he is doing (Mk 11:27-33 par. Mt 21:23-27 par. Lk 20:1-8). It is clear by his actions that he has intentionally bypassed seeking the leadership's sanction. His actions also evoke a set of potentially volatile hopes. In sum, only one of the claimants, either Jesus or the leadership, can really represent God and his people. The Synoptic narrative of the last week has historical coherence.

b. So the temple action raised the likelihood that if Jesus were allowed to continue, then there would be a major disruption of the current stability. If he could walk in and demand reform of the temple, declare its coming destruction and seek to exercise public authority over it, then all the other irritating parts of his ministry[10] would escalate in their potential popular importance. The message Jesus preached was so far-reaching that the leadership recognized its ultimate effect—left unchecked it would represent a remaking of the faith, as they knew it. They found this prospect unacceptable.

c. The strength and certainty expressed in Jesus' claim at the trial meant that Jesus' presence would always cast doubt on the leadership's own authority as well as on the current structure of Judaism, a structure in which the leadership had a major vested interest. In effect, Jesus' preaching and presence challenged and altered the status of many of the major symbols of Judaism, such as the temple and the sabbath, because of the way in which he conducted himself. His call to the nation to cleanse itself evoked the Law and Prophets in a way distinct from current practice. Though engaged in private, the Last Supper shows just how far Jesus was willing to reinvest old traditions with a fresh sense as a result of his presence. Though this meal did not impact Jesus' trial, the fact that Jesus held such a meal and invested it with fresh symbolism showed just how far his teaching sought to go. In all of this, Wright's portrait is credible.

For his part, Pilate, though ultimately responsible for guaranteeing Jesus' execution, was drawn into this dispute as he refused to opt for the protection of a Galilean teacher at the expense of peace with the Jewish leadership.

d. When it comes to Wright's view of Jesus' self-understanding as seen in the events of the last week, I believe two of his three points stand: the defeat of evil and the return of YHWH to Zion.

With regard to the defeat of evil, the presence of God's delivering authority was part of Jesus' ministry before he reached Jerusalem. These acts showed Jesus to be Messiah and indicated the scope of his authority, but how would forgiveness be obtained? For Wright, Jesus realizes that he will go to Jerusalem and die as a result of the claims he is making. Jesus realizes this much earlier in his ministry than, for example, Albert Schweitzer says that Jesus did (*JVG* 609). Two events signify his understanding here: the temple and the upper room. The temple shows a recalcitrant and corrupt present system, ripe for judgment. Jesus declares it will pass away, and in 70 C.E. it did, vindicating his claims. Salvation comes through Jesus the Messiah, the one through whom God "will save Israel and thereby the world" (*JVG* 609-10). The true exodus will come through him as the symbolism at the last meal shows. Passover, not atonement, is the controlling metaphor as this "one-off moment of freedom in Israel's past" is "translated into the one-off moment which would inaugurate Israel's future" (*JVG* 605). All of this was foreseen in his ministry as he fought with sickness, with demon possession or with his opponents on issues about how Israel would achieve national security and hope in ways distinct from taking on Rome. He would take on Rome as well by taking on the forces that stood behind it. Rather than insulting and threatening Rome, he suffered either in silence or with words of forgiveness, an innovation to the martyr tradition, which must be substantially historical (*JVG* 606-7). Evil will be defeated here in this unique one. This is how sins will be forgiven. The early church and the rest of the New Testament have much more to say about these themes, but this is how Jesus presented it initially.

The return of YHWH to Zion is predicated on the inseparable identification between Jesus and YHWH's cause. The identification is rooted in turn on the actualization of God's promise and hope. It has three key elements: the hope for YHWH's return, the speculation that Jesus would be exalted to share his throne and the symbolic language used for YHWH's activity in the world (*JVG* 615).

Exaltation is the topic at the Jewish examination of Jesus that leads to his crucifixion. Jesus' claims here are too much for the High Priest (*JVG* 624-29, 642-45).
The symbols of YHWH's involvement are Shekinah, Torah, Wisdom, Logos
and Spirit (*JVG* 629). The Messiah for Jesus works in all these areas. He would
build, cleanse or rebuild the temple. He would teach and be the enforcer of
Torah. He might be identified with Logos. He would be endowed with Wisdom
as well as the divine Spirit (*JVG* 630). In sum, Messiah "would be the agent or
even the vicegerent of Israel's god, would fight his battles, would restore his people, would rebuild or cleanse the house so that the Shekinah would again dwell in
it" (*JVG* 630). Here is affirmed God's involvement in the whole of the cosmos.

The promised presence of God's kingdom is manifest in the coming of
Israel's God in person and in power. In the proclamation of the coming kingdom,
there is also heard the emphasis that YHWH is returning to Zion. Judaism in the
time of Jesus still looked for such a return, which could also be called "his 'visiting' his people" (*JVG* 622). With the return of YHWH would come as well the
return from exile and the defeat of evil. For Wright all of these three elements
form one interlocking package of the hope Jesus preached. For Wright they all
happened with Jesus' ministry and immediately subsequent vindication.

In support of the thrust of Wright's claim, I can point to another key event
of the last week that indicates that Jesus' authority is the issue. It is the dispute
over the source of Jesus' authority (Mk 11:27-33 par. Mt 21:23-27; Lk 20:1-8).
His reply, in the form of a question, harks back to John the Baptist, whose
authority rested totally outside the official authority structure of the Jewish leadership. If the authority for John or Jesus is not granted from the leadership, only
two alternatives remain: it lacks sanction (and may be from below), or it comes
from above.

Jesus' response leaves the same alternatives in place, but with one important
difference that suggests his reply. The officials were asking him who gave him
permission to do things like the temple act he had just performed. Such authority
over the most centralized symbol of God's presence indicated the extent of
authentication Jesus believed he possessed. It also raised the point that either
Jesus or the leaders represented God, since their views on issues like the temple
were so distinct. If Jesus' way reflects that of God, then virtually automatically the
ways of the leaders represent a crooked path. Seen in these terms, their clash was
inevitable. Jesus' oblique reply by appealing to John is a reply that not only
answers the question but reverses the implication of the alternatives the question
was meant to raise. If Jesus is sanctioned from above, then the leadership is . . . !

The trial scene shows a similar understanding. Jesus' claims here are unique. It also sets up a similar confrontation to the dispute over Jesus' authority. Though Wright is very close to the mark here, I wish to make other points about the extent of Jesus' claim that cohere with his picture and strengthen it. Jesus' claim of exaltation and vindication anticipates an enthronement in heaven. However, this seating is neither merely being received among the righteous nor is it a part of the traditional Jewish messianic expectation. (Wright is not making either of these points, but others do.) Exaltation anticipates a place at God's side. Wright expresses carefully how transcendent this claim is.[11] He allows that it might be and opens the door very much in this direction. Messiah now is seen as "the one who will sit at the right hand of the god of Israel" (*JVG* 551). I think that more can be said about what Jesus' remarks seem to entail and why they were found so offensive.

Here my treatment of strengths begins to bridge over into critique, for I think perhaps Wright has stated this point with subtlety and as a result may have underdeveloped other issues related to Jesus' mission. The claim to sit at God's right hand is a more "heavenlyward" rendering of what probably had previously been read more figuratively as a reference to an earthly king. Whereas Psalm 110:1 probably was read originally as a text about an earthly kingship hope and the vicegerent's role of Israel's ruler, now Jesus applied the pattern of authority asserted there—of an exalted position given from above—to someone who rules not within a theocratic state from a throne on earth but from an exalted seat at the side of God above. What was applied to a human figure on earth now is read as describing an exalted figure at God's side. The metaphor still has its functional quality in that the point is not a chair or a location "up there," but it expresses a vindication and a sharing of divine authority and glory more directly proximate to God in a way Israel's kings did not possess. This escalation in the pattern and promise of scriptural teaching, which this reading contains, surfaces other key questions about the nature of the exaltation proclaimed and what it may eventually bring.

Who can get such a position in heaven? In effect, Jesus' point is not only that God will vindicate him and bring him to a position of authority proximate to God but that he will be given a resident position there. This claim is greater than the claim that one will walk into the Holy of Holies and live there. If this was an offensive claim for the temple setting involving the nonpriestly offering of a sacrifice, as the Maccabean War showed, then think how offensive would be an act that takes place in the heavenly realm, which the temple models! The implication is what really makes for the blasphemy and the immediacy of the reaction to Jesus' remark.[12] It is a claim for transcendent authority, and that implies a future role will emerge from his permanent seating at the side of God. More on this follows below.

In sum, much of Wright's portrait about the key final week stands up to scrutiny, but Jesus' reply at the trial also raises some issues. What questions would one raise about Wright's study?

Questions

The questions that I wish to raise are not an attempt to argue that Wright is necessarily wrong. Rather, with a new paradigm like the one he presents, it is better not to rush too quickly to judgment but to hear out the proposal, which may require some time and exchange to be a mutually profitable undertaking. So I call this section "Questions," because I want to raise some alternatives or discuss some texts within his configuration that might suggest one could come to some slightly different conclusions on some points. I am not extensively footnoting my discussion, as I desire to engage his model rather directly.

I have three areas I wish to probe concerning his portrait of events in this final week: the return-from-exile theme, the strong connection Wright makes between vindication and the fall of 70 C.E. and the issue of pattern in history (what is often called a typological reading of the Scripture). For this last topic, I want to consider the way the fresh emergence of pattern in Jesus' reply involves escalation or fresh twists in the drama of salvation, points to which Wright is often quite sensitive. (See his appeal to the ark of the covenant on *JVG* 621. What was true of Babylon in judgment can now be true of another unfaithful community, Israel: see *JVG* 354-60.) My critique is that Wright's all-encompassing pursuit of the metaphor of Israel's story though the image of the end of exile has been a bit too encompassing. Perhaps some distinguishing in definition can help us here.[13] Some things Jesus claims go beyond that imagery or so alter it that other imagery might be a better summary description of what is claimed. Still other imagery may be needed to supplement this exile metaphor.

1. The return-from-exile theme. As with the other two major themes Wright sees—namely, the defeat of evil and the return of YHWH to Zion—he also makes a strong case for the presence of return-from-exile themes in Jesus' teaching (*JVG* 428-30). I wish to ask whether the issue of the return of YHWH to Zion or even of restoration motifs is significantly distinct from the issue of the return from exile: can one have the first without yet having the second? Perhaps another, possibly better, suggestion could be that return-from-exile language in the New Testament comes in two forms and reflects two phases: one associated with Jesus' earthly ministry, the other tied to imagery looking to the future decisive moment when all nations are placed before him in evaluation. I would argue that the story Jesus tells has a twist at this point. YHWH returns to Zion and even opens the way for return from exile. However, the call for a return from exile is not completely realized until the future. Though imagery associated, for example, with John the Baptist from Isaiah 35 and 40 raises such end-to-exile imagery with YHWH's coming in Jesus (Lk 3:4-6; 7:22-23), the image is not exhausted by such recent application. Rather in Jesus, he redirects Israel in the midst of what will continue to be an exile as the reconstituted and restored people live out their mission still present and scattered throughout the world. There is a biblical and equally metaphorical sense in which the image of scattering remains even in the midst of YHWH's return, as more is still to be done in terms of salvation. Such metaphorical tension, I would argue, fits the general already/not yet patterns of New Testament soteriology.

I believe one could argue that several features suggest this alternative way of stating the third element to the story, especially as Jesus came to understand that his mission was meeting intense rejection.

Many symbols seem to fit here. First, the bulk of Jesus' ministry takes place in Galilee, not in Jerusalem, suggesting that the old central locale for Judaism is less central than one might expect. Granted Jesus does eventually go to the capital, but he goes only to challenge the existing structure and claim the right to make the extensive reforms his ministry already represented. The temple as a house of prayer for Gentiles does not seem to anticipate its ultimate, permanent demise. Second, the challenge of the temple and the suggestion that somehow what Jesus was forming would replace it is not a call to return from exile (at least in one sense of thinking about the metaphor). It is the establishing of a mechanism that would maintain dispersion and yet transform it into the mission-driven structure God always intended as the people's task. The imagery of the disciples as being like sheep scattered when he is struck also suggests nongathering imagery. Third, the thrust of Jesus' associations, compassion and ethic is the call to be a people of light in the midst of a dark world, engaging need where it is found and reflecting the hope of God's activity. Parables like that of the good Samaritan suggest the issue is not return to a place or even to a land. It is a turning to the God who is now engaged in reconstituting the people of God so they can do what God had always intended for them to do wherever he has them. These images should not be read as applied nationally to Israel, but they are appeals to understand why certain kinds of people are sought out in the ministry Jesus has. When Jesus gives a commission at the end of his life, the impulse the disciples initially sense is to go into all the world and look for Jews (see Acts 1—6 and the struggle to get Peter to understand in Acts 10). The call is not to make them return but to make them honor God where they already are. My point is not to argue that Wright should take this language literally and geographically in these contexts but that the image of continued dispersion exists in the midst of God's work of restoration. God can return to Zion and restoration can occur without it being considered an end of exile, at least not yet. The exile image in New Testament fulfillment is more complex than Wright suggests.

I would stress that in saying this, I do not think this says something very different from what Wright means by return from exile. Yet I think the metaphor of the story does not deal with end of exile as much as with a new appreciation of what God is calling on his people to be where he already has them (restoration, yes; return from or end of exile, only perhaps in a limited or initiated sense). They can turn to God and God can return to them without all that is entailed in their gathering having been accomplished. In the gathering yet to come, the exile moves to its consummation. Those texts that mention regathering seem to place it alongside banquet imagery and other themes (see note 15). In other words, the time for ultimate return or regathering in the more traditional sense of Hebrew hope will come later (with another return!). These themes are elements of the story still in the future—a future the church still seems to be reaching toward after Jesus has departed and even after God had acted in judgment against Israel in 70 C.E.

2. The connection between vindication and the fall of the temple. This leads me directly into what surely has been the most controversial of Wright's proposals: his emphasis on vindication and coming being seen in resurrection and the judgment that falls on Israel in 70 C.E. As Jesus heads to his death and anticipates victory, how will triumph come? It is important to stress that Wright's proposal is not a denial of eschatology or apocalyptic, as some have argued. It is a reconfiguration of it in a way he claims is more faithful to the way these categories have worked. Nor do I make this point to argue that the return was a central theme in Jesus' teaching. It was not, as it appears only in a few parables and in even fewer sayings. But the debate is important because it relates to how the victory ultimately comes as well as to how God's vindication and justice will work itself out. It is also important because it is significant to consider whether Jesus laid the groundwork for such hope. What authority and vindication did Jesus conceive of as he submitted to this death, which by all surface appearances should have been the end of his story?

Two points Wright has made here are worth affirming. First, the concerns of apocalyptic treat this history and tell the story of the nation in terms of ultimate vindication. Second, too little importance has traditionally been given to the significance of the fall in 70 C.E. as evidence that God is still working out his plan and as a vindication of Jesus as it relates to Israel and her actions in response to his claims. Whatever else is said about Wright's view of eschatology, his raising this issue and its place in the discussion are worthy of note and appreciation.

Nevertheless, I want to question whether Wright brings the pendulum too far the other way. To make the case, I do not wish to simply argue certain verses in the Jesus tradition teach a return or a coming to earth, for that is what is in dispute. I prefer to make use of two arguments Wright likes to use to get back to the likelihood of what those texts mean. They are (a) that apocalyptic deals with this history and (b) that what the early church explicitly teaches often has seeds in what Jesus taught. If this second principle holds for areas like Christology, perhaps it applies to eschatology as well. If these principles can guide us to see Jesus' aims in terms of how he saw himself, maybe they can help us see how he saw his death, not as an end but as a turning point.

The point coming from the first principle is that Jesus' exaltation places him at the side of God permanently, as I argued earlier for the point of Jesus' remarks in response to Caiaphas. It is the characteristic of eschatology and apocalyptic to present its hope in the form of a final decisive resolution. It is the finality of the hope declared (as well as the certainty that it will come) that gives this genre its persuasive and enduring power. But if this genre points to a decisive resolution and it involves a Jesus who is permanently exalted to the side of God, then the hope anticipates a resolution in the final judgment of God in this history in which Jesus implicitly must share. The fall in 70 C.E. does not qualify as that final event, though it does qualify as a major step along the way. Just as the apocalyptic language in the Hebrew Scriptures referred in the short term to events proximate, the very confidence with which they were expressed caused the text's recipients to see in them an expression of a more ultimate expression of complete shalom. This is where pattern or typology begins to appear in the context of Old Testament hope (more on this below).

To judge Israel in 70 C.E. was still not to remove all the enemies or exercise the complete judgment Jesus contemplated when he spoke of unending suffering for those who turned their back to him. The effect is that a final, decisive judgment on earth in which Jesus shares is implied by the very structure of the genre category.[14]

Now the second principle confirms this reading. I do not think anyone will dispute that the rest of the New Testament anticipates what has been called a second coming. For example, Acts 1:9-11 suggests as much, as does Acts 3:19-22. Undoubtedly, this is more explicitly presented in these other texts. But here is where what Wright argues so eloquently elsewhere can be brought to bear. Where did such a later expectation come from, but from roots Jesus' own teaching supplied? What do the banquet texts or the teaching like the judgment of the nations in Matthew 25 suggest but the arrival of this complete shalom and the final judgment of all the nations after the current exile and alienation are ended? Do not these texts foresee a day in this history when Jesus will play a key role in that final adjudication? Is this not what the theme of Jesus as judge of the living and the dead in Acts connotes (Acts 10:42; 17:31)? Jewish readings in similar contexts anticipate a similar ending, as *1 Enoch* suggests. The motif is an established one in the reflections that grew out of the original story. It resides in both the Jewish and Christian contexts. They are corroborated in the already/not yet emphasis found in texts like 1 Corinthians 15:20-28. They are suggested in the hope Paul apparently clings to for ethnic Israel, despite his earlier warnings of the judgment they face, in Romans 11.[15] They are underscored in the imagery of Revelation 19-22, where we are in a post-70 C.E. setting.

Wright challenges the idea that Jesus taught a second coming with some vigor when he discusses his fresh reading of the parable of the talents/pounds. Wright objects that such a reading "strains probability a long way to think of him attempting to explain, to people who had not grasped the fact of his imminent death, that there would follow an intermediate period after which he would 'return' in some spectacular fashion, for which nothing in their tradition had prepared them" (*JVG* 635).

To this principled objection three quick points can be made. First, we are discussing here whether Jesus taught a second coming, not whether the early church did. All agree on the latter point. So Wright is correct that the appeal to adjudicate the matter must come from factors within Jesus' ministry. Second, it is no argument against an understanding of Jesus that because his audience might not have originally appreciated the remark that he did not teach such things. It is quite possible that Jesus set forth teaching that came to be appreciated once all the pieces of the puzzle came into place. In fact, this is admittedly already the case for his predicted suffering and resurrection, for those who accept the authenticity of such sayings as Wright also eloquently argues. Third, as to the question of whether Jewish tradition left them totally unprepared for a period of decisive judgment, that point can be disputed (see the remark about *1 Enoch* above). Granted, Judaism did not look for a return from heaven, since the Jews debated resurrection itself. But once vindication or resurrection is in place, what is in the way of a return? A Jesus who could appear in a resurrected body and ascend could also return, could he not, to bring judgment in this history?

My argument here is not that other portions of the New Testament teach this, so Jesus must have taught exactly the same thing as well. It is that this particular and more detailed way of expressing this hope in the early church has roots in Jesus' teaching, where he invokes the images of decisive judgment and exaltation permanently to the side of God, alongside teaching about gathering and decisive judgment. Even though it took death and resurrection for them to get his point, the disciples did put it together once all the pieces of the puzzle fell into place and they realized where God had taken him upon vindicating him. These themes and the nature of apocalyptic involving this history suggest that Jesus did anticipate one day when he would share in a decisive judgment. That judgment is pictured by, but is distinct from, the judgment on Israel in 70 C.E. The connection between the two moments of judgment is why Jesus can discuss the two as if they are one event in his eschatological discourse. However, this final judgment also is the natural implication of the claim to sit at God's right hand and be the judge of those who were examining him in those last days. The story of the judgment is an ongoing story whose roots reside in the responses to Jesus taking place in Jerusalem in the fateful week of his execution. What results is both a national judgment in 70 C.E. and the accountability of all to him, an accountability that will be assessed one day when God brings the fullness of righteousness, resurrection and shalom to the earth. This is the ultimate hope to which Jesus alluded, if John 5:24-30 goes back to him. This is why the *palingenesia* Jesus refers to in Matthew 19:28-30 alludes ultimately to the eternal life that comes in the "rebirth" Jesus brings, even though that future new birth has a foretaste in the present. It was this hope that allowed Jesus in part to face the ignominious death to which his arrest and trial would lead. Here is the ultimate regathering and end to exile.

But does this reading distort the story of Daniel 7 as a coming to the Ancient of Days as Wright suggests (*JVG* 524-25)? I would argue not. Yes, Daniel 7 pictures the coming of one like a Son of Man to the Ancient of Days. Yet that enthronement leads to the vindication of the saints on earth, a vindication that will manifest itself in this history. The text portrays a moment, but it is a moment that represents a change in the cosmic structure of the earth and the establishment of a kingdom whose mandate extends into the completion of the task given to it. As a result any event that represents the outworking of that sharing of authority can properly be related to the moment when the sharing began to work itself out. Any exercise of this shared authority and vindication has its roots in the moment that Daniel 7 portrays. For the establishment of a kingdom made not with human hands (reading Daniel 7 as an allusion back to Daniel 2) is the establishment of a permanent kingdom whose victory will one day be manifest over the whole earth in the context of this history. The conclusion, it seems to me, implies a second coming or, at the least, offers a promise that when decisive judgment and final victory leading to shalom come and accounts are reckoned, Jesus will be there to do the accounting. Such ultimate vindication can fit into the concepts of victory and dominion expressed in Daniel 7. So Jesus' last week has very much to do with both redemption and eschatology, both short and long term.

Traditional views of Jesus tend to see the last week in terms of the problem of sin, atonement and cleansing, which also are a part of these events as the ransom saying of Mark 10:45 suggests, as does the probable representational language at the Last Supper. This personal-sin element is incorporated into the view of how redemption comes through Israel by Wright, so much so that some reading him may not think it is present at all for him. In fact Wright, even though he has focused other dimensions of the argument and even though I question his emphasis here, may be sending us down a more balanced track. Our own highlighting of this sin theme has probably served to obscure how important this other eschatological-redemption dimension of Jesus' perspective is in the events of this last week. The hope of resurrection and vindication was important precisely because it meant that Jesus would assume a position next to God and that Jesus would exercise a role in the final say over Israel and the nations. It is a perspective like this that drives later comprehensive claims for Jesus' authority in visions like those in Revelation or in the kerygmatic claims made in Acts that Jesus has been appointed judge of the living and the dead (Acts 10:42-43; 17:30-31). Wright has placed the eschatological emphasis on Israel's story and 70 C.E. I would place it on both 70 C.E. and on what that judgment also represents later for the entire world. So Israel is the gateway to blessing not only in promise but in judgment as well.

   3. *The issue of pattern in history.* This leads to my brief remarks about typology. I believe that the debate over what became the fall of 70 C.E. may represent Wright's hesitation to consider the possibility of the working out of typology, which is a very Jewish way of reading history and pattern. Just as Jesus escalated and developed the picture of vicegerency and exaltation in Psalm 110:1, so he has played with the typological picture of judgment in alluding to the destruction of the temple. What the Israelite king represented in microcosm, Jesus represents to a heightened, cosmic, decisive degree. What the judgment of the unfaithful nation represents in a smaller form is what the heightened, decisive judgment of all nations and people will be like.

   The Jewish story has such patterns in it that permit repetition of the type in a way that links the event to a previous pattern. It can do so and speak as if the event is one, linked by the pattern set up by the correspondence. One event guarantees the other. To see one part is to know the other portion will come. When Jesus evokes the concept of desolation associated with Jerusalem, he is appealing to the example of Antiochus Epiphanes (Dan 11:31). What Antiochus did is the pattern for any act of desecration that also pictures judgment. The association of such a judgment with the day of the Lord means that judgment can appear more than once. After all, the entirety of the pattern is part of the eschatological work of God. Just as imagery of the day of the Lord has patterned typology built into it, so Jesus' remarks about judgment on Israel are a fulfilling, yet typologically patterned, example. Here is the kind of judgment authority Jesus possesses when God totally acts to vindicate Jesus' own claims and delivers those allied to him, both with reference to the nation and later to the judgment that brings his authority before the world. If Wright would apply the typology he sees in other contexts to this scene, I suspect the differences between him and many other interpreters on this question would shrink, though their emphases might still remain decidedly different.

Conclusion

Wright's study is certainly worthy of careful reflection. His proposals represent a sane attempt to explain Jesus' ministry in its original Jewish context and to honor the levels of historical concern that the sources reflect. His pursuit of coherence is certainly the way forward in the study of Jesus from the only sources we possess to make sense of him. Often his guiding us back to the original *Sitz im Leben* is successful, belying the claims of other critics that one must choose between the first setting and one involving only the Evangelists' audience and concerns. Reading the story of the historical Jesus in the coherent way Wright does is not easy. Nuancing is required at virtually every step. Wright is a capable guide. Much in his portrait of the trials and death of Jesus seems historically credible. The questions I raise reflect nothing but respect for the effort and the way these issues have been framed. There is much to learn from here.

I question aspects of his handling of the exile theme and his focus on Jesus' teaching of vindication as aimed at 70 C.E. I would want to say a little more about the Christology reflected in the last week of Jesus' life and the implications that has for the eschatological hope Jesus leaves behind in the shadow of his cross. I suspect, however, that Wright is quite correct to see Jesus as a Jewish figure who was challenging Israel to rethink its story and mission by placing him at its center as bearer and enabler of the promised kingdom of God who was to be exalted. The issues Wright's study raises are neither merely historical nor academic. They represent the portrait of a figure that towers over history and challenges us to consider God in a fresh way. Hopefully Wright's study and the assessment of it will lead all of us to reflect carefully even more about what the life and death of Jesus was all about. What more could an author want from his study of Jesus? Perhaps now we shall more fully appreciate Jesus anew as the uniquely pivotal figure he was both for Israel's history and God's plan.

Seven

Jesus & the Victory of Apocalyptic

DALE C. ALLISON JR.

N T. WRIGHT IS TO BE CONGRATULATED FOR SAYING A NUMBER OF THINGS that very much need to be said today and for defending them with vigor in very entertaining prose. Against a number of important contemporary scholars, for example, Wright correctly insists that apocalyptic eschatology is at the very center of what Jesus was all about. He is also on the mark when he refuses to dissolve that eschatology into atemporal or existential categories. He rightly sees that, in Jesus' proclamation, eschatology is first of all the conclusion of a narrative and that this narrative is the story of God's dealing with Israel.

So far so good, and I could spend the rest of this chapter offering further support for these positions and much else that Wright has to say about matters eschatological. I believe, however, that it shall be more profitable if herein I focus upon a topic on which we do not see eye to eye. Despite the accord that does exist between us, we strongly disagree regarding the nature of apocalyptic language; and it is that disagreement I should like to explore in this chapter—especially as Wright has accused me of misunderstanding the work of George B. Caird (*JVG* 209 n. 38; 321 n. 2; 322 n. 3), whereas I think, with all due respect, that Wright has not fairly grappled with my position. Nonetheless I hope that our conflict in this particular subject does not eclipse the fact that we concur about much of importance.

Wright believes Johannes Weiss and Albert Schweitzer were correct in their conviction that Jesus and his first followers lived within the world of Jewish apocalyptic. Wright equally believes that both Schweitzer and Weiss were wrong in their understanding of that apocalyptic world and that their misunderstanding is shared by many of us within the New Testament guild. Both of these propositions are controversial, but as I happen to agree, as already indicated, with the first, I shall concentrate upon the second, which causes me some difficulty.

The fullest statement of Wright's interpretation of Jewish apocalyptic appears in *The New Testament and the People of God.* In the tenth chapter, which is entitled "The Hope of Israel" (280-338), Wright reviews what Jews in the time shortly before and after Jesus expected their God to do in the future. Again and again two points are highlighted—on the assumption that they have been missed by other interpreters. First, few if any ancient Jews, including those responsible for the apocalyptic literature, were (according to Wright) looking for "the end of the world," if by that one means the end of the space-time universe. They were rather hoping that God would renew the covenant with Israel, rebuild the temple, cleanse the land and raise the dead. Their expectations were decidedly this-worldly. Second, we should reckon with a large measure of metaphor when reading the prophecies not only of the Tanak but also of the later apocalypses. Daniel 7, for example, is not about a supernatural figure employing clouds as a novel means of air transport.[1] We do justice to the cosmic language of apocalyptic when we recognize that it invests historical events with their full, theological meaning.

How do Wright's readings of the Jewish data affect his interpretation of the New Testament? He believes that Jesus used apocalyptic language as (on his interpretation of the evidence) other ancient Jews did. So when, for instance, Jesus warned about the coming judgment, foretold the coming of the Son of Man or uttered the prophecies now found in Mark 13, he was not (despite so many modern readers and scholars arguing to the contrary) envisaging the literal stopping of time or the end of history. Rather he was prophesying, through traditional language and metaphor, concrete historical events of the near future— events that did indeed take place. The apocalyptic judgment fell, through the instrumentality of the Romans, upon Jerusalem for the people's sins. In other words, Jesus' eschatological prophecies have come to pass; they were not about what we call "the end of the world" but rather about the historical fate of the Jewish capital and the Jewish people.

Wright is quick to recognize that his views put him at odds with much learned opinion. He indeed observes that if he is right, then, among other things,

> Mark 13 has been badly misunderstood by the importation into it of ideas concerning the "second coming" of Jesus. There has been a long tradition in mainline Christianity of reading it this way, which has found its way into sermons, books, and even into the headings in many Bibles, and thence into the bloodstream of generations of pious folk. There has been a comparative short tradition within mainline New Testament scholarship, going back particularly to Johannes Weiss and Albert Schweitzer, of endorsing this reading, with one significant difference. Pietism supposes that, in Mark 13, Jesus was predicting his own coming at the end of time, a prediction still to be fulfilled; Weiss, Schweitzer, and their successors have thought that Jesus here predicted the imminent end of the world, and that he was proved wrong. I suggest that both traditions, the old pietist one and the more recent scholarly one, are simply mistaken. (*JVG* 341)

It is clear that Wright's proposal, if correct, requires that one, whether pietist or scholar, rethink quite a bit. But is he correct? My judgment, which I am confident represents mainstream scholarship, is that he is not. That is, the common readings of Mark 13 and of the other eschatological prophecies in the canonical Gospels remain the most plausible readings. I hasten to add that it is often no easy task to determine when, in ancient Jewish texts, we are dealing with metaphor or with something literal; and the supposition that maybe some of us have been misreading certain texts by taking them too literally is a possibility we must face. At the same time, Wright's interpretation may be guilty of finding metaphor where none was originally intended. This reader in any event thinks so, and he has been left with a series of questions. So in what remains I should like to address some of these questions to Wright, in the hope that he might answer them. I think he must if he expects to gain many converts and become the spokesperson for more than a beleaguered minority.[2]

The End of the Space-Time Universe?

Has scholarship in the tradition of Weiss and Schweitzer indeed contended that Jesus looked forward to the end of the space-time universe?[3] And how important is the question? As far as my memory goes, I am unaware of any Gospel scholar who has spoken in this connection of "the space-time universe." This is, to my knowledge, Wright's attempt at exegesis. Is his exegesis correct?

For Rudolf Bultmann, Jesus' eschatology was firmly associated with the apocalyptic literature, which "awaits salvation not from a miraculous change in historical (i.e., political and social) conditions, but from a cosmic catastrophe which will do away with all conditions of the present world as it is."[4] These words might refer to the end of the space-time universe. But they could just as easily be understood to mean, in analogy with Noah's flood, that God will recreate the present world after he destroys it—and I think this is what many have meant when they have written about "the end" or used similar expressions.[5] Here is one very important example: according to Johannes Weiss, Jesus thought the eschatological prophecies were to be fulfilled in the Promised Land, in Israel. It was not a question of the end of the space-time universe but of the radical transformation of the present cosmos, including the saints.[6]

E. P. Sanders, a prominent present-day proponent of a traditional eschatological Jesus, has nowhere to my knowledge ever intimated that Jesus expected the end of the space-time universe. He has instead written that "the big question that recent research poses is not the role of 'the end of the world' in Jesus's view, but rather this: did he think that *God* was going to do something decisive in history"?[7] In other words, what really matters is not exactly what Jesus believed about cosmological states—one doubts, I might add, that he gave them a great deal of thought—but that he longed for, and lived in the light of, a radically new world that only God could bring. Surely this is correct, and it seems to me that, whether or not we speak of the end of the space-time universe with reference to Jesus' eschatology,[8] what matters is that his vision of the kingdom cannot be identified with anything around us. God has not yet brought a radically new world. Specifically, if Jesus hoped for the ingathering of scattered Israel,[9] if he expected the resurrection of the patriarchs[10] and if he anticipated that the saints would gain angelic natures,[11] then his expectations, like the other eschatological expectations of Judaism, have not yet met fulfillment. To this extent we may speak of his "unrealized eschatology."

That the issue of whether Jesus proclaimed the end of the space-time universe may not be as important as Wright implies appears when one considers the classic presentation of an apocalyptic Jesus in Schweitzer's *The Quest of the Historical Jesus*. For the purpose of writing this essay I recently reread the famous chapter nineteen of Schweitzer's book, in which he offers us his reconstruction of Jesus' history. While doing this I asked myself whether, for Schweitzer, Jesus believed in the end of the space-time universe and further how Schweitzer's stance on that issue affects his conclusions. My judgment is that Schweitzer is very unclear on whether Jesus expected an utterly new world or an old world made new. He just does not tell us. This is not strange, for what is crucial to Schweitzer's picture of Jesus is not whether everything in the world will soon be gone but the belief that the messianic woes, the resurrection and the last judgment are at hand. In fact, I cannot see that a single element of Schweitzer's picture has any necessary connection with the world's coming to its end.[12] What matters is the imminent eschatological judgment, which requires a radical response, now.

In Quest of the Historical Metaphor

How can we tell when eschatological language is metaphorical and when it is not? Following Caird, who was here no doubt influenced by C. H. Dodd,[13] Wright has argued that modern readers sometimes find literal meaning where they should instead find metaphor. It is true the *Tanak* contains prophecies that are often understood to use poetic hyperbole and cosmic imagery in their depiction of historical events. One doubts that Joel, or the author of Acts after him, really expected the moon to become bloody (Joel 2:31; Acts 2:20).[14] And surely, as Wright observes, the beasts of Daniel 7 are indeed metaphors: no one was watching the shores of the Mediterranean for the fulfillment of that prophecy.[15] Nonetheless, scholars have often thought, no doubt rightly, that eschatological language often invites a literal explanation. The Qumran War Scroll prophesies a real eschatological battle, complete with literal angels. Has anyone ever suggested otherwise? Papias (in Eusebius *Historia Ecclesiastica* 3.39.12), Justin Martyr (*Dialogue with Trypho the Jew* 80), Irenaeus (e.g., *Against Heresies* 5.32-36), Tertullian (*Against Marcion* 3.24), the Montanists (according to Epiphanius *Hereses* 49.1.2-3) and Lactantius (*Divine Institutes* 7.24-26) all believed, because they interpreted the Old Testament prophecies literally, in a rather worldly millennium involving a far-reaching, miraculous transformation of the natural world.[16] Commodian expected the ten lost tribes to return to the land (*Carmen apologeticum* 941-46). Rabbinic texts even contain the conviction that bones will roll through underground tunnels before being reassembled for the resurrection on the Mount of Olives (*b. Ketubot* 111a). None of this is metaphor.

But what then of Mark 13:24-25? According to these verses,

> The sun will be darkened,
> and the moon will not give its light,
> and the stars will be falling from heaven,
> and the powers in the heavens will be shaken.

Wright, like some others, believes that this free combination of Isaiah 13:10 and 34:4 (which has numerous parallels in apocalyptic literature) is poetry, not literal description (*JVG* 361).[17] Yet, unlike in Daniel 7, there are in Mark itself no clear textual prods to push us in this direction (see note 14), and surely other dramatic events prophesied in Mark 13—wars, famines, earthquakes—are intended as literally as Exodus intends the plagues[18] or as literally as the list of portents Josephus associates with the Jewish war.[19] Further, the Scriptures can, Wright must concede, recount literal heavenly portents. In Joshua 10, the sun really stands still, and in the Synoptic passion narratives the sun literally goes dark. Why then suppose that Mark 13:24 is less prosaic than, let us say, *1 Enoch* 70:6, which foretells that one day the stars "will change their courses and their activities, and will not appear at the times which have been prescribed for them," or that it is less realistic than *Barnabas* 15:8, which says that when the Son of God abolishes the time of the lawless one, God "will change the sun and the moon and the stars" or than Lucan's *Pharsalia* 1.72-80, which envisions stars plunging into the sea at history's end? According to Seneca (*Natural Questions* 3.29), Berosus, the Babylonian astrologer, foretold that "the world will burn when all the planets that now move in different courses come together in Cancer, so that they all stand in a straight line in the same sign." If this is not metaphor, can we be confident that Mark 13:24 is? Should we not understand Mark 13:24 the same way we understand *Sibylline Oracles* 2:200-202 ("But the heavenly luminaries will crash together, also into an utterly desolate form. For all the stars will fall together on the sea"), that is, literally? One wants to ask how Mark, if he had wished to forecast an astronomical disaster, could have forecast it. What more could he have said?

It may be objected that stars are gigantic astronomical objects millions of miles away and that they cannot come crashing to the earth. But is such knowledge to be read into the Bible? The ancients, who lived outside at night much more than modern city dwellers do, were familiar with meteor showers. What reason would a pious Jew have for doubting that God could turn the entire night sky into what we even today call falling stars?[20]

English folklore holds that some people, in accord with their belief in eschatological reversal, have had themselves buried head down so that they will be right side up on the last day. We can all concur that this is bad hermeneutics, an example of the literal swallowing the figurative. Similarly, to return to the ancient world, one can wholly agree with Wright that *2 Baruch* 36—37 is a parable that is not a lesson about forestry and viticulture (*NTPG* 281-82). But one can hardly infer from the appearance of parabolic language in one part of a book that its eschatological prophecies throughout contain nothing besides parables. Consider *2 Baruch* 29:5: When the Messiah comes, the earth will "yield fruits ten-thousandfold. And one vine will be a thousand branches, and one branch will produce a thousand clusters, and one cluster will produce a thousand grapes, and one grape will produce a cor of wine." Now, on the one hand, it would be inane to interpret this without imagination. Prosaic exactitude is not what this text is about. Yet, at the same time, it would be unwise to reduce the language to metaphor. *2 Baruch* 29:5 foretells, in hyperbolic language, a time of unprecedented, supernatural fertility. The physical world will itself be different. Compare Zechariah 14:6-7: "On that day there shall not be either cold or frost. And there shall be continuous day (it is known to the LORD), not day and not night, for at evening time there shall be light."

It is helpful here to keep in mind the distinction between metaphor and symbol. We need not choose between flat-footed literalism and metaphor, for there is the whole realm of real events that are symbolic. "When it was noon, darkness came over the whole land until it was three in the afternoon" (Mk 15:33). The darkness is richly symbolic, but presumably Mark nonetheless thought it historical, not metaphorical. In like manner, when the Gospels depict the Son of Man's coming on the clouds or foretell the general resurrection, it is not crass literalism to think of the redeemer literally flying upon the clouds and of tombs emptying their contents if we also, as we naturally do, perceive the meaning—the triumph of believers, the judgment of the wicked, the fulfillment of prophecy and so on. A literal reading need not be a flat or unimaginative reading. Put otherwise, the literal can be symbolic. There is nothing at all remarkable about this. The White House in Washington, D.C., is simultaneously a literal, functioning residence—a white house—and a famous symbol of many American political realities. In like manner, forecasts of heavenly signs do indeed connote "cosmic significance" (NTPG 283), but that in itself does not imply those signs are metaphors as opposed to literal events that are symbolic.

Elsewhere[21] I have cited an example of the nonliteral use of cosmic or catastrophic eschatological-type language:

> And behold the mountains burned with fire, and the earth quaked, and the hills were disturbed, and mountains were rolled about, and the abysses boiled, and every habitable place was shaken, and the heavens were folded up, and the clouds drew up water, and the flames of fire burned, and thunderings and lightnings were many, and winds and storms roared, the stars gathered together, and angels ran on ahead,

until God should establish the Law of his eternal covenant with the sons of Israel and given his eternal commandments that will not pass away. (Pseudo-Philo *Liber Antiquitatum Biblicarum* 11:5)

Wright himself has cited this text as being in line with his understanding of eschatological language (*JVG* 321 n. 2). But there is reason to reconsider, although this contradicts my previous judgment. The words I have quoted, which develop the scene in Exodus 19:16-18,[22] seem to us moderns obviously to invite a nonliteral reading. It is, however, fascinating to learn that Aristobulus, a Hellenized Jew of Alexandria who applied Stoic allegorical method to biblical exegesis, took Exodus 19:16-18 quite literally. The following, preserved in Eusebius (*Preparation for the Gospel* 10.8), deserves to be quoted at length:[23]

In the book of the Law, it is said that at the time when God was giving the law, a divine descent took place, so that all might see the active power of God. This descent is manifest; and anyone who wants to preserve what is said about God would explain these accounts in the following way. It is declared that "the mountain was alight with fire," as our law code says, because of God's descent. There were the voices of trumpets and the fire blazing beyond all power to resist it. And the number of the entire throng was no less than a million, not counting those outside the prescribed age. They were called to assembly from all around the mountain (the circuit of the mountain took no less than five days) and the blazing fire was observed by them from every vantage point, as they were encamped around it. As a result, the descent was not local, for God is everywhere. And as for the force of the fire, which is exceedingly marvelous because it consumes everything, he showed that it burned irresistibly and actually consumed nothing, which would not have happened unless a divine power had been in it. For, though the place burned furiously, the fire consumed none of the things growing on the mountain, but the fresh green of all the plants remained untouched by the fire. The voices of the trumpets sounded more vehemently together with the lightning-like illumination of the fire, although there were no such instruments ready at hand, nor anyone playing them, but everything came to be by divine provision.[24]

Surely we have to wonder whether—in a world where even an allegorist could find literal, not metaphorical, events in the fire, trumpet and earthquake of Exodus 19:16-18—readers of apocalyptic prophecies might not have expected literal fire, literal trumpets and literal earthquakes?[25]

Wright's views also seem to me to sit uneasily beside Philo. In *De Praemiis et Poenis* 85-88 the allegorist talks about the enmity between humans and beasts. He tells us that no mortal can quell their conflict, for "that is done only by the

Uncreated, when He judges that they are some worthy of salvation, people of peaceful disposition." Someday the "bears and lions and panthers and the Indian animals, elephants and tigers, and all others whose vigor and power are invincible, will change their life of solitariness and isolation for one of companionship, and gradually in imitation of the gregarious creatures show themselves tame," and "thus the age-long and natural and theretofore primary war will be brought to an end through the change which makes the wild beasts tame and amenable." Is it not manifest that at least Philo took the old prophecies of the reconciliation of animals (e.g., Is 11:6-9; cf. Is 35:1-2; Amos 9:13-15) literally?[26] In other words, did he not find in those eschatological texts not just metaphors for the political fortunes of Israel but literal forecasts of incredible events that will some day overtake the natural world?[27]

To Transform but Not Abolish

Has Wright given us a misleading set of options? He tells us (*JVG* 208) that we can understand eschatological language as having to do with (a) the end of the space-time universe, (b) the climax of Israel's history and the end of the space-time universe, (c) the climax of Israel's history and events for which end-of-the-world language is the only adequate set of metaphors even though what is envisaged will take place in space-time history, (d) major events, not specifically climactic within a particular story, for which end-of-the-world language functions as metaphor, (e) the possibility of moving spiritually into a new level of existence, (f) a critique of the present world order, or (g) a critique of the present socio-political scene (*JVG* 208). What I find missing here is precisely my own view, which is, more importantly, that of Weiss and Sanders: it is the view that eschatological language concerns the climax of Israel's history and the remaking—not the end—of the natural world. Because of the way Wright sets things out, we are forced to choose between understanding eschatology in terms of metaphors and understanding it in terms of the end of the space-time universe. But one can refuse the dichotomy.

Jesus and Paul on the Parousia

What is the relationship between Mark 13 and 1 Thessalonians 4:13-18?[28] Wright argues at length that Mark 13 is, from our vantage, not about the future but rather about the past: it came to fulfillment in the events surrounding 70 C.E. Others have previously said the same thing,[29] but they have not won the day. Part of the reason is that there are so many striking parallels between Mark 13 and

Jewish apocalyptic literature[30] that if one associates the latter with the last judgment, as is usually done, then it is natural to associate the former with it too.[31] And the last judgment has not yet come.

Another possible defect appears when Paul is considered. In 1 Thessalonians 4:13-18, the apostle passes on a tradition closely related to Mark 13:24-27.[32] The apostle writes about the coming of the Lord Jesus, who will meet the saints in the clouds. The Synoptic Jesus similarly speaks of the Son of Man's coming on clouds and of the elect's being gathered to him. The point for us is that—so far as I can see, and as far as the commentaries I have consulted go—1 Thessalonians 4:13-18 lends itself neither to being understood as metaphor nor to being a prophecy about 70 C.E. One has great difficulty imagining that Paul was not referring to literal clouds in the atmosphere or that his first readers might have given his words a figurative sense. So an appeal to metaphor when pursuing the meaning of the closely related Mark 13:24-27 (and par.) seems equally out of place. In other words, Paul did not interpret the tradition behind Mark 13:24-27 as does Wright—that is, as a symbolic prophecy of Jerusalem's destruction (*JVG* 360-65). Rather, the apostle construed it as have millenarian Christians down through the centuries: Paul expected Jesus to come on the clouds.

One might also wonder about the implications of 1 Thessalonians 5:2. Paul speaks of the day of the Lord coming like a thief in the night. This obviously refers back to 1 Thessalonians 4:13-18, to the return of Jesus and the resurrection (which cannot be equated with events that happened in 70 C.E.). Presumably Paul's application was traditional, for 2 Peter 3:10[33] and Revelation 3:3[34] also give the simile an eschatological sense. Now this matters because Matthew 24:43-44 uses the very same simile in connection with Jesus' eschatological discourse. So is this not evidence that at least Matthew did not read Mark 13[35] as having been fulfilled in 70 C.E., that he (like Paul) rather saw the coming of the Son of Man as the still outstanding return of Jesus for which one must be prepared?[36] Again, Luke 12:39-40 associates the parable of the thief with the coming of the Son of Man, so those of us who see in 1 Thessalonians 5:2; 2 Peter 3:10; Revelation 3:3; and Matthew 24:43-44 a consistent application to the parousia, understood as the second coming of Jesus, will be strongly inclined to understand the coming of the Son of Man in Luke 12:39-40 accordingly and not as a prophecy of 70 C.E.

The Land and the Temple

Is there tension between Wright's literal and metaphorical inclinations? On the one hand, he is correctly adamant that talk about Israel and the temple cannot be spiritualized away. Prophecies about the land and the temple, whether uttered by Jews or by Jesus, were about the land of Israel and the temple on Zion. They should not be, as they too often have been in the Christian tradition, directly applied to the church. On the other hand, Wright sees the coming of the Son of Man on the clouds of heaven as a figurative way of speaking of the judgment of Jerusalem (*JVG* 360-65), he thinks that the new temple envisaged by Jesus can be equated with Jesus and (perhaps) his followers (*JVG* 426), and he tells us that Jesus and his followers constituted the return of Israel from exile (*JVG* 444). But one who thinks that Jewish eschatology generally has to do with the literal land and the literal temple might also be inclined, one would think, to conceive of the coming of the Son of Man as a literal coming on literal clouds (as in *b. Sanhedrin* 98a), to imagine the new temple as consisting of real stones (as in *1 Enoch* 90:28-29) and to envision the return from exile as a literal pilgrimage from the diaspora (as in *2 Baruch* 78:1-7). Put otherwise, if, as Wright says, Jewish apocalyptic longed for the temple to be rebuilt, the land to be cleansed and the Torah to be obeyed perfectly, then how can the Christ-event be the fulfillment of Jewish apocalyptic hopes? It accomplished none of those things.

When one asks why Wright offers us this mixture of the literal and metaphorical, which evidently leaves the natural world out of account, it occurs that this and nothing else allows him to make 70 C.E. the focus of Jesus' prophecies. The insistence that Jesus' prophetic words were about the nation and land of Israel allows him to refer them to the political events of 70 C.E., while the insistence that we need not be too literal about apocalyptic language permits Wright to identify those political events with the falling of the stars from heaven and the coming of the Son of Man on the clouds.

An Apologetic?

Is Wright's nonliteral interpretation of prophecy an apologetic move[37] with parallels in the history of religions? Rationalizations often appear when a religious movement suffers the falsification of its prophecies. Maimonides, in his reaction against very literal-minded apocalyptic enthusiasm, declared that messianic prophecy is "merely a parable and a figure of speech" (Mishneh Torah 14). More recently members of a Baha'i sect known as "Baha'i's Under the Provisions of the Covenant" circulated a prophecy predicting for 1991 massive earthquakes and a meteor striking the earth. When nothing came to pass, their leader explained that there had been a "spiritual earthquake" created by the apostasy of an important member and that "everything happens on the spiritual plane before it manifests in the physical plane." Earlier, when forecasts that Halley's comet would crash in 1986 failed to materialize, the same leader had this to say: "The spiritual fulfillment did take place. A spiritual stone hit the earth. This stone is the message of the messiahship that only the Bahá'í understand."[38] Even though Wright would vigorously deny that he spiritualizes texts,[39] there is a certain parallel in all this to his comment that the imagery of Mark 13:24-27 is really a way of saying that what these verses envisage will be "earth-shattering" (*JVG* 362; *NTPG* 282) and to his equation of return from exile with something other than the literal return of lost diaspora Jews.

Does Wright believe that if we adopt a more literal interpretation of Jesus' apocalyptic language, then we will be stuck with the embarrassment of an error-ridden Jesus? Is the nonliteral interpretation of biblical prophecy an attempt to circumvent an unwelcome alternative? A Jesus who expected a radical transformation of nature and the last judgment, especially if he spoke as though those things might come in the near future, is not very congenial to either orthodox or modern thought: he raises disturbing questions. But a Jesus who used figurative language to talk about the political events of his day is rhetorically admirable, and he also has the virtue of freeing us from the theological difficulties of the usual apocalyptic Jesus. Schweitzer's Jesus is an offense; Wright's Jesus, by comparison, is a welcome relief. Surely then our suspicions must be aroused.

Parallels of the End

My next question again concerns the general history of religions. Wright's analysis pays no attention to the fact that what we call apocalyptic language is not confined to the Judeo-Christian tradition. The philosopher Seneca wrote:

> Nothing will abide where it is now placed. . . . Time will lay all things low and take all things with it. . . . [It] will level whole mountains, and in another place will pile up rocks on high; it will drink up seas, turn rivers from their courses. . . . In other places it will swallow up cities in yawning chasms, will shatter them with earthquakes, and from deep send forth a pestilential vapor; it will cover with floods the face of the inhabited world, and, deluging the earth, will kill every living creature, and in huge conflagration it will scorch and burn all mortal things. And when time shall come for the world to be blotted out in order that it may begin its life anew, these things will destroy themselves by their own power, and stars will clash with stars, and all the fiery matter of the world that now shines in orderly array will blaze up in a common conflagration. (*Ad Marciam* 26:6-7; cf. *Hercules Oetaeus* 1102-30)

The sort of language Seneca uses in the last sentence is hardly confined to Stoic sources; rather, it appears all over the world throughout history, being very often associated with what the anthropologists call millenarian movements. Ancient heterodox Taoists wrote that a coming deluge of water would introduce terrible epidemics, darkness and earthquakes; that finally the whole earth would be burnt up, including the mountains; and that after all the destruction the Bodhisattva Maitreya would descend from heaven upon a splendid throne and rule a utopia.[40] The *Sibylline Oracles* (2:196-220) envisage heavenly fire falling to burn up the earth, stars crashing from heaven, a great darkness and then the final judgment, conducted by Michael, Gabriel, Raphael and Uriel. The nineteenth-century Amerindian prophet Wovoka and those who participated in the Ghost Dance believed that the near future would bring floods, earthquakes and land-slides and that soon thereafter the ancestors would return.[41] The Melanesian cargo cult leader John Frumm prophesied that his island would become flat and joined to neighboring islands, that the volcanic mountains would melt and fill the valleys, that all sickness as well as all Europeans would disappear and that the natives would become young again.[42]

Now I cannot here enter into detail regarding these and countless other intriguing parallels to biblical prophecy, parallels that reflect a widespread human longing for cataclysmic change. All I wish to do is make the generalization that, to my knowledge, the anthropologists and historians of religion tend to take these predictions at face value; that is, they do not consider them to be metaphors for sociopolitical events, nor do they make a distinction between catastrophic and cosmic language on the one hand and more literal language on the other. Rather, they assume the various prophecies that speak of earthquakes and falling stars and fire burning up the world are indeed about earthquakes and falling stars and fire burning up the world. So my question to Wright is whether this fact troubles him at all, and if not, Why not? Is there not opportunity here to find some light in cross-cultural materials? Can it be irrelevant that, as Lawrence Sullivan has observed, "in nearly all millennial visions the sky tumbles to earth, or the sun, moon, stars . . . plummet from above"?[43] Or are the anthropologists as wrong about worldwide millenarian language as (according to Wright) New Testament scholars are about the New Testament? Or are history-of-religion parallels beside the point for some other reason? My own judgment is that we have so many sim-ilar texts because so many have longed for pretty much the same thing, namely, supernatural judgment and repair of a fallen world; and it would strike me as peculiar to suppose that, whereas ancient Jews and Christians looked into the future and saw metaphorical darkness, metaphorical earthquakes and metaphorical falling stars, so many others who have looked into the future have seen literal darkness, literal earthquakes and literal falling stars.

Prophecies of the End

Although the issue is not crucial for our purposes, one would still like to know how Wright interprets the evidence that suggests at least a few Jews and Christians indeed expected a cataclysmic end of the world in their day and age. The *Sibylline Oracles* 2:196-210 (from a Jewish hand around the turn of the era); 3:75-90 (from the first century B.C.); and 4:171-92 (probably from a Jewish redactor of the late first century A.D.) plainly foretell the unmaking of the physical universe through fire.[44] *Sibylline Oracles* 4:171-92, for instance, says that God will "burn the whole earth, and will destroy the whole race of men and all cities and rivers at once, and the sea. He will destroy everything by fire, and it will be smoking dust." After this will come the resurrection, the judgment and the renewal of the world. That all this is near to hand follows from the context, which has to do with prophecies about the rise of Rome and the destruction of Jerusalem.

What we find in the Sibylline Oracles should not surprise us. For a literal end of the world—the correlation of a literal beginning—already seems to be attested in the Hebrew Bible.[45] It thus stands to reason that Jews profoundly unhappy with their present experience could have hoped for that end to come soon.

One of the writings of the New Testament itself, one should add, envisions cosmic destruction as part of its eschatological scenario. This passage, 2 Peter 3:10-13, deserves to be quoted in full:

> But the day of the Lord will come like a thief, and then the heavens will pass away with a loud noise, and the elements will be dissolved with fire, and the earth and everything that is done on it will be disclosed. Since all these things are to be dissolved in this way, what sort of persons ought you to be in leading lives of holiness and godliness, waiting for and hastening the coming of the day of God, because of which the heavens will be set ablaze and dissolved, and the elements will melt with fire? But, in accordance with his promise, we wait for new heavens and a new earth, where righteousness is at home.

I believe that this should be read literally. I also believe that the author, since he speaks of "hastening the coming of the day of God," hoped that the dissolution of the space-time universe would come sooner rather than later. Here, it seems to me, is exactly the sort of expectation Wright wants to emphasize did not exist or at least was rare. But here it is in the New Testament. What do we make of that? Is 2 Peter under the influence of a "pagan oddity" (*NTPG* 285)? Wright's assertion that belief in a literal end would "contradict creational monotheism" because it implies "that the created world was residually evil" may seem reasonable to us, but it appears to have been missed by more than one ancient author, one of them canonical. Even Genesis, after telling us over and over about the goodness of God's world, soon thereafter tells us that God said to Noah, "I have determined to make an end of all flesh, for the earth is filled with violence because of them; now I am going to destroy them along with the earth" (Gen 6:13). The point is all the more interesting because ancient texts commonly make Noah's flood a foreshadowing of the eschatological judgment.[46]

Is There Yet a Future?

Finally, what does Wright himself think about the eschatological future? Christian theology has always held that, when Jesus came at his first advent, he fulfilled some of the eschatological expectations of Judaism, but that it will take a second advent to fulfill all of them: much was left undone. The reason for this commonplace is that the world around us does not seem to be the world of our hopes and dreams, which is precisely what the world of eschatological promise is supposed to be. The problem of evil has not been solved, and God's will is not done on earth as it is in heaven. The wolf does not lie down with the lamb, and God's kingdom has not come in its fullness. But is not Jewish apocalyptic all about the coming of God's kingdom in its fullness, and all about the wolf and the lamb lying down together, and all about God's will being done on earth as it is in heaven and all about the final resolution of the problem of evil? Is not eschatology the divinely inspired hope for a return to Eden, for a truly perfect world, for utopia? Is it not the solution to the problem of evil written large enough to be read by everybody? But how then can the promises of Jewish apocalyptic be already realized? How can it be that "the decisive 'end' for which Israel had longed had already happened" (*JVG* 322)? Nature is red in tooth and claw. The faithful still pray for the coming of the kingdom. Jerusalem does not dwell in safety. And "every eye shall see him" remains a promise, not a reality. There is no utopia. We should be able to understand the Jew who says that the Messiah cannot have been Jesus because the world is still a mess filled with injustice and agony and evils of all sorts.

Theodicy is at the heart of all apocalyptic, including Jesus' prophecies. So if we still wrestle with the problem of evil—and what reasonable person does not?—then most of what Jesus envisaged in his eschatological prophecies cannot be identified with past events. The last have not become first, nor have the meek inherited the earth. Maybe, in the person of Jesus, we can speak of the initial or proleptic victory of God. But that victory remains agonizingly incomplete,[47] and we cannot, if I may so put it, yet speak of the victory of apocalyptic. For that victory, the final victory, the victory of the Son of Man, has not been won, which is why Christians still wait for it.

Eight

Victory over Violence

The Significance of N. T. Wright's Jesus for New Testament Ethics

RICHARD B. HAYS

*J*ESUS AND THE VICTORY OF GOD CONSTRUCTS A SWEEPING ACCOUNT OF THE JESUS
of history, an account that challenges us to rethink the identity of Jesus
and to situate him afresh within the symbolic world of first-century
Judaism. By anchoring Jesus' identity firmly within Jewish prophetic and apocalyptic thought, N. T. Wright challenges conventional Christian piety (a point
insufficiently appreciated by some readers of the book); at the same time, by seeking to integrate virtually all of the Synoptic material into his historical account of
Jesus, Wright poses an equally sharp challenge to the conventional "pieties" of
historical criticism, which has tended to assign much of this material to later layers of development, up to and including the time of the evangelists.

Every attempt to articulate a normative Christian ethic depends—whether
explicitly or implicitly—on a particular construal of the figure of Jesus, along with
some account of the message that he proclaimed. Thus, because Wright's book
sketches a strikingly original picture of Jesus' aims, it prompts us to ask how this
Jesus might shape or reshape our approach to ethics.

This essay will proceed in four parts:

1. a brief sketch of Wright's account of the Jesus of history, with particular attention to ethical dimensions of his message;

2. some questions about Wright's historical reconstruction;

3. reflections on the possible significance of Wright's portrayal of Jesus for New Testament ethics; and

4. a brief concluding observation on the relation between historical event, canonical narrative and contemporary experience.

Wright's Portrayal of Jesus' Agenda

Wright's portrayal of Jesus stands against the stream of much current historical Jesus research. The notorious Jesus Seminar has Jesus portrayed as a wandering Cynic philosopher, a spinner of mysterious aphorisms. According to their account, Jesus had no particular religious or political program, no interest in the fate of Israel, no sense of himself as a unique figure nor any apocalyptic expectations for the future.[1] Wright, on the other hand, insists that we must understand Jesus as a first-century Jewish apocalyptic prophet. He came proclaiming the kingdom of God, by which he meant, first of all, the restoration of Israel from exile. Wright argues that, even though first-century Jews were living in the land of Israel and had the temple intact, they thought of themselves as being still in exile because they were still under the thumb of foreign oppressors and client rulers. Yahweh had not come triumphantly to restore the Davidic monarchy; consequently, they were still in exile. Second, this proclamation of the kingdom of God entailed the claim that God was about to act or was in fact now acting to bring about the final triumph over the powers of evil and human suffering. And third, as an integral part of this, the proclamation of the kingdom of God meant that Yahweh was about to return to Zion and manifest his glory. Jesus believed, Wright argues, that all these things were taking place in and through his own ministry. In other words, Jesus did not come teaching people how to go to heaven when they die; nor did he proclaim some future cosmic event that would bring about the end of the space-time universe. Instead, all of the apocalyptic language in the Gospels should be read as metaphorical language referring to specific historical events that Jesus expected to happen in the near future, within his own lifetime and that of his immediate followers. At this point, Wright closely follows Albert Schweitzer's classic reconstruction of the historical Jesus—except that Schweitzer understood the New Testament's apocalyptic language literally rather than figuratively. The message that Jesus came proclaiming, Wright suggests, had two quite distinct prongs to it. On the one hand, it was a joyous message of hope and comfort, a message of welcome to sinners; however, on the other hand, it carried a warning of imminent catastrophe: if the people of Israel did not change their ways, divine judgment would come upon them. Wright argues that Jesus stood directly in the tradition of Old Testament prophets like Amos and Jeremiah, proclaiming that a great disaster was going to befall the unfaithful nation of Israel. This portrayal of Jesus places him solidly "on the ground," within the context of the political and religious history of first-century Judaism.

It also makes clear that Jesus was engaged in a powerful critique of first-century Judaism. The main elements of this critique are as follows. First, Jesus criticized Judaism because of its narrowness, its insistence on clinging to election as a matter of privilege and acting in a manner that was hostile and heedless toward the pagan world. Such behavior was a betrayal of Israel's divinely appointed vocation to be a light to the nations, as declared in Isaiah (e.g., Is 49:1-6). Second, Jesus castigated his Jewish contemporaries for their commitment to nationalistic violence. On Wright's reconstruction, the revolutionary resistance movement against Roman rule was a powerful force bubbling up throughout first-century Judaism. Even the Pharisees, Wright argues, were committed to programs of revolutionary zealot violence, though they are not portrayed this way in the Gospels.

Against all of this, Wright proposes, Jesus came proclaiming a new way of being the people of God, a new construal of Israel's worldview symbols. Jesus' critical attack focused on practices surrounding the identity-defining symbols of the Second Temple Jewish worldview, particularly on sabbath, food laws and worship in the Temple—all of which were signs of the exclusivity that Jesus was criticizing. (The omission of circumcision from this list of symbols is a striking datum that demands further explanation; the Synoptic traditions offer no hint that Jesus ever spoke critically about the practice of circumcision.) In the last part of the book, Wright discusses Jesus' aims and beliefs, what we would call Jesus' own self-interpretation. Wright argues that, in his final journey to Jerusalem, Jesus was intentionally enacting, in his own person, Israel's return from exile, the defeat of evil and the return of Yahweh to Zion. He believed he was the Messiah and that "the fortunes of the people were drawn together onto himself and his own work" (*JVG* 481).

When Jesus went to Jerusalem for his final confrontation with the authorities, he undertook three great symbolic actions. The first great symbolic action was the overturning of the tables and the driving of the moneychangers out of the temple. Wright interprets this as an act of judgment, prefiguring the destruction of the whole system of temple worship. The second great symbolic action was the Last Supper, which symbolized a new exodus, a new coming to freedom and a manifestation of the delivering power of God. Finally, Wright argues that the crucifixion was itself a prophetic, symbolic action, which Jesus knowingly and deliberately undertook as a way of enacting God's judgment on the unfaithful people Israel and, at the same time, of bringing about the final defeat of the power of evil. That is a very quick sketch of Wright's lengthy and complex construction. In the context of that sketch, let us consider the ethics of Jesus within Wright's account.

Most relevant to our concerns is Wright's outline of the message that Jesus proclaimed in a chapter called "Stories of the Kingdom: Invitation, Welcome, Challenge and Summons" (*JVG* 244-319). Wright emphasizes that Jesus' teachings about the kingdom of God can be understood only within the framework of a particular narrative about Israel and about Jesus' own climactic destiny within that narrative. Consequently, the obedience for which Jesus called was intelligible only in response to Jesus' distinctive way of retelling Israel's story. An excerpt from the beginning of that chapter gives an overview of the way in which Wright sees Jesus' proclamation as pertinent to the question of ethics. He writes,

> Jesus' . . . kingdom-narratives carried as part of their story-line the sense that his hearers were invited to see themselves as the "Israel" who would benefit from his work; and also, to some extent at least, as the "helpers" who would have an active share in that work. With that invitation there went a further implication: the returned-from-exile Israel must conduct itself in a certain fashion. Nor was this simply a general set of rules, a new abstract "ethic." The unique and unrepeatable nature of Jesus' own sense of vocation extended to those who followed him. They were summoned to specific tasks, which had to do with his own career and project.
>
> The *story* of the kingdom thus generated an appropriate *praxis* among those who heard it and made it their own. . . . Jesus' appeals, commands, and so forth are to be seen not simply as "new teaching" in the sense of a few new moral rules or theological principles, but as part of the underlying story he told, which aimed to produce in his hearers a realignment of their own praxis, necessarily involving a realignment of the other elements of their worldview also. (*JVG* 245, emphasis added)

This quotation articulates a conviction that is foundational for Wright's interpretation of the actions of all historical agents: all praxis is grounded in particular worldviews that are expressed through symbols and stories. Thus *ethics* is best understood not merely in terms of rules and principles; rather, it is best understood as the practical outworking of particular narratives in the lives of particular human communities.[2] Consequently, in order to grasp the nature of Jesus' program and the claim it made on his followers, we must recover the narrative framework that made it meaningful within first-century Jewish culture. The importance of this point—the close linkage between story and praxis—is considerable, and we shall return to it later in this essay. Out of Wright's lengthy discussion of Jesus' kingdom practice and worldview, I want to highlight five salient points of special interest for our questions about New Testament ethics.

1. Jesus clearly understood himself to be calling and forming a community. He was gathering what Wright calls "cells" of followers (*JVG* 276). Unlike the Essenes who withdrew into the caves at Qumran to live a separated life, Jesus' followers were living in the midst of the people, but nonetheless they were cells of a gathered community living in a distinctive way as an "alternative Israel" (*JVG* 317) defined particularly by their allegiance to Jesus.

2. This community was a new covenant community, and it was therefore to be characterized by the renewed heart, a changed heart (*JVG* 282-87). In accordance with the new-covenant promise of Jeremiah 31, the law was to be written on their hearts; one implication of this is that they were to enact forgiveness among themselves. An important piece of evidence for Wright's argument is Jesus' prohibition of divorce. To the Pharisees interrogating him, he says, "Of course, we know that Deuteronomy 24 allows divorce, but Moses gave you that law because of the hardness of your hearts. But it is not to be so now." Jesus was proclaiming a new state of affairs among his followers: hardness of heart was no longer to prevail, for the people of the new covenant are given new hearts.

3. This new-covenant people was not to make common cause with the resistance movement. Instead, they are called to the way of creative nonviolent resistance (*JVG* 290-91). This is a major theme that Wright hammers home again and again. Jesus' followers must not engage in the ultimately self-destructive effort to revolt against Roman authority.

4. These followers were called to live by the jubilee principle among themselves (*JVG* 294-95). Within their cell communities they were called to forgive economic debts and to pool resources.

5. *This community was to be a light to the world* (*JVG* 289). Jesus envisioned the redrawing of Israel's boundaries (*JVG* 307) so that these communities would become a light to the Gentiles and reach out to the world as the Old Testament prophets had envisioned that God's glory would do. Jesus envisioned that after his death, this community would go on "*implementing* what he had achieved" by becoming "Isaianic heralds, lights to the world" (*JVG* 660). Their witness had to be not just in words but through actions, in praxis.

In sum, Wright pictures Jesus as a man of action, the organizer of a movement. He was seeking to give his followers a new vision of their identity that would transform their behavior. For those who would follow Jesus, as Wright summarizes the matter, "the aim is not simply to believe as many true things as possible, but to act in obedience, implementing the achievement of Jesus while spurred and sustained by true belief" (*JVG* 660). Such a picture of discipleship has inescapable consequences for Christian ethics.

Some Questions About Wright's Historical Reconstruction

The purpose of this essay is not primarily to offer a critical response to Wright's historical theses. (Other contributors to this volume have posed critiques of various particular points in Wright's picture of the historical Jesus and his program.) Nonetheless, because the normative ethical implications of Wright's account are so closely linked to his historical reconstruction, no critical assessment of his proposal can omit some engagement with historical issues. Therefore, I want to list five points, without going into detail about them, where I think that Wright's overall historical construction is open to challenge—or where some nuancing might be required.

1. *Did "the great majority of Jesus' contemporaries" among the Jewish people understand themselves to be "still in exile, in all the senses that really mattered"* (*JVG* 445)? It seems to me that Wright has overstated his case on this point. Certainly, many first-century Jews hoped for the eschatological intervention of God. They still hoped for a radical renewal, perhaps even for the restoration of an autonomous monarchy, but the holding of such hopes does not necessarily mean that they thought themselves to be in exile. Certainly the Qumran community, living in an isolated settlement on the shores of the Dead Sea, regarded themselves as living in exile, but this self-understanding was precisely one of the distinctive features of their communal identity. They had deliberately withdrawn from participation in the mainstream of Jewish life and temple worship;

consequently, the exile metaphor resonated deeply with their experience. Whether a similar sense of living in exile was characteristic of Judaism more broadly, however, is doubtful.

More to the point, what is the evidence that Jesus thought in such terms? In Wright's discussion, apart from his revisionary interpretation of the parable of the prodigal son as a parable about Israel's exile and return (e.g., *JVG* 126-29), there is very little direct evidence of this motif in Jesus' teaching. Rather, Wright's characteristic line of argument is to suggest that Jesus' proclamation of the kingdom of God and of the forgiveness of sins as well as his acts of healing—when interpreted against the background of Old Testament prophetic texts—are all implicitly linked with the hope of return from exile (e.g., *JVG* 227, 268-74, 428-30). I do not deny that Jesus could have made the metaphorical link between his own activity and these exilic prophecies of hope, preeminently Isaiah 40—55. If he did so, however, it remains an unstated presupposition of the traditions that have come down to us through the Gospels, rather than an explicit emphasis of Jesus' teachings.

2. Did Jesus teach a realized eschatology? Wright's reinterpretation of eschatology and of Jewish apocalyptic language tends to focus on the claim that Jesus fulfilled everything through his death and resurrection; consequently, it leads to the virtual evaporation of any element of future hope in Christian proclamation. Consider, for example, the following passage:

> [Jesus] believes himself, much as John the Baptist had done, to be charged with the god-given responsibility of regrouping Israel around himself. But this regrouping is no longer a preliminary preparation for the return from exile, the coming of the kingdom; it *is* the return, the redemption, the resurrection from the dead. (*JVG* 132, emphasis original)

Wright has done a great deal of very provocative exegetical work to support his case, but statements such as the one just cited fail to account for the pervasive future-oriented eschatological expectation in early Christianity, including the expectation of a future resurrection of the dead, which also nearly disappears from Wright's reconstruction of Jesus and his teaching. The historical issue is how to account for the apparent disconnection between Wright's account of Jesus' message and the early church's subsequent insistence, even after the resurrection of Jesus, that "we hope for what we do not see" (Rom 8:25), a final redemption of the created order from its bondage to decay.

3. *Were the Pharisees violent revolutionaries?* Wright may exaggerate the degree to which Jesus' contemporaries, especially the Pharisees, were committed to a program of armed revolution against Rome. If Wright is wrong about this, then it becomes questionable whether he is correct in emphasizing Israel's espousal of violence as a central cause for Jesus' announcement of judgment on Israel. A good case can be made that some Pharisaic Jews, in their "zeal" for the Law, were willing to follow the example of Phinehas (Num 25:1-13) by employing violence against their fellow Jews in order to purify the covenant people; Paul's persecution of the church (i.e., the early Jewish-Christian community) is strong historical evidence for this phenomenon of intra-Jewish violence. It is quite another matter, however, to claim that Pharisees were programmatically committed to violent revolution against pagan rulers. Indeed, the evidence of both the New Testament and of Josephus[3] seems to suggest a very different picture of the Pharisees as scrupulous observers of the oral traditions surrounding the Torah who were content to wait patiently for God to intervene and set things right.

4. *Did Jesus believe that Israel had a vocation to be a light to the nations and that his own ministry was to have the effect of opening the kingdom of God to the Gentiles?* If so, why did the first generation of his followers find the mission to the Gentiles to be such a controversial and threatening topic (see Acts 10—15; Gal 2:11-21)?

5. *Did Jesus interpret his own impending death as the fulfillment of prophecy?* Wright attributes to Jesus an elaborate interpretation of his own death in terms of Old Testament prophetic images and typologies. Readers acquainted with my work on the interpretation of the Old Testament in the New Testament[4] will rightly anticipate my critical sympathy with Wright's effort to understand New Testament traditions within the literary and theological framework of the Old Testament. Nonetheless, his construction is vulnerable because of its unqualified attribution to Jesus of a complex christological hermeneutic, including the claim that he saw his own death and vindication as the fulfillment of the promise of Yahweh's return to Zion. For many scholars, it is easier to believe that these complicated typological interpretations emerged over time, after the fact, as the early church tried to understand the significance of Jesus' death. Simply at the level of historical argument, Wright has not convincingly demonstrated why his attribution of these ideas to Jesus is to be preferred to the more conventional view of critical scholars—that the fully developed christological typologies found in the

Gospels are best attributed to the interpretative activity of the church in the interval of forty years or more between the events and the evangelists' telling of the story.

I myself would answer the first three of these five questions in the negative, plead ignorance on the fourth and offer a cautiously qualified "yes" to the last. To justify my differences from Wright on these issues would take me far afield from the purpose of the present essay; indeed, it might require me to write a book equal to his in scope. Thus, for now my questions must remain queries for the reader to consider. To dispute these points, certainly, is to challenge some of the major underpinnings of Wright's work. Nonetheless, even with the appropriate demurrals and qualifications made, Wright's construction remains substantial and illuminating, and it helps us to think about the Jesus of history in fresh ways. Our immediate task is to reflect on how such fresh thinking might be of importance for Christian ethics.

Wright's Jesus: Ethical Implications

In light of these preliminary summaries and queries, I turn now to some comments on the significance of Wright's account for our understanding of New Testament ethics. It must be remembered that *Jesus and the Victory of God* presents itself not as a set of normative proposals about Christian doctrine and ethics but as a historical investigation; therefore, the ethical implications of the book are mostly implicit rather than explicit. Thus, I offer here some preliminary reflections about ways in which Wright's historical proposals might be constructively appropriated by communities that look to Jesus for direction and ethical guidance. I will first highlight four positive contributions of Wright's approach and then raise three fundamental questions.

1. Wright's emphasis on the integral relation between worldview, story and praxis is of great significance for ethical reflection about the Jesus tradition. Wright helps to move us beyond the study of disconnected, disembodied aphorisms; he helps us see that the significance of Jesus' parables and teachings can be comprehended only in relation to some overarching account of the storied world within which Jesus lived and moved. Without such a narrative context, the teachings become free-floating enigmas that can be interpreted at the whim of the reader to mean almost anything (as the recent history of scholarship attests). By developing a sustained reading of Jesus within a particular first-century Palestinian Jewish setting, Wright provides a controlling framework that helps us locate and understand the individual teachings. For example, Jesus' prohibition of divorce (Mk 10:2-12 and par.) is not a harsh new law stricter than the law of Moses but an announcement of the kingdom, a vision of new-covenant community in which hardness of heart is healed and infinite reconciliation is possible. Or, to take another example, one cannot isolate principles such as love or justice from their narrative matrix in Israel's Scripture. To understand what Jesus means when he calls his hearers to love God and love their neighbors as themselves (Mt 22:34-40), we must grasp that Jesus is simultaneously reaffirming the Torah (e.g., Deut 6:4-5 and Lev 19:18) and calling for participation in a renewed Israel that will understand the meaning of love preeminently in light of Jesus' own self-sacrificial example. In short, Wright's account of Jesus demonstrates that we cannot think of ethics apart from discipleship. We cannot ask in a vacuum what is good or right to do, nor can we be sufficiently guided by tables of rules or general ethical principles. Instead, we must ask what it means to become a follower of this particular man Jesus, to take up his agenda, to allow our praxis to be generated by the story that he told and lived.

2. Wright's construction of the historical Jesus does a great service for New Testament ethics by stressing the theme of continuity with Israel and Israel's heritage. Jesus was not rejecting or abolishing Israel; rather, he was proclaiming Israel's renewal and healing. This is a matter of great significance for the ethical issue of how Christians should understand their relation to the Jewish people. If Jesus' activity pointed toward the creation of a restored Israel, proleptically figured in the community of his disciples, then insofar as the church maintains the continuity of its life and witness with the historical Jesus, it will necessarily seek continuity with Israel's story. Our identity ought to be grounded in the traditions of Israel, and we must continue to wrestle with issues posed by Israel's election and Israel's unfaithfulness. The struggle with the tension between Israel's election and Israel's unfaithfulness was central to Jesus' career, and it must remain central for the church. In this respect, Wright's portrayal of Jesus points us in a direction far more fruitful for ethical reflection than do rival accounts of Jesus that downplay his embeddedness in Israel's identity. In *The Moral Vision of the New Testament*, I have devoted a lengthy chapter to the problem of the church's attitude toward Judaism as an ethical issue[5]; although studies of New Testament ethics have rarely recognized this issue, Wright's work forces us to come to grips with it somehow. The difficulty is that Wright has focused the problem without (yet) providing a solution. What justification, if any, does Wright's account leave for the existence of the Jewish people after the death and resurrection of Jesus? By emphasizing so strongly that Jesus took the destiny of Israel upon himself, enacting both their punishment and their restoration, Wright leaves the empirical people of Israel with no role to play—or so it appears. It is the church, the followers of Jesus, who are left to implement the victory that he achieved. But what then of the Jews as a continuing people who have endured in history long after the destruction of the temple, living in (literal) exile from their land for almost 1,900 years and now (literally) returning from exile to a secular state of Israel that bears strikingly little resemblance to the ancient prophetic vision of justice and peace in Mount Zion?

This theological problem is hardly unique to Wright's program; it has long vexed Christian theology, beginning with Paul's letter to the Romans. Still, anyone who wants to go forward with the construction of normative Christian ethics by building on the christological foundation that Wright has laid will have to confront this issue of the relation between the people of Israel and the movement that Jesus founded, which very quickly became overwhelmingly Gentile in composition. Does Wright's account give us any safeguards against the idea, articulated by Christian apologists from the second century onwards, that the destruction of the temple in 70 C.E. was God's final judgment of Israel, God's rejection of the Jewish people?

3. Wright has also made a major contribution by highlighting Jesus' critique of violence. In Wright's construction, this is central to Jesus' message and mission. It is not simply a matter of a few isolated sayings sprinkled among others ("turn the other cheek" and so on). Instead, Jesus' fundamental critique of Israel had to do with their adopting the ways of pagan violence. Wright articulates this view repeatedly and forcefully:

> Jesus denounced, as no better than pagans, not only those who compromised with Caesar by playing his power-games, *but also those who compromised with him by thinking to defeat him with his own weapons.* Those who take the sword will perish by the sword. . . . His kingdom-announcement, like all truly Jewish kingdom-announcements, came as the message of the one true God, the God of Israel, in opposition to pagan power, pagan gods, and pagan politics. But, unlike the other kingdom-announcers of his time from Judas the Galilean to Simeon Ben Kosiba, Jesus declared that the way of the kingdom was the way of peace, the way of love, the way of the cross. Fighting the battle of the kingdom with the enemy's weapons meant that one had already lost it, in principle, and would soon lose it, and lose it terribly, in practice. (*JVG* 595, emphasis original)

Thus the programmatic rejection of violence is integral to Wright's portrait of Jesus. His movement embraced the politics of peace, and this politics was constitutive of his own messianic identity. At the heart of this reading of the Gospels stands Wright's interpretation of the crucifixion as a symbolic action deliberately embraced and performed by Jesus, an act of martyrdom vividly symbolizing the consequences of violence:

> Jesus believed it was his god-given vocation to identify with the rebel cause, the kingdom-cause, when at last that identification could not be understood as endorsement. Israel was in exile, suffering at the hands of the pagans; the Roman cross was the bitterest symbol of that ongoing exilic state. He would go ahead of his people, to take upon himself both the fate that they had suffered one way or another for half a millennium at the hands of pagan empires and the fate that his contemporaries were apparently hell-bent upon pulling down on their heads once for all. The martyr-tradition suggested that this was the way in which Israel would at last be brought through suffering to vindication. Jesus' riddles, binding the fate of the nation to his own fate, suggested strongly that he intended to evoke and enact this tradition. (*JVG* 596)

To the extent that this becomes a historically persuasive account, I would hope that it might move the church to give deeper consideration to the importance of Jesus' renunciation of violence. Christian theology, by overlooking the specific political character of the death of Jesus in the setting of first-century Palestine, has usually failed to perceive that the rejection of nationalistic violence was of central importance in his message. Wright's account, on the other hand, even if it exaggerates the extent to which Israel in Jesus' time was "a hotbed of nationalist revolution" (*JVG* 596), rightly recalls readers of the New Testament to understand the teaching and practice of Jesus as the way of peace. One might wish that Wright had placed his work in dialogue with John Howard Yoder's important analysis of *The Politics of Jesus*—with which it shares substantial similarities—and thereby drawn out more fully the normative implications of the picture that he has drawn. Perhaps we can await his discussion of this question in future installments of his multivolume work.

4. Finally, Wright's portrayal of Jesus performs a signal service for New Testament ethics by emphasizing Jesus' agenda of building a community that will put his vision of the kingdom into practice. The community of Jesus' followers is to be characterized by a strong sense of communal life; they are to forgive, to share their goods, to reach across ethnic and national boundaries and, of course, to live as a nonviolent community. This vision cannot be carried out by isolated individuals seeking to cultivate a private spirituality; instead, all these practices are essentially relational. Wright's focus on community formation is a very important corrective to the Jesus Seminar's fictive picture of Jesus as a wandering philosopher who cared nothing about community. At the same time, it is also a tremendous challenge to the church at the end of the twentieth century, a church hypnotized by Enlightenment mantras about the rights of the individual and wallowing in postmodern self-indulgence. To take Wright's Jesus as the starting point for Christian ethics would require us to see ethics as an inalienably ecclesial discipline, an inquiry about how our common life might faithfully embody the vision of the kingdom that appears in the Gospels. We would have to ask ourselves how our church communities might become the authentic "cells" of followers that Jesus was seeking to organize. To ask this question would immediately force us to deal, for example, with the jubilee principle and to initiate practices of sharing economic resources more freely within the community.

Having recognized these four positive contributions of *Jesus and the Victory of God* to the task of ethical reflection, I turn now to pose three major questions about matters left unresolved by Wright's book.

1. What about the cross? In *The Moral Vision of the New Testament,* I wrote, "Jesus of Nazareth died on a cross. Those who follow him can hardly expect better treatment from the world. Insofar as the community of faith follows the path of the Jesus of history, it should expect suffering as its lot."[6] Indeed, I argued there that the cross is a focal image for discerning the unity of New Testament ethics: all the New Testament writers bear witness to Jesus' self-sacrificial death as a paradigm for our obedience to God. It remains unclear to me, however, whether Wright's account of Jesus' understanding of his unique vocation might undermine appeals to the image of the cross as an ethical paradigm. I do not mean to suggest that Wright intends any such result. Nonetheless, the more that he emphasizes the radically vicarious character of Jesus' death and resurrection—the fact that Jesus goes alone to the cross to enact Israel's punishment and vindication in his own person—the more one wonders whether the whole drama of suffering and triumph is already complete. Does Wright's portrayal make the cross a one-time event of obedience for Jesus only, focused on one distinct historical moment of crisis? Does Jesus in his own person enact God's judgment and God's victory in such a way that he exempts others from suffering? Wright's discussion in *Jesus and the Victory of God* is not very clear about that point. (Again, I emphasize that the book does not aim to answer such questions and that my query is an attempt both to read between the lines and to foresee the shape of future volumes in Wright's planned six-volume work.)

2. *Closely linked to this issue is a theological problem: how can we understand the fact that the power of evil continues to hold sway in the world?* Wright himself sees this difficulty near the end of the book and writes movingly about it: "The real problem . . . is this: Jesus interpreted his coming death, and the vindication he expected after that death, as the defeat of evil; but, on the first Easter Monday evil still stalked the earth from Jerusalem to Gibraltar and beyond, and stalks it still" (*JVG* 659).

Again, this problem dogs all Christian theology and ethics; it is not a distinctive problem for Wright. If, however, we accept Wright's portrayal of Jesus as believing that redemption and resurrection were already achieved in his regrouping of Israel around himself and if we accept his controversial exegesis of passages traditionally thought to refer to Jesus' second coming as references to Jesus' accomplishment of Yahweh's return to Zion in his own actions, we will find it correspondingly more difficult to give coherent answers to this question—unless, of course, we simply say "Jesus was wrong," which is clearly not what Wright wants to say. To put the point more concisely, the realized eschatology of Wright's account enhances the internal tension of the theodicy question virtually to the breaking point. Surely this is a matter that Wright must address as the rest of his opus unfolds.

3. *My final question is this: how does the specific historical agenda of Jesus that Wright sketches relate to what we are called to do today?* Wright contends that the teachings of Jesus in the Gospels are not timeless, general moral admonitions. Rather, they are particular directives for Israel at a particular moment of historical crisis. As we have seen, Wright suggests that "the unique and unrepeatable nature of Jesus' own sense of vocation extended to those who followed him. They were summoned to specific tasks, which had to do with his own career and project" (*JVG* 245).

My question, then, is how do we get from there to here? Wright has not told us. There is very little explicit hermeneutical reflection in *Jesus and the Victory of God*. In fairness to Wright, we must keep reminding ourselves that this book is only part two of a projected six-part series of volumes on early Christianity. Presumably, Wright intends to get to hermeneutical questions eventually, but he has not done it yet. Still, he has given us some clues, and here is my hunch, as I read him: story is the key. Those of us who live now, even many generations later, continue to live out the next act of the drama, as he puts it, "implementing the achievement of Jesus" as heralds who bear witness to the story through obedient action. We do not necessarily do exactly what Jesus did, but we have to carry on this story. If that is correct, Wright's account of the historical Jesus proves, in the end, deeply congenial to my proposal that New Testament ethics necessarily involves metaphor making. Living faithfully requires a continual retelling of the story in and through our own lives, which correspond, in an indirect but analogical way, to the character of the New Testament stories. The ethical question for us, then, becomes this: how do we form the life of our communities so that we carry on the story of return from exile, the story of a restored alternative Israel and the story of the victory of God?

Should the Jesus of History Command Our Obedience?

Of course, some readers might immediately protest that historical reconstructions of Jesus have no legitimate role to play in the formulation of Christian doctrine and ethics. From Martin Kähler to Luke Timothy Johnson, some interpreters have insisted that "the real Jesus" is the Jesus disclosed in the church's kerygma and/or in the church's experience of a risen and exalted Lord. There are two variants of this argument. One variant, represented by Johnson, contends that we encounter Jesus not through historical inquiry but through encountering his transforming power in our lives. The other variant, represented by Karl Barth and Hans Frei, contends that the identity of Jesus is irreducibly disclosed by the canonical narratives. These two variants stand in some tension with one another, but they concur in regarding it as a category mistake to use historical reconstructions of events behind the New Testament texts as a basis for the formulation or critique of normative Christian teaching. Such a position, if consistently developed, would necessarily hold that Wright's book, whatever its merits as a historical account, is actually of no importance for Christian ethics.

Although *Jesus and the Victory of God* does not extensively treat such issues, Wright rejects a strict dichotomy between history and theology.

> Christianity does itself a radical disservice when it appeals away from history, when it says that what matters is not what happened but "what it means for me." . . . We must not back away from history, or seek to keep the theological handbrake on to prevent history running away with us. A truly first-century Jewish theological

perspective would teach us to recognize that history . . . is the sphere where we find, at work to judge and to save, the God who made the world. (*JVG* 661-62)

Consequently, Wright intends his account to offer more than the solution to a historical puzzle; his description of the historical Jesus is meant to challenge and edify the community of those who profess faith in this historical figure. The Jesus of history is relevant for Christian ethics because we live in that same sphere where God is still at work; we inhabit the same continuum of history in which Jesus also lived and moved. Jesus defined the agenda for his followers, with whom we stand in direct historical continuity. At both ends of the spectrum, past and present, Christian faith deals with real-world events, real history. According to Wright, then, the victory of God is to be implemented in human community; it is not something that happens in an otherworldly sphere.

All of this is grounded theologically in the Christian doctrine of the incarnation. Because the Word became flesh, because Jesus was a human being, our human historical finitude is redeemed. At the same time, because Jesus was a human being, his history may be investigated using the tools of historical research in just the same way that we might investigate the historical life of any other human being, whether Socrates or Julius Caesar or Martin Luther or Martin Luther King Jr.

The difficulty, of course, is that our historical reconstructions—especially of figures from the ancient past about whom we have limited sources of information—are always uncertain and provisional. Each of the ancient Gospel writers assembled traditions about Jesus into a coherent narrative that interpreted his significance for the church in the writer's own time; the task of the historian is to ask what events lie behind these narratives. Therein, however, lies the challenging problem: the historian's account will never simply be identical with the canonical narratives, for it will always be a new constructive narration. This observation holds even for an account like Wright's, which tries to retain as much of the Synoptic data as possible.

Some critics will castigate Wright for being too conservative by seeking to incorporate so much of the canonical material in his portrait of Jesus. My point, however, is a different one: even in retaining this material, Wright transforms it hermeneutically in ways that are not fully reflected upon in *Jesus and the Victory of God.* Rather than winnowing the Synoptic accounts and throwing away the chaff, Wright understands his task as a historian to be the task of imaginatively recontextualizing the Synoptic material within a larger story, the story of Israel as understood in Second Temple Jewish sources. In order to help us understand this story, Wright does a good deal of filling gaps, connecting dots and sketching background. The result is a new narrative that greatly amplifies the canonical Gospels, seeking to allow us to hear these stories as Wright believes they would have been heard by Palestinian Jews in the first century. (Notice in the above quotation how Wright appeals to a "truly first-century Jewish theological perspective" as normative.) But how is this perspective to be related to the rather different tradition of interpretation embodied in the church's subsequent tradition? One might argue that the two perspectives are somehow complementary or mutually correcting, but Wright leaves us guessing about this at the end of his book.

My guess is that Wright regards his historical account as a recovery of the historical roots of the Christian faith; to use a different metaphor, his account is a historical lens through which we should reexamine the shape of Christian teaching in order to see it more clearly. This would mean that his reconstruction would not replace the canonical narratives; rather, it would lead us back to those narratives again and again with new eyes. I have suggested above some of the implications of this program for Christian ethics, particularly with regard to the question of violence. If the victory of God accomplished in Jesus was a victory over violence and nationalism, then all subsequent Christian accommodations of violence and nationalism are betrayals of Jesus' agenda, surrenders of territory won for us by the one we call Lord. If indeed Wright intends that his revisionary historical account should become the critical norm for shaping and revising Christian ethics, future volumes in his project will have to articulate more fully what such a reshaping would entail. Even though the challenges of such a hermeneutical undertaking are formidable, they are to be preferred to the post-Kantian (and ultimately docetic) project of erecting an impassable barrier between faith and history.

Those who find Wright's historical portrayal of Jesus unpersuasive owe us an alternative account. Those who do find Wright's Jesus historically compelling must decide whether he was a fanatic false messiah or whether he was what he believed himself to be. If we decide the latter, we owe him (Jesus, that is, not Wright!) worship and obedience, the sort of obedience that will continue to "implement what he achieved" in communities that embody the obedience of faith.

Nine

Reality, Symbol & History

Theological Reflections on N. T. Wright's Portrayal of Jesus

ALISTER E. MCGRATH

Y ANY STANDARDS, N. T. WRIGHT'S SERIES OF VOLUMES ENTITLED CHRISTIAN Origins and the Question of God promises to be one of the most significant works of New Testament scholarship and theology on its completion. Even after the publication of the first two volumes in the series, its significance has been firmly established and accepted. In part, this significance is grounded in the sheer weight of the scholarship that Wright deploys and the broad scope of the enterprise that he has undertaken. In an age in which much New Testament scholarship is fragmentary in nature, focusing on isolated elements of the New Testament or its themes, Wright's comprehensive approach ✓ must be welcomed as a salutary antidote to the tunnel vision that so often seems to characterize modern New Testament scholarship.

I must make it clear from the outset that I am not, at least by my own perception, a member of the professional guild of New Testament scholars. I have always regarded New Testament theology as essential to the discipline of Christian theology and have taken a particular interest in Paul's doctrine of justification and its development within the Christian tradition.[1] I am simply a theologian who has long lamented the artificial divide that has opened up between New Testament scholarship and systematic theology, and I have deeply regretted the tendency of both New Testament scholars and theologians to perpetuate this situation by studiedly ignoring the potential interface of their enterprises. One of the reasons why Wright's work is so fascinating and important is that he is aware of the broader implications of his work and is not afraid to explore them.

In the last few decades, evangelicalism has shown a new willingness to engage with major academic and scholarly questions.[2] Although it is clear that this development still has some way to go,[3] it is equally evident that evangelicalism now feels able to engage the academy from a position of strength and commitment. Wright's book is clearly an important stimulus in this matter, not least in that it reaffirms the basic themes of traditional Christology at a time when this has been called into question by others, often on somewhat questionable grounds. Wright's masterly defense of the historicity and theological reliability of the Synoptic Gospels in the face of the somewhat artificial schemata of the Jesus Seminar and others has been—and deserves to be—welcomed by evangelicals. Yet Wright's work also poses a challenge to evangelicalism. In the course of its long and rich history, evangelicalism has reached a series of understandings of the significance of the death and resurrection of Jesus Christ. Wright's project calls these into question, at least in aspects of their detail.

This raises a significant and difficult question: Are evangelical New Testament scholars under some kind of family obligation to repeat what their forebears affirmed? Or are they under an absolute obligation to determine what Scripture says, even if this may prove to be in tension with what the evangelical tradition held, and held dearly? There is no contradiction in speaking of an "evangelical tradition of Pauline interpretation," in that evangelicals have fallen into certain set patterns of thinking about the cross and resurrection of Christ. Wright's book invites us to consider whether these are, as a matter of fact, quite as biblical as we would like to think. This is a deeply unsettling challenge.

It is possible that some evangelicals may respond to this by repeating what evangelicals of the eighteenth century affirmed, followed by comparing Wright's views to theirs. Where they are seen to differ, it may be concluded that Wright does not represent an evangelical perspective. While this may satisfy some, it is deeply inadequate. It basically rests upon the fallacious and indefensible assertion that evangelicals have always got things right in the past and are for that reason excused from critical examination or correction. As the Reformers affirmed so strenuously, we are under an obligation to constantly reexamine our ideas and values against Scripture and to avoid the complacency and laziness of thinking that the parrot-like repetition of the past ensures orthodoxy. As J. I. Packer pointed out in a careful and wise study of the role of tradition within evangelicalism, we must be prepared to submit all our ideas to the court of Scripture and verify them on its basis.[4] Wright's challenge is to ensure that our views do indeed represent a biblical perspective. Evangelicalism is principally about being biblical, not about the uncritical repetition of past evangelical beliefs.

This essay will focus on one of the most interesting and potentially one of the most significant aspects of Wright's enterprise—the question of the interaction of reality, history and theology. The question is specifically addressed in *New Testament and the People of God*, and the approach adopted in this earlier work can clearly be seen as underlying and undergirding the analysis offered in *Jesus and the Victory of God*. We shall explore this question by focusing on three themes that arise directly from Wright's work to date: the relation of New Testament scholarship and Christian theology, the issue of critical realism and its theological significance and the implications of Wright's approach for theologies of the atonement.

The Relation of New Testament Scholarship and Christian Theology

As we have seen, one of the more worrying aspects of late twentieth-century theology has been the tendency for New Testament scholars and systematic theologians to tread separate paths and attend their own conferences, offering us a somewhat disturbing picture of an intellectual apartheid that calls out to be challenged and removed. Wright's enterprise can be seen as a sustained challenge to this position, not least by bringing together critical scholarship, historical contextualization and theological reflection.

For Wright, Christian theology is to be distinguished from theology in general by its particularity—its focus upon the Christian story.

> Christian theology tells a story. . . . The story is about a creator and his creation, about humans made in this creator's image and given tasks to perform, about the rebellion of humans and the dissonance of creation at every level, and particularly about the creator's acting, through Israel and climactically through Jesus, to rescue his creation from its ensuing plight. (*NTPG* 132)

It will be clear that this narrative approach immediately secures a connection with Scripture and that it does justice to its historical and narrative character in a manner that contrasts sharply with the rather abstract and self-referential approach offered, for example, by Louis Berkhof in his *Systematic Theology*. It will also be clear that Jesus is placed firmly in continuity with the history of Israel.

Wright sets out three general considerations that indicate the organic connection between biblical studies and theology (see *NTPG* 137-38). First, it is clear that theological ideas were important to New Testament writers, such as Paul, making it imperative that those who study those writers understand "what made early Christians tick." As Wright points out, "one cannot study Paul seriously without enquiring as to his worldview, mindset, basic and consequent beliefs, and practical aims and intentions" (*NTPG* 138). Second, theological analysis allows the alleged "neutrality" of the interpreter to be challenged in that it discloses their prior convictions and working assumptions. Finally, theology inevitably connects up with "the stories contained in the Bible" if it is to retain and justify its distinctive character as Christian theology. "To be truly Christian, it must show that it includes the story which the Bible tells, and the sub-stories within it. Without this, it lapses into a mere ad hoc use of the Bible, finding bits and pieces to fit into a scheme derived from elsewhere" (*NTPG* 138). Although proof-texting (the somewhat simplistic justification of theological claims on the basis of isolated texts, dislocated from their contexts) is now widely recognized as failing to honor and do justice to Scripture, Wright's comments still need to be heeded.

This emphasis upon the manner in which Christian theology relates to the Christian story indicates the importance of the tradition deriving from that story for theology. One of the most distinctive features of recent theology has been the recognition that there is no such thing as a view from nowhere; all theological and philosophical systems relate to historically mediated traditions. This view, especially associated with Alasdair MacIntyre, has been of major importance in shaping the general outlook now widely known as critical realism. In what follows, we shall explore Wright's use of this approach.

The Status of Biblical Statements: Critical Realism

To what do biblical statements refer? According to one popular reading of the situation, those statements relate solely to ideological and cultural issues and agendas, and they have no external referents. Theology is simply an ideational cocoon woven to protect the interests and identity of the group that created it, and it has no genuine significance beyond that group. One thus finds occasional reference to such notions as the "ideology of the Johannine community," meaning something like "the ideas invented by the Johannine community to justify its existence and mark it off from other communities." This, it must be stressed, is related to a wider trend in intellectual culture in general, which seemed to uncritically accept the idea that any form of theological realism was outdated and unfashionable.

Especially during the 1970s and 1980s, some religious (and antireligious) writers argued that God and religion were human constructs, and they proceeded to the conclusion that human dignity and freedom could be advanced by deconstructing both notions.[5] Reality is something that we construct, not something to which we respond. As Don Cupitt, perhaps the most noted popular critic of any form of religious realism, asserts, "We constructed all the world-views, we made all the theories. . . . They depend on us, not we on them."[6] The suggestion that religious worlds are purely human constructions (and may thus be reconstructed in manners congenial to the *Zeitgeist* or the concerns of the postmodern self) clearly has an attraction for many; nevertheless, it remains a contested issue. Wright offers a sustained challenge to this suggestion.

One of the most important issues dealt with by Wright is the status of biblical or theological statements concerning God. The importance of this matter is indicated at several junctures, for example in relation to the complex and contested issue of the role of "facts" in history (*NTPG* 88-92) or the manner in which the reader and the text interact (*NTPG* 61-64). Wright affirms that texts refer to something beyond themselves. The texts cannot be taken to reflect ideas that are free human creations, but the texts are a response to and are governed by a reality that lies beyond them. Wright develops a form of critical realism in his defense of this proposition, which is of considerable theological importance, in addition to being significant in relation to engaging trends in New Testament scholarship.

For Wright, *critical realism* can be defined as follows:

> [Critical realism] is a way of describing the process of "knowing" that acknowledges the *reality of the thing known, as something other than the knower* (hence "realism"), while also fully acknowledging that the only access we have to this reality lies along the spiralling path of *appropriate dialogue* or *conversation between the knower and the thing known* (hence "critical"). This path leads to critical reflection on the products of our enquiry into "reality," so that our assertions about "reality" acknowledge their own provisionality. Knowledge, in other words, although in principle concerning realities independent of the knower, is never itself independent of the knower. (*NTPG* 35)

Wright contrasts this with what he terms *naive realism* or *positivism*, on the one hand, and *phenomenalism*, on the other (*NTPG* 32-34).

Wright's commitment to critical realism reflects a growing interest in this approach to the nuanced issue of our grasp upon reality, and it shows a clear awareness of its potential for Christian theology (in general) and New Testament scholarship (in particular). Although there is at present no consensus on this matter, it is important to note the preponderance of forms of realism within the pre-Enlightenment tradition of theologizing and the growing commitment to forms of realism within Reformed, Roman Catholic and Orthodox circles. William P. Alston's[7] remarkable recent defense of philosophical and theological realism from within the Reformed tradition will serve as an example of the growing influence of realism in such circles, to which other examples could easily be added—such as Thomas F. Torrance[8] in relation to theology, John Milbank[9] in connection with the relation of theology and social theory, and Ian G. Barbour[10] and Wentzel van Huyssteen[11] in their discussion of the relation of religion and science. Wright's major analysis resonates with a significant trend within Christian theology as a whole, which we could loosely designate as a *rediscovery of the ontological finality of reality*. Theology is a discipline that aims to give an account of something that has an existence independent of us, even if the forms we are obligated to use to represent and describe that reality may owe something to our cultures, personalities and histories.

The central distinction of importance that lies behind Wright's analysis may be said to be the one between idealism, on the one hand, and realism, on the other. The former, while not denying that such things as physical objects exist in the world, holds that we can have knowledge only of how things appear to us or are experienced by us, but not as they are in themselves. Perhaps the most familiar version of such an approach is that espoused by Immanuel Kant, who argues (although not with total consistency) that such physical things are to be considered as appearances or representations, rather than as things in themselves.[12] The idealist will thus hold that we can have knowledge of the manner in which things appear to us, through the ordering activity of the human mind; we cannot, however, have knowledge of mind-independent realities. In developing our ideas, we are therefore building on foundations that already exist in the human mind.

Realism, on the other hand, will argue to the effect that experience is knowledge of something independent of human minds. *Realism* is, however, a term that is perhaps as easy to use as it is difficult to define. Three brief definitions could be offered of the central realist thesis, each of which will find its defenders:[13]

1. The world is mind-independent.

2. (Only) nonmental entities exist.

3. Mental and nonmental entities exist.

Each of these statements embodies a realist thesis, although it will be clear that there is a significant difference in the level of commitment and manner of formulation which they adopt. The first definition certainly gets to the heart of the matter, in that it directly counters George Berkeley's denial of the real existence of unperceived things; nevertheless, it is wise to draw a distinction between reality and mind-independence, which is embodied in the second and third definitions.

As Wright is clearly aware, the natural sciences are potentially important dialogue partners in this discussion (*NTPG* 37). It is therefore important to explore the basic elements of this approach to the issue. Richard Boyd sets out the central theses of what he terms "scientific realism" as follows:[14]

1. "Theoretical terms" (or "non-observational terms") in scientific theories are to be thought of as putatively referring expressions. Scientific theories should thus be interpreted "realistically."

2. Scientific theories, interpreted in this realistic manner, are confirmable and are in fact often confirmed as approximately true by ordinary scientific evidence interpreted in accordance with ordinary methodological norms.

The historical development of the mature sciences is largely a matter of successively more accurate approximations to the truth concerning both observable and unobserved phenomena. Later theories tend to build on the observational and theoretical knowledge embodied in earlier theories. The reality that scientific theories describe is largely independent of thoughts or theoretical commitments.

There can be little doubt that most natural scientists espouse a range of opinions that are recognizably realist in their core affirmations, reflecting a common commitment to the ontological finality of the natural order.[15] The fundamental notion is that there is some mind-independent reality of which we are obligated to give an account on the basis of that reality itself, to the extent that it can be known to us and by us. A similar notion underlies Wright's approach, which operates on the assumption that there is an extramental world of reality that governs our thinking and to which we are obligated to respond. At the same time, Wright insists that we must take due account of the influence of a cluster of (assumptions) that shape the manner in which we articulate this reality.

At this point, Wright draws upon the growing interest in narrative theology and in particular the manner in which stories shape our mental worlds. For

Wright, the manner in which we articulate reality is shaped by the story that controls our thinking. Critical realism can thus be said to see "knowledge of particulars as taking place within the larger framework of the story or worldview which forms the basis of the observer's way of being in relation to the world" (*NTPG* 37). Although this point may initially seem somewhat contorted, it is becoming increasingly widely accepted (although in varying forms) within the theological community. Critical realism can be argued to operate on a series of assumptions, including the following:

1. Reality exists independent of our mental activity.
2. Reality is intelligible and is capable of representation.
3. Theoretical terms (such as *neutrinos* in the natural sciences and *God* or *salvation* in theology) refer to this reality.
4. An interpretative community is involved in the shaping of the manner in which reality is represented.

It is the latter aspect of critical realism that is of major importance to our study, and it requires a little explanation. In recent years, both philosophers and theologians have come to realize the importance of community and tradition in the process of interpretation and the advancement of understanding. MacIntyre has stressed that the Enlightenment-inspired model of an isolated individual thinker, free to make intellectual judgments devoid of any explicit or implicit pre-commitments, is little more than a fantasy:

> The history of attempts to construct a morality for tradition-free individuals . . . has in its outcome . . . been a history of continuously contested disputes, so that there emerges no uncontested and incontestable account of what tradition-independent morality consists in and consequently no neutral set of criteria by means of which the claims of rival and contending traditions could be adjudicated.[16]

What is true of the quest for an indisputable morality is true also for the intellectual quest in general. The Enlightenment quest for a universal rationality, free of the limitations of culture and history, has failed.

Both the thinkers of the Enlightenment and their successors proved unable to agree as to precisely what those principles were which would be found undeniable by all rational persons. One kind of answer was given by the authors of the Encyclopédie, a second by Rousseau, a third by Bentham, a fourth by Kant, a fifth by the Scottish philosophers of common sense and their French and American disciples. Nor has subsequent history diminished the extent of such disagreement.

Consequently, the legacy of the Enlightenment has been the provision of an ideal of rational justification which it has proved impossible to attain.[17]

MacIntyre argues for the need to return to the idea of a tradition-centered rationality. There is no "view from nowhere," no rationality that is untainted by history and culture.[18] For MacIntyre, this means a renewed understanding of the epistemological and moral importance of a community and of tradition.

At this point, Wright does more than make helpful suggestions concerning the epistemological status of theological statements; he indicates the role of the early Christian community in shaping the manner in which reality would be represented. Jesus can thus be thought of as retelling the story of Israel as his own story (*JVG* 466), culminating in his winning, as God's representative, the final victory in the final battle. Wright argues that Jesus can be seen as standing within an existing communal tradition (or range of traditions) concerning the kingdom and that Jesus simultaneously reaffirms and redefines that story-shaped tradition (*JVG* 591-92). The early Christian community continued that task of interpretation, by thinking through its own identity and role in the light of its perception that it was "the continuation of Israel in a new situation" (*NTPG* 457-58). Wright's emphasis on the role of the early Christian community takes full account of the praxis, symbols and stories of that community (*NTPG* 359-443) and avoids the purely theoretical approach associated with some accounts of the development of early Christian doctrine.

Wright's constant emphasis on the role of the community in relation to the Christian story should be noted at this point as an aspect of his adoption of critical realism. Theological reflection is clearly understood to take place within a tradition, which embodies world-views expressed in, and to some extent constituted by, stories and their associated symbols (*NTPG* 122-24). The same themes have emerged as important within theology as a whole, particularly in the postliberal school. The writings of George Lindbeck and Stanley Hauerwas have stressed the importance of community and tradition for theology and ethics respectively.[19] Theological and ethical reflection are undertaken within a tradition-shaped community. A similar point is made by Thomas F. Torrance in his discussion of "the social coefficient of knowledge," where he notes the importance of a community in relation to the acquisition and interpretation of knowledge.[20] There are also clear parallels between the approach here adopted by Wright and the related approach found in Milbank's major study of the relation of theology and social theory. Milbank advocates the notion of "a true Christian metanarrative realism."[21]

The essential point emerging from this discussion is that Wright regards the New Testament—and, by implication, those theologies that base themselves upon it—as reflecting something real that is beyond the text and the reader. Wright's critical realism affirms that ontological finality is to be sought in the reality of God and that the New Testament stories and symbols are thus to be seen as relating to the greater reality of God. There can be no doubt that evangelicals will welcome and resonate with this affirmation, just as they will welcome Wright's important criticisms of the Jesus Seminar and the Third Quest.

Up to this point, our primary concern has thus been Wright's understanding of the status of theological statements. Yet the content of those statements is also of importance, not least in that (as Wright presents them) they do not sit entirely easily with the settled evangelical views on matters of some importance. In *Jesus and the Victory of God*, Wright offers an important contribution to the contemporary discussion of the doctrine of the person and work of Christ. In what follows, we shall offer a critical analysis of Wright's approach, considering in particular its impact upon evangelical thinking.

Wright and the Evangelical Tradition: A Critical Exploration

As noted earlier, Wright makes it clear that a close connection exists between biblical scholarship and Christian theology. The artificial distinction that has been created between biblical studies and theological reflection is to be deplored. Given this strong commitment to maintaining the interrelatedness of biblical studies and theology, it is clearly appropriate to explore how Wright's portrayal of Jesus can be appropriated by systematic theology, on the basis of the assumption that New Testament scholarship has implications for systematic theology.

It may be noted that many evangelical theologians resist such an idea, although perhaps more in practice than in theory. A casual examination of a work of popular evangelical theology, such as Wayne Grudem's *Systematic Theology* (which is subtitled *An Introduction to Biblical Doctrine*) indicates a marked preference for reading the New Testament through the controlling framework of existing evangelical ideas rather than dealing with some of the issues of New Testament interpretation that have been thrown up in recent years. Although published in 1994, Grudem does not mention E. P. Sanders or the major debate on Pauline interpretation that has resulted.

There are doubtless good reasons for failing to mention this debate, which has momentous implications for evangelical theology. For example, some of the issues are quite technical and are difficult to explain to a popular readership. However, many would feel that its significance must be recognized and the issues addressed. If Sanders or Wright is correct, Martin Luther is wrong. Although many evangelicals have only a slight grasp of Luther's theology, often tending to impute their own views to him, their perception of his significance is iconic: Luther was the man who began the Reformation. It is no refutation of either Sanders or Wright to point out that they disagree with Luther. The important issue for evangelicals is what Paul meant, not what Luther thought Paul meant. A Christian doctrine that rests on a misreading of Scripture (as the Reformers, for example, held to be the case with the medieval church's understanding of the role of Mary) must at least be critiqued and possibly be rejected.

The program undertaken by Wright is thus of significance to evangelicalism in that it is clearly a labor of love, dedicated to the rediscovery of the authentic biblical perspective on Jesus, with implications for the Christian understanding of the person and work of Christ. Wright makes the point that Protestantism has tended to concern itself with Pauline theology rather than with the ministry of Jesus, often seeing the ministry of Jesus as being theologically subordinated to the ideas of Paul (*JVG* 13-15). This point is in itself of major importance: a common criticism directed against evangelicalism is that it tends to ignore the life of Jesus, and concentrate on Paul's ideas about his death and resurrection.

In one sense, it is difficult to offer a full account of Wright's understanding of these issues, for a full discussion of the doctrines will not be publicly available until the third volume of the Christian Origins and the Question of God series, dealing with Pauline theology, makes its appearance. Nevertheless, Wright dealt with some of the general themes relating to these doctrines in his earlier study *The Climax of the Covenant,*[22] and he has indicated that his approach in that later volume will be an extension of what is to be found earlier. I will therefore make use of this earlier work in exploring some issues in the concluding section of this paper.

There can be no doubt that Wright regards much Protestant thinking concerning the identity and significance of Jesus to be defective, partly on account of its failure to address the Jewish context of the New Testament (both in relation to Jesus and Paul). This is seen as a general failure, which extends to evangelicalism, rather than a specific failing on the part of evangelicalism itself. Perhaps the most effective way of bringing out the potential tensions between Wright's approach and those associated with classical evangelicalism is to explore the manner in which Galatians 3:10-14 is to be understood. Wright argues that this cannot be seen as a systematized and abstract statement but that it is to be placed in a specific context. The critical question, according to Wright, that Paul addresses at this point concerns the blessings promised to the Gentiles through Abraham. Does not the law make void the promises to Abraham and his offspring, in that the blessings are obviated by the curse, so evidently confirmed in the events of the exile? The basic argument that Wright deploys is that the death of Christ provides a means by which the curse over Israel is removed, so that the blessing can now reach its intended recipients. This emphasis upon the pattern of exile and restoration, as well as Wright's interpretation of the Roman occupation of Palestine as a continuation of the exile theme, is one of the more distinctive features of Wright's approach. Although I am not a New Testament scholar, I have to confess misgivings concerning the extent to which Wright elevates the exile-restoration pattern to such a significant (possibly even controlling) extent. However, my concern here will be to explore what Wright does with it and to attempt to assess its theological importance.

Wright's exposition of the atoning death of Christ thus focuses on Christ as the redeeming representative of Israel. This can be seen in his careful analysis of Galatians 3:13, in which he asserts that Christ died at this specific moment in history not for Jews and Gentiles alike but specifically to redeem Israel.

Because the Messiah represents Israel, he is able to take on himself Israel's curse and exhaust it. Jesus dies as the King of the Jews, at the hands of the Romans whose oppression of Israel is the present, and climactic, form of the curse of exile itself. The crucifixion of the Messiah is, one might say, the quintessence of the curse of exile, and its climactic act. The context thus demands the first person plural for which Paul has been criticized by some and misunderstood by others: he is not here producing a general statement of atonement theology applicable equally, and in the same way, to Jew and Gentile alike. Christ, as the representative Messiah, has achieved a specific task, that of taking on himself the curse which hung over Israel and which on the one hand prevented her from enjoying full membership in Abraham's family and thereby on the other prevented the blessing of Abraham from flowing out to the Gentiles. The Messiah has come where Israel is, under the Torah's curse (see 4:4), in order not only to be Israel's representative but Israel's redeeming representative.[23]

The assumptions that lie behind Paul's affirmations at this point could be summarized as follows:[24]

1. Israel as a whole is under the curse if she fails to keep the Torah.
2. Israel as a whole failed to keep the Torah.
3. Therefore Israel is under a curse.

Wright argues that the effects of this curse can be seen in Israel's period of exile in Babylon and, supremely, in the cross of Christ, in which the curse of exile reached its climax.[25] Christ is thus to be seen as the one who bears the curse of Israel, and in doing so, he removes it. For Wright, Paul is quite clearly affirming that Israel is under a curse as a consequence of her failure to live as God's true representative. In *Jesus and the Victory of God*, Wright develops this argument, focusing particularly on how Isaiah 53 illuminates the manner in which Jesus saw himself as the one would redeem Israel (*JVG* 602-3).

Wright thus argues for the introduction of a stimulus to the rethinking of the concept of atonement, in a manner that both reaffirms the existing tradition and, at the same time, redefines it.

> There was, then, no such thing as a pre-Christian Jewish version of (what we now think of as) Pauline atonement-theology. There was a variegated and multifaceted story of how the present evil exilic age could be understood, and how indeed it could be brought to an end, through certain persons embodying in themselves the sufferings of Israel. Jesus, therefore, was not offering an abstract atonement theology; he was identifying himself with the sufferings of Israel. . . . The symbolism and story-telling of Jesus make sense only within this Jewish world, but they play their own strange and unique variation on their dark theme. What Jesus did and said stands out a mile from what early Christianity said about him and his execution, but early Christian atonement-theology is only fully explicable as the post-Easter rethinking of Jesus' essentially pre-Easter understanding. (*JVG* 592)

Elsewhere, Wright notes how some of Jesus' parables that hint at his coming death are "remarkably free of any later Christian atonement-theology" (*JVG* 566). The suggestion (which is not fully developed in Wright's project thus far) would appear to be that Pauline atonement theology is an imposition upon the words and deeds of Jesus (although it should not be inferred from this that such a development is to be regarded as *improper*).

So what are the implications of this for our understanding of the benefits of Christ's death and resurrection for Gentiles? As the redemptive representative of Israel, Jesus is able to remove the curse from this people, and as a result he unleashes the blessings to the Gentiles originally promised through Abraham. Wright's interpretation of Paul at this point allows him to argue that the true restoration of Israel involves the invitation of those outside Israel to share in its blessings. The mission to the Gentiles can thus be understood as an invitation to join the new and restored covenant community,[26] whose benefits are available through faith rather than through works of the law (in the technical sense of the term).

The implications of this approach for traditional evangelical theories of the atonement will be clear. Traditional evangelical approaches to Galatians 3:10-14 might take the following forms.[27] The first approach might be to argue that Paul is making a universal affirmation of the sinfulness of humanity, perhaps along the following lines:

1. All who fail to obey the law are cursed.
2. As a matter of fact, no individual obeys the law fully.
3. Therefore all are cursed.

Christ could therefore be understood as bearing the curse that has descended upon all of humanity as a result of its failure to obey the law. Christ thus removes this curse from all people by means of his death upon the cross. Yet Wright argues that this is not what Paul intended and that this cannot be sustained by exegesis of the passages concerned.[28]

A second approach might be to focus on Paul's doctrine of justification by faith and to assert Paul argues that those who seek self-justification by human achievement are under a curse. In this case, the phrase "works of the law" is understood to mean something like "human effort" or "human achievement." This could be set out as follows.

1. Some seek to achieve their own salvation by "works of the law."
2. This is an arrogant attempt to establish a claim upon God.
3. Such people are under a curse.

For Wright, this interpretation simply cannot be sustained. The phrase "works of the law" must be understood to refer to works within and under the law of Moses. Paul must be interpreted on his own terms rather in terms of historic Protestant categories.

Paul is not here speaking of those problems with which existentialist theologians have wrestled—"achievement," "accomplishment" and the like— nor yet with those traditional in Protestantism, "legalism" (or "nomism"), "self-righteousness" and so forth. Nor is he offering an abstract account of "how one gets saved." His argument, in outline and in detail, makes little sense if read in this way.[29]

At this specific point, Wright clearly finds himself in sympathy with the views of Sanders, who argued that works of the law are not to be understood as the means by which Jews believed they could gain access to the covenant; for they already stood within it. Rather, these works are an expression of the fact that the Jews already belonged to the covenant people of God and that they were living out their obligations to that covenant. Sanders thus rejects the opinion that "the righteousness which comes from the law" is "a meritorious achievement which allows one to demand reward from God and it thus a denial of grace." "Works of the law" were thus understood as the basis not of entry to the covenant but of remaining inside the covenant.[30]

This cuts the ground from under much of the traditional evangelical reading of Paul, which has tended to interpret Paul as making universal affirmations concerning humanity—for example, its sinfulness and tendency to believe that salvation may be achieved or purchased by human attainment or merit.[31] The general approach adopted by most evangelical authors is that Paul is here critiquing a general characteristic of fallen humanity—the desire for self-justification, autonomy and gaining acceptance on account of achievement and merit. Wright sees Paul's polemic as directed against any understanding of the law—and of its associated works of the law—as a "charter of national privilege" for Judaism. For Wright, Paul's arguments are directed against any idea that the specifically Jewish concept of works of the law can safeguard the covenant relationship. As Wright points out, the demarcating mark of the new-covenant family, embracing both Jew and Gentile, is faith—the faith of Abraham.[32] The term "works of the law" is thus to be understood as a *terminus technicus*, having a specific reference to ideas within Judaism that would have been understood by Paul's original readers and that has been misunderstood by subsequent readers who are unaware of the Jewish background to Paul's thought at this point.

It is important to appreciate at this point that it is not merely evangelical interpretations of the phrase "works of the law" that are called into question by Wright. Having studied the development of the Western interpretation of Paul on justification over a period of 1,800 years, I have to report that, until recently, virtually every writer within that tradition of interpretation treated the notion of works of the law in this manner, irrespective of whether the interpreter is Protestant or Catholic, evangelical or not. It is for this reason that the general line of interpretation developed by Sanders, which is echoed in (yet modified by) Wright, is of such significance.

The importance of this point can be further appreciated by considering the nature of salvation itself. Wright stresses that Jesus does not consider his mission to be construed in historically abstract terms. For example, in his important discussion of Matthew's account of the Last Supper, Wright argues that the notion of "the forgiveness of sins" is no abstract idea but is specifically linked with the historical situation of Israel:

Once again we must stress: in its first-century Jewish context, this [i.e., "forgiveness of sins"] denotes, not an abstract transaction between human beings and their god, but the very concrete expectation of Israel, namely that their nation would at last be rescued from the "exile" which had come about because of their sins. Matthew is not suggesting that Jesus' death will accomplish an abstract atonement, but that it will be the means of rescuing YHWH's people from their exilic plight. (*JVG* 561)

Throughout Wright's analysis, this theme can be discerned. Theological interpreters of the New Testament have improperly converted specific, historical and communal hopes and expectations into timeless, abstract and historically detached ideas, which lack the substance of their original context. In that original context, they are embedded in a matrix of concrete historical particularities relating specifically to Israel, and they lack the abstraction and contextual detachment that later Protestant theology has apparently imposed upon them.

What, then, of the cross—a theme that has been of major importance to traditional evangelical theology and spirituality and that serves as the symbol of the Christian faith? Wright is clear that symbols are a significant element of world-views, and he is fully aware of their importance, particularly as boundary markers (*NTPG* 122-26). In his careful analysis of the symbols of Israel's identity—such as the temple, sabbath, food, nation and land—Wright argues that Jesus can be seen to challenge the symbols of Israel as a means of proclaiming judgment against Israel (*JVG* 415-17). This theme is naturally linked with that of the God of Israel's becoming king.

When Jesus came to Jerusalem, he symbolically and prophetically enacted judgment on it—a judgment which, both before and after, he announced verbally as well as in action. The Temple, as the central symbol of the whole national life, was under divine threat, and, unless Israel repented, it would fall to the pagans. Furthermore, Jesus, by making this claim in this way, perceived himself to be not merely a prophet like Jeremiah, announcing the Temple's doom, but the true king. (*JVG* 417)

In continuity with the prophetic tradition, Jesus thus "set his face against the central institutions and symbols of Israel" (*JVG* 428). In their place, Jesus offered a new series of symbols as signs of the renewal that lay ahead as a result of God's restoration of the covenant community (*JVG* 428-37). Jesus was thus the agent of God's restoration of Israel, and part of his means of achieving this goal was the critique of the symbolic system of the time:

Jesus was claiming to be speaking for Israel's god, her scriptures, and her true vocation. Israel was trusting in her ancestral religious symbols; Jesus was claiming to speak for the reality to which those symbols pointed, and to show that, by her concentration on them, Israel had turned inwards upon herself and was being not only disobedient, but dangerously disobedient, to her god's vision for her, his vocation that she should be the light of the world. . . . A clash of visions, incarnated in a clash of symbols, led to confrontation. (*JVG* 442)

Wright thus identifies a *symbolic confrontation* between Jesus and the Judaism of his time and deftly brings out its importance. Jesus' vision "involved the loss of cherished ancestral symbols" (*JVG* 466), which was viewed as totally unacceptable by his Jewish opponents of the time.

The early Christians did not accept any of the symbols of Judaism, but they gradually came to replace them with that of the cross. The process by which this took place is complex and not fully understood.[33] Yet the cross remains the central Christian symbol. Wright himself is clear that the process of acceptance of this symbol took place at an early stage:

The early Christians . . . gave allegiance to none of the regular symbols of either Judaism or paganism. What did they put in their place? . . . Already by the time of Justin Martyr one symbol had become so associated with the early Christian movement that Justin could mount a polemically tendentious argument about it, suggesting that all people give it tacit allegiance. The symbol in question is the cross. . . . Within a short time the cross became the central Christian symbol, easy to draw, hard to forget, pregnant in both its reference to Jesus himself and in its multiple significance for his followers. (*NTPG* 366-67)

Wright locates the "central symbolic action" that offers the key to Jesus' understanding of his own death in the Last Supper, which both recalled the Passover event and affirmed Jesus' own role as the central character in the drama of the divine restoration of Israel (*JVG* 554-59). Wright interprets this meal as both signifying Jesus' identification of himself as the means of Israel's divine redemption and affirming the hope of the return from exile through the renewal of the covenant.

Wright argues that the renewal of the covenant in this manner would involve suffering and death and that such ideas were firmly embedded in the biblical tradition up to this point (*JVG* 576-92). As a matter of historical fact, Jesus died upon the cross. Wright's account of how the cross relates to the overall story of Jesus is significant and merits close attention.

Jesus believed that it was his god-given vocation to identify with the rebel cause, the kingdom-cause, when at last that identification could not be misunderstood as endorsement. Israel was in exile, suffering at the hands of the pagans; the Roman cross was the bitterest symbol of that ongoing exilic state. He would go ahead of his people, to take upon himself both the fate that they had suffered one way or another for half a millennium at the hands of pagan empires and the fate that his contemporaries were apparently hell-bent upon pulling down on their own heads once for all. The martyr-tradition suggested that this was the way in which Israel would at last be brought through suffering to vindication. . . . The "messianic woes" tradition indicated that this suffering and vindication would be climactic, unique, the one-off moment when Israel's history and world history would turn their great corner at last, when YHWH's kingdom would come and his will be done on earth as it was in heaven. The central symbolic act by which Jesus gave meaning to his approaching death suggests strongly that he believed this moment had come. This would be the new exodus, the renewal of the covenant, the forgiveness of sins, the end of exile. It would do for Israel what Israel could not do for herself. (*JVG* 596-97)

This complex and important passage brings out Wright's perception that Jesus intended to share Israel's sufferings as the key action in the divinely appointed plan of redemption for Israel and the world. The cross was thus a symbol of Roman power and a reminder of the exile of Israel at the hands of pagans. Jesus took upon himself the fate that he had declared for Israel (*JVG* 608). The resurrection can be regarded as a symbol of the return from exile (*JVG* 127-28, 255-56), so that the pattern of crucifixion and resurrection can, so to speak, be seen as reflecting that of exile and restoration.

It is difficult to assess the theological significance of this approach, for we must await its fuller analysis in later volumes of the Christian Origins and the Question of God series. Nevertheless, some preliminary comments would seem to be in order.

1. Wright argues that the cross and resurrection are to be correlated not with theological abstractions but with certain very specific and concrete aspects of the history of Israel. The pattern of cross and resurrection, reflecting that of exile and restoration, has determinative significance for Israel rather than a universal significance for all of humanity—except in that all of humanity are implicated in Israel's destiny, on account of the promise to Abraham.

2. It would therefore follow from this that it would not be correct to interpret the cross and resurrection as "abstract systematized statements"[34] but rather as specific to the situation Israel faced, including its exile under the Romans. Wright frequently comments on the manner in which an atonement theology has

been imposed upon the cross and resurrection, and he clearly believes that its fundamental sense is limited.

3. Wright asserts that while the cross is indeed a symbol of suffering and death, its specific historical significance is to be linked with its Roman associations. It is a symbol of Israel's exile as much as of Christ's sufferings.

4. Wright asserts that while Christianity has traditionally seen the cross as being of central symbolic importance, Wright's analysis suggests it is the Last Supper that possesses the greater symbolic weight, not least in relation to Jesus' own perceptions and intentions and especially in the manner in which he understands his own story as relating to that of Israel itself.

As I have stressed, a fuller analysis of Wright's views must await the publication of later volumes, in which it is to be hoped that we will find a detailed study of the relation between the history and intentions of Jesus, as presented by Wright, and Paul's theology of atonement. Nevertheless, the more specifically theological issues that Wright's analysis raises for evangelicals at this early stage could be summarized as follows.

1. The death of Christ can indeed be thought of as being "for others," but it is to be understood as having corporate significance for the people of Israel, not individual significance for sinners. Wright argues that the death of Jesus is linked with the notion of the covenant, so that Jesus can be seen as a redemptive representative of Israel, bearing her specific curse and making it possible for her as a people to achieve her intended destiny. It is not correct to think of the death of Jesus as having significance for individuals, except insofar as they are members of the covenant people of God. This therefore raises the question of how a non-Jew becomes a member of the people of God; for Wright, this question relates to the doctrine of justification by faith.

2. Traditional Protestant (and hence evangelical) ways of systematizing the meaning of the cross and resurrection are thus called into question. Notions such as the forgiveness of sins are not to be interpreted as global and timeless construals; they are specifically related to the history of Israel and thus have concrete referents (the return from exile) within that history. The question of how one relates this specific historical context to, for example, that of modern Western non-Jews thus becomes problematic and requires careful attention.

3. The individualism that has been so characteristic of much of evangelicalism, particularly in North America, is called into question. On the basis of a set of individualist assumptions, probably ultimately deriving from the late Renaissance, evangelical interpreters of Scripture have tended to assume that the biblical message is addressed to them as individuals, dealing with issues such as

personal sin, personal destiny and an individual relationship with God. It would not be correct to say that Wright dismisses these as distortions; nevertheless, it is clear that his understanding of concepts of sin, salvation and identity are corporate, grounded in the identity, history and purposes of Israel as the people of God.

4. At least on the basis of the analysis thus far in Wright's project, our attention should perhaps be directed toward the Last Supper rather than the cross. Of course, in one sense, this absolute distinction cannot be maintained, in that the Last Supper anticipates the cross as much as the cross is continuous with the narrative of the Supper. But in terms of the traditional symbolism, Wright shifts the emphasis in a manner that some evangelicals might find unsettling (and even a little sacramental). It must be pointed out immediately, however, that we await Wright's detailed discussion of Pauline theology and especially Wright's understanding of the role of the Last Supper commemoration within Paul's overall vision of Christianity.

To these points we must add the highly significant and contentious issue of the meaning of works of the law, noted earlier, which calls into question traditional Protestant understandings of the doctrine of justification by faith.

Wright has thus lobbed a hand grenade into the world of traditional evangelical theology. It is far too early to determine whether this grenade will explode and cause fatalities or whether it will prove to be the kind of explosion that generates mild and polite interest within academic seminar rooms and fails to impact the broader world of evangelical theology. In fact, in many ways this paper represents a request for clarification, which may be expected to be forthcoming in due course. Like all interim reports, it can easily be outdated and rendered irrelevant by subsequent events. Yet such reports also serve another purpose: to set an agenda that it is hoped will help in the process of clarification and development. At point after point in this paper, I have had to indicate the need to await clarification in future volumes.

Yet I must end on an appreciative, even expectant, note. Wright's project is like a gadfly to evangelical theology. It is an irritant, a stimulus, that demands we reexamine our ways of thinking and interpreting Scripture, particularly Paul's writings, to see whether we have fallen into settled and lazy ways of thinking that, in the end, fail to do justice to the New Testament. A favorite slogan of later-Reformation writers was that the Reformed church must be *ecclesia semper reformanda*—that is, a church that is always reforming itself. Reformation, rightly understood, is not a once-for-all event whose ideas are to be set in stone but an ongoing process of reexamination and reconsideration, forced upon us by the priority of the biblical text over our provisional interpretations of that text. Wright obliges us to read the New Testament again and to take the profound risk of allowing our most settled ideas to be challenged in the light of the biblical witness. The price of being biblical is to constantly return to the Bible, sometimes with anticipation and at other times with trepidation, in that our present ideas may find themselves rendered questionable. It is a price that I, for one, am glad to pay.

Ten

Methodological Naturalism in Historical Biblical Scholarship

C. STEPHEN EVANS

N T. WRIGHT'S *JESUS AND THE VICTORY OF GOD* IS ONE OF THE MOST IMPRES-
sive examples of biblical scholarship I have ever had the privilege of reading. The book is full of original insights and
arguments and manifests deep learning as well as many years of pondering
the relevant biblical texts. Furthermore, the book presents us with a portrait
of a historical Jesus that has clear relevance and value for theology, including
theology that wishes to remain within orthodoxy. Though Wright is careful
throughout to avoid anachronistically reading back into Jesus' own actions
and self-understanding the formulations of later creeds and theologies, he
gives us a Jesus who thinks of himself as and claims to be God's chosen Messiah, the one appointed by God to act on God's behalf to end the captivity of
Israel and redeem Israel by his sacrificial death. Israel's own vocation is seen
in turn as ultimately universal; the redemption of Israel is the victory of God,
the inauguration of the kingdom of God that will bless all peoples of the
world.

Such a Jesus is no namby-pamby, self-effacing teacher of abstract ethical principles. Rather, Wright's Jesus has the boldness to call for faith in himself and loyalty to himself and to identify those who oppose him as servants of "the satan," be they Pharisees or priests. While such a Jesus is far from thinking of himself in Chalcedonian terms, it is not hard to see why, on Wright's account, the earliest Christians began to worship Jesus. It becomes possible to think about how the church could have begun the process of reflection on the life, death and resurrection of Jesus that led to Chalcedon. Although Wright's account contains elements that many will find surprising and perhaps disturbing, it is an account that on the whole provides a Jesus conducive to orthodox theology. I myself found the account to be powerful and persuasive for the most part, though I often found myself agreeing with a point while disagreeing somewhat with the implications Wright wished to draw out from that point.

To show that Wright's version of the historical Jesus is on the whole one that is helpful for orthodox Christology, one has merely to compare it with the portraits of Jesus by John Dominic Crossan, Burton L. Mack or, to mention a scholar much closer to Wright, E. P. Sanders. However, I am confident that Wright himself would insist that his historical narrative be judged primarily not in terms of its value for theology but for its plausibility as history. As a Christian believer and clergyman, he would presumably be glad for the value of the history for theology, but in the book he frequently charges that theological agendas have led to historical mistakes, both on the part of those pushing those agendas and those resisting them.

An excellent example of this is the following: "If I am right, the church, not least in its would-be orthodox moments, has regularly read language in which Jesus referred to YHWH's return to Zion (as part of his understanding of what he himself was doing) as referring to the 'second coming'" (*JVG* 660). One of the passages Wright has in mind here is Luke 9:27, with its corresponding texts in Mark 9:1 and Matthew 16:28: "But truly I tell you, there are some standing here who will not taste death before they see the kingdom of God." As Wright sees things, "to read this saying as though it were a prediction of Jesus' 'return,' or of the 'parousia' in some Schweitzerian end-of-the-world sense, is simply to fail to think historically" (*JVG* 470).

Here Wright argues that many Christians, in their zeal to provide a foundation for the doctrine of Jesus' return, have in fact misunderstood the historical narrative surrounding the last days of Jesus. At the same time, some critics, reading the relevant passages in a similar way, have argued either that the passages are not authentic (since Jesus would never have predicted his own second coming) or else that they are authentic and show Jesus was deluded or mistaken (since he predicted that the definitive arrival of the kingdom of God would occur very soon).

Wright gives the impression that he thinks that theology will be better off if we give the historian his or her due and let the historical chips fall where they may. Yet it is apparent—and unorthodox scholars will certainly point this out soon if they have not done so already—that Wright himself has theological concerns that lurk beneath the surface of his text, which now and then extend into clear view. Just a few sentences after the one quoted above, in which Wright deplores the way a concern to establish a scriptural basis for the doctrine of the second coming has led to what he sees as the misreading of certain key texts, he notes the greater value of these texts in developing the even more fundamental doctrine of the incarnation: "Those who have desired to explore and understand the incarnation itself have regularly missed what is arguably the most central, shocking and dramatic source material on that subject, which if taken seriously would ensure that the meaning of the word 'god' be again and again rethought around the actual history of Jesus himself" (*JVG* 661).

Wright's claim that reading such passages as predictions of a second coming is a failure to think historically raises the question as to what it *means* to "think historically." In what follows I propose to examine Wright's implicit answer to that question. I wish to defend several theses. Since these theses are interlinked, I shall discuss them as a package and not serially. However, it may be helpful to set them out first as distinct claims:

1. The historical method generally followed by Wright (with some important exceptions to be noted) is essentially similar to that defended by Ernst Troeltsch and Van A. Harvey, and this method is the dominant method employed by historical biblical scholars.

2. This historical method incorporates a commitment to what is usually termed "methodological naturalism."

3. The method Wright employs is one that Christian scholars should be free to use; it is a method that is valuable in a number of respects, heuristically, pragmatically and for apologetics.

4. The method Wright employs should not be identified as the historical method all historical scholars must use, and it is a mistake to claim that historical conclusions not attainable by this method are illegitimate. Specifically, Christian scholars should not claim or give the impression that all reasonable historical beliefs must be derived from such a method.

Troeltsch's Historical Method

Biblical scholarship in the twentieth century has been dominated, methodologically, by the kind of perspective articulated around the beginning of the twentieth
century and end of the nineteenth by thinkers such as Troeltsch and F. H. Bradley and articulated and defended more recently by Harvey.[1] Harvey argues that
this kind of historical inquiry is bound to be problematic from the viewpoint of
traditional Christian orthodoxy not because of any particular empirical findings
but simply because of the principles a good historian should follow.[2] On Harvey's
account, Troeltsch himself thinks there are three such principles: the principle of
criticism, the principle of analogy and the principle of correlation.[3]

The *principle of criticism* I take to be a conglomeration of several ideas,
including the following: the historian should base all historical claims on evidence; the historian should treat evidential sources, especially written narratives,
with an attitude of suspicion and skepticism; and the historian should adopt an
open and tentative attitude toward conclusions, always viewing them as more or
less probable and open to revision in light of further evidence.[4]

The *principle of analogy* seems to be a kind of principle of the uniformity of
natural causes, applied both to nature as a physical system and to human actions.
On this view, the basic causal forces do not change over time. The natural laws
that are observed to operate at the present time have always determined the
course of the physical world. This would include whatever psychological laws are
determinative of human behavior, though Troeltsch is far from denying the
importance of human culture, which varies so greatly from society to society.

The *principle of correlation* is another causal principle. Essentially, this principle says that the historian must look at historical events from within a causal
nexus. All historical events must be understood as emerging from a complex of
preceding events and flowing into a complex of consequences. This principle may
seem perfectly platitudinous, but it gains bite if the "before and after" causal
nexus is understood to consist solely of natural events. The natural world, including the historical world, is thus seen as a closed system in which no events are to
be attributed to causal powers that transcend the system.

Now it seems to me that these methodological principles involve an acceptance of what could aptly be called "methodological naturalism." The historian
who follows these principles may not be committed to naturalism in a metaphysical sense. The historian may believe in God personally and may even believe that
God performs miracles. However, if the historian believes in such miracles, he or
she must regard such beliefs as things "accepted by faith" or "accepted by virtue of

being a Christian," and not as a belief that can be warranted on historical grounds.

As will become evident in what follows, even the category of methodological naturalism is complex. As I understand it, methodological naturalism is linked to the employment of the principles of Troeltsch or of rules similar to those. However, it is important to distinguish between two different attitudes toward these rules, which define two different types of methodological naturalism. For what we might call the "type one" methodological naturalist, these rules are somehow binding or obligatory on historians, such that one who does not follow them is not practicing good history. For the "type two" methodological naturalist, these rules simply prescribe a method that can be followed and may be valuable to follow, without regarding that method as obligatory for historians. At the conclusion of this paper, I shall criticize "type one" methodological naturalism, but I wish to endorse methodological naturalism in its "type two" form. In a broad sense, ignoring the distinction I have just made, we can characterize any research done in accordance with Troeltsch's principles as research that conforms to methodological naturalism.

It is not too difficult, I think, to show that most historical biblical criticism is conducted along these lines. It is not surprising that some prominent members of the Jesus Seminar and others critical of orthodox views should take such a view. But it must be noted that relatively moderate biblical scholars are committed to the same kind of methodology. John P. Meier, for example, in dealing with miracles is careful to claim that the most he can do is argue that a historical figure such as Jesus was *believed* by his contemporaries to have performed miracles.[5] To affirm the occurrence of a miracle is to go beyond the competence of a historian, who must conduct her or his investigation as if the outcome were the result of what Meier calls an "unpapal conclave," an imaginary meeting of a Protestant, a Catholic, a Jew and an agnostic who must reach some kind of agreement.[6] In a similar manner, Luke Timothy Johnson, in commenting on what he sees as my own proposal to widen the concept of history so as to include the supernatural, argues that the "real difficulty" is "the effect on the very idea of history once it has been so expanded. What happens is that history ceases to be a mode of knowledge accessible to any person of good will and decent abilities at weighing evidence, and becomes the private preserve of Christian apologists, that is, a form of 'myth.'"[7]

Johnson's quotation here explicitly raises the question as to the nature of historical scholarship. Is it the case that to gain historical knowledge one needs only to be a "person of good will" who has "decent abilities at weighing evidence"? I think that Johnson is quite mistaken about this. The main reason is that the notion of weighing evidence is quite complex. How evidence should be weighted depends on, among other things, one's assessment of the honesty of a source and upon one's general background beliefs, including metaphysical beliefs. For example, if one is convinced, as was Friedrich Nietzsche, that Paul is fundamentally a devious, power-hungry example of the kind of person Nietzsche called a "decadent," then one's assessment of Paul's accounts of what he had received from the tradition will be quite different than would be the case if a person considers Paul to be an admirable, even if flawed, man of spiritual insight and discernment. For another example, if one thinks events that cannot be naturally explained simply cannot occur, then any testimony in favor of miracles will be dismissed in advance. The dismissal of miracles in such a case does not result simply from being a "person of good will" who "knows how to weigh evidence" but from metaphysical beliefs that not everyone shares.

I make this point because it shows that Johnson is confused about the justification for the kind of methodological naturalism he advocates and also because it usefully illustrates a kind of naive view of historical methodology from which Wright is free. Wright's view of historical methodology is far more sophisticated than this, as we shall see. However, despite the differences, I shall argue that Wright also seems committed to a kind of methodological naturalism.

Johnson's comments suggest one possible justification for methodological naturalism: that the method is neutral and thus provides common ground for scholars of differing religious viewpoints. This justification has some merit, but its merits extend, I believe, only to type-two methodological naturalism. The justification is half right. The ground may be common, but it is not neutral, since it reflects the metaphysical views of one faction—albeit the dominant faction within academe, namely, those committed to some form of naturalism. As we shall see, the quotation from Johnson points to a good reason for employing methodological naturalism *some of the time for some scholars*. It is a method that turns out to be useful for both apologetic and pragmatic reasons. Thus, Wright's use of the method can be shown to be justifiable and valuable. However, Christians have every reason to deny that a person who wishes to find historical truth is best off relying on methodological naturalism all of the time, and there are no good arguments for methodological naturalism as a method that is universally binding on good historians. Christian scholars such as Wright who employ this method should therefore be careful to frame their reliance on the method carefully and to make it clear that they are not suggesting historical truth can be determined only through such means.

Wright's Apparent Rejection of Methodological Naturalism

What reasons do I have for thinking that Wright employs methodological naturalism in *Jesus and the Victory of God*? Paradoxically, I must first discuss some reasons for thinking that Wright *rejects* such a methodological naturalism. So far as I know, Wright does not explicitly discuss the issue and commit himself with respect to it anywhere in *Jesus and the Victory of God*. He does explicitly discuss such methodological issues in the first part of that book's predecessor, *The New Testament and the People of God*. In that work, he argues *against* what I term methodological naturalism. In fact, he says, following lines similar to those I have employed myself, we should not dogmatically claim that the philosophies of the Enlightenment are binding upon historians:

> Nor is it to say that if we are to read the gospels as they stand, "miracles" and all, we must frankly admit that we are ceasing to do "history" and are now doing something else, namely "theology," or a kind of meta-history. Only if we have devalued "history" so that the word now *means* "the positivist recounting of those sorts of events which fit with an eighteenth-century worldview, and which seem to have actually happened," would we need to think that. (*NTPG* 93)

In this earlier work, Wright shows a sophisticated yet balanced perspective on a number of key philosophical issues. For example, on the basic epistemological question concerning the nature of knowledge and the relation of the knower to the world, Wright adopts a "critical realist" position (*NTPG* 31-46). This position acknowledges that human knowledge of the world is always shaped by "subjective" factors, including the idea that knowing occurs within the framework of a worldview: "It [critical realism] acknowledges that all knowledge of realities external to oneself takes place within the framework of a worldview, of which stories form an essential part" (*NTPG* 45). However, Wright claims, to my mind correctly, that such an epistemology does not preclude striving to know that external reality as it really is. The fact that God has created us in his image gives us hope that knowledge is possible, a knowledge that must be seen as a gift from the Creator (*NTPG* 45).

Wright is thus far removed from the kind of narrow empiricism sometimes designated as "positivism." And this can be seen in his historical method. There is, for example, no trace in Wright of the kind of naive empiricism I would describe as inductivism. The inductivist insists that we must simply start with individual facts and use these to build up generalizations. In biblical scholarship concerning the Gospels, the inductivist would be the type of scholar who begins with individual pericopes, or even individual sayings, and attempts to establish which are authentic and which are not, relying on "criteria of authenticity." The assumption behind this is that once we have an authentic core of "facts" we can then proceed to develop generalizations about what Jesus taught or did. Wright clearly sees that this procedure is doomed to failure, because it is impossible to determine which individual sayings or pericopes are authentic in isolation from one's broader views about Jesus. The facts cannot be settled in isolation from broader theories. Even a criterion so apparently objective as multiple attestation cannot be applied in isolation from one's theories about the relations the Synoptic Gospels have to each other and to Q (if Q existed), to the dating of the fourth Gospel, to *Thomas* and to many other factors. Similarly, the criterion of dissimilarity, even if one thinks it a reasonable criterion, depends for its application on one's theories about the characteristics of the early church and first-century Judaism.

Because he recognizes the way theories and facts are interconnected, Wright not only rejects a simple inductivism; he also moves beyond the kind of empiricism in which hypotheses are developed (perhaps creatively rather than inductively) and then verified (or falsified) by facts. Wright sees that theories do not face experience individually but collectively; theories form webs, to use the kind of metaphor popularized by W. V. Quine.[8] Because theories are interconnected in this way, verification and falsification are not simple affairs, and it always possible to "save" a theory by making suitable modifications elsewhere in the web, though at some point such modifications, particularly if they seem *ad hoc*, begin to make the whole web implausible.[9]

The weblike nature of theories can also function positively, however. A major thrust of Wright's own approach is that a biblical scholar must develop a comprehensive narrative, which can not only explain or account for all the data but enables us to see coherence and meaning so incidents and sayings that were enigmatic now make sense as part of an overall account. A nice example is found in his treatment of the sayings and symbolic actions attributed to Jesus in the upper room before his crucifixion:

> And, just as in relation to the Temple we discovered that a good many of Jesus' sayings, clustered around the incident, functioned as riddles which explained the symbol, so we find in this case several sayings which, though cryptic in themselves, collectively point in one particular direction. Finally, as before, the symbolic action,

and the riddles which explain it, create a historical context within which other material can settle down and, through coherence with the larger picture, make itself at home. (*JVG* 563)

Within the framework of this sophisticated epistemology and its accompanying view of historical methodology, it is not surprising that Wright is able to recognize even the importance of worldviews in historical scholarship. For webs of theories cannot ultimately be divorced from the background beliefs that scholars bring with them to their activities as theorizers.

It is safe to say, then, that there is nothing in Wright's epistemology that compels him to be what I have called a type-one methodological naturalist. I suspect in the end he is not this type of methodological naturalist; I shall discuss below some of what he has to say about the resurrection that could be interpreted to point beyond such a view. Nevertheless, it seems to me that *Jesus and the Victory of God* does, for the most part, conform to the dictates of this historical method. He is at least a type-two methodological naturalist, and in this work he does conform to Troeltsch's methodology. In the next section, I offer some evidence for this claim.

Wright's Implicit Reliance on Methodological Naturalism

Wright's reliance on methodological naturalism can be seen in at least three areas: his treatment of miracles, of prophetic insight and of Jesus' self-awareness. I shall discuss each of these in turn.

1. Miracles. An obvious place to turn to see whether Wright employs a methodological naturalism is his treatment of miracles, or the "mighty works" of Jesus. The first thing to notice here is that the subject is not a prominent item of discussion. In a book that contains 662 pages of text (not including appendix, bibliography and indices), the subject of miracles takes up only eleven pages. While Wright certainly does not ignore miracles—and there are a few other mentions of the subject—the sustained discussion of miracles can be found on pages 186-97. In a book that is long and in which certain themes are discussed repeatedly, the miraculous deeds of Jesus do not appear to play a very prominent role in the interpretation of Jesus' life.

One might be tempted to take Wright's introduction to his discussion of miracles as a step away from Troeltsch-type methodological naturalism. For Wright begins by noting approvingly that the Third Quest for the historical Jesus has moved away from the nineteenth-century rationalism that tried to eliminate the "mighty works" of Jesus (*JVG* 186). It appears, rather, that Wright wants to claim that historical research must affirm miraculous deeds as part of Jesus' ministry: "More thoroughgoing recent history has been coming to the conclusion that we can only explain the evidence before us if we reckon that Jesus did indeed perform deeds for which there was at the time, and may well be still, no obvious 'naturalistic' explanation—to use that terminology for the moment" (*JVG* 186). Wright goes on cautiously to urge us not to adopt uncritically the philosophical assumptions of the Enlightenment:

> It is prudent, methodologically, to hold back from too hasty a judgment on what is actually possible and what is not within the space-time universe. There are more things in heaven and earth than are dreamed of in post-Enlightenment philosophy, as those who have lived and worked in areas of the world less affected by Hume, Lessing and Troeltsch know quite well. (*JVG* 187)

So far it would appear Wright does not wish to be identified with Troeltsch.

Nevertheless, there is less here than meets the eye. Traditional Christian thinkers, whom Wright labels "pre-critical," a term loaded with Troeltschian meaning, have generally viewed the miracles of Jesus as attesting that God was indeed working through and speaking through Jesus, a sign that the claims made by Jesus and his close followers could be believed on divine authority. Thomas Aquinas, for example, in discussing how a true revelation from God could be recognized, points to the importance of "signs produced in a supernatural way, which alone fittingly gives witness to divine inspiration; for a visible action that can be only divine reveals an invisibly inspired teacher of truth."[10] Wright explicitly distances himself from any such appeal to the miraculous:

> The appeal for suspension of judgment, then, cannot be used as a Trojan horse for smuggling in an old-fashioned "supernaturalist" worldview under pretence of neutrality; this is sometimes done by conservative apologists, who are often interested at this point, not in Jesus himself, but in miracles as test cases but [sic] for whether the Bible is believed to be "true" or not—a position that brings its own nemesis. (*JVG* 187)

It is not clear what is wrong with a supernaturalist worldview other than the allegation that it is out of date. Perhaps Wright thinks that supernaturalism is a "non-Humean worldview in which a (normally absent?) god intervenes in the world in an apparently arbitrary and irrational fashion" (*JVG* 187). If so, his worries are founded on confusion and a gross caricature of traditional views. The supernaturalism of Aquinas certainly does not involve a God who is normally absent from the world intervening in an arbitrary and irrational fashion.

Supernaturalism, insofar as it is linked to Christian orthodoxy, must not be confused with deism. The question it is designed to answer is, rather, this one: Is the natural world, with all of its powers, a self-contained system, existing "on its own," so to speak; or is that natural world, with all of its regularities, an expression of the power of a personal being who transcends that natural order, while being immanent within it as well? God thus conceived is never "absent" from the natural world, and the overwhelming majority of "pre-critical" Christian thinkers have recognized this clearly. Within the framework of supernaturalism thus conceived, the question of miracles is not whether God from time to time intervenes in a world where God is not normally present but whether God, besides continually conserving the natural created world that he providentially orders, also can perform special actions that manifest his intentions in a more direct and personal manner than what might be called his routine activity does.[11]

It is, I believe, because of his worries about supernaturalism that Wright in fact adopts a form of methodological naturalism, despite his initial brave words about not being bound by Enlightenment thinking. It is clear from Wright's words that he does not wish to be committed to *metaphysical* naturalism. However, one can reject a dogmatic form of metaphysical naturalism and still be committed in practice to a methodological naturalism as the proper stance for historians to take, as Meier, for example, does.

Meier, as already noted, claims that historians can, as historians, neither affirm nor deny the reality of miracles, though they can try to discern whether a person's contemporaries *believed* that the person performed miracles. This is clearly not a commitment to metaphysical naturalism. Still, however neutral this stance may appear, in practice it means the historian must not interpret or explain events as the result of special divine activity. Any actual explanations offered must, therefore, be natural ones. Thus, the historian who follows Meier's rule also conforms to Troeltsch's principle of correlation.

Several items can be cited as evidence that Wright's stance is in reality much like Meier's. Take, first, the claim that "few serious historians now deny that Jesus, and for that matter many other people, performed cures and did other startling things for which there was no obvious natural explanation" (*JVG* 188). We might pause just a bit to wonder about the truth of this claim. Is it really true that most historians agree that Jesus and "many other people" have performed cures and other actions for which there is no obvious natural explanation? However, even if Wright is correct about this, the thrust of the passage is to "naturalize" the signs that Jesus is alleged to have performed. Far from being a sign of special divine authority or power, the signs of Jesus are now to be grouped with actions performed by "many people." (And presumably, since the agents are many, the acts are not infrequent either.) Since most people think of miracles—at least the kinds of "authenticating miracles" Jesus is alleged to have performed—as relatively rare events, the thrust of this passage is toward naturalizing the works of Jesus. Wright seems to be saying that Jesus' mighty acts can be considered by historians because they are part of a broader class of human actions.

This tendency toward naturalization is confirmed by Wright's decision to classify the mighty works of Jesus as a form of magic, at least in an "extended sense" (*JVG* 190). Wright appears sympathetic to the claim that there is no objective way to distinguish Jesus' miracles from magic. Many commentators want to make a sharp distinction between magic and miracles, but Wright appears to agree with Crossan that the distinction is primarily one that reflects values rather than causal explanations (*JVG* 189-90).[12] Mighty works regarded as beneficial and sanctioned by religious authorities are described as miracles (and therefore attributed to God), while those that are not so regarded are stigmatized as magic. In neither case does Crossan think of the acts as necessarily to be explained by supernatural causes. The distinction between miracles and magic cannot be drawn as a distinction between acts due to God and those due to trickery, or acts due to God as opposed to those due to evil spirits. Rather, magic and miracles are seen as the same type of event, but they are described differently because our attitudes toward the events is different. The distinction is analogous to the way a bombing could be described by one person as the act of a courageous freedom fighter and by another as the act of a cowardly terrorist.

Wright seems to accept Crossan's attempt to widen the meaning of "magic" to "include any mighty work performed outside an official context" (*JVG* 190). From the point of view of the historian, the mighty works of Jesus then fit into the broader category of magic, a type of event in principle explainable by natural causes.

We cannot tell "by further scrutiny of the mighty works themselves," whether Jesus was, in the pejorative sense, merely a magician or whether his activity in some sense represented the coming of the kingdom of God (*JVG* 191). The traditional view of Jesus' miracles was that their supernatural character itself was evidence of divine authority, as when Nicodemus is reported to say to Jesus, "Rabbi, we know you are a teacher who has come from God; for no one can do these signs that you do apart from the presence of God" (Jn 3:2). From the perspective of Crossan (and Wright), our decision as to whether Jesus' acts are miracles, to be thus attributed to God, is grounded in a judgment about the meaning of Jesus' life as a whole, and it does not appear that the miracles themselves can be decisive in determining that meaning.

I am inclined to agree that our decision about the miracles is tied closely to our views about the narrative as a whole. However, I don't see why in some cases the miracles themselves could be not be a key part of the evidence that determines our view of that meaning. We have here another instance of the hermeneutical circle. It is true that our reading of the part will always be shaped by our reading of the whole, but we must not forget that our reading of the whole is equally derived from our reading of the parts. And for many readers, the supernatural character of parts of the narrative is a key element that points to the fact that Jesus did indeed come from God.

Wright is careful not to claim that there is nothing unique or different about Jesus' mighty works. He says that one can't decide the question as to the nature of the works merely by looking for parallels in the history of religion (*JVG* 191). (Interestingly though, his own attempt to argue for the historicity of these works seems to depend on classifying them as a type of action performed by "many other people.") And he says that "for the most part" Jesus appears not to have used the same techniques as other magicians of his time (*JVG* 191). Still, the upshot of his discussion seems to be that Jesus' mighty works are a type of magic, a natural category of actions that historians of varying worldviews may use in understanding them.

That Wright's argument for the historicity of Jesus' mighty works represents no break with methodological naturalism can also be seen from the fact that he several times appeals to a "consensus" among historians. "Many scholars from widely differing backgrounds now accept that Jesus did remarkable 'mighty works'" (*JVG* 194). Here Wright seems to appeal to something like Meier's unpapal conclave. And since Wright explicitly notes that this consensus will include historians who think that miracles do not occur and that therefore natural explanations of the miracles (as psychosomatic, for example) are possible, the historical acknowledgment of the mighty works cannot represent any kind of break with methodological naturalism. This type of consensus view is important in that it has a strong bearing on which events are taken to be historical. It seems no accident to me that the mighty works accepted as authentic are almost always those, such as exorcisms, that can be given a plausible natural explanation.

The thrust of Wright's treatment of miracles is then something like the following: historians have good evidence for the claim that the contemporaries of Jesus regarded him as performing "mighty works" (a term open to interpretation in various ways). The best explanation of this fact is that Jesus did in fact do such works. Some people (his followers) regarded these works as signs of divine authority; others (his opponents) regarded the works as magic. Though Wright is less forthcoming on this point than I would like, it seems to me his final view is similar to Meier's. As historians, we are unable to say that these works are due to the power of God, though perhaps we are also unable to say dogmatically that they are not. As religious (or antireligious) human beings we may of course feel the need to say something more.

2. Prophetic utterances. A second area where I believe an implicit commitment to methodological naturalism can be seen in Wright's work concerns what I shall term "prophetic utterances." These are sayings attributed to Jesus that have usually been interpreted, by orthodox Christian believers at least, as indicating some kind of insight resulting from divine inspiration. Examples would be sayings predicting future events, such as the destruction of Jerusalem, or sayings implying other kinds of knowledge that suggest a knowledge that is not naturally obtainable, such as knowledge of Jesus' own preexistence.

An excellent example is the discourse Jesus is reported as having given in Mark 13:5-37. This passage has frequently been read as a prophetic oracle about "the last days" prior to Jesus' own return. Jesus warns his disciples that "many will come in my name and say, 'I am he!' and they will lead many astray" (Mk 13:6). He predicts that before these things will happen "the good news must first be proclaimed to all nations" (Mk 13:10). Prior to the end there will be a terrible time of tribulation: "For in those days there will be suffering, such as has not been from the beginning of the creation that God created until now," so that "if the LORD had not cut short those days, no one would be saved" (Mk 13:19-20). However, for the sake of God's elect, the days will be shortened, and the culmination will see " 'the Son of Man coming in clouds' with great power and glory," while "he will send out the angels, and gather his elect from the four winds, from the ends of the earth to the ends of heaven" (Mk 13:26-27).

I think it is fair to say that if one thinks Jesus is the divine Son of God or even if one thinks him merely to be God's supreme prophet and agent, it is reasonable to interpret this discourse as referring to future events that could not be known through natural insight alone. Orthodox believers naturally think that the prophetic utterance is a reliable one, though much of it is clearly yet to be ful-filled. Many critical historians, such as Albert Schweitzer, have interpreted the discourse as evidence that Jesus was suffering the delusion that the end of history was about to occur. Wright, however, thinks that this tradition of reading is "sim-ply mistaken" (*JVG* 341). Jesus is not speaking about the end of human history; nor is he speaking about his own second coming. (Both of these are things that a human being could not know about except through some kind of divine inspira-tion or revelation.) Instead, Wright says that Jesus is referring to his own impending visit to Jerusalem. It takes no special divine insight, of course, for Jesus to know what he intends to do.

The dramatic, apocalyptic character of the discourse is explained by Wright in the following manner. Jesus is discussing the future overthrow of Jerusalem, and he uses the apocalyptic language he chooses "to evoke the full resonances of Old Tes-tament prophecy and to invest the coming events with their full theological signifi-cance" (*JVG* 340). No special divine insight is needed to know that Jerusalem will be destroyed by the Romans, according to Wright, one needs only ordinary human shrewdness and political wisdom. For example, for Jesus to know that when Jerusa-lem fell there would be false messiahs "did not take much guessing" on the part of Jesus, since "at a time of great national crisis . . . there would always be those who would set themselves up as YHWH's anointed" (*JVG* 360). "The prediction in Mark 13.2 ('There will not be left here one stone upon another, that will not be thrown down.') is neither new nor unexpected. It is the sort of thing that many sec-tarian Jews of the time might well have thought or said" (*JVG* 344). All that we must assume in order to account for Jesus' predictions—which are, in Wright's view, about the destruction of Jerusalem by the Romans—is that Jesus had an accurate view that the Jewish people of his day were moving toward a rebellion against Rome and that Jesus had enough understanding of the military might of Rome to know that this revolt would prove disastrous. On Wright's view, Jesus invests these prognostications with theological significance, but no ascription of special supernatural aid is necessary to understand how the predictions them-selves could be made.

3. Jesus' self-understanding. Many other examples of this tendency to natu-ralize prophetic discourse in Wright could be given. Next, I wish to comment on the similar treatment that is given to Jesus' own self-understanding, Jesus' aware-ness of his own vocation. Here Wright comes close to openly committing himself to a naturalistic methodology:

"Awareness of vocation" is by no means the same thing as Jesus having the sort of "supernatural" awareness of himself, of Israel's god, and of the relation between the two of them, such as is often envisaged by those who, concerned to maintain a "high" christology, place it within an eighteenth-century context of implicit Deism where one can maintain Jesus' "divinity" only by holding some form of docetism. Jesus did not, in other words, "know that he was God" in the same way that one knows one is male or female, hungry or thirsty, or that one ate an orange an hour ago. His "knowledge" was of a more risky, but perhaps more significant, sort: like knowing one is loved. One cannot "prove" it except by living by it. (*JVG* 652-53)

This passage is noteworthy for a number of reasons.

It seems remarkable that Wright can know not only what Jesus believed about himself but the manner in which the knowledge was obtained and the degree of certainty he possessed. One cannot but wonder here whether or not the traditional practice of reading back into Jesus the characteristics of the historian and his or her friends is not happening again. Our age is certainly an age characterized by uncertainty, and we tend to admire individuals who maintain convictions in the face of intellectual doubts. Is this really a characteristic likely to be much in evidence in a first-century Palestinian Jew, to ask the kind of historical question Wright himself likes to pose?

That this passage is not an anomaly is seen from Wright's treatment of the agony of Jesus in Gethsemane. Without any real evidence that this is so, Wright speculates that the source of Jesus' suffering was his own anxiety that he might be deluded: "he must have known that he might have been deeply mistaken" (*JVG* 609). It is surely right that if I claimed God was acting through me to defeat "the satan," I would worry a lot about whether I was right. It is not clear to me, however, why Jesus, if he were indeed the divine Son of God, must necessarily be in the same boat. It seems to me that this move of Wright's is driven by a kind of methodological naturalism. Any knowledge Jesus may have had must have been obtained in the normal way, the way you and I obtain our knowledge. You and I would worry about whether we were right if we thought God had marked us out for such a special role; Jesus must have had the same kind of worries. This seems to me to be an application of Troeltsch's principle of analogy.

Wright's comment above about supernatural knowledge on the part of Jesus embodies the same kind of muddle we saw earlier in the way Wright described supernaturalism in general. Wright seems to think any claim that Jesus had supernatural power or that he was even a channel for supernatural power implies a deistic view of the universe, one in which God is not normally active in the world but intervenes from time to time. However much this may reflect the views of some misguided fundamentalists (to whom Wright may be reacting), it is an indefensible caricature of classical theism, which holds that though God is always present in the natural world through creative, conserving and providential activity, God can also act in special ways that point directly to his character and intentions.

The Resurrection: An Exception to Methodological Naturalism?

One possible exception to my claim that Wright implicitly follows a principle of methodological naturalism is his treatment of the resurrection of Jesus. Strictly speaking, there is almost no treatment of the resurrection in *Jesus and the Victory of God.* The subject comes up only at the end of the book and is given only a few paragraphs.

Nevertheless, there is a hint in these few paragraphs that the resurrection might be treated differently. Here, Wright tells us that "the relevance of Jesus . . . becomes radically different depending on whether one accepts or rejects the witness of the early church to his resurrection" (*JVG* 659). This statement is cryptic and might be taken in a number of ways. However, one possibility is that Wright is here hinting that in his promised sequel to *Jesus and the Victory of God* he will make the resurrection central to his account. All I can do is speculate at this point about what Wright intends to do. However, I hope that by this statement Wright is signaling an intention to view the resurrection in a way similar to the way traditional Christians viewed all of the miracles associated with Jesus (though of course traditional Christians also tended to give the resurrection unique significance). That is, it is possible that Wright intends to argue that the resurrection, as a miraculous event that must be of divine origin, could be seen as validating Jesus' mission, as declaring that Jesus "had in principle succeeded in his task" (*JVG* 660). If this conjecture about Wright's program is correct, it is a bit unclear why he should pour out such scorn earlier in the book on supernaturalists who see other miracles of Jesus as having a similar function.

What I find most interesting about the above quote is the idea that acceptance of the resurrection is a matter of accepting the witness of the early church. This might be taken as an admission that in this one case at least, the Christian is not limited to the conclusions of the critical historian. For one of the marks of such a critical historian, according to people like Troeltsch and Harvey, is that one never simply accepts the testimony of an authority, but does so only when critical history has investigated the matter and pronounced judgment. If it might be permissible simply to accept the testimony of the early church with respect to the resurrection of Jesus, then it appears it might be permissible to do the same thing for other aspects of the story of Jesus.

In any case, even if Wright does intend to give the resurrection a special treatment in his sequel, it is difficult to isolate the resurrection and treat it as an exception. If we insist that the stance of the critical historian is the only proper one to take toward the life of Jesus, then it seems this attitude should be extended toward the resurrection. If one rejects methodological naturalism and argues that historical evidence could support belief in the resurrection, then it appears the same should be said about other miracles, which could be understood as events that could only be viewed as divine actions and not simply as magic or mighty works. If one accepts methodological naturalism, then seemingly it would not be possible to base belief in the resurrection on a historical case. Rather, one would either have to reject belief in the resurrection or else have to say that belief is not based on critical historical results. In either case consistency would dictate that the same possibility be extended to other aspects of the life of Jesus. On the basis of the scanty remarks about the resurrection in *Jesus and the Victory of God*, it is not possible to say which way Wright will go in his promised sequel, though presumably as a clergyman, he will want to maintain belief in the resurrection on some basis.

Can Methodological Naturalism Be Theologically Justified?

Wright's remark that viewing Jesus as having supernatural power or insight leads to docetism might also be taken as implying a kind of theological justification for methodological naturalism when one is studying Jesus historically. I refer here to Wright's cryptic suggestion (quoted above) that those who interpret Jesus as saying or doing things that show supernatural power are misguidedly trying to defend Jesus' divinity, but in reality they fall into docetism (*JVG* 652-53). Should we say that those who attribute supernatural power to Jesus are docetists, perhaps unintentional ones? Surely not. A docetist is someone who denies the real humanity of Jesus. However, it in no way follows that because someone regards Jesus as possessing supernatural powers expressed through miracles or prophetic insight therefore Jesus' humanity is being denied or compromised. Perhaps this would be the case if someone said that Jesus were *only* capable of supernaturally qualified actions and not capable of any ordinary human ones, such as sleeping or eating, but that is surely not what the traditional Christian has in mind when Jesus is understood to have supernatural power. The docetist is someone who denies the humanity of Jesus; one does not become a docetist merely by affirming the divinity of Jesus. Docetism would follow from the recognition of supernatural power only if such powers were inconsistent with being human. Such a claim is manifestly implausible, however, since there are many prophets who have been believed to have performed miracles and enjoyed prophetic insights, such as Elijah, and no one thinks that one should question their humanness.

Although one cannot argue that one must be a methodological naturalist in order to avoid docetism, one might think that such a methodology is entailed by some theological commitments. Clearly, this is so. If, for example, one has (or believes one has) theological reasons for thinking that God would never perform a miracle, then it would appear reasonable to proceed as if miracles did not happen. I myself do not believe, however, that there are any good theological grounds for such a view.[13]

In particular I want to argue that a commitment to what is called "kenotic Christology" does not lead to any such methodology. The kenotic christologist believes that when the Second Person of the Trinity became incarnate and fully human, he divested himself of some of the classical theistic attributes such as omnipotence and omniscience in order to share fully in the limitations of our human condition. One might think that such a Christology, since it is committed to seeing Jesus as living as an ordinary human, would rule out miracles, prophetic insight or supernaturally mediated self-awareness. This would, however, be a mistake. The kenotic christologist by no means has to reject all exercise of supernatural power on the part of Jesus. Rather, the consistent kenoticist will regard the exercise of supernatural power on the part of Jesus as dependent on the power of God the Father, with whom the Son remains united and on whom the Son in his humanness is completely dependent. On the kenotic view, if Jesus performed miracles, he did so in ways similar to the way in which other prophets have done miracles, even though Jesus himself is more than a prophet.

Actually, as the above discussion implies, the whole discussion of Christology in this context is a bit of a red herring, since no claims to divinity follow directly from the exercise of supernatural powers. Many prophets and apostles have been alleged to have performed miraculous deeds and exercised supernatural insight—with no suspicion of any claim to divinity. The supernatural deeds and insights of Jesus, to the degree that they have apologetic value, have value as attesting that he is indeed a true prophet of God and that his claims are to be believed. It is only if those claims explicitly or implicitly lead to claims of divinity that the miracles have a logical tie to Christology.

Thus, if my neighbor performs apparent miracles, this would not by itself warrant my believing that my neighbor is divine. However, if my neighbor Joe claims to speak on behalf of God, the miracles would give me at least some reason to think he is speaking truthfully. Of course, if part of the content of what Joe says is that he has some special relation to God, or even is God, the miracles would then be relevant to the overall assessment of the claims. I myself would think that the miracles, even if well attested, would not be sufficient taken alone to warrant belief in Joe's divinity. However, they might nevertheless be an important, even necessary, part of any case to be made.

Is Methodological Naturalism a Valuable Tool for Christian Scholars?

I have argued that Wright seems committed, in practice, to a methodological naturalism. However, I now wish to make it clear that I do not see this claim as a *criticism* of Wright. To the contrary, it is partly his use of this method that makes his book interesting and valuable, both historically and theologically.

Methodological naturalism, as I conceive it, does involve a search for common ground of a sort. However, in an enterprise such as historical biblical scholarship, the common ground will necessarily be scanty; such common ground will be a kind of lowest common denominator, and such a stance is by no means neutral but is the home turf of the naturalist who thinks that this stance accurately captures the way things work in reality. One may well wonder why a Christian researcher would limit himself or herself to such common ground. I might, for example, think I have some knowledge relevant to the subject that is not shared by other researchers. Why should I not make use of such knowledge?

For some purposes, there is no good reason why I should not. However, if my goal is to engage my fellow researchers in a scholarly conversation and to possibly convince them of my views, or at least get them to think more favorably about those views, then I must appeal to considerations that will be effective for that task.

Methodological naturalism can then be viewed as analogous to a strategy employed by Christian philosophers, and for that matter secular philosophers too, a great deal of the time—the strategy of hypothetical thinking. As a Christian philosopher, I may believe that morality consists of objective obligations rooted in divine commands. Suppose, however, I am engaging in conversation some atheistic philosophers who are inclined to be moral relativists. I wish to argue that moral obligations are objective. I could attempt to convince them that morality is objective by changing their minds about God's reality. But suppose I think that is not very feasible, directly. I may then proceed to argue with them on their own grounds, by trying to show that even if we do not assume the existence of God, then it would still be reasonable to believe in objective moral obligations. By bracketing my belief in God's reality, I may hope to produce an argument they will find convincing, or at least one that will give them reasons to think differently about morality. I have no guarantees, of course. Common ground cannot always be found. If I fail to convince them, I should not think this failure necessarily means I do not know that moral obligations are real. But even if I think that this belief in moral objectivity is best grounded in a belief in God, I may still look for other reasons for the belief—reasons that could be convincing to an atheist or an agnostic. If I convince my atheist friends that moral obligations are indeed real and objective, then perhaps I may even then proceed to argue that they ought to consider the possibility that these obligations are grounded in the reality of God. Such a long-term hope is still compatible with a short-term methodological naturalism.

There is therefore nothing objectionable, and possibly a good deal to be gained, when believing Christians who are historical biblical scholars seek to show what kind of knowledge about Jesus can be achieved, even when one is limited to evidence that would be admissible to a naturalist. Wright's work is a good example of this, I think. For he tries to show, and I think makes a strong case, that even from the limited perspective of the methodological naturalist, one can rightly believe that Jesus made strong claims to be the Messiah, the Anointed One, who saw himself as engaged in a crucial battle with "the satan," a battle in which God's promises to Israel and the salvation of all human peoples were being decided. Jesus saw his own death as an atoning one in which God would win a great victory, and he saw this victory as one through which his followers would form a new and true Israel. Of course this is far from Chalcedon. But no one thinks that such later doctrinal developments were present from the beginning. The question is whether the church was right to draw the implications from the story that it gradually drew. A historical case such as Wright's offers, I think, a lot for the orthodox theologian who wishes to argue that the church was right to think through the meaning of Jesus' life, death and resurrection in the way that it did.

So I conclude that a historical study of Jesus employing methodological naturalism is not merely intellectually interesting. It is not only a case of seeing whether a lot can be done with skimpy tools, as when a logician tries to build an intricate system with just a few postulates. Nor is it simply like a weight lifter who attempts to hoist a heavy barbell with one hand tied behind his back as a demonstration of strength. Rather, methodological naturalism can be justified on several grounds. First, the method may be heuristically valuable. If we look on the story of Jesus in this purely "natural" way, we may see things we would otherwise miss or be inclined to misinterpret. For example, it seems likely to me that Wright is correct when he argues that at least some of the utterances in which Jesus has been thought to describe the second coming are in reality about his impending visit to Jerusalem. Maybe this hypothesis would not have occurred to Wright if he had not been proceeding methodologically in the way he did. Second, the method can be justified pragmatically. It is a recognized method that scholars in this field follow, and it seems plausible that Christians who wish to be part of the scholarly debate must be able to employ the method and actually do so in a skilled manner. Finally, since the method is one that enables one to engage non-Christian colleagues on common ground, it may make possible a historical case for matters crucial to Christian faith that has apologetic value.

The Limitations of Methodological Naturalism

Wright deserves then not criticism but rather praise for skillful use of methodological naturalism in developing a historical account of the life and death of Jesus of Nazareth. However, there are times when Wright appears to go beyond using this historical method to suggest a much stronger claim: that such a method is the best or even the only means of ascertaining the historical truth about Jesus of Nazareth. To use the categories developed earlier, he appears to go beyond type-two methodological naturalism to a type-one version. Perhaps Wright would not in reality endorse such a claim, but his rhetoric at times lends credence to it. In any case, whether Wright holds the view or not, it is important to see that this claim is far from obviously true; I would go so far as to say that from a Christian perspective it appears obviously false.

I here assume that those who hold orthodox Christian beliefs have certain historical beliefs as either part of those Christian beliefs or as direct implications of them. For example, someone who thinks that Jesus' death on the cross was an atonement for human sin must *eo ipso* believe that Jesus did indeed die on the cross. I take it as virtually certain that the overwhelming majority of Christians who have held such historical beliefs have not held them on the basis of critical, historical scholarship that conforms to the canons of methodological naturalism. This is completely obvious since such scholarship did not exist before roughly the nineteenth century and since then has been limited to a relatively small group of scholars and educated intellectuals.

If most Christians have not held their historical beliefs about Jesus on the basis of critical historical scholarship, on what basis have they held their beliefs? I believe the answer is that for the most part that they have relied on *testimony*. They have accepted the testimony of those who have told them the story contained in the Gospels, either in preaching or writing, or the testimony of the writers of the Gospels themselves. Hearing testimony and believing that testimony is of course one of the most basic ways human beings acquire beliefs and, I would argue, knowledge. To this very ordinary form of belief acquisition, two refinements should be added. Some theologians, notably including John Calvin, have insisted that when the testimony about the Gospel is believed, it is because of the work of the Holy Spirit, who adds an inner "witness" or "testimony" that confirms or strengthens the natural mechanism of believing another person. Others have emphasized that the testimony in question is one certified by the church, and this provides an added reason for belief on the part of those who consider the church to be a reliable authority in such matters. Obviously, there is no contradiction in holding that both the church and the Holy Spirit could function in this way so as to certify the testimony about Jesus.

Now if Jesus is a religiously significant individual and if the historical truth about Jesus is part of what is religiously significant—such that a person's religious life would be seriously damaged or impaired in some way for not knowing that historical truth—then it seems utterly implausible that historical critical study would be the only way of coming to know about such truths. For example, suppose that orthodox Christians are right in believing Jesus to be a divine Savior, and suppose that eternal life is to be found in believing in Jesus. It seems ridiculous to suppose that God would make eternal life dependent on understanding the historical truth about Jesus and, at the same time, to suppose that this historical truth is something that would only be discovered by a small group of scholars almost two thousand years after Jesus lived.

It seems likely then that if the historical truth about Jesus is truly religiously significant, critical historical study would not be the only means of discovering that truth. Indeed, it seems likely that some such method as Christians have traditionally followed would be far more likely as the normal route to such knowledge.

In *Jesus and the Victory of God*, Wright sometimes writes as if the true story of Jesus is only now being discovered for the first time, using the resources of critical history. However, it seems to me that this could only be true if the story is one that has no real religious significance. It is easy to imagine that there might be many details of the story of Jesus that are not religiously essential, and with respect to those, it might well be that the critical historian's methods are the preferred ones to employ to gain knowledge, though I am not sure that this will always be the case. With respect to what is truly religiously significant, however, think how improbable the following scenario is: Suppose Jesus was in fact God's Messiah who came to redeem Israel and, through the fulfillment of Israel's calling, also liberate the human race (as Wright himself seems to think Jesus saw himself), and yet none of his earliest followers or later ones truly understood him, until the whole matter was studied by critical historians in the twentieth century.

If I am right in my supposition that this is most unlikely, then from the viewpoint of Christian belief, the note of condescension and sometimes even contempt that Wright at times expresses toward those who rely on tradition seems unwarranted. He speaks very little about tradition as such but speaks quite a bit about what he terms "naive traditionalism" (e.g., *JVG* 81). Thinkers who look at the study of Jesus with self-conscious theological aims and motivations are pejoratively described as "pre-critical" (*JVG* 104). At times Wright seems to take satisfaction in developing interpretations of Jesus' actions and words that differ dramatically from those traditionally given by the church. In principle, it must be said that Wright could be correct; tradition can err, and even councils can be mistaken. However, it must be said that to the degree that Wright's reading of the narrative is absolutely original, it seems less probable that it could be true, insofar as the reading is seen as an attempt to describe the significance of Jesus' life in a way that is useful for orthodox Christian theology.

In the end I suspect that Wright does not really think his reading of the life of Jesus is so original as he suggests; I would guess he would want to see consistency with the teachings of the apostles, the biblical writers and early church. I certainly do not think it is genuinely different *in essence* from traditional views, and I mean that as praise. It may be that the implied reader and intended audience of the book are critical biblical scholars such as members of the Jesus Seminar who see orthodox conclusions as *prima facie* evidence that one is not being intellectually honest. Perhaps for such readers Wright wishes to say, "Look, I too am a tough-minded historical scholar willing to break fearlessly with theological orthodoxy." However, if this is what is going on, there is a danger that the rhetoric intended to appease such a reader will give a misleading impression to his other readers. If Wright's reading is truly completely original and the church has been mistaken about Jesus all along, it is hardly likely that the church can be what it claims to be—the people of God whom Jesus came to establish. Such a conclusion would surely be awkward to a clergyman such as Wright.

There is a difference, I believe, between theology and other academic disciplines with respect to the value of originality. The physicist or psychologist who comes up with an absolutely original yet powerful theory rightly takes pride in this accomplishment. It seems to me that originality cannot function in the same way or have exactly the same value for Christian theology. We do value originality in a theologian, but we do so, primarily I think, because the theologian we regard as original understands and articulates the same truths as earlier theologians but does so in a new way, or because she or he sees new implications in those truths or finds new ways of expressing them or applying them to contemporary problems. Originality with respect to such basic questions as the identity of Jesus would, however, be somewhat suspicious.

One might think that this criticism is misguided because I am judging Wright as a theologian when his own view is that history must be independent of theology. History must go its own way and let the theological chips fall where they may. This is correct, but one of the claims Wright wants to make is that this kind of autonomous historical study is ultimately beneficial for theology. For "history, especially the history of first-century Judaism, is the sphere where we find, at work to judge and to save, the God who made the world" (*JVG* 662).

I believe that Wright is both right and wrong about this, because of a confusion that bedevils the English word *history*. Everyone recognizes, and Wright certainly knows, that *history* can refer to "what actually happened" but also "the accounts given by historians about what happened." Now it is certainly true that history in the first of these two senses is crucial for Christian faith, and any older brother who would turn away from history in this sense has departed from the Father's true house. Christians should agree that to know God we must pay attention to the history of first-century Palestine in this sense of *history*. However, it does not follow from this that history in the second sense is essential for Christian faith, *especially if by "historical account" we mean "history done within the limits of methodological naturalism."* For Christians there is no reason to think that the historical accounts about Jesus produced by this method, legitimate and valuable as they may be for pragmatic and apologetic purposes, give us our best access to the historical events in first-century Palestine as they actually occurred.

Wright is certainly correct to say that "we must not back away from history, or seek to keep the theological handbrake on to prevent history running away with us" (*JVG* 662). However, he makes this remark in the course of a discussion of critical history as practiced since the Enlightenment. It is simply not clear to me why Christians should agree that the only thing qualifying as history (in the sense of a serious account of what happened) should be this kind of history.

This means the drumbeat of criticism that Wright maintains toward historians who allow theological insights to shape their historical work is unwarranted. If one thinks that one knows certain theological truths about Jesus, why should not that knowledge be employed as background knowledge that shapes the way the historical evidence is interpreted? Of course such a strategy may not be valuable apologetically or when one is seeking common ground with non-Christians; in that case a strategy of methodological naturalism may be more valuable. But suppose one is not doing apologetics but is merely wishing to discover the truth? In that case, why not make use of any insights one has, regardless of the source?

I am sure that Wright advocates this autonomy of history over against theology because he fears a situation in which the theologian "is allowed to inflict his or her point of view on to unwilling material" (*JVG* 117). The historian's work cannot be "reduced to terms of the historian's own antecedent beliefs or worldview" (*JVG* 117). This is a reasonable concern. Wright is certainly correct to say that a genuine historian must be open to evidence such that "the observer has to be prepared to change his or her mind" (*JVG* 117). However, this is not a good reason to isolate history from theology or to exclude theological insights when one is doing history. Wright's own epistemology specifically admits that historical research cannot be done in a positivistic fashion that insulates it from questions of worldview. Furthermore, he rejects both the inductivist account of history as founded on atomic "facts" and even the simple "verificationist" and "falsificationist" views, because he sees that theories are embedded in webs and that the plausibility of a theory is related to its overall coherence and explanatory power relative to all of the data. I do not see any principled reason why one could not make progress toward historical truth by taking account of all that one knows, including one's theological knowledge. Nor do I see why Wright should deny this. Tactically, he may be wise to argue on the grounds that he chooses to defend. However, it is important not to allow a concession made for the sake of discussion to become a presupposition.

Eleven

A Historiographical Response to Wright's Jesus

LUKE TIMOTHY JOHNSON

*A*SSESSING N. T. WRIGHT'S *JESUS AND THE VICTORY OF GOD* IN ANY SPECIFIC respect is daunting for a number of reasons. The most obvious is that its 662 pages offer a portrait of Jesus that is both highly detailed and extensively, perhaps even exhaustively, argued. Wright's exposition, furthermore, is intricately interconnected at every part. The explanation of each part depends on the overall construal, while the overall construction evokes in support the steadily mounting bits of evidence that have been adduced. Wright's approach is thoroughly synthetic rather than analytic. He thinks of his procedure in terms of testing a hypothesis (*JVG* 131-33). Others might think that Wright's search for a singular and simple explanation runs the risk of circularity and totalization. In either case, his presentation more easily invites affirmation or dissent with regard to the whole than it does a critical assessment of the parts.

Adding to the difficulty of response, the volume under consideration represents only the second part of a six-volume project whose overall target is purportedly the question of "God" in the New Testament. Evaluating Wright's historical reconstruction of Jesus must take into account the argument already established in *The New Testament and the People of God* (as his constant references to that volume as support for positions in the present volume make obvious), but in principle it ought also to consider the further stages, which have yet to appear. The publication of *What Saint Paul Really Said*[1] amplifies somewhat the brief sketch of Paul found in *The New Testament and the People of God,* but the interdependent character of Wright's argument means that the evaluation of any portion apart from the whole is hazardous.

In this essay I take up Wright's historiographical method and practice in his two major volumes already in print, because these are so critical to the fair evaluation of his overall project. It is in considering how he goes about doing history that the most searching questions might be raised concerning the adequacy of his reconstruction.

Placing Wright's Project

Recognition is due to Wright's accomplishment: the project thus far completed is marked not only by size and ambition but also by great energy and intelligence. This is, by any measure, a significant contribution to the entire historical Jesus debate. Nor is it the case that Wright develops his argument in a scholarly vacuum. His engagement with other scholars is lively if sometimes uneven. He gives a great deal of attention to what he calls the "traffic on the Wredebahn," represented by the Jesus Seminar, Marcus Borg and John Dominic Crossan (*JVG* 28-82). In light of this, his failure give anything other than passing recognition to John P. Meier's monumental historical Jesus project[2] is all the more striking and puzzling, particularly when Wright agrees with Meier in significant ways (e.g., the eschatological character of Jesus' ministry) and, especially, when in some cases (e.g., the miracle stories) Meier's general discussions are so rich and useful. In contrast, Wright's debt to the late Ben F. Meyer's work on *The Aims of Jesus* is frequently and gratefully noted.[3]

Wright's work is also remarkably consistent in its adherence to a theoretical model. The model was worked out in part two of *The New Testament and the People of God* (31-144) and is followed faithfully in Wright's reconstruction (see *JVG* 125-44). This model seeks to cover both the complexity of the data and yet retain simplicity (*NTPG* 99-100). Simplicity is achieved primarily by a heavy emphasis on the "continuity of the person" or "consistency in thought" (*NTPG* 107-9). Wright's model demands coherence between story, symbol and praxis in an individual as well as in a specific culture, and it assumes that questions, controversies, aims and intentions equally reveal a consistent internal logic (*JVG* 139). The strength of the model is its simplicity and clarity. The weakness, I will argue, is that simplicity is achieved at the cost of a more adequate reading of the evidence. But Wright cannot be faulted for failing to present his theory from the start.

Wright's portrait of Jesus, finally, has considerable plausibility. He follows Albert Schweitzer rather than William Wrede in regarding the Synoptic Gospels as fundamentally reliable sources for the historical Jesus, and he follows Schweitzer rather than the Jesus Seminar in taking "Jewish eschatology as the key to understanding Jesus" (*JVG* 123).[4] He differs from Schweitzer primarily in his this-worldly, political understanding of Jewish eschatology. Wright follows E. P. Sanders in taking Jesus' praxis as the starting point for historical reconstruction and agrees with Sanders on the pivotal importance of Jesus' symbolic action in the temple.[5] He differs from Sanders primarily in giving considerable credit to the Gospel accounts of Jesus' conflicts with Pharisees and in attaching such controversies to a different political agenda. At the very least—and this is no small thing—Wright convincingly demonstrates that the pieces of the Gospel tradition dismissed by the New Quest can be used as the basis of an equally plausible construal of Jesus sponsored by the Third Quest. As mention of his scholarly antecedents indicates, Wright's portrait of Jesus is significant not so much for its novelty as for its reclamation of a reading currently less in favor and for its attempt to secure that reading by showing how it makes better sense of all the data.

Despite the different result, however, Wright's project resembles those of other Jesus Questers in two critical respects. First, the choice of pattern very much determines the selection and interpretation of the pieces. This does not, on the surface, appear to be the case on either side: the New Quest makes a great commotion about its scientific process of isolating the authentic pieces of the Jesus tradition analytically and then moving to the resulting portrait, whereas Wright is clear about his use of the pattern of the prophet and does not appear to make any real systematic discrimination among traditions with regard to reliability. In both cases, however, appearances deceive. The Lukan parable of the prodigal is a good example. It is the master parable for Robert W. Funk, the pure representation of the vision of Jesus, even though it does not meet any of the fabled criteria for authenticity.[6] But it is equally important for Wright not because it has passed any tests but because it can be read (at least to his satisfaction) as an allegory of the same master-script that Jesus both follows and enunciates—the script of Israel's exile coming to an end in the triumph of God (*JVG* 125-31).

A second way in which the New Quest, as represented by Funk and his associates and the Third Quest, as represented by Wright, agree is on a set of uncritical assumptions concerning history.[7] Both have remarkable confidence in the
historian's ability to move from literary judgments to historical conclusions when
working with ancient sources. The New Questers think they can dissect sayings'
material into discrete slices. Wright thinks he can align the sayings of Jesus with
specific prophetic passages in such fashion as to reveal Jesus' own intentions.
Both tend to elide the critical distinction between historical reconstructions—
always a fragile and creative task entirely dependent on the accidents of source
survival—and "what really happened." In Wright's case, this manifests itself most
in language that declares what Jesus hoped to accomplish, as though tentative
guesses in the direction of the probable goals of reported actions could lead,
largely by way of repetition, to confident assertions concerning Jesus' specific and
coherent aims (e.g., *JVG* 132, 163, 167, 309 n. 246, 604-11).

Finally, both Wright and the New Questers are confident that history has
implications for theology—that is, history has a normative function. It is not
Funk but Wright who declares, "If Jesus was as Reimarus, or Schweitzer, or
Sanders, have portrayed him, then the church needs at the very least to revise its
faith quite substantially" (*NTPG* 22). Wright is even more insistent than any of
the New Questers that history and theology must cohere: "I wish in the present
work to share the concern of [Questers like Reimarus] for rigorous historical
construction, and also to work towards a new integration of history and theology
which will do justice, rather than violence, to both" (*JVG* 122).

In his preface, he declares, "At every stage I found myself coming face to face
with historical problems, and (since I could not abandon my basic Christian beliefs
without becoming a totally different person) with the question of how, if at all, history and belief might cohere"; and he concludes that in the process of his investigations, "my view of Jesus within his historical context has substantially developed
and changed. So, *inevitably*, has my understanding of what Christianity itself actually is, and the nature of my belief in it" (*JVG* xv, emphasis added). Note the word
inevitably: in the "integration" of history and theology, it appears that historical
construction is the dominant factor to which theology must conform.

In the conclusion to the present book, Wright states, "A truly first-century
Jewish theological perspective would teach us to recognize that history, especially
the history of first-century Judaism, is the sphere where we find, at work to judge
and to save, the God who made the world" (*JVG* 662). The statement is remarkable on a number of counts, not least in its understanding of God's revelation, as

well as for its easy equation between "history as scholars' historical reconstruction of the past" and "history as what happened in the past." But I cite it here simply to note how unabashedly Wright asserts the fundamentally theological character of historiography on Jesus, which, for him, has high stakes: "if [New Testament theology] does not contain the decisive proclamation of Jesus, it cannot itself be the be-all and end-all of the divine revelation, the ultimate locus of authority, the 'thing' that all the study of the New Testament is bent towards finding" (*NTPG* 23, emphasis original).

As I have pointed out in another place, these assumptions about history and historiography stand in need of serious challenge.[8] At the heart of the historical Jesus debate are the epistemological issues that are suppressed or bracketed by Third and New Questers alike:

1. the limits of historiography as a way of knowing
2. the need to define what is meant in any specific instance by the "historical"
3. the non-normative character of historical reconstruction apart from the decisions of contemporary communities

Unless and until Questers of any stripe seriously engage the epistemological challenge, conceptual confusion and methodological imprecision will continue to haunt the entire enterprise.

Historiographical Comments

It is tempting—but impossible—to take on Wright's historiographical practices in detail, particularly since the sheer length of his argument may well tempt other readers to leave unattended its major weaknesses. In a review of *The New Testament and the People of God*, I pointed out several traits that were already problematic in that volume, above all the tendency to create an artificially unified worldview out of the complex world of first-century Judaism.[9] That tendency is even more prominent in *Jesus and the Victory of God*, as it necessarily must be, if Wright is to follow the logic of his model. Readers need to be aware, however, of the fallacy of moving from the observation that certain prophetic and Second Temple texts contain a theme concerning exile and God's victory to the empirical claim that "in Jesus' day many, if not most, Jews, regarded the exile as still continuing" (*JVG* 126; see also xvii, 445). One cannot simply move from the presence of a literary theme (even a frequent one) found in literature that happens to have been preserved to a shared psychology among a populace; above all, one cannot make an empirical claim that such an outlook was present among "many, if not most, Jews" in Jesus' day.

A handy checklist for the errors in historiographical argumentation found in Wright's work is David Hackett Fischer's *Historians' Fallacies*,[10] which I was reading concurrently with my study of Wright's *Jesus and the Victory of God*. Fischer does not provide a complete compendium, but he seeks to encourage better thinking among historians by noting the sorts of errors in logic made by famous practitioners of the craft. Fischer would have termed Wright's illicit elision from the literary to the empirical as one of two forms of fallacy—either the "aesthetic fallacy" (if it works logically, it must have happened factually) or the fallacy of generalization he calls "statistical sampling" (if some people thought this way, everyone must have thought this way).[11]

Another form of erroneous historical logic identified by Fischer is the "black and white fallacy," which he defines as the "misconstruction of vague terms" either by obscuring differences or artificially sharpening them. The form this fallacy takes in Wright is in his habit of forming of false alternatives. "If Jesus is not the last prophet," says Wright, "he is a false prophet" (*JVG* 364). Really? Are those truly the only alternatives available? More precisely, Wright has here committed the fallacy of the excluded middle or "false dichotomy."[12]

Similarly, after stating that "most first century Jews would have seen themselves as still, in all sorts of senses, 'in exile,'" Wright continues, "I would ask critics to face the question: would any serious-thinking first-century Jew claim that the promises of Isaiah 40—66, or of Jeremiah, Ezekiel, or Zechariah, had been fulfilled?" (*JVG* xvii). Even if we refrain from asking which of the many promises and predictions Wright has in mind, we must still note that he excludes the possibility that the very *issue* of fulfilling these promises may not have been posed by most Jews in the first place, not least because they did not inhabit the eschatological story line that he has made normative.

Perhaps the most egregious example of black-and-white fallacy is the way Wright tends to caricature any understanding of religion that is not, by his definition, political. On the same page, he contrasts the "contours of second-Temple Judaism" to the "bland and anachronistic landscape of moralism," and he opposes a "claim about eschatology" to "a piece of 'teaching' about 'religion' or 'morality,'. . . the dissemination of a timeless truth" (*JVG* 433). His favorite negative epithet is, in fact, "timeless" (see *JVG* 650), indicating once more how "history" in this work is not only one mode of knowing but an entire value system already heavy laden with theological significance (cf. *JVG* 122).

Earlier, Wright dismisses the view that Jesus might have taught "a different sort of religion, namely, an interior spiritual sort" in this fashion: "This is clearly no good. If it were true, Jesus would have been simply incomprehensible, a teacher of abstract and interior truths to a people hungry for God to act within history. The people were asking for bread and freedom, not thin air" (*JVG* 92); and, a few pages later, "in such a world, to be non-political is to be irrelevant" (*JVG* 98). Now these statements are patently disconfirmed by much ancient evidence, most obviously in the many forms of Gnostic spirituality within Hellenism, Judaism and Christianity. They also show circularity in argumentation.[13] Not only does he caricature the religion of the interior as "thin air" but he unfairly suggests that such a religious posture is less "political" than one preoccupied with social arrangements, when in fact, the Epicurean withdrawal from public in the name of a quietist piety could be regarded as having significant political implications (see Plutarch *Against Colotes*). More striking still, these citations show that the issue for Wright appears to be less whether Jesus did or did not do something than whether it has matched Wright's understanding of what he *should* have done in order to be a politically relevant—and therefore, in his judgment, religiously significant—figure of the first century.

The notion that the majority of Jews still thought of themselves as "somehow in exile" and that all "authentic Jews" were searching for a restoration of Israel on the historical (that is, political) plane is central to Wright's entire reconstruction. He states in his preface that he is "not attempting to reduce everything to a single theme" but that he is using the term exile as "a shorthand" for the "expectation that Israel's god would once again act *within her history*" (*JVG* xviii, emphasis original). I pause here first to observe how the phrase "God acting in history" works well rhetorically but—as shown by Rudolf Bultmann's famous response to Oscar Cullmann's *Christ and Time*—is conceptually very fuzzy.[14] More to the point, Wright's subsequent use of exile exemplifies what Fischer terms the "fallacy of ambiguity," defined as "the use of a word or an expression which has two or more possible meanings, without sufficient specification of which meaning is intended."[15] Precisely because the term functions as a kind of symbolic shorthand, Wright is able to draw all kinds of equations and inferences that a more precise usage might disallow. Thus, his discussion of the forgiveness of sins (*JVG* 268-74) might just barely be brought within the theme of "return from exile," but it is neither a necessary part of that theme nor explicable only in terms of that theme.

I conclude these comments on Wright's historiographic practices with his treatment of the Pharisees (*NTPG* 181-203; *JVG* 369-442). In the Gospel accounts, the Pharisees obviously play a key role as opponents of Jesus over matters of the law. They neither express nor are given any specific eschatological views. If they consider themselves, as did "most Jews in Jesus' day," as still in exile, the Gospels do not say how. Neither does the Jewish historian Josephus—our other major source of knowledge of the Pharisees—emphasize their eschatology, except to distinguish them from Sadducees with respect to their belief in the resurrection. Josephus mostly stresses the Pharisees' concern for the strict observance of the laws, thereby agreeing with the Gospels as well as with Paul, who is our only first-hand Pharisaic voice of the period before the war of 66-70 C.E.

If all this evidence is taken at face value, then the Gospel accounts make good sense. The Pharisees appear in the stories concerning them fairly much as they are described by Josephus, the disputes over the observance of Torah fit within a context of intra-Jewish dispute over the meaning of allegiance to God, and the opposition between Jesus and the Pharisees could well have escalated to a point where he was vulnerable to serious criticism and worse. In none of this would there be a need for diverging eschatological visions or competing political agendas.

Wright, however, is particularly given to that fallacy Fischer calls "the fallacy of one-dimensional man."[16] In this case the one dimension is political. Authentic Judaism must also be a political Judaism. The Gospels must therefore be read against the backdrop of a revisionist view of the Pharisees and of Wright's own conviction that everything Jesus said and did must fit within a specific eschatological script. Following Jacob Neusner's argument that the Pharisees began in politics and ended in piety,[17] Wright gathers all the evidence from Josephus of Pharisaic involvement in anti-Roman activity before 135 C.E. Fair enough. It's not a great deal, but it's some. It should be pointed out, however, that there is no connection drawn in the sources between such activity and any Pharisaic ideology. In other words, the involvement of Pharisee X in a struggle against Pilate may or may not have been because he was a Pharisee. It may equally be the case that Rioter Z was a choleric and revolutionary fellow who also happened to be a Pharisee. But for Wright, all human activity must flow consistently from some group ideology or story. Any resistance to Rome by a Pharisee must therefore represent a Pharisaic political posture.

Wright then takes the tensions between the House of Shammai and the House of Hillel within the Pharisaic movement[18] also in political terms, with the stricter Shammaites now representing an even stronger line of resistance to Rome than the Hillelites. Once more, note the elision: being stricter in *halachah* must equal a more resistant political posture as well. Then, Wright takes the usual assumption, that the House of Shammai was more numerous and powerful before 70 C.E. than the House of Hillel, to argue the Pharisees as a whole during the time of Jesus were so hard-line against Rome that they were virtually equivalent to Zealots. Finally, since all praxis must flow consistently from a story, the Pharisees can be seen as sponsoring a restoration from exile that was actively resistant to Rome, not only ritually but if necessary also by force.

Having (literally) created this portrait of the Pharisees, Wright can then portray the conflicts between them and Jesus in terms of rival political programs for the restoration from exile. Jesus' inclusionary ministry is one of passive resistance and nonviolence, involving the reinterpretation of the social symbols of Judaism. The Pharisees advance a program of restoration that is exclusionary and confrontational, willing to exercise violence in order to protect the traditional understanding of symbols and restore the kingdom to Israel. Since the conflicts between Jesus and the Pharisees involved politics from the start, it is much easier to understand the conflicts between such political programs as leading to a political resolution through a choreographed state execution.

As I stated from the start, Wright has managed to construct a plausible scenario. But historiography—as Wright himself recognizes—must move from the plausible (it is possible and it makes sense) to the probable (there is a stronger reason for thinking it happened this way and not some other way), and the only way to the probable is through the assessment of specific historical evidence. In his presentation of the Pharisees, I would argue that Wright has stretched the evidence very far indeed, making a secondary element in one source (Josephus) into the dominant and defining element of the Pharisees. In the process, Wright is forced to conclude that *all* of our sources—Josephus, the Gospels, the Talmud and presumably also Paul—have, for reasons of their own, suppressed this political dimension (*NTPG* 202).

In short, at some critical junctures, Wright has taken those pieces of evidence that fit his overall schema and rejected or reinterpreted the pieces that don't. Thus he says concerning Josephus' emphasis on the Pharisees' belief in the resurrection, "This belief, however, is not merely to do with speculation about a future life after death. As we can see from some of the early texts which articulate it, is bound up with the desire for a reconstituted and restored Israel" (*NTPG* 200). Note how slippery this is: if the resurrection is "not merely to do" with the future life, it nevertheless certainly does at least have much to do with it! Josephus, furthermore, does not connect this belief to a hope for political restoration.

And the texts that Wright claims to be "bound up with" a restored Israel (Ezek and 2 Macc) are not specifically Pharisaic. In 2 Maccabees, furthermore, the specific passages dealing with the resurrection of the Maccabean martyrs (2 Macc 6—7) are not in the least connected to a this-worldly restoration of Israel's political fortunes.

Historians must—and often do—stretch the limits of evidence in order to find meaningful patterns or to test hypotheses. But they must expect to be challenged if they do it on this scale. Wright relies on supposition, tenuous links and possible combinations for his construction. But positive evidence is lacking where he most needs it. He has not made the historical case concerning the Pharisees. Instead, he has committed what Fischer calls "the historian's fallacy," which is the tendency to assume that what the historian knows the subjects of inquiry also must have known and acted upon as well.[19]

Suppose we grant that each and every Pharisee espoused the ideological views Wright ascribes to the Pharisees as a whole and that each and every Pharisee acted upon these views with utter consistency, as part of a coherent political program (and if we grant this, we are granting more than any serious historian should). We would by no means thereby grant that each and every Pharisee thereby also knew that this was what they were doing—not to mention that the Pharisees could recognize in Jesus' symbolic actions a political program that was in some ways akin but in other ways inimical and threatening to theirs—so that all of the Pharisees responded to Jesus on this basis and this basis alone.

Likewise, suppose we granted that Jesus had the entire eschatological scenario ascribed to him by Wright in his head at every moment, that he acted consistently with that scenario in all his actions and that he even *knew* that this was what he was doing. We could by no means thereby allow that Jesus also knew *their* program in detail and that he shaped his own program consciously as a counter to that of the Pharisees, so that it shared their dream of restoration but eschewed their violent methods.

Wright has the characters in the Gospels acting out a script that was available to none of them because it has only been constructed by contemporary scholars. It would have been far better if he had heeded his own salutary warning:

> We have no means of knowing whether Caiaphas would have been aware of the speculations on this point which we have already studied. (We may remind ourselves that we do not know who in the first century read which non-biblical books; also, that there may have been dozens or even hundreds of texts familiar then

and subsequently lost). Nor do we have any idea whether Jesus had himself been influenced by the non-biblical texts we have studied, or whether his own use was original to himself, albeit parallel to others roughly contemporary. (*JVG* 643)

A good reminder, needing only the addition of "biblical writings" to make it adequate. Yet Wright proceeds to ignore his own warning in his ever more elaborate speculations about what might have been. The length of his argument, with its insistent repetition of points that have not been demonstrated but only asserted, places Wright in proximity to that form of "fallacy of substantive distraction" Fischer lists under arguments *ad Verecundiam* ("appeal to authority"), namely, "a thesis which is sustained by the length of its exposition."[20]

The Gospels and Christian Origins

I move now to a substantive review of two elements in Wright's project that are interconnected and critical to the evaluation of his historical Jesus. The first is his relatively uncritical use of the Gospels as sources; the second is his (so far) minimalist view of the resurrection.

1. The Gospels as sources. In *The New Testament and the People of God* (371-443), Wright provides his most sustained account of the compositions in the New Testament, under the (not surprising) rubric of "stories in early Christianity," treating in turn the four Gospels, Paul and Hebrews before considering form criticism. Although he considers some basic themes in these materials, his single organizing thesis is that they all represent subversions of Israel's shared story. In other words, his partial survey of New Testament literature serves mainly to make a point that no one would dispute, namely that these compositions represent reinterpretations of the symbolic world of Torah. What Wright does *not* do in this section is consider the difficult critical issues concerning literary relationships between the sources, nor does he assess the difficulties their respective forms of the "story" present for historical reconstruction. He spends considerable time demonstrating what needs no proof and no time dealing with what most requires attention.

At the beginning of *The New Testament and the People of God*, Wright asserts that "Jesus' own theological beliefs cannot be read off the surface of the text" (22), a statement that appears to respect the difficulties of getting at Jesus' ideas and motivations through the evangelists' literary representations. Subsequent statements, however, move in another direction. He insists that the Synoptic writers considered themselves to be writing a "history of Jesus" (*NTPG* 397) in which the perspective of the resurrection was not determinative (*NTPG* 398).

This history of Jesus, furthermore, was of a special sort; the early church "told Israel-stories about him" (*NTPG* 401), and the Gospels "are, in fact, Jewish-style biographies, designed to show the quintessence of Israel's story played out in a single life. . . . The Gospels are therefore the story of Jesus *told as the story of Israel in miniature*" (*NTPG* 402). Yet, "the evangelists' theological and pastoral programme has in no way diminished their intent to write about Jesus of Nazareth" (*NTPG* 403). In these statements, Wright seems intent on maintaining the character of the Gospels as accurate historical records basically unaffected by literary shaping, while at the same time he is insisting that they tell the story of Jesus as the story of Israel in miniature.

The only way these tensions can be reconciled is if Jesus himself was following a scriptural script such as Wright has proposed and if the Gospels are "performances" of that basic script. But to suppose this is to ignore the most obvious thing about the Gospels: they not only place the emphasis differently, they are truly different scripts. If Wright wants to avoid the deconstructive path of the New Questers and work with the New Testament compositions as stories, then he must deal with each of their stories in all its specificity, *before* seeing how some historical script might underlie them.

Just as his analysis of sources consisted simply in assertions supportive of his central thesis, Wright fails to supply a rationale for the way he actually uses the New Testament as evidence for his historical reconstruction. Why, for example, has he made no use of the historical evidence in Paul's letters concerning the human Jesus? Even more pertinently, why has he not dealt with John as a source for the historical Jesus? In his preface, Wright admits that his reconstruction "has been conducted almost entirely in terms of the synoptic tradition," but he provides no reason why he has not even considered John's possible use. I will return to this point, for Wright's plea that he omitted John in the interest of brevity and his hope that he might be able to work with John in the future simply do not suffice (*JVG* xvi).

In his use of the Synoptics themselves, moreover, Wright appears to be bound by no consistent principle of selection or use. He relieves himself of the necessity of taking differences between accounts seriously by appealing to the premise that stories circulated in oral tradition in slightly different forms (*JVG* 133-36). He can construct major parts of his thesis by the use of one of the Gospels without seriously taking that composition's literary and religious interests into account. Note, for example, it is Luke-Acts that provides Wright with the framework for his presentation of Jesus as prophet—the theme is much less developed in the other Synoptics. It is

Matthew's Sermon on the Mount that he takes as his text for Jesus' teaching, rather than Luke's Sermon on the Plain, even though large sections of that discourse are clearly peculiar to Matthew. It is Mark's apocalyptic discourse that he takes as Jesus' version, even though Luke's differs in significant ways. He provides no reason why he follows now one Gospel and now another; indeed, he fails even to acknowledge that this is his procedure.

More disturbing is his sometimes casual assessment of material. See again the basic prophetic mindset he attributes to Jesus. After listing the passages referring to Jesus as a prophet (*JVG* 164-65), Wright notes that these include statements from triple tradition—Luke, Matthew and John. He does not state why in this case John's evidence is significant. Then he claims that "apart from Acts 3.22 there is nothing in the New Testament, outside the gospels, about Jesus as a prophet." Actually, Acts 7:37 could be added, as could Revelation 19:10. Wright then asserts that although the Gospels have a "Moses-typology," they have only tangential allusion to the specific idea of a "prophet like Moses" (*JVG* 166) In fact, however, John's Gospel has a specific and important "prophet like Moses" theme (Wayne A. Meeks' important monograph is missing from Wright's bibliography),[21] and the most substantial scholarship on Luke-Acts in the past thirty years has demonstrated just how central the theme of the prophet like Moses is to Luke's work.[22] The point here is that Wright's assessment of the data—and above all his failure to reckon with the specific compositional tendencies of the sources—undercuts his confident assertion that "we are here in touch with firmly authentic tradition, preserved against all the tendencies that may be presumed to have been at work" (*JVG* 165-66).

At times Wright will take the specific wording in a specific Gospel passage as a critical clue to Jesus' intentions. On Mark 13, for example, he writes, "The scriptural background is in fact threefold, and very instructive for *what we must hypothesize as the mindset of Jesus, reusing Israel's prophetic heritage, and retelling its story, consistently with his entire set of aims*" (*JVG* 349, emphasis added; see the entire argument in detail, *JVG* 349-60). At other times, he can ignore the clear statement of the source in favor of his own reading. Thus, although the Synoptics clearly identify John with Elijah, Wright insists that "Jesus adopts the style of, and consciously seems to imitate, Elijah" (*JVG* 167), even though his evidence for this is drawn only from the stories in Luke that all scholars recognize as specifically Lukan redaction. Wright treats the Gospels as reliable reports of Jesus' actions and words and intentions when they agree with his thesis; when they do not, he ignores or corrects them in light of the master story that Jesus "must" have been following.

2. Christian origins. Corresponding to Wright's inconsistency with regard to the sources is his minimalist understanding of the resurrection. I do not mean to suggest that the resurrection is less than critical for Wright; he agrees with Sanders that Jesus' followers would not have survived longer than those of John without the resurrection (*JVG* 110). The resurrection was "the only reason they came up with for supposing that Jesus was anything other than a dream that might have come true but didn't" (*JVG* 659). The relevance of Jesus, continues Wright, depends entirely on what view one takes of the resurrection. I call his view "minimalist" because Jesus' resurrection is described primarily as the resuscitation of Jesus as an individual, rather than an eschatological event affecting his followers as well, and as something that served to ratify who Jesus already was rather than cause a fundamental process of interpretation of his paradoxical life and death: "The resurrection thus vindicates *what Jesus was already believed to be*" (*NTPG* 400, emphasis original). Wright clearly emphasizes continuity, rather than discontinuity, between the earthly ministry of Jesus and the resurrection.

Wright's understanding of the Gospel accounts and of the resurrection comes together in the statement at the end of this book, which comes as close as anything to addressing the transition between Jesus and the faith of the church:

> But if he was an eschatological prophet/Messiah, announcing the kingdom and dying in order to bring it about, the resurrection would declare that he had in principle succeeded in his task, and that his earlier redefinitions of the coming kingdom had pointed to a further task awaiting his followers, that of *implementing* what he had achieved. (*JVG* 660, emphasis original)

Once more, then, continuity. But is this, in fact, what we find in our earliest evidence concerning Christian convictions about Jesus?

It is impossible to review all the New Testament evidence here, but it can be stated with considerable confidence that the New Testament compositions apart from the Synoptics show few traces of continuity with Jesus' understanding of his mission (as Wright sketches it). In *What Saint Paul Really Said*, Wright presents a maximal case for such continuity, depending heavily on Romans and portions of Galatians and Philippians.[23] And even in these letters (which do not constitute all of Paul) the evidence is stretched uncomfortably to fit the thesis that Jesus and Paul were reading from the same scriptural script concerning God's triumph.

Most of Paul, and most of the New Testament literature in general, focuses on Jesus as the risen Lord, that is, as the powerful source of life and the victor over the cosmic forces that hold humans captive to sin and death. These writings do not slight Jesus' humanity in the least. Jesus' humanity is significant, however, not because of what he said or did as a prophet of Israel but because of how he revealed God's reconciling work for humans in the pattern of his life. It is not the prophetic vision of Jesus that is cited as normative; it is his character as the obedient son who gave his life in service to others. When Paul refers to "the mind of Christ" (1 Cor 2:16), he gives no indication that he means Jesus' understanding of Israel's story and how he was to bring it to completion; Paul means, instead, an attitude or disposition of heart that expressed itself in self-donative service. And if one were to ask Paul whether it were more important to know where they were in the story line of God's triumph in history or to live lives worthily of God in imitation of Jesus, Paul's answer would emphatically be to focus not on what is next but on what should be done now. And if this is the case with Paul—who does after all, maintain a passionate connection to Israel as a people and a lively sense of God's eschatological victory—it is even more the case in the other New Testament epistolary literature. The risen Lord is worshiped as the source of eternal life for all who believe in him; his humanity is the pattern for obedient faith in God.

Wright could object to this by observing that this epistolary literature was addressed primarily to Gentile believers and, in any case, was preoccupied with the implementation of what Jesus had achieved rather than with the memory of his mission and vision. It is the Gospels, he might say, that provide the definitive evidence for a clean continuity between Jesus and the church's understanding of him. But precisely here is where Wright's lack of a critical analysis of the Gospels, and above all his failure to account for John, weakens his argument. If one follows the two-source solution to the Synoptic Problem (the literary relationship between Matthew, Mark and Luke), then Mark's story line is the basic source for both Luke and Matthew (to which Q offers sayings material as a supplement but not an alternative story line). If one prefers Matthean priority, then Luke used Matthew, and Mark epitomized them. In either case, we have basically only *one* "Synoptic witness" to the portrayal of Jesus in Wright, not three. The question therefore becomes urgent: why should this version be preferred to John as providing historical access to the words, deeds and even self-consciousness of Jesus? The question becomes even more acute when it is noted that there are at least as many links between John and Paul as there are between Paul and the Synoptics. Just as with Wright's standardized "story of Israel" the complexity of first-century Judaism is reduced to a single eschatological strand, so with Wright's "historical Jesus" the complexity of witnesses to Jesus is reduced to a single Synoptic strand. And *that* strand, as I have indicated, has been reduced even further by Wright's distillation of the distinctive witnesses of Matthew, Mark and Luke into a single voice.

There is still a further difficulty with Wright's position, for in fact none of the Synoptic Gospels as such contain precisely the Jesus he now puts before us. In order to come up with his Jesus, in fact, Wright needs to abstract some elements from each of the Synoptic Gospels and amplify these elements by aligning them with a presumptive master story. No less than the New Questers, despite his apparent greater fealty to the Gospel narratives, Wright ends up enucleating his simple Jesus from their more complex compositions. And if this is the case—if Wright's Jesus never existed until Wright constructed him—then serious questions must be put to his claim to have gained access to the very perceptions of Jesus[24] as well as to his premise that the resurrection simply validated who Jesus had been all along. If none of Wright's chosen sources, the Synoptic Gospels, got it right, then who did? Only Wright himself?

Another Approach to the Jesus of the Gospels

I began this essay by stating that Wright's portrait of Jesus had considerable plausibility, as it does. In fact, his portrait of Jesus is not that far from the one constructed by the evangelist Luke, for whom also Jesus is above all a prophet. But Wright's work is flawed in the same way the work of the New Questers is flawed—by his trying to go past the limits established by the evidence. By trying to establish an absolutely clear and consistent historical Jesus, Wright paradoxically ends with another in a series of sociological stereotype Jesuses, one who must think and act in accordance with the role assigned him. By trying to prove too much, Wright commits any number of fallacies and ends up with a position that is logically and historiographically unsound.

Like those he opposes, Wright distorts an essentially complex process by trying to make it simple. He dislikes those views of the resurrection that emphasize its radical character because such a view seems to establish nothing but discontinuity between the early church and Jesus. And he is partly correct. In his reaction, however, he goes much too far in the other direction, ending with an emphasis on continuity that is simply not credible or consistent with the evidence of the sources taken as a whole. Above all, Wright cannot demonstrate that scriptural prophecies and the Synoptic accounts "fit like a glove" (*JVG* 602) simply because the Gospel writers themselves made that fit, especially since Paul, Hebrews, 1 Peter and, above all, the Gospel of John all offer interpretations of Jesus that resemble those in the Synoptics with respect to their use of the symbolic world of Torah but that differ in the texts they employ and the specific images they create.

I would suggest that a more useful path to the *rapprochement* Wright seeks between history, literature and theology is to recognize the distinctive and inter-dependent role played by each rather than reduce them to one. I would also suggest that the construction of the multiple images of Jesus in the New Testament results not from a simple, linear process but from a complex and dialectical one.

We can begin by recognizing there are a number of important points concerning the human Jesus that can be established historically—that is to say, with a high degree of historical probability. And, as I have suggested, these points are compatible with the basic lines of a prophetic ministry that proclaimed the rule of God, that called people to repentance as part of a faithful Israel, that included the outcast of society and that involved preaching, teaching, and healing. There is every reason to think that Jesus was baptized by John in the Jordan, that he chose special followers, that he performed a prophetic gesture in the temple, that he shared a last meal with the disciples and that he was executed as a messianic fig-ure. Properly historical evidence is sufficient to make these statements. There was, in a word, a Jesus to remember, and we can say some things about him.

But then we must also recognize the critical importance of the resurrection, which was far more than a simple resuscitation from the dead. The sources them-selves witness that the resurrection involved as much discontinuity as continuity, demanding that Jesus be viewed in a new way because of his present life as pow-erful Lord. The memory of Jesus after his death was inevitably selected and shaped by the experience of the church, above all by the experience of the resur-rection, which was understood not as something that happened only to Jesus in the past but especially as something that touched those who worshiped him in the present. The memory of Jesus past could not but be affected by the experience of Jesus present. If there was a Jesus to remember, then, this was also a Jesus remembered through the influence of that power the Christians called the Holy Spirit.

From the first, the process of remembering Jesus involved seeing him in the light of scriptural prophecies. There is no reason to think that Jesus did not him-self refer to the Scripture with reference to his mission. But we cannot demon-strate that he did or which texts he himself might have used. What the evidence does make clear is that from the very beginning, as shown primarily by Paul's let-ters, the significance of Jesus—if you will, the theological appreciation of Jesus—was mediated by an interpretation of Jesus that read him into Torah and read

Torah into his work and his death and his resurrection. It is even possible that the church learned this practice from Jesus. But it is imperative to note that the only interpretations we are able to verify are those made by the compositions themselves. These rereadings of Scripture took a variety of forms, as we see by comparing Romans to Hebrews, 1 Peter to Revelation. We see it also by comparing the Gospel of John to the Gospel of Matthew or the Gospel of Luke. The texts chosen are different, the resulting themes are different, but the instinct to read Jesus through Scripture remains constant.

This process of interpreting Jesus through and in Torah reaches one form of crystallization in the narrative Gospels now found in the New Testament. And here is where the specifically literary character of these narratives must be taken seriously. It will not do (to use one of Wright's favorite phrases) to assert that each of the Synoptic Gospels "more or less" tells the same story. That is obvious from their literary interdependence. But what is equally clear from a close reading of each of the Gospels is that each Gospel's own way of interpreting Jesus through Torah is distinctive. Each of them gives its own meaning to the work of Jesus and, above all, its own interpretation of Jesus vis-à-vis the people Israel. Nor will it do to ignore that diversity by choosing from all these Gospels (and only them) those elements that fit the master plot Wright has discerned in the Scripture, thereby creating a single story that is not found as such in any of them.

Indeed, if we were to look for a unifying element in the Gospels (including that of John), it would be found not in the historical details of Jesus' activity, nor in the Scriptures that are brought to bear on that activity, but in the deep agreement concerning the basic character of Jesus as obedient servant and the basic character of discipleship as following in the path that he followed. In a word, it is not the historical specificity of Jesus' words and deeds but rather the pattern of humanity he reveals within his historical specificity that forms the heart of the Gospel story.

A proper appreciation of the dialectical process by which the Gospels came into being would recognize the historicity of Jesus as a first-century Jewish man who acted as a prophet. It would recognize the radical change in the perception of Jesus brought about by his scandalous crucifixion and his surprising resurrection into God's own life, a change in perception that led to a reexamination of the Scripture in the light of these experiences. It would recognize, finally, that the Gospel narratives contain a variety of images of Jesus, each of which contains some elements of historical fact and event, each of which testifies to his powerful presence as Lord, each of which advances an understanding of discipleship in imitation of his suffering service and each of which clothes Jesus richly and diversely in the garments of Torah.

Despite its great energy, ambition, and intelligence, Wright's *Jesus and the Victory of God* yields neither a rendering of Jesus nor an account of the Gospels that is convincingly historical. At best it is an inventive exercise in one of the aspects of the theology of the Synoptic tradition.

Part Three

Responses

Twelve

An Appreciative Disagreement

MARCUS J. BORG

N T. WRIGHT OCCUPIES AN UNUSUAL PLACE WITHIN CONTEMPORARY JESUS scholarship. In conservative Christian circles, he is somewhat of a hero. His lectures attract large numbers of people, and he is widely read by evangelical scholars, clergy and laity. Yet he is also in prolonged and vigorous conversation with moderate and liberal Jesus scholars and is recognized as one of the "players" to be reckoned with. I know of no one else who so prominently and ably engages both groups.

Moreover, he is brilliant. Indeed, he is among the half dozen most brilliant people I have met in my life (and I do not include myself in that group). His knowledge of scholarship is encyclopedic, as anybody who has read his footnotes knows. He analyzes and synthesizes a vast amount of material. To say the obvious, I am most impressed.

And he is a very good friend. Thus I will call him "Tom" in the rest of this chapter; it seems unnatural and remote to call him "Wright."

Yet despite how deeply impressed I am, and despite our friendship, I disagree in foundational ways with Tom's portrait of Jesus. Our ways of seeing Jesus and our disagreements are exposited side by side in a book that we have recently coauthored, *The Meaning of Jesus: Two Visions*.[1] My understanding of his position and my response to it are thus based not only on the first two volumes of his projected six-volume Christian Origins and the Question of God series but also on what he says in the book we have written together.

To speak about how I see my role in this present volume, I note that the majority of contributors are from the more conservative side of the historical and theological spectrum. Their essays are marked by careful scholarship and consistent lucidity, and I have enjoyed reading them. They also provided me with a window into a way of seeing Jesus quite different from my own.

My place on the historical spectrum is moderate to liberal, with the choice of adjective depending upon the vantage point from which I am seen. Moreover, I am a member of the Jesus Seminar, the only member to be included in this volume. This suggests to me that my role is to some extent to articulate a point of view otherwise not represented in this book. Of course, I will speak about how I see Jesus and Christian origins, and I will not seek to speak for all of moderate and liberal scholarship. But my contribution also reflects understandings widely shared by other moderate and liberal Jesus scholars.

On the theological spectrum, I am also probably best seen as a moderate to liberal or "neoliberal." And in this essay, I will speak both historically and theologically, indicating when I am doing each.

A Traditionalist Jesus

What makes Tom's understanding of Jesus so important in the contemporary discussion in both the academy and the church is that he provides historical support—indeed, I would say brilliant historical support—for what might be called a traditionalist view of Jesus. I don't know that it can be done better. Tom argues on historical grounds that Jesus understood himself to be the Messiah, saw his own death as salvific and was raised physically from the dead. Tom thus grounds both Christology and atonement theology in the self-understanding and intention of Jesus.

I call this view traditionalist because it is the image of Jesus held by virtually all Christians until the Enlightenment, before which the Gospels were generally seen as straightforward historical documents. There was no reason to think otherwise. This understanding of Jesus has remained dominant in much of Christianity and was learned by most of us who grew up in the church. Associated with the conservative wing of the contemporary church, it is also held by many thoughtful traditionalists.

My own view might be called revisionist, both historically and theologically. Historically, my view leads to a revision of the traditionalist understanding of Jesus: I attribute central elements of the traditional view to the voice of the early Christian community, not to Jesus. Theologically, this leads to a different understanding of the relationship between history and theology. Christology and atonement theology are not grounded directly in the awareness and intention of Jesus but in the early Christian movement's experience of and affirmations about Jesus. Thus, within the church, my view is associated with moderate and liberal voices.

I am not completely happy with describing the contrast between Tom and me as the contrast of traditionalist versus revisionist. I value tradition very highly myself. Moreover, elements in Tom's view might reasonably be considered revisionist. For example, Tom treats a number of passages commonly seen as second-coming sayings as referring to something else. Nevertheless, the contrast between traditionalist and revisionist does name a real difference.

The conversation between Tom's traditionalist position and moderate to liberal revisionist views is a major conversation going on within the church today, especially in mainline denominations. The conversation also goes on in the minds of many individual Christians who grew up with a traditionalist view (in either a popular or more sophisticated form) but who now find central elements of it no longer persuasive and compelling. Many are seeking an alternative to the traditionalist view that can be combined with deep Christian commitment.

I turn now to describing in greater detail Tom's historical case for a traditionalist understanding of Jesus. I begin with his argument that Jesus understood himself to be Israel's Messiah.

Messianic awareness. Though Tom grants that explicit claims by Jesus to be the Messiah are relatively scarce in the Synoptic tradition, he argues that such claims are massively implicit in Jesus' words and deeds. Jesus' use of eschatological imagery, his entry into Jerusalem, his prophetic act in the temple, and his Last Supper all suggest that Jesus saw himself as the Messiah whose vocation was to bring about the climax of Israel's history.

So far as I know, Tom does not indicate when or how Jesus came to think this about himself. Did Jesus think so already in childhood? Did he think so before going to the Jordan and being baptized by John? Or is it something he realized through his association with John? Was Jesus' messianic awareness something that came to him as a mature adult, or was it there from early childhood?

Indeed, Tom claims more than messianic awareness for Jesus. He argues that Jesus, with cryptic parables and sayings, indicated his awareness that he was doing and being for Israel what only God could do and be for Israel. Not only a messianic claim but also a claim to be the functional equivalent of God are thus part of Jesus' self-understanding.

Salvific death. Tom also argues that Jesus saw his death as intrinsic to his messianic vocation. Importantly, Tom does not claim that Jesus saw his death as a sacrifice for sin in the sense articulated by later substitutionary atonement theology. Rather, he links Jesus' vocational understanding of his death to Jesus' conviction that the real return from exile had not yet happened. In order for the exile to end, the final enemy had to be defeated. That enemy was "the satan," not Rome or the domination system. Tom argues that Jesus saw his death as the means whereby God would defeat the satan, thereby making the real return from exile possible.

Thus, if I understand Tom's position correctly, he locates at least the germ of the *Christus Victor* understanding of Jesus' death in the awareness and intention of Jesus himself.

Physical resurrection. Tom argues vigorously for the historical factuality of the empty tomb and the transformation of Jesus' corpse into a new kind of physicality. He rightly rejects the notion that Easter is about the resuscitation of Jesus' body. Resuscitation means the resumption of previous existence—a resuscitated person resumes the life he or she had before and will die again some day. Whatever Easter is about, it is not about that.

But Tom does claim that Easter did involve something happening to the physical body of Jesus. It was changed into a state of "transformed physicality," thereby leaving the tomb empty. For Tom, much is at stake in this claim, both historically and theologically.

Historically speaking, Tom argues that we cannot account for the rise of early Christianity without the historical factuality of the empty tomb and the transformation of Jesus' corpse into a new kind of physicality. And thus, in his interlocking argument, the rise of early Christianity also becomes evidence for the empty tomb.

Theologically speaking, the stakes are very high. Tom has said that if he became convinced that the empty tomb was not historically factual and that nothing remarkable happened to the corpse of Jesus, he would resign his ordination as an Anglican priest and do something else. For Tom, it seems that no less than the truth of Christianity is at stake.

An Alternative View

Along with the majority of moderate to liberal Jesus scholars, I am skeptical about all the above. Most of us see things very differently. Foundational to our different way of seeing is our understanding of the Gospels. To use my own way of putting this view, which is widely held by Jesus and Gospel scholars, I describe the nature of the Gospels with two compact statements.

First, I see the Gospels as a developing tradition. As such, they contain earlier and later layers. Such a conclusion flows directly out of the fairly standard scholarly understanding of the relationships among the Synoptic Gospels. I am persuaded that this widely accepted and familiar view is correct. Mark is the earliest of our existing Gospels, and Matthew and Luke both used Mark. I also am persuaded of the existence of Q. Though I regard Q as the product of a developing tradition, I am skeptical that we can divide it into earlier and later layers with any degree of confidence. I am also skeptical that we can infer very much about a Q community from the contents of Q. But I think there was a Q.

Tom basically sets aside the question of Gospel sources. To be sure, he demonstrates his familiarity with the history of scholarship about the sources and mounts arguments against the common understanding. The result is that he brackets the question of Synoptic relationships and justifies doing so by pointing to the lack of unanimity among scholars. He concludes that we can know more about Jesus than we can about the origin and development of the Gospels.

Instead, using his method of hypothesis and verification, he essentially treats all of the Synoptic tradition as potential data for integration into an overarching hypothesis about the historical Jesus. Indeed, I am not aware that he says "Jesus did not say this" or "Jesus did not do this" or "This did not happen" about a single Synoptic pericope.

Second, I see the Gospels as a combination of *history remembered* and *history metaphorized.* Though the terminology is my own, I think the majority of moderate to liberal scholars agree with the distinction I am making. *History remembered* needs little explanation. Some things are in the Gospels because they happened and became part of the memory of the early Christian movement.

History metaphorized needs a bit more explanation. The phrase, as I use it, has two subcategories. The first subcategory comprises Gospel stories that report things really said or done but that, because of the way the stories are told, give the accounts metaphorical meaning as well. For example, I think Jesus really did restore sight to some blind people. But the way the stories are told also gives them a metaphorical meaning. To illustrate this claim, we can examine the meta-phorical meaning suggested by Mark's placement of the stories of the blind man of Bethsaida (Mk 8:22-26) and blind Bartimaeus (Mk 10:46-52). The two stories frame the great central section of Mark's Gospel: Jesus' teaching about the way of discipleship as he makes his final journey to Jerusalem. As the framework for this section, the two stories suggest that regaining one's sight involves seeing the way of Jesus. The way of Jesus, the path of discipleship, involves following him to Jerusalem, the place of death and resurrection, of endings and beginnings. More-over, the central section itself provides another example of history metaphorized: Jesus really did make a final journey to Jerusalem (history remembered), and the way the story is told metaphorizes it into a story of discipleship.

The second subcategory of history metaphorized comprises purely meta-phorical narratives. Here there is no particular historical event behind the story. In these cases, the history being metaphorized is the historical significance of Jesus as a whole. In my judgment, examples of material in this category include the stories of Jesus' birth, his multiplying loaves, his walking on water, his stilling the storm, his changing water into wine and his raising of Lazarus.

The basis for my judgment that these narratives are purely metaphorical is in part the use within the stories themselves of what seem to me obviously symbolic elements drawn from Israel's history and the Hebrew Bible. My judgment also involves a metahistorical factor: Are there limits to the spectacular? Are there some things that never happen anywhere? I think there are, even though I am not sure what the limits are. Amazing things happen, marvels happen, wonders hap-pen. But as a historian I cannot accept that Jesus' ability to "do the spectacular" was unique and without parallel.

To put that differently, if I became convinced that at least a few people have been able to walk on water, then I would be willing to take seriously that Jesus may have done so. But as a historian, I find myself unable to say that the life of Jesus involved spectacular happenings of a magnitude without parallel anywhere else. Thus for this reason also, I see a number of Gospel stories in the second sub-division of history metaphorized: as purely metaphorical narratives that are not grounded in a specific historical event but that nevertheless truthfully express the significance of Jesus.

With a portion of the above, Tom agrees, though without accepting my ter-minology. He affirms, of course, that the Gospels contain history remembered. He also affirms that the story of something that happened can be told in such a way as to give it rich metaphorical meanings and that some Gospel stories are history metaphorized in this sense. But he rejects the notion that the Synoptic Gospels contain history metaphorized in the second sense of the term, namely, that they contain purely metaphorical narratives. What is reported, even if the story has metaphorical resonances, really happened.

Thus there are two major disagreements between Tom and the majority of his mainline colleagues (including me) about the nature of the Gospels. We disagree about whether there are earlier and later layers in the Gospels and whether we can discern such layers. And we disagree about how much of the Gospels is history remembered and how much is the metaphorization of the story of Jesus.

Developmentally I ascribe the material most central to Tom's reconstruction of Jesus' messianic vocation to the post-Easter period and thus to voices within the early Christian movement. Moreover, like Jesus, these early Christians often spoke in the language of metaphor and metaphorical narratives. Early on, it seems to me, we Christians metaphorized our history. In subsequent centuries, we have often historicized our metaphors.

These disagreements about the nature of the Gospels are the major reason that Tom's reconstruction of the historical Jesus is unpersuasive to a majority of moderate to liberal scholars. Earlier I spoke of Tom's bracketing the question of Synoptic relationships. I would put it more strongly: Tom positively needs the common scholarly understanding of Synoptic relationships to be wrong. His reconstruction depends on seeing most (all?) of the material in the Synoptic Gospels as equally early, indeed as going back to Jesus, and as only modestly shaped by the early Christian movement after Easter.

And, of course, if one does see the Synoptics as Tom does, then Jesus did think of himself as the Messiah and did see his death as central to his vocation. As all the readers of this volume know, this is the way Mark, our earliest Gospel, portrays Jesus. In Mark's account of Jesus' final journey to Jerusalem, Jesus three times speaks of his upcoming death as necessary and purposeful. Moreover, in Mark, Jesus knew he was the Messiah, even though an explicit messianic claim is not part of his public proclamation.

But are these features of Mark reflective of the pre-Easter Jesus? Or are they more plausibly seen as the interpretive voice of the post-Easter community? To me and a majority of my colleagues, they seem more likely to be the latter. I turn now to the reasons for saying so, organizing my exposition around the two key ingredients of Tom's understanding of Jesus' messianic vocation: messianic awareness and vocational death.

Jesus' Self-Understanding: Messianic or Not?

Rather than answering "messianic" to this question as Tom does, my own answer is "probably not." I take seriously Mark's silence about an explicit messianic affirmation being part of Jesus' public message. Rather, according to Mark, on only two occasions does a messianic exchange occur, both of which are in private, not in public: the conversation with Peter and the disciples at Caesarea Philippi (Mk 8:27-30) and the scene before the High Priest (Mk 14:61-62). Thus, in Mark's account of Jesus' public message and activity, Jesus did not speak of being the Messiah.

I also take seriously a demonstrable tendency of Matthew and Luke to add messianic and other christological language to the basic narrative that they take over from Mark. As a historian, I must therefore take seriously the possibility that the two passages in Mark that do contain an explicit messianic interchange may well be the product of this demonstrable tendency of the developing tradition.

Moreover, those two passages have particular features that compel historical caution. The scene before the High Priest has a number of difficulties that give one pause. As has long been noted, there are problems imagining that such a trial (or even hearing) could have occurred at night and at the festival of Passover. There are the important questions raised by John Dominic Crossan: Would the highest Jewish authority have bothered to grant a trial or hearing to a peasant? And even if so, how would the followers of Jesus have known what was said? To paraphrase Crossan, those who knew what happened between the arrest of Jesus and his execution didn't care; and those who cared about Jesus are unlikely to have known.[2]

But even setting aside these questions, one must still address the content of the exchange itself, which has three elements. The first two are part of the High Priest's question: "(1) Are you the Messiah, (2) the Son of God [the Blessed One]?" The third element follows Jesus' affirmative answer to the first two: "I am; (3) and you will see the Son of Man seated at the right hand of the Power, and coming with the clouds of heaven." This third element is understood by most scholars (rightly, in my judgment) as referring to Jesus' second coming.[3]

Thus, the scene portrays Jesus as the Messiah and Son of God who will come again, which sounds very much like an early Christian confession of faith. According to Mark, Jesus is condemned to death for what is essentially a Christian confession of his significance. In short, does the scene sound more like history remembered or more like the post-Easter voice of the community? It is, of course, impossible to be certain that it is a post-Easter creation. But equally, if not more so, it is impossible to be more than moderately confident that the inter-change in Mark reflects what was said on the last night of Jesus' life. The most I can imagine saying in answer to a question about the historical factuality of this scene is "Perhaps, perhaps."

The other explicit messianic interchange in Mark is the scene at Caesarea Philippi. Here, of course, it is Peter and not Jesus who makes the affirmation. Though Mark almost certainly intends the reader to understand that Jesus accepts Peter's affirmation, Jesus does not do so explicitly. Instead, he orders the disciples "not to tell anyone about him." It is instructive to compare Matthew's development of the scene: he makes explicit Jesus' acceptance of Peter's confes-sion. Rather than saying nothing to Peter, the Jesus of Matthew commends Peter and declares his confession to have come from God.

But let us return to Mark. Does the scene at Caesarea Philippi report a pre-Easter event, or is it a post-Easter creation that Mark uses as an epiphany to dis-close the identity of Jesus as he begins his final journey to Jerusalem? Whatever one's answer, it seems to me that it needs to be a "soft" judgment, one with a low degree of certainty.

Given all of the above, I cannot, as a historian, be confident that a messianic affirmation can be traced back to Jesus himself. Yet I can be confident that the community after Easter proclaimed Jesus to be the Messiah and indeed spoke of him with the most exalted language known in the Jewish tradition. I grant that it is possible Jesus thought of himself as the Messiah; but if I had to bet one way or the other, historical caution would lead me to bet that the affirmation and procla-mation of Jesus as Messiah are a post-Easter development.

Importantly, I do not see the truthfulness of the claim that Jesus is the Messiah as being dependent upon his having said so or thought so himself. I assume the other contributors to this volume would agree with the underlying principle upon which this claim is based. To illustrate that principle, I do not think that the truth of "Jesus is the light of the world" or "Jesus is the Word made flesh" is dependent on Jesus' having thought of himself or spoken of himself in these terms.

Moreover, as a Christian, I affirm that the early Christian movement got it right. Jesus is the Messiah (and the light of the world, the bread of life, the Wis-dom of God, the Word made flesh and so forth), even though I do not think that these claims were part of his teaching and, thus, I doubt that he saw himself as such.

I see the christological language of the New Testament as language of con-fession and commitment. To say Jesus is the Messiah, the Wisdom of God, the

Son of God, the Word of God and so forth, means to see him as the Messiah, the Wisdom of God, the Son of God and the Word of God. Such confession and commitment is constitutive and definitive of Christian identity.

The cumulative claim made by this language is impressive and important: Jesus is, for those of us who are Christians, the decisive disclosure of two things. First, he shows us (reveals or discloses) what God is like. In the words of Colossians 1:15, Jesus is the image—the icon—of the invisible God. And, second, Jesus shows us what a life full of God is like. He discloses what the Word made flesh, the Wisdom of God incarnate, the Spirit of God embodied in a human life, looks like. In Jesus, we see both what God is like and what a life full of God is like.

Thus, on historical grounds I am uncertain (and ultimately doubtful) that Jesus saw himself as Messiah. But theologically, I do not think anything major is at stake. I do not see that it has significant theological consequences. The truth of Christian claims about Jesus does not depend upon being able to ground those claims in Jesus' own sense of himself.

Jesus' Death: Vocation or Consequence?

Tom's view has already been briefly described: Jesus saw his own death as central to his messianic vocation. In Jesus' own mind, his death was purposive, for he believed it would be the means whereby God would bring about the climax of Israel's history and the real return from exile.

I see Jesus' death as consequence, not vocation. That is, his execution was the consequence of what he was doing, but it was not the purpose of his vocation. To use an analogy from the twentieth century, I see the shootings of Gandhi and Martin Luther King as the consequence of what they were doing and not as an intended part of their vocation. I do not mean that they were oblivious to the possibility of premature death or that they never thought about it. Both had to be aware that what they were doing (their vocation) could easily get them into fatal trouble, and yet they courageously continued to follow their vocation in spite of the potential consequence. But neither would have seen their deaths as a necessary part of their vocation. So also I see the death of Jesus. I do not see Jesus' death as part of his own intended purpose.

Rather, I see the purposive understanding of his death as retrospective interpretation, not as prospective intentionality. The salvific interpretation of Jesus' death originated after Easter as the early followers of Jesus sought to give meaning to what had happened. To state a claim about which I will soon say more, I see five different post-Easter interpretations of Jesus' death in the New Testament, all of which I regard as powerfully true.[4] Indeed, I find them to be more persuasively and compellingly true as the voice of the community than if I were to think of one or more of them as going back to the mind of Jesus. I turn now to explaining why.

I grant that our earliest narrative Gospel presents Jesus' death as central to his vocation. In strong contrast to his picture of Jesus' silence about his messiahship, Mark portrays Jesus explicitly telling his disciples of the necessity of his death as they journey to Jerusalem. In the threefold prediction of his passion, the Jesus of Mark does not simply say that the authorities may very well take action against him and even kill him; he says that this must happen—he must undergo great suffering and be killed. The other Gospels and the rest of the New Testament agree: Jesus' death was central to his purpose.

Given this consistent affirmation, why be skeptical that this goes back to Jesus' own sense of vocation? A minor reason, a further feature of Mark's Gospel, that makes one wonder if Jesus did speak so openly and clearly about the necessity of his upcoming death is that Jesus' death seems to have taken the disciples by surprise.

Much more important to me is a probability question about a comprehensive matter. Which is more probable—that the community after Easter was responsible for seeing meaning and providential purpose in Jesus' death or that this goes back to Jesus himself?

That the community sought to find providential meaning in Jesus' death, and that it did so very soon after Easter, seems obvious. Unless one thinks that all five (and perhaps more) of the post-Easter interpretations of Jesus' death go back to Jesus himself, one has to grant that the community did give meanings to his death. His early followers sought to see purpose in the death of this person whom they loved and whom they also believed God had raised. Thus the process of interpretation was manifestly going on from a very early date. This realization creates a prima facie case for considering the possibility that all such interpretations are post-Easter.

To continue, I have great trouble imagining that Jesus could have thought his death was the central purpose of his vocation and the means whereby God would defeat the final enemy and bring about the real return from exile. The issue is not really about the sanity of Jesus (though I have raised that question in another context).[5] Nor is the issue whether some Jews near the time of Jesus could see the death of a martyr as an atoning death. I think Tom is right: some could. Rather, the issue is how we reconcile the claim that Jesus saw his death this way with what else we may reasonably affirm about Jesus.

Treating this issue involves us not in the consideration of individual texts but in holistic historical reflection. Namely, how persuasive is Tom's historical reconstruction as a whole, including its corollaries? I will treat this question in two stages.

I begin by briefly using my own understanding of Jesus as a way of illustrating my first point. I see Jesus as a Spirit-filled healer, wisdom teacher, social prophet and movement founder. With much or all of this, Tom agrees—and he also argues that Jesus saw his own death as central to his vocation. But how does one put this together? Was Jesus doing the activities associated with each of the features in my list (healing, teaching an alternative wisdom, indicting the domination system, forming a remarkably boundary-shattering movement) "on the side," as it were, even though his real vocation was his death? Or were these activities, taken together, his vocation—with his execution the unintended (even if anticipated) consequence of what he was up to?

The second stage invites reflection on a necessary corollary of Tom's position: Jesus somehow had to arrive at this understanding of his death. But when I try to imagine Jesus seeing his death as the means whereby God would defeat the final enemy and bring about the real return from exile, I run into difficulties. I wonder, why would Jesus think this? The only answer I can imagine is that Jesus had put together a scenario in his own mind about what the real return from exile required (namely, his death). That scenario would presumably have been created from a pastiche of Hebrew Bible texts.

Set aside for the moment the question of whether Jesus possessed scribal literacy (the level of literacy required to read an unpointed Hebrew scroll). Imagine that he did. Why would he have arrived at this reading of texts from the Hebrew Bible? How could he have become convinced that his death would be the way God would bring about the real return from exile? I can imagine Jesus' arriving at such a conclusion if there were texts in the Hebrew Bible that spoke explicitly of the death of the Messiah as the means whereby God would bring about the final victory. But there are no such texts. So why and how would Jesus create such a scenario? It strikes me as a very odd notion.

Whereas I find the origin of this notion virtually inexplicable when I try to imagine it as originating before the death of Jesus (that is, in the mind of Jesus himself), I find it completely explicable when I imagine it happening within the community after Easter. The death had happened; it cried out for meaning. Looking back on Jesus' life from a post-Easter vantage point and looking back on the Hebrew Scriptures in light of the climax of the story, it is easy to imagine the process whereby providential purpose was ascribed to what had happened.

I illustrate my claim by compactly describing the five interpretations of Good Friday and Easter that I have developed more fully elsewhere.[6]

Rejection/vindication. The rulers of this world, those at the top of the domi- nation system, said "no" to Jesus and what he was up to by executing him; they rejected him. The resurrection is God's vindication of Jesus: God said "yes" to Jesus, and "no" to the domination system. Jesus is Lord, and they aren't.

Defeat of "the powers" (Christus Victor). In his life, Jesus battled with "the powers"; in his death, "the powers" swallowed him up. But God in Christ (especially in the resurrection) defeated the principalities and powers.

Incarnation of the path of transformation. Jesus' death and resurrection embody and reveal the path of return to God: dying to an old way of living and being born into a new way of being. Here Good Friday and Easter symbolize the way of return that Jesus himself taught and that those in the early Christian community experienced.

Incarnation of the depth of God's love for us. For this interpretation to work, the completed Christian story of Jesus as God's beloved Son must be in place. How much does God love us? So much that "for us" and "for our salvation," God was willing to sacrifice that which was most dear to God.

Sacrifice for sin. In the context of the temple's claim to have an institutional monopoly on the forgiveness of certain kinds of sins and impurities, the claim that Jesus was the sacrifice for sin subverts the temple's claim—the sacrifice has already been made. The temple's claim is negated. Positively, the language proclaims the immediacy of access to God apart from institutional mediation: the "once for all" sacrifice has already occurred.

All of these interpretations make enormous sense to me when I view them as the product of the early community. They are central to the community's proclamation of the significance of what had happened in Jesus. I see them as profoundly meaningful ways of continuing to talk about the significance of Jesus in our time. But when I try to imagine one or more of them as central to how Jesus saw his vocation, I cannot imagine why he would have thought so.

I note one more corollary of Tom's position: if Jesus did believe that his death would bring about the defeat of the final enemy and the real return from exile, Jesus was wrong. It didn't happen. The real return from exile did not occur. The final enemy was not defeated. The conditions of life for Israel (and the world as a whole) remained unchanged. Unless one radically metaphorizes this language, which I gather Tom does not want to do, this seems to be a corollary of Tom's understanding of Jesus.

I mention this not because it counts in a historical argument. In fact, the desire that Jesus not be wrong should not be a factor affecting historical judgment. Rather, I mention this because of a perception of mine. I think some Christians are attracted to Tom's position because he does ground the saving significance of Jesus' death in the intention of Jesus himself. Continuity between the historical Jesus and church doctrine is achieved. Less noticed, however, is the price: Jesus thought his death would accomplish something that manifestly was not accomplished. As Tom sees it, Jesus was wrong about that which was most central to Jesus' vocation.

Both Jesus' messianic awareness and salvific death seem, to me and many of my colleagues, to be post-Easter developments. In a book on Paul, Tom argues convincingly that Paul saw Jesus as "the climax of the covenant."[7] In his work on Jesus, Tom in effect argues that Jesus saw himself (including his death) as the climax of the covenant. But Tom's treatment of the historical Jesus strikes many of us as a retrojection of early Christian understandings back into the mind of Jesus himself.

Two More Issues

In this final section, I want to treat two more issues. The first is Tom's understanding of Jesus as prophet. He and I agree that Jesus was a prophet. "Social prophet" is one of my major categories for constellating the traditions about Jesus; as such, I also speak of Jesus as prophet of the kingdom of God. In addition to what I affirm, Tom emphasizes that Jesus was a prophet of apocalyptic eschatology, a claim that I and a significant number of my colleagues deny.

At first glance, this seems like a major difference. But by "apocalyptic eschatology," Tom means something quite different from what most scholars have meant. To Tom the language of apocalyptic eschatology as Jesus used it was a way of investing events in the space-time world with their ultimate significance. Thus the language of apocalyptic eschatology really means "climactic" or "decisive." Ascribing it to Jesus becomes a way of saying that Jesus saw himself as being and doing something of climactic and decisive significance. It virtually becomes christological language, and it is a key element in Tom's argument that Jesus saw himself as the Messiah.

Thus for Tom the language of apocalyptic eschatology no longer means what Albert Schweitzer meant, or what Rudolf Bultmann meant, or what advocates in our own day such as E. P. Sanders or Dale Allison mean.[8] Given that the expectation of the imminent and dramatic arrival of the kingdom of God as a manifestly supernatural event is no longer part of what Jesus expected, I am unclear whether Tom's understanding of Jesus as prophet of the kingdom of God is sharply differ-ent from my own understanding and that of others who see as I do. The differ-ence may in fact be christological and not be about apocalyptic expectation.

The second issue concerns Easter. Here I do not want to rehash the argu-ments about whether the story of the empty tomb and the Gospel stories of the risen Christ appearing to his followers should be regarded as historically factual accounts that go back to eyewitnesses and thus to the earliest layers of the tradi-tion.[9] Rather, I will summarize my own understanding of Easter and then raise questions about two aspects of Tom's position that puzzle me.

For me, whether or not the tomb was empty, and whether or not something happened to the corpse of Jesus, is irrelevant to the truth of Easter. Positively, I see the truth of Easter as grounded in the continuing experience of Jesus as a liv-ing reality after his death. I think the followers of Jesus really experienced him after his execution and that they did so in a variety of ways. There were visions. There was a sense of his continuing presence. There was a sense of the power that they had known in him continuing to operate. I take very seriously the phenom-enology of Christian religious experience, both in the first century and subse-quent centuries. Such experiences are the historical ground of Easter.

And, importantly, I see the central meaning of Easter to be more than sim-ply that people experienced (and continue to experience) Jesus as a living reality. What differentiates the experience of Jesus after his death from experiences of a deceased loved one (or from Elvis sightings, for that matter) is that there is some-thing about the experience of the risen Christ that leads to the affirmation, "Jesus is Lord." Easter means not only that Jesus is a figure of the present and not just of the past; it also means that Jesus is Lord, raised to the right hand of God, now one with God.

The first of Tom's claims about Easter that puzzles me is his argument that Jesus' body was changed into a state of "transformed physicality." Thus the resur-rection was "physical," even though it was not a resuscitation of Jesus' corpse. About the latter point we agree, but I have difficulty with the claim that Jesus' resurrected body exists in a state of "transformed physicality." The problem is not so much that I cannot believe the claim but that I cannot imagine what it means.

To be sure, I understand part of what Tom means. He means that the tomb really was empty: the corpse of Jesus was transformed. And he means that Paul's contrast between a *sōma psychikon* and a *sōma pneumatikon* should not be seen as the contrast between a "physical body" and a "spiritual body" but as the contrast between "a body animated by soul" and "a body animated by spirit."[10] Both bodies, he argues, are physical.

But when I try to imagine what a body in a state of "transformed physicality" is, I run into difficulty. The difficulty is compounded when Tom says, as I have heard him say, that the risen Christ continues to exist in a state of transformed physicality. What can this mean? Does a person in a state of transformed physicality occupy space and have weight? Is a person in such a state able to eat and digest food? Does a person in such a state perhaps need food—not just during the forty days between Easter and ascension, to use the timetable supplied by the book of Acts, but even now?

To echo Paul, I feel like a madman asking such questions. "Yes" answers strike me as ridiculous. Surely the risen Christ through the centuries does not occupy space and have weight, eat and digest food, and so forth. But if "no" answers are given to these questions, then a further question arises: what is the difference between a state of transformed physicality and a state of nonphysicality?

Or have I misunderstood? Does Tom mean simply that the followers of Jesus had experiences of Jesus in bodily form? If so, I have no problem with the affirmation. I take seriously that Christians from the earliest days to the present sometimes have experiences of Jesus appearing in visual form. This is what visions are. Does Tom mean more than this? His language suggests that he does.

The second puzzle I have about Tom's position is theological. What is at stake theologically in seeing the empty tomb and the Gospel appearance stories as historically factual accounts? I have already noted that for Tom, the theological stakes are very high indeed. Nothing less than the truth of Christianity is at stake.

But is that really the case? Does the truth of Christianity depend upon the tomb's really being empty? Is the truth of Christianity in principle falsifiable by the discovery of Jesus' skeletal remains, however impossible such a discovery might be? Would we need to say that Christians throughout the centuries who have experienced the living Jesus were all mistaken? Do we not know on other grounds that Christianity is true?

Christianity has functioned from its beginning and in the centuries ever since as a sacrament, a mediator of the sacred, a means whereby God and the risen Christ come to us. It has been a means whereby millions have been brought into and nurtured by a relationship with God as known in Jesus. As a sacrament of the sacred, Christianity has been the means whereby compassion and even saintliness have been generated in the lives of many. Surely its truth is not dependent upon whether a camera could have photographed an empty tomb on Easter morning.

This puzzlement leads me to my concluding section. In this essay, I have spoken primarily about why Tom and I see the historical Jesus differently. Yet in writing our book together and in the conversations that accompanied and followed the process, Tom and I also discovered centrally important areas of agreement. These are described in the concluding chapters of our book, in which we each speak about the vision of the Christian life that flows out of our ways of seeing Jesus.

In his concluding chapter, Tom brilliantly describes a Christian life that takes Jesus seriously as centered in worship and mission. He then develops his vision of such a life under four categories: *spirituality, theology, healing* and *politics.* I agree with everything he says in three of his categories: spirituality, healing and politics.

Our disagreement is primarily in the category of theology. There, our disagreements about the historical Jesus become a theological disagreement. We disagree not only about how much is historical but about how much needs to be historical. What theological weight should be given to our historical differences? Does it matter, theologically, whether Jesus thought he was the Messiah? Does it matter, theologically, whether Jesus saw his death as salvific? Does it matter, theologically, whether the tomb was empty?

To all of these questions, Tom's answer is "yes," and mine is "no." I don't want to be misunderstood here. I'm not saying that history doesn't matter. For the Jewish and Christian traditions, history matters greatly. Moreover, I think that what we can glimpse of the historical Jesus matters greatly, for it helps to give content to what a life full of God looks like. But I don't think the truth of Christianity is dependent on "yes" answers to these three historical questions. Rather, the truth of Christianity is grounded in its ability, its capacity, to be a sacrament of the sacred, a mediator of God as known in Jesus Christ.

Thirteen

In Grateful Dialogue

A Response

N. T. WRIGHT

*A*N ACTOR, THEY SAY, DOESN'T MIND WHETHER HE'S PLAYING THE HERO OR THE villain, as long as his name is up in lights. Authors aren't quite like that; the high compliment of having a whole book devoted to the discussion of one's work is finely balanced by the probing, intelligent questions and by the occasional thud of a blunt instrument on the back of one's head. Having for years valued the motto *qui s'excuse, s'accuse,* I am eager not to add fuel to the fire with lame explanations of "what I really meant." Nor do I like the style of writing whose main theme is "if only professor so-and-so had read what I said on page 594 note 203, he could never have accused me of such-and-such"—though I confess that there were several times, as I read these essays, when that sort of sentence sprang unbidden to mind, and there will inevitably be some near equivalents in what follows. I have, however, been asked several specific questions, and courtesy and gratitude demand that I should try to answer them. As one of my heroes, Ernst Käsemann, once said, "In scholarship as in life, no one can possess truth except by constantly learning it afresh; and no one can learn it afresh without listening to the people who are his companions on the search for that truth. Community does not necessarily mean agreement."[1]

It isn't possible, of course, to go through each essay point by point; and that would be very boring, anyway. Much of what has been said by way of summary of *Jesus and the Victory of God* and indeed of *The New Testament and the People of God* is on target; many of the questions are ones that I have often asked myself. Only occasionally did I rub my eyes and say, "How could you have thought that I meant *that?*" Only once did I look up my lawyer's telephone number. What I propose is as follows:

1. I will make some preliminary remarks about the sort of task I thought I was attempting, in the hope of clarifying a few methodological questions.

2. I will briefly discuss first-century Judaism, not least the controversial notion of return from exile.

3. I will reexamine the even more controversial issue of the referents of apocalyptic language, especially as regards Jesus himself.

4. Lastly, but of course most importantly, I shall attend briefly to the wider questions relating to Jesus himself.

In all of this I offer my warmest thanks to the editor, contributors and publisher for the attention they have paid to my work and for the many gratifying things they have said.

History: What It Is and How We Do It

In *The New Testament and the People of God,* set within a section in chapter four on method and especially epistemology (topics most contemporary New Testament scholars simply ignore), I described in detail what I meant by *history* and how I proposed to go about studying it. I neither suppressed nor bracketed these issues but discussed them in detail. I was careful to distinguish literature, history and theology while leaving them in their properly differentiated and dynamic mutual relationships. Since no one has yet engaged, far less attempted to refute, my arguments there, I am not too anxious about gadflylike criticisms that sting the surface but do not touch the substance.

One of the main points to emerge concerns the distinction and interrelation between our perceptions of things and the way things actually are. What I called "critical realism" (itself, of course, a slippery term, though I define carefully what I mean by it) offers an account of how we can take full cognizance of the provisionality and partiality of all our perceptions while still affirming—and living our lives on the basis of—the reality of things external to ourselves and our minds. This method involves, crucially, the telling of stories within the context of communities of discourse.

In the study of history this involves, of course, the well-known distinction between history as "what actually happened" and history as "what people write about what actually happened" (*NTPG* 81ff.). Having made this distinction, I was quite careful thereafter not to elide these two senses. It is tedious, when using the word *history*, to have to specify which type of history one means ("history-E" and "history-W," for instance, indicating "event" and "writing"), but for clarity I shall sometimes do this in what follows. One might have hoped that the context would make it obvious. What happens, of course, is that the latent phenomenalism that still passes for sophistication (among those unaware of the excluded middle between naiveté and skepticism) lures people into the cheap putdown: "Oh, we aren't so naive as to think that this actually happened" or "We have grown up now, and we can see that this is simply a literary construct." Or whatever. In vain do we offer actual arguments that (say) Jesus' temple action and the riddles that surround it simply cannot have been invented by the early church; these arguments go unnoticed. It is assumed that, since we are not conforming to a certain type of fashionable doublethink, we must simply be asserting historicity ("history-E," of course) in the teeth of a cleverer reading of the evidence.

This appears in what has become a familiar double bind to those of us engaged in historical Jesus research. If one's construction looks for a moment anything like what we find in one or more of the Gospels, one is smartly told (even if one has foreseen this objection and argued carefully for several pages against it) that this is, of course, only a reflection of Synoptic theology and that it doesn't, or may not, relate to Jesus. If, however, one ventures to suggest that the "history-E" of Jesus might be different in certain ways from the first-century versions of its "history-W" (for instance, if one suggests that the early church came to believe in the second coming but that Jesus never said anything about it), one runs into the opposite protest: Where did this great gulf come from? By what arrogance do we pretend to know better than they did? Sometimes, as in Luke Timothy Johnson's article, the two objections are combined, despite the fact that they cancel each other out so neatly.[2] I want to insist that, a priori, we do not know whether the evangelists got it right or got it wrong and, indeed, that those are not the only alternatives. Part of the point of all historical study is to recognize that all "history-W" is written from one particular angle, involving particular selection and arrangement. Nobody ever "tells it like it was," because all events, from the fall of a leaf to the fall of an empire, are too complex for that. All "history-W" therefore involves fresh selection, fresh rearrangement, not in order to prove that previous "history-W" "got it wrong" as regards "history-E" but in order that people of our own generation may glimpse afresh the "history-E" that previous "history-W" was trying to unveil.

Two further issues follow from this, relating to points raised by several essayists. First, it is no proper objection to a historical proposal to say, "If this were true, why has nobody thought of it before?" Quite apart from the fact that if that objection were ever to be allowed, all historical work (other than that involving fresh evidence) would wither on the vine; do we really want to tell our doctoral students (as Oscar Cullmann was reportedly told as a postgraduate) that all the problems are now solved and that they had better study something else? Or does our discipline not recognize (not least because of the rapid spread of early Christianity beyond the cultural, as well as the geographical, borders of Judaism) that many things in the New Testament were actually opaque to, say, the second-century church—things that we, with a cautious use of the excellent Jewish materials now available to us, are able to see in a fresh and arguably probable historical light? It is not only possible but highly likely that things which were extremely clear to first-century authors were rapidly forgotten in the very different subsequent circumstances and also that we have to reconstruct them with labor and great care.

This relates, of course, to certain features in particular, not least the objections to the return-from-exile theme (about which more anon). Do I detect here, thinking in terms of Thomas Kuhn's famous analysis, the faint smell of burning paradigms? And do I sense the alarmed reaction of those who had invested heavily in them and who still prefer them even though these paradigms have less explanatory power, and indeed a higher degree of combustibility, than originally supposed? Of course, all new paradigms face the charge of being mere shallow innovations. Their worth has to be proved. But their defenders never have an easy time of it; and the reasons for this have at least as much to do with nonacademic human factors as with serious attention to either "history-E" or "history-W." On we go around the old circle—of course, just because you're criticizing it doesn't mean the paradigm is correct; likewise (fair's fair), just because it's new doesn't mean it's wrong. What counts is argument, not assertion (a distinction New Testament scholars are often surprisingly loath to make, both in analyzing the New Testament itself and in commenting on each other's work).

Second, is my work in any sense "apologetic"? Dale Allison thinks it is, and he suggests that my reading of apocalyptic language in particular is an example of the rewriting of prophecies that failed to happen.[3] Stephen Evans thinks it may be, and he suggests that this would validate my use of a soft form of "methodological naturalism." Well, my work is and it isn't. I should have thought that my rereading of Jesus' apocalyptic language was quite enough to show that I was not trying to curry favor with the conservative establishment or to prove that one particular type of Christianity was true after all; at precisely this point I am at my most revisionist. However, it is true that I believe, as Johnson is cross with me for believing, that if the "historical-E" Jesus really was a first-century Jewish revolutionary or if he was neither more nor less than a Galilean *hasid* or a Cynic sage, then Christianity really would be based on a mistake. I do believe, in other words, that the historical question raised by the Enlightenment is important and cannot be waved aside, or escaped from by a retreat into the golden world of either the tradition or a private spirituality. At this point I may simply refer readers to what I say in the preface to *Jesus and the Victory of God* (esp. p. xv) and to the chapter entitled "Knowing Jesus: Faith and History" in the book that sets out the debate between Marcus Borg and myself.[4]

All historians have worldviews; we all have to look out on the world through something, from some angle. Part of the challenge of history, and what makes it exciting, is to discover that there are more things in heaven and earth than are dreamed of in our own worldviews, whether those views are post-Enlightenment rationalist, traditional Christian (of whatever sort) or any other. As Alister McGrath rightly sees, I have myself undergone a quite drastic process of rethinking traditional Christian thought-forms and language in the course of my study of the New Testament. This has been (do I really need to stress this?) not because I have applied rationalistic or reductionist thought-forms to it, and certainly not because I have been a crypto-Troeltschian, as Stephen Evans supposes, but because I have done my best, in constant dialogue with the texts, to hear what the texts themselves are saying (however unfashionable that may sound) and not just what my traditions tell me they ought to be saying. *Ecclesia catholica semper reformanda* is a noble ideal, but it is a painful one to live up to. I do not think (despite Craig Blomberg's intriguing suggestion) that I have described an "evangelical" Jesus; indeed, the reaction of many evangelicals to several aspects of my proposal would suggest otherwise. But I do think, as many contributors have seen, that the Jesus I have described, one whom I believe belongs substantially in "history-E" and not merely "history-W," can be seen as the starting point for mainstream orthodox Christianity, not as a strange figure left behind by the significantly different Christ of the church's faith. I am glad that some contributors saw this point quite clearly.

The task to which I gave myself, then, was that of studying "history-W" with the intent of coming as close as I could to "history-E." I described and frequently referred back to the method by which I proceeded: that of hypothesis and verification. The tests for a hypothesis are, in principle (though see below), the same as in the natural sciences: getting in the data, simplicity and shedding light on other areas. What counts in each case is of course contested, but I provided a discussion of and answers to that question, and none of the criticisms I have received suggests to me that I was mistaken. Historical hypotheses characteristically come in the form of narratives, in which chains of events, connected by personal character and the contingent rough-and-tumble events of real life, form a complex web of cause and effect.

The move from historical sources (literary, archaeological, numismatic and so on) to larger hypothetical statements about what people believed is a matter of induction, not deduction—or, as some philosophers have put it, of "abduction" or "inference to the best explanation" (one variety of abduction). There is considerable philosophical discussion of how such a move may be made and of how hypotheses created by this method may then be appropriately tested. I have tried to stay within these developing guidelines. I recognize, of course, that a skeptic, standing in the tradition of David Hume above all, can almost always find a way of doubting even the move to the broad hypothesis, let alone the arguments that can then be advanced to support it. New Testament scholarship has for too long been in thrall to just such a methodological skepticism, which is not, at this level, a skepticism about such things as miracles (see below) but an epistemological skepticism about engaging in induction or abduction at all: that is, an insistence on deduction as the only valid form of reasoning. That, I think, is why some people accuse me of merely asserting things when what I have done is advance hypotheses that are then quite rigorously tested. Very few such skeptics are actually consistent; almost all go on, having rejected other people's conclusions on the grounds that they were not deduced logically from the data, to propose alternative frameworks of their own, not noticing, it seems, that they are sitting on thin air, having themselves just sawn off the branch.

Of course, the historian, unlike the natural scientist, is not concerned with the discovery of laws or theories that would enable one to offer predictions about the future. This is a major point of difference, I think, between my work and that of either type of "methodological naturalist." Cause and effect, in other words, do not mean the same in history as they do in the natural sciences. Science studies what always happens (compare Ernst Troeltsch's principle of criticism and analogy);

history studies what happened once and once only. To flatten out the method I articulated and used into a variety of that articulated by Troeltsch is therefore invalid, though I realize that to a professional philosopher all that I said in *The New Testament and the People of God,* and all I have said here, remains at best an inadequate beginning. I console myself with the knowledge that my work goes considerably further than the work most New Testament scholars have done.

In particular, the philosophy of history developed by R. G. Collingwood—standing on the shoulders of Heinrich Rickert, Wilhelm Dilthey and Benedetto Croce—emphasized historical thought as "the re-creation of past experience." I gave special attention to this point; it remains of great interest and importance, though I do not think any reviewer has yet even mentioned it. The historian's task, as seen by Collingwood, is "to 'rethink' or inwardly re-enact the deliberations of past agents, thereby rendering their behavior intelligible."[5] This has, of course, no analogy in the natural sciences. The historian, working in this way, does indeed seek to explain why people behaved as they did, trying to establish something not unlike a causal nexus between worldviews, mindsets, beliefs and aims on the one hand and intentional actions on the other (another whole section of my method to which none of the contributors drew attention, far less commented on). But this is some way off from Troeltsch's "principle of correlation," which is precisely, as Stephen Evans points out, to do with "solely . . . natural events."

Of course, it is open to anyone to object a priori that we can never know the sort of things that Collingwood and his followers, myself included, are trying to discover; just as it is possible to allow that we might in theory be able to discover such things while objecting to a particular set of proposals. Some have seen a quasi-psychologizing lurking in Collingwood's proposal (I specifically ward off this charge in *JVG* 479-81); others have urged that, when all is said and done, this style of "explanation" does after all have some analogy with those of the natural sciences. (This is a point my own account acknowledges. I see historical method as a distinct branch of how we know things, standing in a cousinly relation to the natural sciences while having some distinct features of its own.) There is, of course, a great deal more to be said here. But if we are to talk about historical method, this is the discussion we need to have. It has not yet taken place, to my knowledge, in the main guild of New Testament scholarship. To engage in it would be to honor the memory of its greatest exponent in our field, the late Ben F. Meyer.[6] He and I and others have made some proposals and have shown how they work in practice. I await comment and engagement.

The main reason why anyone, Christian or otherwise, would want to undertake the historical task is that the sudden rise of Christianity is, to put it bluntly, extraordinary and demands an explanation. The more specific reasons why Christians ought (in my view) to engage in this task have to do with the historical questions raised, but not yet answered, in the last two hundred years. Call these reasons apologetic if you like, but if the alternatives are pious closed-mindedness on the one hand or helpless capitulation to post-Enlightenment rationalism on the other, the word *apologetic* ceases to have much sting. Negatively, it has been said time and again that the picture of Jesus in the Gospels is historically incredible and that Christianity is, therefore, based on a mistake. Theologians from Martin Kähler to Luke Timothy Johnson have denied the inference, saying that Christianity is unaffected by the Gospel's inaccuracy and unreliability. Most, myself included, accept that the inference is valid: if the Gospels got it wrong, Christianity is indeed ill founded. However, positively, it should be clear that the church's use of the Gospels prior to and indeed since the rise of so-called critical historiography has given scant attention to what the Gospels themselves are saying about the actual events of Jesus' life and his kingdom-proclamation. It should also be clear that therefore the church is, in effect, sitting on but paying no attention to a central part of its own tradition that might, perhaps, revitalize or reform the church significantly were it to be investigated. This is *not* a matter of saying that theology must conform to every last hypothetical reconstruction ("history-W"), an impossible task in any case. Rather, as historians approximate to "history-E," that history itself—Jesus himself, in other words, as a figure of "history-E" and *not* simply of the historians' approximations—confronts, disturbs and beckons us in new ways. This need not ultimately involve going behind the Gospels or contradicting them; it must involve understanding what they are saying about Jesus within the world of first-century Judaism, not within the imagination of subsequent piety (or indeed impiety).[7] To rule out this possibility a priori, and to content oneself with a nonhistorical Christ of faith, seems to me not only deeply counterintuitive but also demonstrably false to New Testament Christianity.

Problems, of course, remain. My explanation for why John plays little part in the book remains thin (*JVG* xvi), though not as thin as Johnson implies. I was contributing to a complex debate in which the Synoptics were the main subject matter. I do think, however, that to rule John out altogether a priori as a historical source is a mistake. Nobody in the current debate seems to read C. H. Dodd or Percy Gardner-Smith or even J. A. T. Robinson, let alone to engage with them; rather they rest content with century-old shibboleths about the nonhistorical nature of John. If I am even half right about the Jesus of the Synoptic tradition (and I don't rule out noncanonical sources a priori, either; I just don't think, as a historian, that they have very much to offer), this old scholarly tradition is ripe for reconsideration, though neither I nor most of my colleagues in today's "Jesus debates" are equipped for this task. I sometimes think my critics were really asking for a 1,200-page book.

Jews and Their World in the First Century

In part three of *The New Testament and the People of God,* I gave as full a description of first-century Judaism, in many of its multiple varieties, as almost any other New Testament scholar has done in recent times. (The obvious exception, from whom I have learned a great deal, is of course E. P. Sanders.) Johnson's criticism (in a review of *NTPG* and repeated in his article in this volume) that I omitted some strands is technically true. I didn't discuss Philo and the viewpoint he represents, nor did I give much consideration to other Diaspora Judaism. But this criticism is, for our present purposes, trivial. Nobody thinks that studying Philo and the Diaspora might help us get closer to Jesus within "history-E." I resist the suggestion that I have simplified or flattened out first-century Judaism. Nor did I simply describe what was there in the literary sources. What we know about first-century Judaism we also know from archaeological sources, coins and so on; and what we know enables us to mount a plausible historical hypothesis not only about what the writers of certain texts thought and believed but also, as Sanders has massively demonstrated, about what the majority of "ordinary Jews" thought and believed. We know about some of their popular movements. We know the symbols and the festivals that gave characteristic expression to their worldview. By assembling what we know and by studying it in context, we can infer, as a working hypothesis (abduction again), what that worldview was, fully allowing for all kinds of local variations and even denials (e.g., the Sadducees' denial of some things that many other Jews believed and worked for).

Of course there must have been a full spectrum of first-century Jews, from those who did all these things unreflectively (including plotting and attempting violent revolution) through to those who could have articulated their reasons, not least in terms of biblical metanarratives. Of course there must have been plenty of people who were anxious about, or who avoided contact with, movements of thought and action that the majority embraced. But I am in good company with much mainstream scholarship on first-century Palestinian Judaism in arguing that many Jews, including Jesus, regarded themselves as living within a narrative world that we can, in principle, reconstruct and in arguing that many others, who might not have been so articulate, ordered their lives around the symbols and symbolic praxis that embodied and sustained this narrative world.

This world is not the same as ours. I am anxious when, for instance, Klyne Snodgrass, objecting to my reading of some of the parables on the grounds that we are not sure whether Jesus and his hearers thought in the way I suggest, proposes instead ways of thinking that look to me suspiciously like contemporary Christian generalizations. Of course this is not an either-or situation. Many contemporary Christian generalizations stand in some relation—which we can, in principle, describe—to many strands in Second Temple Judaism. But New Testament scholarship has been allowed for too long to "explain" biblical passages in terms of the assumption that Jesus' hearers were thinking in the same categories as were late-Western persons, whether Christian or not. The day I was drafting this passage I came upon the following, in a new book about St. Patrick:

> Can an account of the human experience of the divine communicate that experience to someone who does not share the same understanding of the universe . . . ? This is as true of the documents that make up the New Testament as it is true of Patrick, but Christians today have heard the Gospels so often that their foreignness is passed over, or we are so used to accommodating them into our view of reality that we do not notice that we hear them in a way very alien to that of the audience for whom they were first written.[8]

While not wishing, then, to deny continuity between the original meaning of the text and our own reading of it, I insist that we must learn to live within the "foreign" world of Second Temple Judaism if we are to understand the New Testament; that this task, though difficult, is not impossible; and that the best way of accomplishing it is by studying not simply literary works but the worldview (praxis, story, symbol, question-and-answer) of the society as a whole, which is reflected in our extant sources but embraces a much wider circle of life.

The mass movements in the century or so before and after Jesus of which we have knowledge turned, again and again, toward anti-Roman revolt. Of course there were differing degrees and different agendas for how to cope with the present time and for how to be a loyal Jew granted the way things were. I spelled all that out in considerable detail. There were, however, constant factors, which emerge as much in symbolic actions as in literary remains: gathering in the wilderness, for instance, or symbolically crossing the Jordan. To a people who celebrated Passover annually and who regularly retold the narrative of the exodus, that could only mean one thing. When this "new exodus" motif is combined with a counter-temple theme—as many have argued for various movements within Second Temple Judaism, including those of John the Baptist, Jesus and the early church—we find ourselves in the thick of what Sanders called "restoration eschatology." This is an appropriately loose term to denote various movements that could locate their different agendas within the broad hope that Israel's god[9] would act decisively to restore the people's fortunes and to reestablish them as in the days of old. Sometimes, but not always, those visions of the days of old included the hope for a revived monarchy. Exodus, temple, kingship: a powerful combination. There is plenty of evidence that a large number of Jews in the period of roughly 100 B.C. to A.D. 140 embraced and acted on something like this vision. This was the context within which words like salvation meant what they meant.

We must conclude, then, (a) that most Jews of Jesus' day did not believe (to put it mildly) that they were living in their ideal world; (b) that the failure of their world to live up to their hopes had a good deal to do with foreign overlordship, which ultimately might be got rid of by violent action; and (c) that their god was committed to bringing about their liberation. Of course, as I have frequently pointed out, some were profiting comfortably from the system of Roman occupation. The Sadducees, on the one hand, and the Herodian court, on the other, were presumably not dissatisfied—though Martin Goodman's powerful and detailed argument for aristocratic involvement in the war of A.D. 66-70 needs to be taken seriously.[10]

The spectrum of positions among the Pharisees (for which, by the way, there is excellent support in some recent scholarship, including work by Jewish writers)[11] means that not all of them would have been involved in "zeal." But this was clearly one strong option for many, and there is actually no major problem in reconstructing (by appropriate abductive method) the hypothetical symbolic and narrative world within which such activity took place. This is not assertion, as is suggested by those for whom nothing except Humean deduction counts as argument; it is a hypothesis that has been proposed, tested, supported by evidence and defended against alternative construals of the evidence and that emerges as a highly probable reading. It is ironic to be criticized for being uncritical because one takes sources at face value and then, almost in the same breath, for being too clever because one reads all the sources critically.

In all of this, I, in company with a good many other writers of all shades of opinion, am restoring to the debate the sociopolitical dimension that, ever since the Enlightenment, has been screened out in favor of "purely religious" readings.

To insist on including this dimension is not to suggest that everything is either really or merely political; far from it. It is simply to integrate that which should never have been disintegrated in the first place—that is, if we are interested in "history-E." For example (to mention only one consideration), in a world where the fastest-growing religious cult was that of Caesar, religion was bound to involve politics and vice versa. But that is, of course, only one particular example of a much broader phenomenon.

One difference some have seen between many late-Western worldviews and most Second Temple Jewish ones is that those who inhabited some versions of the latter were demonstrably conscious of living within a long and overarching narrative, the story of Israel, Israel's god and the pagan world. However, things are not quite that simple. There are several people in late-Western culture who think of themselves as living within a large historical narrative, too. Post-Enlightenment Western persons frequently think of themselves as riding the crest of a historical wave whose earlier story includes the ancient world, the Dark Ages, the Middle Ages, the Renaissance, the Reformation (in some tellings, not all), the Enlightenment and, in some cases now, Postmodernity. Part of the problem, perhaps, is not so much that we do not think of ourselves as living within a narrative but that we think of ourselves as living within a *different* one. Even those who remain ignorant of the detailed story of the periods I have just mentioned are often dimly aware that we live in something called "the modern world," as opposed to the "olden days," and that there are certain implications of this (modern medicine, air travel and so on).

One difference between the controlling story which many of us in the West now take for granted as "our" story, and the large story that Jesus' contemporaries told themselves, is that, so far as I know, nobody in the Dark Ages thought they were in the Dark Ages, waiting for the light to dawn, and nobody in the Middle Ages thought in a puzzled sort of way about why they were still in the Middle Ages and about when the long-awaited Renaissance might appear. These were retrospective constructs. There are, of course, plenty of cults, plenty of individuals and plenty of whole societies that have lived with a sense of incompleteness or worse and that have told stories about their history in which they are living within a longer narrative that includes a glorious distant past, an undesirable present and an exciting future. Marxism has characteristically told a narrative of that sort; so have many cargo cults and other millenarian movements. But the large common narrative we tell ourselves about Western civilization (which, incidentally, is seldom written down in full but, instead, is taken for granted on the edge of a thousand casual remarks; I suspect some scholars, studying our period two millennia hence, would deny the existence of this common story because it could not be proved deductively) tends to assume that we are living in the "good" period, which *follows* a "worse" one. Whether because of long memories of the Magna Carta, or because of a latent "Whig view of history," or because of some semi-Darwinian sense that, despite all evidence to the contrary, "things are getting better," we tell the story as one of developing freedoms.

The narrative told by Jesus' contemporaries was not like that. It was sometimes about things getting worse before they would get better. In particular, it was about "the present evil age" and "the age to come." This is well known and well documented. This controlling narrative was deeply shaped by Scripture. Those who either read the Scriptures for themselves or heard them read in synagogue, those who sang the Psalms or heard them sung, those who reenacted the old festivals and told and sang the stories that went with them, those who told stories of the great kings and prophets of old and longed for things to be once more as they were then—all these and many besides were formed by these stories to belong to a larger story, the one that contained them all. This narrative made sense of the world, gave depth and meaning to the present and, above all, gave hope for the future. It was the story of Israel and its god and of their ongoing and often checkered relationship. And, since Israel's god was also the creator of the whole world, it was also the story of the world, particularly of the pagan nations with whose stories Israel's so often, and so fatefully, interacted.

Before I develop this vital line of thought any further, let me pause for one comment. A good deal of contemporary Christian thinking, not least among some biblical scholars, has assumed that what the texts "must" be talking about is the eternal salvation of the individual, which is seen not primarily as someone living within ongoing history but as someone who might as well be living at any time and in any place. This viewpoint has for so long been read into the first-century texts that some find it flatly counterintuitive to read them any other way. It is precisely at points like this that the historian has a responsibility to challenge prevailing assumptions. That is what I have tried to do in my writings and am trying to do now. It is remarkable how difficult it is to get people to hold in their minds, even for a minute, a way of looking at reality that is different from the way to which they have become accustomed—even when there is a mass of historical evidence encouraging them to do so.

The crucial point is to see that for an average Second Temple Jew (I know perfectly well how difficult it is to construct such a figure, but unless we explicitly try we shall construct an anachronistic one by stealth instead) what mattered more than his or her own isolated, individual "salvation" was the whole future direction of the purposes of YHWH for Israel and the world; or, to put it another way, what mattered was when and how the present evil age would come to an end and the new age be born. *That* this would happen was ensured by the old promises, not only in the Pentateuch but also in the Prophets. To believe in Israel's god was to believe that these promises would one day come true, to live within a story that had a future in which they came true. How and when it would happen was a matter of ongoing, sometimes bitter, debate. Insofar as people looked for a "salvation" for themselves as individuals—which I would not for a moment deny—that hope fell within the larger picture of God's future for the whole nation.

The point, then, which I have tried to make in several places and which still seems puzzlingly obscure to several of my readers—though it is as clear as day to others—is that many Jews of Jesus' day were aware of living within a larger narrative ("history-W," or at least "history-O," that is, oral history) about Israel's "history-E"; that Jesus' kingdom-announcement makes sense within this same narrative; and that they located themselves at a particular moment within that narrative. The location in question—the place in the scheme where they thought they were living—was a historical period characterized by several overlapping and interlocking phenomena. Israel's oppression at the hands of foreigners was central, and it was interpreted (by those who, we must remember, believed that Israel's god was the Lord of the nations) in terms of YHWH's strange dealings with Israel. The present time was not outside YHWH's control; rather, as the prophets had taught, it was to be seen as the result of YHWH's temporary judgment on Israel, which would eventually come to an end.

This scheme can be seen to good advantage in a central and critical passage in the book of Daniel, namely chapter 9. This is the more important because it was almost certainly Daniel 9 (probably in combination with Daniel 2 and 7) to which Josephus referred when he spoke of an oracle in the Jewish Scriptures which predicted that, at that time, a world ruler would arise from Judea, thereby causing countless multitudes of Jews to join the revolt of the mid-60s of the first century A.D. Daniel 9 is the only passage from the likely candidates that offers a specific chronological sequence, and we know from Second Temple sources that it was widely used for exactly such purposes.[12]

Daniel 9 contains the prayer of Daniel in Babylon, inquiring after the time when Jerusalem will be rebuilt. It expresses the belief, common to Jeremiah and other writers on the same subject, that what had happened to Israel was not an accident and did not mean that YHWH had overlooked his promises to Israel. What had happened, had happened within the covenant: Israel had sinned, and YHWH had allowed this evil to befall his chosen people. But, by the same divine covenant faithfulness, Israel would be restored, albeit through difficult and perilous times (Dan 9:24-27), climaxing with the cessation of the sacrifices and the setting up of "an abomination that desolates"—a phrase most readers of the New Testament will at once recognize from Mark 13:14 and Matthew 24:15.

Among the many vital points that emerge from Daniel 9 and from a consideration of how it would be read in Jesus' day, we must highlight one in particular. The chapter opens with Daniel's meditation on the prophecy of Jeremiah, according to which Jerusalem would lie desolate for seventy years.[13] When Gabriel gives Daniel his answer, however, the seventy years have become seventy *weeks of years*, subdivided into seven, sixty-two, and one (Dan 9:24-27). Jeremiah's prophecy has been reinterpreted in precisely the text that we have good reason to suppose was a vital one for Jews of Jesus' day and the next generation; and what it says, beyond all cavil, is that *the "exile" is extended beyond the time of Israel's actual sojourn in Babylon*. This chimes in exactly with the portrait of the "returning exiles" under Ezra and Nehemiah: we are slaves, they say, in our own land, and we are this because of our own sins.[14] What slaves need is, of course, a new exodus, which is what Daniel 9:15-19 implies. And when this comes, it will "finish the transgression, . . . put an end to sin, and . . . atone for iniquity" (Dan 9:24).

Craig Evans has shown, in his article in the present volume, that this perception of where the Jews were in God's timetable characterized a wide spread of Second Temple Jewish self-perception. It is by no means confined, as is sometimes suggested, to Qumran, though it is strongly in evidence there.[15] Since I thought I had made all this clear at least twice—and since it is quite evident that many readers have not picked up the point—I am anxious about trying to say it again, but I must: most of Jesus' Jewish contemporaries believed that the exile was still continuing and that what they needed and longed for was the real return from exile.[16]

Many of the objections that have been raised to this notion, in this volume and elsewhere, are completely beside the point, telling me in effect not that I was wrong but that I had failed to make myself clear. To point out, as some have done, that many Jews were living in the land of Israel and worshiping in the temple (so how could they think of themselves as being in exile?) is about as helpful as objecting to the Enlightenment philosophers' self-perception by showing that, despite the label they gave to their movement, they still lit candles every evening, proving that they knew they were really in the dark. The more subtle probing of Richard Hays's question—whether this idea of continuing exile goes rather with the experience of groups like Qumran who actually were exiled—likewise fails to grip the point that emerges from the biblical base of Daniel 9, Ezra 9 and Nehemiah 9: the sense that the Babylonian exile was simply the beginning of a longer period of history, *one in which the same political and theological conditions applied and to which the same word*—exile—*could therefore appropriately be given.* In the massive annotation supplied by Craig Evans and the volume of essays edited by James M. Scott it is demonstrated that this self-perception was indeed widespread and that it lay at the heart of the Second Temple Jewish belief that, despite being back in the land geographically, despite having the temple rebuilt after a fashion, despite the regular worship and sacrifices and despite even the establishment of the Hasmonean dynasty as a more or less independent monarchy, YHWH had not yet acted as he had promised to do. Israel had not yet "returned" from *the period of history* characterized by the suffering and oppression which, according to the prophets, had resulted from the national sin.

When I use the word *exile* in this sense, then, it refers to *a period of history with certain characteristics,* not to a geographical situation. To the objection that this is somewhat misleading, since *exile* inalienably refers to geography, I reply that our task as historians is not to dictate to our subjects how they ought to have thought and spoken, but to think ourselves into the thoughts of the period. When we do this, we find Daniel 9, and a host of clustering ideas that radiate out from it, near the center of the worldview and the self-perception of many (not all) Jews of Jesus' day. Daniel 9 declares that the period of exile has continued long after the Babylonian exile and that it will be brought to its climax in the strange events which concern the abomination of desolation and the cessation of sacrifice, and, yet more strangely, "an anointed one" who "shall be cut off and shall have nothing" (Dan 9:26); and, not strangely at all, the time when "the troops of the prince who is to come shall destroy the city and the sanctuary" (Dan 9:26). We note, by the way, that in Daniel's highly influential scheme the seventy weeks, which are by definition the prolongation of the period of exile, *include* the rebuilt sanctuary of the Second Temple period. The writer, and presumably his Second Temple readers, knew perfectly well that the extension of the seventy years of Babylonian exile to the seventy weeks of years of exile included, and indeed mostly consisted of, time when Jews were back in the land worshiping in the rebuilt temple.

It is not, then, merely a matter of Jesus' making a "metaphorical link" (Hays's phrase) between his own activity and the exilic promises of hope. Here, interestingly, my debate with Hays echoes some earlier ones that he and I have had about Pauline theology, debates in which his recent commentary on 1 Corinthians represents a striking further move forward.[17] It is not a matter of detached echoes, which produce a dehistoricized typology, but rather of historical sequence: if it is true that many, even most, of Jesus' contemporaries thought of themselves in the way I have described and if it is true (as seems to me incontrovertible) that the phrase "kingdom of God" is a shorthand for not only the hope for return from exile but several other aspects of "restoration eschatology," we are fully justified in looking for evidence that Jesus held the view I have described and that he (like many other Jews, according to Josephus) believed the scheme of Daniel 9 would shortly reach its climax. When, in that light, we find the puzzling and dangerous word about "the abomination of desolation" in Mark 13 and Matthew 24, do we not have a prima facie case for saying that Jesus intended to hook in to Daniel's scheme of thought? Hays himself has taught us how, in a proper disciplined fashion, we may hear the scriptural echoes that a particular phrase can evoke when quoted in a first-century text. This is not, of course, a complete argument, but it is a straw in the wind that indicates how the full gale of discourse would blow if it had more space.

I do not think, therefore, that I have, in McGrath's words, elevated the exile-restoration pattern to too high a place. Indeed, part of the point is that it isn't a *pattern*, as though we were talking about mere typology, something that happened once or possibly more in the past and that now needs to happen again. Nor is it simply an image, a metaphor in the sense of an abstract idea (see below on metaphors and their referents).[18] We are talking about something that has *not* yet happened (from the perspective of a first-century Jew), namely, the fulfillment of Daniel 9 and all the other passages that cluster round the theme. *Exile* thus means, more or less, "the present evil age" as opposed to "the age to come."[19] It is a period of history, like the Middle Ages or the Dark Ages. Just as *middle* and *dark* in those phrases are, of course, metaphors, and yet the periods were real periods of years and centuries, so *exile* in the sense I am using it is, of course, a metaphor (since its meaning transcends geographical exile, the normal literal reference), but the period is a real period of actual human history.

Exile was not, then, merely an idea in people's minds that could be called up if individuals or groups thought it a useful way of describing their own particular moment or situation. It sums up the set of images, clustered together in Daniel and many other places, through which Second Temple Jews explained their present plight, saw it as going back to the Babylonian exile in particular and applied to it the great promises of "return" that they found in Isaiah and elsewhere.

The Eschatology of Jesus

All of this brings us at last to the great question that has dominated not only several of these essays but also many reviews and public discussions: how are we to talk sense, and historical sense at that, about Second Temple eschatology and apocalyptic? And how are we to locate Jesus on that map with the right balance of appropriate double similarity and dissimilarity—that is, so that he makes sense both as a first-century Palestinian Jew and as the one from whom Christianity took its origin and so that he is recognizably saying something different both from what his contemporaries had said and also from what the church said after Easter?[20]

It is vital to begin with some technical terms—not, first and foremost, the dreaded words *eschatology* and *apocalyptic* themselves (though goodness knows they have caused us enough problems and still do),[21] but rather the much-abused word *metaphor* and the other terms that cluster around it.[22] Many who use the word *metaphor* and its cognates in this debate seem to me to employ it in a very imprecise and misleading way. People can of course use words however they wish; but if we are to understand one another, let alone move toward agreement, it is vital to be clear at precisely this point. (I take comfort in the knowledge that the sixteenth-century Reformers faced exactly the same problem, that of saying what they meant by metaphor and of deciding which biblical passages were to be taken metaphorically in discussing, among other things, the sentence "This is my body.")

Strictly speaking, the opposite of *metaphorical* is *literal*. These two words refer to *the way words refer to things*, not to the things themselves. Confusion arises, not least in present discussions, because this pair is regularly muddled up with the words *abstract* and *concrete*, which indicate not *the way words refer to things* but rather *the sort of things words refer to*. Thus "Plato's theory of forms" refers, *literally*, to a doubly abstract entity (the forms themselves, by definition, are abstract, and the theory is an abstract idea about those abstractions). If I say

"Plato's whole box of tricks," intending to refer to that same theory, I am referring *metaphorically* to the same abstract entity (or entities). Alternatively, if I talk
about "my car," I am referring *literally* to something concrete; and if I say "my old
tin can," I am referring *metaphorically* to that same concrete entity.[23] Matters are
made much worse because, in popular usage, *literally* is regularly used to add
emphasis to a sentence without any serious intent to mean what it says ("we were
literally driving at the speed of light"; "my grandfather is literally as old as the
hills"). We are thus bereft of the literal meaning of *literal,* and we find ourselves
wallowing in all too many metaphorical meanings of *metaphorical.*

The problem comes to a head in one or two essays in particular. Allison
(pp. 131-32) seems to use *metaphorical* to mean abstract; for when he says that it
would be unwise to reduce the language of *2 Baruch* to metaphor, it is the word
reduce that puzzles me. He then fills the linguistic gap by using the word *symbol*
and its cognates.[24] Thus when he accuses me of forcing a choice between understanding eschatology in terms of metaphors and understanding it in terms of the
end of the space-time universe (p. 134), he is first forcing his shrunken understanding of metaphor on to me and then rejecting it. Revealingly, in order to do
this he has to truncate the relevant sentence in *Jesus and the Victory of God* (*JVG*
208, point 3): I there speak of "a new and quite different phase *within* space-time
history." This is, after all, very close to what Allison then goes on to describe as
his own view (and, he says, that of both Johannes Weiss and E. P. Sanders): the
view that "eschatological language concerns the climax of Israel's history and the
remaking—not the end—of the natural world." That is quite a vague statement,
which needs more precise nuancing, but I would not be unhappy with it as a general guide to the meaning I perceive as well.

Has Allison been fighting a shadow all along in his opposition to the reading
of apocalyptic that I and others have expounded? He may or may not be right in
his apparently revisionist reading of Albert Schweitzer, but it is certainly the case
that most people since Schweitzer have taken the great doctor to be saying that
Jesus was expecting the actual end of the space-time universe. If Allison wants to
carve out some hermeneutical space between that view and the belief that nothing much happened except what happened in people's heads and hearts, he is
welcome; but he will find me (as well as George B. Caird and others) there ahead
of him. I am quite happy to think that some apocalyptic texts, and some of their
readers, did envisage actual stars falling from the sky and so on; the question is,
how were these texts, the ones Jesus and the early Christians drew on, being read
in this period, and what did Mark and the others think they meant? If Mark had

intended us to read his thirteenth chapter as an account of physical stars falling from the sky, why has he so carefully told us that Jesus was answering a question about the fall of Jerusalem? But that something was to happen in the concrete world through which everything that mattered was changed—on that, as will appear, we agree, though not, I think, in our view of what it was.

Matters get still worse when the confusion between *metaphorical/literal* and *abstract/concrete* is compounded by association with a further pair: *spiritual* and *this-worldly* (or *historical,* or various other near-synonyms).[25] Somewhere here, too, belongs *cosmic,* as in Paul Eddy's essay (pp. 47, 55), where he speaks interestingly of "a literal cosmic personal enemy" and "a literal cosmic Son of Man" and suggests that to refuse this dimension is to "spiritualize" the restoration of Israel that Jesus was promising. Eddy elsewhere (p. 44) proposes "a 'non-natural' inbreaking of God, a divine intervention of such *cosmic* qualities and proportions, that—although the cosmos itself would remain—to call it purely 'historical' in Wright's sense would be woefully inadequate" (emphasis original). These are challenging and important comments, and I need to tease out my response to them a bit further. To take the last one first: the trouble with *cosmic,* I think, is that it seems to carry three overlapping but by no means identical meanings: "cosmic-S," meaning "supernatural" or at least "non-natural"; "cosmic-D," meaning "relating to direct divine activity, unmediated by historical process"; and "cosmic-C," meaning "relating to the entire creation, especially outer space." When we then start talking of Jesus (and/or "the Son of Man") flying about on a cloud in mid-air and when we use the word *cosmic* (or "literal cosmic"!) in relation to such an event, which sense are we employing? Are we not in danger of confusing nonterrestrial events ("cosmic-C") with supernatural events ("cosmic-S"), and are we not hoping that by putting them together we might somehow arrive at direct divine intervention ("cosmic-D")? And is not this a massive non sequitur?

This complex linguistic confusion is, I believe, the surface noise covering up a much deeper problem, which is how we conceive of reality in general and of divine action within the world in particular. This is obviously of particular relevance to the subject matter of first-century eschatology. If we were to believe that events in our world belonged within a simple continuum of physical or quasi-physical causes and effects, into which no divine power could ever "intervene," then the meaning of both *spiritual* and *cosmic* would be affected. We might of course read eschatological and apocalyptic language (e.g., the sun and moon being darkened, the coming of the Son of Man) as an indication that the writer clearly believed in a supernatural, "interventionist" deity, while we do not; or we might suggest that the writer's viewpoint approximated more to ours, seeing such language simply as a metaphor for certain striking things that happen within the unbroken continuum of cause and effect.

Stephen Evans is quite right that I am firmly committed to rejecting this way of conceiving the question, though I think he is somewhat idealistic in claiming that the word *supernatural* is being misused if we understand it in that setting. Of course classical Christian theism, standing on the shoulders of biblical Judaism, developed subtle and sophisticated ways of thinking and speaking about divine action within the created order. But the word *supernatural* itself and related terms such as *miracle* are now, I believe, firmly allied to the notions (derived from Enlightenment Deism among other places) that the world is indeed a closed continuum, that God is normally absent from it but that God might from time to time intervene into it (breaking the "laws of nature" as he does so). So firm is this alliance that the mere mention of such words has become next to useless for people who do not want to invoke that model at all but who want to work instead within precisely that more nuanced classical theism of which Stephen Evans speaks. This is a matter of judgment about current usage; in rejecting this post-Enlightenment sense of *supernatural* I am not at all committed to saying that God does not work within history. Far from it. I am rejecting one model (which I think Stephen Evans also rejects), and I am, with some sorrow, abandoning language that once did not, but that now does, invoke that model for most Western listeners.

There is of course no commonly agreed conceptuality, still less is there language to express it, to talk about the ways in which the God we know in Jesus Christ and by the Spirit does act in relation to the world to which he is in so many senses always present and from which he nevertheless remains mysteriously distinct. The ancient Jews developed language systems to cope with this: God's Word, Wisdom, Spirit, Law, Presence, Glory, and even Righteousness, Love, Salvation— the list goes on, with varying degrees of personification in various texts. The Christians fell heir to this tradition and made rich and fresh use of it. But one of the things that their view of Jesus suggests to us is that it is in the "ordinary" events of Jesus' life and death, just as much as in the "extraordinary" events, that we should recognize the presence of the true God. It was a patristic misunderstanding, picked up again by Enlightenment apologists, to suppose that the miracles "proved" Jesus' divinity; most of Jesus' mighty deeds are paralleled in the Elijah and Elisha stories, and nobody supposed that those great prophets were "divine."

What then, now that we have attempted to clear some of the conceptual rubble out of the way, are we to say about what Second Temple Jews expected to happen, about the language they used to express their hopes and about how Jesus and the early church developed both the hopes and the language?[26]

I repeat what I have said often enough: we have no reason to suppose that any Jews for whom we have actual evidence expected that the space-time universe was going to come to a stop ("the end of the world" of popular imagination). However "cosmic" their language, they clearly envisaged events *after which* there would still be recognizable human life on the recognizable planet, albeit in drastically transformed conditions. Since one of the conditions that needed drastic transformation was their political and social situation, and since so many of them (goaded, as Josephus says, by apocalyptic oracles) took part in military uprisings to try to speed this transformation on its way, we must conclude that they did not make a sharp division between transformations wrought by God alone and those wrought by his obedient people. Their sacred texts, after all, spoke of many different kinds of divine deliverance, some of which happened while Israel merely stood still and watched, others of which happened through great battles.

In particular, we have no reason to suppose that any Second Temple Jewish reader of Daniel 7 would have read the passage about the Son of Man coming on the clouds as referring to anything other than the vindication of Israel after suffering, and perhaps the triumph of a particular Israelite, the Messiah. I can hardly stress this point enough, since though I have made it many times it still seems not to have got through. Several essayists continue to refer to the quotations from Daniel 7:13 in Mark 13 and 14 and parallels as though this point had not been made.[27] Several still read Mark 13 as though it "must" really be about an end, a transformation, that has not yet taken place, even though the question with which the chapter opens, and for which the previous chapters have exactly prepared us, is about the fall of Jerusalem and the temple in particular.[28]

Perhaps a comment about the nature of the discussion may be allowed at this point. I sense a huge anxiety in many contributors: a fear that, if they concede the point that Mark 13 is basically about events in the first century, something will be irreplaceably lost from their theology. Since the writers I have in mind all give allegiance to a high view of Scripture, let me beg them to let Scripture say what it says, to not force it to say something else (remember McGrath's warnings about Scripture standing over against all our traditions!) and to contemplate with equanimity the task of reconstructing a Christian theology of the future from those texts that surely speak of it—Romans 8, 1 Corinthians 15, Revelation 21—22 and so on— rather than from those that are unlikely at best. Of course, we are at liberty to invoke a *sensus plenior* reading if we wish. But it is heavily ironic for conservative

Protestants to pull that rabbit out of the hat; and those who have pressed me personally to allow for second-level meanings in Mark 13 and its parallels, meanings that make the passage refer not only to first-century events but to events yet to come, seem clearly to be looking for a let-out, a way of focusing not on what the passage refers to but on something else. How can this be loyalty to the text?

What matters, then, is first to ascertain how Daniel 7 was being read in the first century. Fortunately, through Josephus and *4 Ezra* in particular, we have some idea. This is the point of my earlier discussion about language. It was being read metaphorically, to refer to concrete events within ongoing history and to invest those events with their theological ("cosmic-D") significance. The concrete events in question would of course be huge, unmistakable, transformative; nothing would be the same again. Of course, not everything in Daniel 7 was read metaphorically: in the phrase "four beasts," the beasts are metaphorical, with concrete referents (world empires), but the number four was meant literally. And so on. Ideally one would need to go through every text inch by inch and tease out such nuances. But my basic point is that there is no evidence for anyone supposing that the denouement of Daniel 7—the Son of Man's coming to the Ancient of Days—was intended literally; and, even if they had supposed it to be so, it would have referred to an upward movement, not a downward one.

Two texts are quoted against me, purporting to show that the early Christians read Mark 13 in the way that I say Jesus did not intend. (By the way, the argument "the early church said such-and-such, therefore Jesus must have meant such-and-such when he used similar words" is not, shall we say, the most secure piece of logic in the world.) John 3:13 speaks of "the Son of Man" as having *already* come down from heaven; here the "coming down" is surely a reference to the incarnation. Then 1 Thessalonians 4:16-17—two verses that seem to me to have wielded a tyranny over New Testament interpretation out of all proportion to their significance, let alone their intelligibility—are reckoned to support the "traditional" reading of the coming of the Son of Man in Mark 13 and elsewhere. About this a little more needs to be said.

First, the passage gives no support to traditional views of the "rapture." The meeting with the Lord "in the air" is the kind of meeting in which citizens go out of the city gates to meet, at some point down the road, their Lord who has come from the mother city. They will not stay out in the country but will bring him back. They have come to welcome him, to escort him with honor into the city. Otherwise, in Paul's paragraph, what becomes of the dead who have been raised (to inhabit, one must assume, the renewed creation, which according to Romans 8 will be set free from its bondage to decay when God's children receive their new bodies)? The whole point of the paragraph is to comfort those whose loved ones have died; the destiny of the dead who are to be raised, and of the still-alive who are to meet the Lord in the air, must ultimately be to share the same continuing existence.

Second, though there are some clear parallels with the so-called Synoptic apocalypse, they by no means force us to conclude that Paul was thinking of "the Son of Man coming in clouds" when he spoke of "the Lord himself . . . descend[ing] from heaven." In 1 Thessalonians it is not Jesus' downward travel but the saints' upward travel that is accompanied by clouds. If Paul is here reinterpreting Daniel 7, he is envisaging the coming of the Son of Man as being now fulfilled not in the descent of Jesus but in the ascent of the still-alive saints.

Third, when Paul sets out substantially the same scenario in 1 Corinthians 15:51-52, instead of speaking of the saints' being snatched upward to meet the Lord in the air, he simply says that they will be "changed." This is of course in line with the theme of the whole chapter, which is not about comfort for the bereaved but about the nature of the resurrection body and about the continuity and discontinuity between the present body and that which is to come. But it shows well enough that we should be cautious before taking the densely apocalyptic language of 1 Thessalonians 4 literally in every respect. Please note, I do not say that it does not refer to concrete events; nor do I say these events are not of cosmic significance; I merely note that the way this language is used in all other texts known to us encourages us to suppose that it is highly figurative and not to be pressed for a literal, photographic account of that which is yet to happen.

Fourth, although I do believe there was a good deal of continuity between Jesus and Paul (something I have not yet written very much about), I regard it as illegitimate in principle, and very difficult in practice, to conduct historical Jesus research by arguing from something in Paul's writing to something that Jesus "must have meant." Such a move would in any case be laughed out of court by some of my main debating partners. In any case, the two verses in question in 1 Thessalonians 4 offer a complex and unique statement on a subject which Paul can elsewhere describe quite differently. Precisely because the resurrection made such a huge difference to everything, we must assume that Paul saw the world in a new light; the undoubted continuities of theme and matter are held within a framework of great discontinuity, which does not mean that Paul or the others were misrepresenting Jesus but rather that they believed him to have been much more than a great teacher whose ideas they should simply pass on. They believed he had accomplished the unique and decisive act for which Israel and the world had been waiting. Everything was now different. They now had different things to say, not because they were being disloyal to Jesus but precisely because they were being loyal.

That, indeed, is the point—a point well made, of course, by Allison himself in an earlier work.[29] The early Christians believed that the world *was* now a different place, that the God of Israel had acted decisively and uniquely within history; that actual, concrete, non-abstract events had taken place which *did* mean that God's kingdom had arrived in Israel, in creation, in a new way. Of course this "inaugurated" eschatology still had a vital and lively future element. Attempts to line my theology up with the flattened-out "realized eschatology" of Dodd are simply naive. But what few seem able to grasp is that the early Christians regarded the world as a different place *because Jesus of Nazareth had been bodily raised from the dead.* This was, for them, the great apocalyptic event that had already taken place, which pointed to great apocalyptic events that had not yet taken place but that now surely would. They scoured their linguistic and theological cupboards for metaphors adequate to express what had happened; but they believed it had happened within concrete history.

I did not discuss the resurrection of Jesus in *Jesus and the Victory of God* because I recognized, finally (and with one eye on considerations of space), that the book was basically about the mindset of Jesus as he went to the cross. I saw that the question of what happened next, vital though it is to any complete understanding of Christian origins, does not affect the question of how we understand what Jesus did, said and thought up to that point. I intend to address the question head-on in the next volume in the series, which should also put paid to the (frankly very funny) suggestion by Johnson that I hold a "minimalist" view of Jesus' resurrection. Why Johnson thinks I describe the resurrection as a "resuscitation" (p. 219) I don't know. Why he thinks I restrict its significance to Jesus as an individual I can't imagine. What he means by the "radical character" of the resurrection is not clear. And why he supposes I "dislike" such a view (p. 221) I have no idea. It is strange that Johnson, who is so skilled as an exegete of first-century texts, has such trouble reading one or two texts by a twentieth-century colleague that he must needs first invent a view for me to hold and then tell me off for holding it. If, of course, he means that when the early Christians said, "Jesus is risen from the dead," they were referring not to something that had happened to Jesus but to an experience that they had had, then not only is it he who is the minimalist but it is he who is inventing a story that none of the New Testament writers corroborate.

Far more important than addressing this set of misunderstandings, I think, is to clarify the way in which I think about the following:

1. how the early church believed that Jesus had, in fact, been vindicated
2. how the early church believed that Jesus would be vindicated in the future
3. how Jesus himself thought about his overall vindication from his pre-Calvary perspective
4. how the early church, faced with the total surprise of Jesus' resurrection, set about rethinking its traditional Jewish expectations
5. how this squares with the post-Easter perception that the world has not, after all, been healed

This is near the heart of a good deal of puzzlement among my readers, including the most sympathetic. I recognize now, much better than I did before, where this puzzlement has come from, and I hope to be able briefly to sort it out.

1. How the early church believed that Jesus had, in fact, been vindicated. The early church clearly believed that Jesus had been vindicated by the resurrection: "God has made him [Jesus] both Lord and Messiah" (Acts 2:36). "[Jesus Christ] was declared to be the Son of God [i.e., Messiah]. . . by the resurrection from the dead" (Romans 1:4). Jesus had already been vindicated. The resurrection was more important to them than any other single event; it is more true to say that they saw themselves (and knew and felt themselves) to be living in the first days of God's new world than to say that they saw, knew or felt themselves to be living in the last days of God's old world.

The resurrection of Jesus, in fact, offers the best available correlation to the point made by several essayists, notably Blomberg and Allison, that the Jewish expectation envisaged actual transformation within the concrete world. Actual transformation had indeed taken place, in a single, close-up, dramatic incident pregnant with cosmic meaning ("cosmic-D," of course) and life-transforming power. It was because they believed this had happened to Jesus (and because its meaning, and transforming power, was already flooding their own lives)[30] that the early Christians also believed in the coming transformation of the whole creation through the Spirit of Jesus (Rom 8).[31]

2. How the early church believed that Jesus would be vindicated in the future. The early church also continued to tell the story of Jesus' confrontation with the temple and its hierarchy, and to see that story as coming to its denouement in the temple's destruction, which would prove that Jesus had spoken the truth and thus was vindicated as a true prophet. They continued to use "apocalyptic" language about this forthcoming event, not least presumably because Jesus himself had done so. And they looked outwards to events on a far larger scale: the renewal of heaven and earth, the "exodus" of the whole creation, God's defeat of death itself. Of such matters only small hints can be found in the sayings of Jesus.[32]

3. *How Jesus himself thought about his overall vindication from his pre-Calvary perspective.* My view was, and remains, that Jesus shared the belief of many of his contemporaries: Israel's god would act decisively within history to fulfill his promises, to liberate Israel and thereby to set the whole world to rights. Moreover, Jesus believed that it was his task and vocation to bring about these events, in the ways that I have described at length. But the texts do not go very much further. They look to me much more like the result of the early church's refusal to read its own post-Easter eschatology back into his mind, and its recognition that he remained ignorant, as he himself said in this context, of how precisely things would work out. That, it seems, is part of what it meant to be the Messiah, part of the strange humiliation of which the cross itself was the climax. I believe, in other words, that we can credibly reconstruct the mindset of Jesus going to the cross, believing that Israel's god would vindicate him after his death—in other words, would raise him from the dead—and, moreover, believing that his solemn warnings about Jerusalem and the temple would also come true and function as a large-scale public vindication.[33] But because Jesus, as a Second Temple Jew, believed that YHWH's acting to redeem Israel would also be the means of setting the world to rights, it is reasonable to assume that, out beyond his own unique and specific task, he trusted that the creator God would use this victory to accomplish his will for all creation. There are hints that he did indeed believe this. There are signs (such as Romans 15:8-9) that the early church thought in these terms as well. But there are also very strong signs that the main emphasis of Jesus' teaching about the future was designed to be about the *immediate* future, and that this immediate future contained for him, as a matter of huge concrete and symbolic importance, the destruction of Jerusalem.[34]

4. *How the early church, faced with the total surprise of Jesus' resurrection, set about rethinking its traditional Jewish expectations.* The so-called second coming is built into the apostolic witness from the beginning, and for an excellent reason:

Jesus had been raised from the dead, and the Spirit had been poured out on the believers. But none of the other things that they might have expected to occur had taken place. The world had not visibly been put to rights. The early church held on firmly to both sides of the apparent paradox: the end had happened; the end was yet to come. Paul writes from prison about his present suffering at the hands of persecutors and also about the triumphant victory that Jesus won on the cross over the principalities and powers.[35] This is utterly characteristic. Both sides must be given the same stress.

Where did the early church's future hope begin? Whatever one makes of the stylized narrative in Acts 1, the suggestion that from very early on the church came to believe that Jesus, bodily risen from the dead, was now alive in God's space ("heaven"), and that he would appear again in the future, accords with all the other evidence we have. Many of my critics, faced with this, will say at once, "Well then, so why could they not have got this teaching from Jesus himself?" (so, e.g., Blomberg, pp. 296-97 n. 81, and Bock, p. 121). The answer of course is that they could, in principle; but it would be nice to see some solid evidence that Jesus did actually speak of this second coming in the way that is normally supposed. It simply will not do to go back to Daniel 7 again as though the question were now settled that it could refer, on Jesus' lips, to a downward movement rather than to an upward one (which is of course itself metaphorical). Just as Jesus had nothing, or next to nothing, to say about several other topics of hot interest in the early church—the Spirit, for instance, or circumcision, or speaking in tongues—so we do not need to postulate that he said much about the ultimate future of the cosmos, let alone his role within it. The parallel with my argument about Jesus' messiahship simply does not hold. There was no reason to regard a recently crucified man as Messiah, even if he had been raised from the dead, unless he had shown signs of claiming that status beforehand. There was no reason, however, for Jesus to provide his hearers with a detailed breakdown of the sequence of events, following his own death, through which he would be vindicated and the world would eventually be put to rights. Indeed, there was every reason not to.

We should recognize that the early Christians, in speaking of that ultimate future as they naturally and rightly did, were doing so from a position different from that of the pre-Calvary Jesus. For them, the "end" had now begun; and that beginning told them a good deal about the shape of (so to speak) the end of the end. In the climactic statements of Romans 8, 1 Corinthians 15 and Revelation 21—22, we see a vision far greater than the etiolated little eschatologies of some modern Protestant or evangelical debate. The second coming is but one part of a much greater whole. The entire creation will be set free from its bondage to decay; and when that happens the central, most wonderful feature of the picture will be the personal presence (for which the Greek, of course, is *parousia*) of Jesus. All this I, with the early church, most firmly believe. But I do not think that Jesus said much about this himself before his death. And—though God is free to do whatever God wants, and who knows which old metaphors may not come out of their cages when he does so—I do not think that he will arrive in the newborn world riding downward on a cloud.

   5. How this squares with the post-Easter perception that the world has not, after all, been healed. Several essayists, looking anxiously at my (as it appears to them) overrealized eschatology, reminded me of the point I made myself as strongly as I could in the last chapter of *Jesus and the Victory of God*: evil was not wiped off the earth at Easter.[36] Nor did the early Christians suppose it had been. But they were absolutely convinced that a great—no, not *a* great, *the* great—victory had been won in Jesus' crucifixion and resurrection.[37] This belief alone makes sense, after all, of why this odd little quasi-messianic sect even survived, let alone flourished, let alone arrived in Rome within a generation proclaiming its crucified Messiah as the world's rightful Lord, its new emperor. An eschatological reading of Jesus demands, I believe, that we get used to thinking in terms of the dialectic between achievement and *implementation*. Jesus did not come to teach an abstract ethic that the church should just go on teaching. He came (to borrow two illustrations from another book) to compose the score for others to sing, to provide the medicine for others to administer.[38] To point out tartly, as some no doubt will do, that much of the singing has been out of tune and that many of the patients have not improved is to say nothing whatever about the mindset of Jesus. To use the failure of the church as a lever to rewrite the history of its Lord would pass beyond irony toward blasphemy.

What Jesus Did and Said, and What It Meant

We come at last to the questions that have been raised—other than that of "Jesus' teaching about the future"—concerning the picture of Jesus' public career that I have offered in *Jesus and the Victory of God*. There are many issues I would gladly take up, were there still more space. I persist, for instance, in thinking that there are good contextual as well as theological reasons why "the one you should fear" in Matthew 10:28 and Luke 12:5 is the satan, not God. I persist in thinking that Jesus' temple action was an acted parable of its coming destruction and that the reason was not only the corruption of the officials but also the way the temple had come to function (as in Jeremiah's day) as a symbol of national security that somehow left out of account obedience to YHWH.[39]

In particular, I persist in my reading of the parables, and of certain key ones in particular. I was glad and grateful that Klyne Snodgrass accepted my reading of the parable of the sower, and I acknowledge that it might have been better to say that the parable evokes, rather than saying it "is a retelling of," the larger narrative about the kingdoms of the world and the kingdom of God (*JVG* 232). I do not think, however, that Snodgrass is right to say that I have distilled the theology of the parable of the prodigal son and applied it to Israel; rather, I think it is he who has made the parable "about" something much more general than it originally was. The "kingdom forgiveness Jesus embodied" (Snodgrass's summary, p. 70) was precisely, if I and others are right, all about God's restoration of Israel. When Snodgrass goes on to say that "first-century Jews were the initial hearers, but these are parables of the kingdom" (p. 70), it is the word *but* that bothers me: "the kingdom of God" was a first-century Jewish concept whose referent was precisely the restoration of Israel. I am perfectly happy that the challenging parables should be applied to "humanity preoccupied with mundane pursuits," but that seems to me *our* wider application of Jesus' much more focused telling.[40]

I did not expect an easy ride, of course, with the parable of the pounds/talents. I do want to insist, however, in company with Johnson (I am glad we are able to agree on something), that Luke at least did not think the parable was about an eschatological delay. Luke's introduction (Lk 19:11: "because he was near Jerusalem, and because they supposed that the kingdom of God was to appear immediately") not only *can* be understood in terms of "Yes, it's coming, but are you sure you really want it?"—rather than "No, it's not coming for a long time yet"—but simply *must* be taken this way, in view of Luke's own scene later on in the same chapter, when Jesus, in tears on the donkey, pronounces over the city the judgment that, in the parable, is meted out on the wicked servant, "because you did not recognize the time of your visitation" (Lk 19:44). The kingdom has come—indeed, Israel's god has come back to claim what was his—and his people have ignored him. I agree with Snodgrass (p. 76) that the dual focus on present and future is characteristic of all New Testament eschatology; but in Luke 19 the focus is on the present and on the immediate future that will follow as a result.

Now to one of the largest lacunae in *Jesus and the Victory of God*: the miracles. I was aware that my discussion was brief and that more could have been done, as Stephen Evans (p. 188) rightly comments. I was uncomfortably aware that to take the subject further would have necessitated a much more substantial discussion of method and presupposition than would have been possible within the already bulging seams of the book. I had listened to Colin Brown's lectures on the subject in Oxford in 1993, and I knew the vast ranges of issues involved. Where I was quite clear was that even if we suppose Jesus to have done exactly what the Gospels say he did, this should not be taken as a "proof" of his "divinity." That is not to "naturalize" his "mighty works"; rather it is to note that in the Scriptures it is prophets who do these kinds of things and to note further that, as Moses discovered, the magicians of Egypt could imitate him. As Jesus himself and the author of Acts were aware, other people besides Jesus were capable of performing exorcisms. I accepted Crossan's distinction between "miracle" and "magic" for the sake of the discussion, drawing the sting of it in the way I developed the argument. Stephen Evans is right to say that, in the end, my view is not too unlike that of John P. Meier (and Johnson is right to say that I do not use Meier as much as I might have done; but how many more footnotes did he want?); but the meaning of Jesus' "mighty works" must remain, as Evans sees, a function of the interpretation we give or indeed of the interpretation Jesus himself gave to his life as a whole.

Which leads us, by a somewhat circuitous route, to what I intended, and planned structurally, to be the climax of the book: the three chapters (eleven, twelve and thirteen) on messiahship, the cross and the return of YHWH to Zion. I make here two preliminary comments.

First, I find it remarkable how comparatively little interest has been shown, by other reviewers as well as the present essayists, in either the detail of the argument or its overall thrust. If what I have set out here is anywhere near the truth, it ought to be of considerable significance for all sorts of debates and discussions in biblical and systematic theology, which have only been hinted at in the present volume.

Second, I also find it remarkable how few critics have seen the point of the historical method I used in these three chapters.[41] It is precisely here that the well-worn objection to discovering the aims of Jesus (that all we can really find out is the theology of the evangelists) meets a counter-objection: the sayings in question are in most cases cryptic, riddling and dark, so that many commentators declare themselves at a loss to understand them. (Think, for instance, of the green tree and the dry in Lk 23:31.) This holds true for all three categories: messianic sayings, sayings about the cross and words about the return of YHWH to Zion. By themselves these sayings would yield, and to many interpreters have yielded, little. Yet put them in the context of the central and decisive actions of Jesus—his temple action, the Last Supper and the entire last journey to Jerusalem—and they come to life with power and consistency. At the same time, the sayings in question simply do not make sense as emanating from the early church. The early Christians were neither cryptic, riddling nor dark when it came to Jesus' messiahship, his saving death or, ultimately, his divinity. Until this argument is addressed, I cannot but regard the reiteration of the standard objection as beside the point.

In the discussion of the crucifixion, two questions stand out from these essays (apart from the tendency of some writers to turn this, too, into another discussion of the second coming; is the meaning of the cross so taken for granted in some theological circles that nothing new can be learned?). First, let me address the question raised by McGrath (whom I first met, over twenty years ago, a few yards from the spot where I am writing these words): Have I succeeded in making the Last Supper more important than the crucifixion itself? At this I was troubled, and I cast in my mind what manner of saying this might be. There is no possible way I could have meant what McGrath suggests, and I am still puzzled that anyone could think I did. My argument was, rather, that the Supper was Jesus' deliberate signpost, pointing to the reality. Signposts are vital if you want to know where you are and where you are going, but they are not the thing itself. If a visiting student, wishing to study with Dr. McGrath, were lost in the wilds of North Oxford, the large sign saying "Wycliffe Hall" would correctly inform her that she had arrived at her destination. But if she sat down in front of the sign, expecting thereby to acquire a theological education, she would be disappointed. The Supper was Jesus' careful sign, more accurate in its symbolic narrativity than any theory could ever be, of the meaning he intended his forthcoming death to bear. I believe it remains the first and finest index of that meaning. But it was and is the cross itself, replete with its own multiple symbolism, that stands at the center.

Second, let me address the question interestingly raised by Eddy (p. 55): If Jesus dies, as I say, as the representative (and in a sense the substitute) of Israel, the Israel that has turned its back on YHWH, why does Jerusalem still have to fall? This is, in a sense, the historical version of the old universalist conundrum that if Christ died for the ungodly (as Christian tradition since Paul has always said), why are not all the ungodly automatically saved (as Christian tradition since Paul has usually denied)? I do not have a good answer for this mystery, but I do not regard this as a fatal objection to the proposal. There is a sense in which, seen from the point of view I have proposed, the first atonement theology in the early church is that of Peter on the day of Pentecost: "Save yourselves," he said, "from this corrupt generation" (Acts 2:40). In other words (read through the lens I propose), the Messiah has died, at the hands of the pagans, the death toward which you are rushing, and he has made a way through to the new age for which you have longed; abandon the course upon which you are set, and discover instead the way, his way, of peace and life. That thought may, perhaps, be part of the meaning of Galatians 2:20 ("The Son of God, who loved me and gave himself for me"). There was, I think, more to it than that, but not less.

The central question of all—the one that the talk-show hosts always want to know about, and rightly so—concerns the relation, if that is the word, between Jesus and God. Here I am grateful to Eddy in particular for his clear restatement (pp. 58-59) of what I was trying to say. Yet problems still remain. There is obviously a lot more to be said about enthronement and its implications. I fear that some writers, both conservative and radical, are operating with a rather too woodenly traditional view of what it might mean to speak of Jesus as being in any sense "divine." Once again we think, if we are not careful, as the heirs of the long Deist years. We need to rediscover, through coming to a fresh understanding of Jesus himself, just what it might mean to make such a claim.

A sign that this exercise is still not complete is when assumptions are made about what Jesus' "divine self-understanding" ought to have been like and what it ought to have prevented. Why, for instance, does Blomberg find it "disturbing" (p. 37) to think that Jesus must have known he might have been mistaken? Is it not far more disturbing to muzzle the texts that say, clearly enough, that Jesus faced exactly that question? Is it not good orthodox theology to say, with the letter to the Hebrews, that he was tempted in every way as we are? Why does Stephen Evans miss the point so disastrously (pp. 195-96), supposing that I was simply arguing from what it would be like for us, in our "age characterized by uncertainty," if we were faced with the situation Jesus was in? I was, rather, trying to make sense (in the context, be it noted, of an argument against those who said the whole picture was nonsense) of the mindset of Jesus as evidenced in the texts: texts that tell of temptation, of seeing the satan at work in a remark of his closest associate, of Gethsemane (for if that is not an account of someone facing the possibility that they might be mistaken, I do not know what it is), of the mocking on the cross and of the final cry of abandonment. (Whatever other echoes that cry may have, it is the height of trivialization to say that Jesus was merely quoting a piece of Scripture with a happy ending.) Jesus knew, as all Jews knew, that it was failed messiahs who ended up on crosses.[42] Let me be blunt. Unless we do business with these texts, we have not really begun to consider what it might mean for God to become human. To marginalize or minimalize them because they do not conform to our idea of what God or what the self-knowledge of one who believed himself in some sense divine ought to be like is not only to be deeply unbiblical or even antibiblical; it is to insist on learning the meaning of the word *God* from somewhere other than Jesus himself.

Am I then saying, as Eddy asks (p. 57), that Jesus, in one sense, embodied Israel in making the true response to YHWH and, in another, embodied YHWH in returning at last to Israel? Yes. I do not see anything ultimately problematic about that. Indeed, though this was certainly not the route by which I came to this position, I see this as the historical focal point of the generalized and much later dogmatic statement that Jesus was perfectly human and perfectly divine.

Once again, however, it is not the case that Jesus was, did or articulated something that merely exemplified some larger truth that would be, as it were, the "real point." Statements beginning "Jesus came to teach us that . . ." or "Jesus was trying to show us that . . ."—though often containing some truth and sometimes even great wisdom—all ultimately miss the point. This is the difference between truly eschatological readings of Jesus, in my sense, and ultimately non-eschatological ones (even if they spend thousands of pages inventing "end-time" scenarios for Jesus to "teach"). Jesus came to bring to its climax, its great issue, the story of YHWH and Israel. He believed that this was the focal point of the story of YHWH with the world. Like his ancestor Jacob, he wrestled with God and with humanity.

His followers believed that he had prevailed. That belief, grounded in the resurrection—nothing else will do, historically, to explain the rise of the church—always was, and still is, self-involving. And that self-involvement, finding itself grasped by a Jesus-shaped love known as the Spirit of Jesus, must mean—can only mean—working to implement in the world the achievement of the cross. That is what inaugurated eschatology is all about. What I still cannot understand, though, is how some critics insist, on the one hand, that whatever else Jesus' resurrection might mean it was not an event within space-time history and, on the other hand, that nothing has really *happened* to inaugurate the actual, concrete new creation awaited by Jesus' contemporaries. Of course, if you bury the key piece of evidence, you can make a case for a while. But things don't stay buried long in the kingdom of God.

Part Four

Conclusion

Fourteen

From (Wright's) Jesus to (the Church's) Christ

Can We Get There from Here?

CAREY C. NEWMAN

*T*HE DIVINITY OF JESUS[1] IS A FUNDAMENTAL BUILDING BLOCK OF CHRISTIAN THE-
ology. Indeed, if the early church councils are to be heard at all, the
divinity of Jesus may be fairly considered to be *the* chief cornerstone.
Without the deification of Jesus there would not be a Trinity; and, at least theo-
retically (if not also historically), Christianity ceases to be Christianity when
Jesus is not confessed and worshiped as divine.[2] The divinity of Jesus is thus one
of the few issues in the study of Christianity that touches—and sometimes
drives—the work of nearly every scholar, regardless of discipline. Scripture scholars, theologians, philosophers and church historians all must, in the end, grapple
with this issue (or its implications) in one way or another. N. T. Wright's *Jesus
and the Victory of God* is no exception. It, too, wrestles with the complex theological relationship among Jewish monotheism, the historical Jesus and the church's
divine Christ.

But the divinity of Jesus is as historically vexing as it is theologically crucial.
Any assertion about this doctrine's theological centrality has a provocative, historical

correlate: the early Jesus movement (first?) *became* Christianity when regular, public and sanctioned devotion was offered to Jesus alongside of, and *as,* the *monos theos* of Judaism.[3] This last statement raises any number of important questions, not the least of which is "Of all the affirmations Christians cherished, what caused them to make, or why did they willingly make, the divinity of Jesus a, or the, confessional litmus test?"

The traditional answer has been to observe that the formal confessions about the Godhead were simply making explicit the convictional logic inherent in (or implied by) the New Testament.[4] But, in the end, this response does not really satisfy, for it only serves to drive the Trinitarian debate further back in time, to the first days of the Christian movement[5] and, potentially, even to Jesus himself. Given the liturgical constraints of Jewish-style monotheism—Yahweh is only one true god; only worship him—the questions "when was Jesus first worshiped?" and "what precipitated his worship?" and "was the worship of Jesus a legitimate development of Judaism?" become all the more intriguing.

Admittedly, asking these questions of *Jesus and the Victory of God* is a bit unfair. To do so is to seek answers to questions that are still in the process of being explained. While *Jesus and the Victory of God* is written in light of and, sometimes, in open conversation with the larger issues of Christian origins, Wright does self-consciously restrict himself to what can be shown about Jesus. Stated plainly, *Jesus and the Victory of God* is about the vocational aims of Jesus and not about the theology of the early church. The volume should be judged for what it is. Wright has yet to square his take on the world of first-century Judaism (as detailed in *NTPG*) and his portrait of Jesus (in *JVG*) with Paul and the apostolic theology of the early church (to be examined in volumes three through six of the Christian Origins and the Question of God series). This noted, however, it is fair to situate the Christology implied by *Jesus and the Victory of God* and to raise a question or two that, given this work, Wright must at some point address in full.

Just why did the lowly Jewish prophet become the object of public veneration? Answers vary, as a quick survey of some representative scholars shows. Some think Judaism already possessed the divine circuitry for the deification of Jesus (or any other messianic figure). For example, J. C. O'Neill argues that the Christian notion of the Trinity can be found in pre-Christian Judaism.[6] Equally provocative is Margaret Barker's contention that ancient Judaism was originally ditheistic—Judaism always had two divinities, El and Yahweh[7]—and that the Jewish High Priest was, in some cases, worshiped as Yahweh's incarnation.[8] In either case, Jesus is fitted into an already existing pattern; the only challenge, historically, is identifying him as the divine figure.

Most scholars, however, locate the bulk of christological innovation within the postresurrection community of Jesus' followers, as does Marcus J. Borg in his essay in this volume. But here a great division occurs. For some, the deification of Jesus occurred early (a matter of weeks or months after his death) and went to the very heart of Christian identity; for others, the worship of Jesus occurred much later and was not a decisive factor in the "partings of the ways" between Judaism and Christianity. An example of the former, Martin Hengel points to the church's creative, exegetical activity in which Jesus began to replace God in the spontaneous singing of hymns.[9] Larry W. Hurtado, while not discounting Jewish tradition (especially speculation about intermediary figures) or the profound implications inherent in the ministry of the historical Jesus, argues that it was religious experience that caused the first Christians to break with their Jewish past and worship Jesus.[10] While also acknowledging that the roots of the church's full Christology can and should be traced to Second Temple Judaism, James D. G. Dunn parts company with Hengel and Hurtado by understanding the deification of Jesus as occurring relatively late (ca. A.D. 100) and construing this event as peripheral to Christian identity.[11]

Still others think that the Christian deification of Jesus cannot be explained in terms of Judaism or the critically reconstructed Jesus tradition. This version of Christian origins also has two branches. Some consider the church's veneration of Jesus to be nothing short of the paganization of Christianity. For example, P. M. Casey argues that the worship of Jesus as the *kyrios* first took place in the Gentile churches, under the influence of Hellenistic culture. According to Casey, the veneration of Jesus is a correlate of and reflects the incremental movement from a Jewish communal identity to a fully Gentile one—from understanding Jesus as a Jewish prophet to a Gentile Lord.[12] James M. Robinson and Helmut Koester (and many of the Jesus Seminar members) contend that Jesus was quite un-Jewish (or at least not very Jewish) and that Christianity came out of the gate pluriform. Jesus' deification, ultimately, was a politically expedient decision made by later theologians. Jesus (of history) only became the Christ (of faith) due to third- and fourth-century politics.[13]

Allowing for the natural idiosyncratic variations of individual authors, five discernible models of christological innovation begin to appear. They can be summarized as follows.

1	2	3	4	5
The possibility of a second divine being, even a divinized human, was already present within Judaism.	However suggestive biblical and Jewish tradition may have been and whatever Jesus may have thought about himself privately, he did not make his deity part of his public ministry.	Despite the speculation about intermediary figures, the deity of the Messiah was not part of the Old Testament or Jewish tradition, Jesus did not teach it himself, nor was Jesus' divinity a defining characteristic of the early church.	Speculations about heavenly beings during the Second Temple period reflects a decisive weakening of historic and prophetic Jewish-style monotheism.	Depending on wisdom tradition, Jesus is best understood as a wandering Cynic philosopher.
Jesus appeals to and follows the already established pattern within Judaism of his day. That is, by word and deed Jesus explicitly identifies himself as a (or the) divine intermediary figure of Jewish tradition.	Jesus was first acclaimed as divine in (and because of) the worship experiences of the church.	Real innovation occurred in the late first century (ca. 100 C.E.) as a legitimate outworking of both the Jewish tradition and the Jesus tradition.	The historical Jesus recovered the ethical tradition of prophetic monotheism. He died a Jewish prophet.	Early Christianity is characterized by wide diversity and no observable theological boundaries.
Jesus' claims for divinity went to the very heart of his life and teaching and thus became the source of controversy with other Jews during his life time. The Gospels reflect Jesus' sustained attempt to prove himself to be a (or the) divine Messiah.	This innovation occurred early and was a (or the) major source of controversy between Jews and Christians that ultimately caused the formation of two communities.	The issues separating Christianity and Judaism were halachic in character (and not christological).	Real innovation in Christianity occurred under the influence of Gentile religion, when Jesus was first hailed and celebrated as a divine being.	The decision to include Jesus in the Godhead was finally a political one, representing the majority tradition that sought to silence other (equally authentic) brands of Christianity.

It is precisely at this point that Wright's full-dress portrait of the historical Jesus makes yet another important contribution to the study of Christian origins. Wright's answer to the question "How did Jesus become the object of veneration?" stands somewhere between (or straddles) positions one and two listed above.

Against Wilhelm Bousset, John Dominic Crossan and many of the Jesus Seminar, Wright sees Christianity as a genuine outworking of Jewish monotheism. However, while acknowledging the suggestive character of Second Temple speculations about heavenly intermediaries, Wright, against O'Neill and Barker but with Hurtado, does not think that Judaism ever conceived of a second divine being—heavenly or otherwise (*JVG* 477-78, 508 n. 116, 526, 529 n. 182, 627). Further, with Hurtado and Hengel (but against Dunn, Casey, Robinson, Koester and Geza Vermes), Wright does agree that the worship of Jesus occurred very early, was an important feature of Christian identity and should not be construed as an imposition from outside influences (*JVG* 104, 118, 612).

However, against Hurtado and Hengel, Wright isolates Jesus (and not the early church) as the real source of innovation. In so doing, Wright extends to Jesus the courtesy normally accorded Paul, Luke, John and, more generally, the early church. Wright insists that Jesus was a creative theologian (*JVG* 478-79, 519).

Chapter thirteen of *Jesus and the Victory of God* is key to Wright's argument at this point. Wright contends that Jesus fulfilled the long-awaited return of Yahweh to Zion. Jesus' triumphal entry to Jerusalem, his action in the temple and his last meal with his disciples were all symbolic actions that fit into a larger story. Part of that story-world entailed Israel's hope for Yahweh's return to Zion. Jesus fulfilled that hope. According to Wright, as part of his vocational aim, Jesus sought to enact the climactic moment of Yahweh's return to Zion in Israel's storied history, thereby implying that he was the (true? unique? full?) embodiment of Yahweh.

If Wright is correct in this assessment, he just may have isolated a passable, historical bridge from the vocational aims of the historical Jesus to the unprecedented worship praxis of the early church. What Nils A. Dahl did in nailing down the church's proclamation of Jesus' messiahship in history (Jesus died on the cross under the title "King of the Jews"),[14] Wright hopes to do for the church's worship of the resurrected Christ (the historical Jesus symbolically acted in ways that encouraged, even demanded, his postcrucifixion veneration). Moreover, Wright may have shown why the church wound up at Nicaea: it was Jesus who first headed his followers down that path.

However, despite Wright's carefully nuanced arguments, I deeply suspect that many readers, on both sides of the theological fence, will doubt whether Wright can get us "there" (the church's high Christology) from "here" (his take on the historical Jesus). On the one hand, some, still languishing in the grip of a profound and pervasive confessional skepticism, will look askance at *Jesus and the Victory of God.* To them this book is a prime example of a historical study gone awry. Ignoring the wealth of scriptural precedents to which Wright appeals, they will simply charge him with smuggling in the accepted Christology through the back door, thereby imperiling the historical honesty of the work.

On the other hand, more confession-oriented scholars, while marveling at Wright's theological courage, will fear *Jesus and the Victory of God* to be a historical wrecking ball. Wright's dogged insistence on rooting Jesus in first-century Judaism yields a convincing picture of Jesus as a prophet and messiah—but how much more? In fact, while seeking to answer the anticipated criticisms of the skeptics, Wright repeatedly belittles what he calls "traditional orthodoxy."

> The Divine Saviour to whom *they* [orthodox Christians] pray has only a tangential relationship to first-century Palestine, and they intend to keep it that way. He can, it seems, be worshiped, but if he ever actually lived he was a very strange figure, clothed in white while all round wore drab, on his face a perpetual faraway expression of pious solemnity. This icon was one means by which Victorian devotion tried to cope with Enlightenment rationalism, though arguably its use conceded the main point at issue (the non-identity of Jesus with the worshipped Christ). (*JVG* 9-10, emphasis added)

> For the church, . . . Jesus was the divine Christ. . . . The icon was in place, and nobody asked whether the Christ it portrayed—and in whose name so much good and ill was done—was at all like the Jesus whom it claimed to represent. (*JVG* 16)

Wright simply cannot abide an orthodoxy that all too easily equates the terms "Messiah" and "God" (*JVG* 94, 104), that inappropriately appeals to miracles as evidence of Jesus' divinity (*JVG* 186) and that uncritically pictures Jesus as wandering around "inviting Galilean villagers to embrace a body of doctrine" (*JVG* 263). Wright warns that an orthodoxy unwilling to engage in serious historical research is really an elder brother in desperate need of methodological reconciliation with a once wanton, but now humbled, historiography (*JVG* 137). It simply "will not do for the elder brother (orthodoxy) to set terms and conditions for the return of the younger (history)" (*JVG* 197).

To those who would hide behind confessional and Enlightenment apologet-ics, Wright insists that Jesus' public ministry was not, in the first instance, an attempt to prove that he was sharing God's very nature. Jesus' calls for repentance and allegiance, his offers of forgiveness and even his miracles do not prove he was divine. These acts show that Jesus was the chief protagonist in a story that has reached its climactic moment (*JVG* 257).

But herein lies a deep irony: at the very moment Wright makes Jesus a cred-ible, crucifiable, apocalyptically minded, first-century Jewish prophet and mes-siah, he renders him less credible as the object of devotion (on par with Yahweh) for the first-century church. That is, the more Jesus is historically comparable to Isaiah, Jeremiah and John the Baptist (prophets) and to other messianic figures (e.g., Simon bar Kochba), the less it seems likely that this Jesus would wind up as the focus of public, sanctioned, organized and regular worship. It is not at all clear how Jesus, the prophet to Israel, and Jesus, the Messiah of Israel, become Jesus, the Lord of the church. The shoulders of Wright's Jesus do not appear to be sturdy enough to bear the christological weight the church willingly placed upon them. Wright appears to have dissolved all the potential ontological ele-ments of Christology into narrative. That is, for Wright, Christology is simply this: Jesus is the chief protagonist in the stories he tells and enacts.

Unless, of course, there is more to the story than Wright has told us in *Jesus and the Victory of God.* And there is. For example, it remains to be seen just how the resurrection figures into the chain of events Wright has linked together. We wait to hear whether, for Wright, the resurrection is a vindicating event (confirm-ing what was already known in public about Jesus) or a revelatory event (disclos-ing new information about the crucified prophet and Messiah) or both. We wait to hear about how what was implicit in the ministry of Jesus (his special relation-ship with Yahweh) became the focal point of the church's liturgy. We wait to hear a full accounting of how the narrowly focused story of Israel's prophet and Mes-siah turns into a story about the universal significance of a cosmic Lord. Claim-ing that Jesus somehow enacts Yahweh's return, while suggestive and possibly even necessary, is not a sufficient explanation of the claim "Jesus, the Christ, is Lord." There must be more to the story.

Contributors

Dale C. Allison Jr. is associate professor of New Testament and Early Christianity at Pittsburgh Theological Seminary, Pittsburgh, Pennsylvania. He is the author of several books, including *The End of the Ages Has Come* (1985), *The Jesus Tradition in Q* (1997) and *Jesus of Nazareth: Millenarian Prophet* (1998). He is coauthor with W. D. Davies of *A Critical and Exegetical Commentary on the Gospel according to St. Matthew* (3 vols, 1988, 1991, 1997).

Craig Blomberg is professor of New Testament at Denver Seminary, Denver, Colorado. He is the author of several books on Jesus and the Gospels, including *The Historical Reliability of the Gospels* (1987), *Interpreting the Parables* (1990) and *Jesus and the Gospels: An Introduction and Survey* (1997).

Darrell L. Bock is research professor for New Testament at Dallas Theological Seminary, Dallas, Texas. His work on Jesus and the Gospels include commentaries on Luke in the Baker Exegetical Commentary on the New Testament and the IVP New Testament Commentary Series and a monograph on *Blasphemy and Exaltation in Judaism and the Final Examination of Jesus*.

Marcus Borg is Hundere Distinguished Professor of Religion and Culture at Oregon State University, Corvallis, Oregon. His well-known studies on Jesus include *Conflict, Holiness and Politics in the Teachings of Jesus* (1984), *Jesus: A New Vision* (1987), *Meeting Jesus Again for the First Time* (1994) and, with N. T. Wright, of *The Meaning of Jesus: Two Visions* (1998).

Paul R. Eddy is instructor in biblical and theological studies at Bethel College, St. Paul, Minnesota, and a Ph.D. candidate at Marquette University. His article "Jesus as Diogenes? Reflections on the Cynic Jesus Thesis" was published in the *Journal of Biblical Literature* (1996).

C. Stephen Evans is William Spoelhof Scholar and professor of philosophy at Calvin College, Grand Rapids, Michigan. In addition to his many publications in philosophy, he is the author of *The Historical Christ and the Jesus of Faith: The Incarnational Narrative as History* (1996).

Craig A. Evans is Director of Graduate Program in Biblical Studies and the Dead Sea Scrolls Institute at Trinity Western University, Langley, British Columbia. He is the author of numerous studies on Jesus and the Gospels, including *Jesus and His Contemporaries: Comparative Studies* (1995) and (with James A. Sanders) *Luke and Scripture: The Function of Sacred Tradition in Luke-Acts* (1993). His edited volumes include (with Bruce Chilton) *Studying the Historical Jesus: Evaluations of the State of Current Research* (1994) and (with Stanley E. Porter) IVP's forthcoming *Dictionary of New Testament Background* (2000).

Richard B. Hays is professor of New Testament at The Divinity School, Duke University, Durham, North Carolina. He is the author of several important studies in the New Testament, including *Echoes of Scripture in the Letters of Paul* (1989) and *The Moral Vision of the New Testament: A Contemporary Introduction to New Testament Ethics* (1996).

Luke Timothy Johnson is the Robert W. Woodruff Professor of New Testament and Christian Origins at the Candler School of Theology, Emory University, Atlanta, Georgia. His well known New Testament studies include *The Writings of the New Testament* (1986), *The Real Jesus: The Misguided Quest for the Historical Jesus and the Truth of the Traditional Gospels* (1996) and *Religious Experience in Earliest Christianity: A Missing Dimension of New Testament Studies* (1998).

Alister E. McGrath is professor of historical theology at Oxford University and principal of Wycliffe Hall, Oxford, and a leading evangelical theologian. His numerous and wide–ranging historical and theological studies include *Iustitia Dei: A History of the Christian Doctrine of Justification* (2 vols., 1986), *The Genesis of Doctrine: A Study in the Foundation of Doctrinal Criticism* (1990), *The Intellectual Origins of the European Reformation* (1987) and *Evangelicalism and the Future of Christianity* (1995).

Carey C. Newman is academic and reference book editor at Westminster John Knox Press and author of *Paul's Glory-Christology: Tradition and Rhetoric* (1992).

Klyne R. Snodgrass is Paul W. Brandel Professor of New Testament Studies at North Park Theological Seminary, Chicago, Illinois. He is author of *The Parable of the Wicked Tenants* (1983) and other studies on the parables.

N. T. Wright is Canon Theologian of Westminster Abbey and was formerly dean of Lichfield Cathedral, Lichfield, England. He is a leading figure in the contemporary Third Quest of the historical Jesus. The first two volumes of his multivolume study of Christian Origins and the Question of God are *The New Testament and the People of God* (1992) and *Jesus and the Victory of God* (1996). He is coauthor with Marcus Borg of *The Meaning of Jesus: Two Visions* (1998).

Notes

Throughout the notes, the abbreviation *NTPG* refers to N. T. Wright, *The New Testament and the People of God*, Christian Origins and the Question of God, vol. 1 (Minneapolis: Fortress, 1992) and the abbreviation *JVG* refers to N. T. Wright, *Jesus and the Victory of God*, Christian Origins and the Question of God, vol. 2 (Minneapolis: Fortress, 1996).

Chapter 1: Right Reading, Reading Wright
[1]A portion of the first part of this essay appeared as "(W)righting the History of Jesus: A Review Essay of *Jesus and the Victory of God*," *Critical Reviews of Books in Religion* 10 (1997): 121-44.
[2]See, e.g., William E. Arnal and Michel Desjardins, eds., *Whose Historical Jesus?* Studies in Christianity and Judaism (Études sur le christianisme et le judaisme) 7 (Waterloo, Ont.: Wilfrid Laurier University Press, 1997).
[3]For example, Elisabeth Schüssler Fiorenza, *Jesus: Miriam's Child, Sophia's Prophet: Critical Issues in a Feminist Christology* (London: SCM Press, 1994).
[4]N. T. Wright, *Jesus and the Victory of God*, Christian Origins and the Question of God, vol. 2 (Minneapolis: Fortress, 1996).
[5]N. T. Wright, *The New Testament and the People of God*, Christian Origins and the Question of God, vol. 1 (Minneapolis: Fortress, 1992).

Chapter 2: The Wright Stuff
[1]Stephen C. Neill and N. T. Wright, *The Interpretation of the New Testament, 1861-1986* (Oxford: Oxford University Press, 1988).
[2]N. T. Wright, *Who Was Jesus?* (London: SPCK; Grand Rapids, Mich.: Eerdmans, 1992).
[3]The best detailed explanation of the appropriation of this philosophical methodology for New Testament studies appears in Ben F. Meyer, *Critical Realism and the New Testament*, Pittsburgh Theological Monograph Series 17 (Allison Park, Penn.: Pickwick, 1989). Others have used such terms as the "hermeneutical spiral" (e.g., Grant R. Osborne, *The Hermeneutical Spiral* [Downers Grove, Ill.: InterVarsity Press, 1991]) and "hypothesis verification" (e.g., Gordon R. Lewis and Bruce A. Demarest, *Integrative Theology*, 3 vols. [Grand Rapids, Mich.: Zondervan, 1987-1994]) to refer to different aspects of the process involved.
[4]As, e.g., in Stephen D. Moore, *Literary Criticism and the Gospels* (New Haven and London: Yale University Press, 1989). For a parallel, holistic model, as in Wright, see, e.g., Mark A. Powell, *What Is Narrative Criticism?* (Minneapolis: Fortress, 1990).
[5]See esp. John Dominic Crossan, *The Historical Jesus: The Life of a Mediterranean Jewish Peasant* (San Francisco: HarperSanFrancisco, 1991); Marcus Borg, *Jesus: A New Vision* (San Francisco: Harper and Row, 1987).
[6]I agree with Wright on both major issues though have come to slightly more conservative results after my historical investigations. See Craig L. Blomberg, *Jesus and the Gospels: An Introduction and Survey* (Nashville: Broadman and Holman; Leicester, U.K.: Inter-Varsity Press, 1997); Luke Timothy Johnson, *The Real Jesus: The Misguided Quest for the Historical Jesus and the Truth of the Traditional Gospels* (San Francisco: HarperSanFrancisco, 1996).
[7]William Wrede, *The Messianic Secret* (German original: Göttingen: Vandenhoeck & Ruprecht, 1901; English translation: London and Cambridge: James Clarke, 1971); Albert Schweitzer, *The Quest of the Historical Jesus: A Critical Study of Its Progress from Reimarus to Wrede* (London: A & C Black, 1906).

[8]E. P. Sanders, *Jesus and Judaism* (London: SCM Press; Philadelphia: Fortress, 1985); Ben F. Meyer, *The Aims of Jesus* (London: SCM Press, 1979).

[9]As shown dramatically in Robert W. Funk, Roy W. Hoover and the Jesus Seminar, *The Five Gospels: The Search for the Authentic Words of Jesus* (New York: Macmillan, 1993); Robert W. Funk, *Honest to Jesus: Jesus for a New Millennium* (San Francisco: HarperSanFrancisco, 1996).

[10]See Burton L. Mack, *A Myth of Innocence: Mark and Christian Origins* (Philadelphia: Fortress, 1988).

[11]Compare the review by Ben F. Meyer of Crossan in *Catholic Biblical Quarterly* 55 (1993): 575-76; and N. T. Wright, "Taking the Text with Her Pleasure," *Theology* 96 (1993): 303-10.

[12]In my opinion, ultimately Borg is still more indebted to the untenable bifurcation of the Jesus of history versus the Christ of faith, as so often in the New Quest, esp. in his dependence on the reductionist historiographical dualism of Van A. Harvey, *The Historian and the Believer: The Morality of Historical Knowledge and Christian Belief* (New York: Macmillan, 1966). For a thorough refutation of and alternative to Harvey's approach, see C. Stephen Evans, *The Historical Christ and the Jesus of Faith* (Oxford: Oxford University Press, 1996). I am grateful to Borg for making clear his dependence on Harvey in private correspondence and conversation.

[13]See esp. F. G. Downing, *Cynics and Christian Origins* (Edinburgh: T & T Clark, 1992).

[14]The most detailed critique of the hypothesis of a Cynic Jesus, elaborating on these and related criticisms, is Gregory A. Boyd, *Cynic Sage or Son of God?* (Wheaton, Ill.: Victor, 1995).

[15]For a thorough survey and critique of the criteria of authenticity most commonly used, see Craig A. Evans, "Authenticity Criteria in Life of Jesus Research," *Christian Scholar's Review* 19 (1989): 6-31.

[16]Compare esp. Anthony E. Harvey, *Jesus and the Constraints of History* (London: Duckworth, 1982).

[17]Citing J. Michael Wallace-Hadrill, *The Vikings in Francia* (Stanton Lecture, 1974), p. 8.

[18]As I have argued elsewhere, to insist that those who attempt to argue for authenticity must prove their case beyond reasonable doubt via corroborating evidence of some sort is usually to insist that they marshal a quantity of data that is simply unavailable. Given the paucity of what has been preserved from the ancient world, the only approach that can hope to avoid an almost total historical agnosticism is that which gives writers who have demonstrated themselves reliable where they can be tested the benefit of the doubt in those areas where they cannot be checked. See Stewart C. Goetz and Craig L. Blomberg, "The Burden of Proof," *Journal for the Study of the New Testament* 11 (1981): 39-63.

[19]I have tried to argue this point in some detail with comparative examples from the literature about Alexander the Great, Josephus's histories and parallel narratives in Samuel—Kings and Chronicles. See Craig L. Blomberg, "The Legitimacy and the Limits of Harmonization," in *Hermeneutics, Authority and Canon*, ed. D. A. Carson and John D. Woodbridge (Grand Rapids, Mich.: Zondervan, 1986), pp. 135-74.

[20]Sanders, *Jesus and Judaism*, pp. 61-76.

[21]Meyer, *Aims of Jesus*.

[22]W. K. Wimsatt and M. C. Beardsley, "The Intentional Fallacy," in *The Verbal Icon*, ed. W. K. Wimsatt (Lexington: University of Kentucky Press, 1954), pp. 2-18.

[23]On which see esp. Larry W. Hurtado, *One God, One Lord: Early Christian Devotion and Ancient Jewish Monotheism* (Philadelphia: Fortress, 1988).

[24]In *NTPG* (346-57) Wright employs a similar strategy to move backwards from the second century into the first through a series of undeniably historical events relevant to the rise of the early church and attested in noncanonical literature.

[25]See, e.g., René Latourelle, *Finding Jesus Through the Gospels* (New York: Alba House, 1979), pp. 229-32.

[26]Kenneth E. Bailey, "Informal Controlled Oral Tradition and the Synoptic Gospels," *Asia Journal of Theology* 5 (1991): 34-54 (reprinted in *Themelios* 20 [1995]: 4-11).

[27]It is interesting that my own work on interpreting the parables also derived initially from a reading of the story of the prodigal son, which then functioned as a hypothesis to be tested elsewhere (Craig L.

Blomberg, *Interpreting the Parables* [Downers Grove, Ill.: InterVarsity Press; Leicester, U.K.: Inter-Varsity Press, 1990], initially following Pierre Grelot, "Le pére et ses deux fils: Luc XV, 11-32," *Revue biblique* 84 [1977]: 321-48, 538-65). It might have been more persuasive if Wright had moved immediately to demonstrating how other parables of Jesus read most coherently as depicting a similar return from exile, thus offering a critical mass of data generating his hypothesis from the core of almost undisputed authentic Jesus material. He does so much later in *JVG*, especially with the parable of the sower (Mk 4:3-9 and par.; *JVG* 230-39), but it is not clear that this is the best parallel he could have chosen. Other parables that he passes over very briefly (*JVG* 232, 234) actually make his point more clearly—esp. the parables of the wicked tenants (Mk 12:1-12 and par.) and the great banquet (Lk 14:16-24).

[28]See esp. R. David Kaylor, *Jesus the Prophet* (Louisville, Ky.: Westminster John Knox, 1994); Edward P. Meadors, *Jesus the Messianic Herald of Salvation* (Peabody, Mass.: Hendrickson, 1997), pp. 72-96.

[29]Esp. Jesus' birth ca. 4 B.C.E., growing up in Nazareth, being partly trilingual, beginning his public ministry in the context of John the Baptist's work, calling for repentance, announcing the kingdom, teaching in parables, effecting healings and exorcisms, sharing table fellowship with socially diverse people, calling disciples, the dramatic temple incident, incurring the wrath of the Jewish religious establishment, being handed over to the Romans, being executed for insurrection and his followers' believing him to be raised from the dead.

[30]See, classically, Norman Perrin and Dennis C. Duling, *The New Testament: An Introduction* (New York and London: Harcourt Brace Jovanovich, 1982), pp. 405-6, 412-25, for both the list and the criteria used to establish it.

[31]Ben Witherington III, *The Christology of Jesus* (Minneapolis: Fortress, 1990), p. 131.

[32]See esp. Jeremiah 26:12-15, probable background for Matthew 27:25.

[33]For extensive detail, see Craig A. Evans and Donald A. Hagner, eds., *Anti-Semitism and Early Christianity* (Minneapolis: Fortress, 1993).

[34]Does this trajectory recognize that if one starts with "Jesus the prophet," a fuller Christology necessarily follows, thus compelling them to deny even this relatively minimalist category?

[35]Compare Blomberg, *Interpreting the Parables,* pp. 29-69, 134-44.

[36]For detailed corroboration, see John P. Meier, *A Marginal Jew: Rethinking the Historical Jesus,* 2 vols. (New York and London: Doubleday, 1991-1994), 2:509-1038. Particularly significant is Meier's conclusion (2:630): "The curious upshot of our investigation is that, viewed globally, the tradition of Jesus' miracles is more firmly supported by the criteria of historicity than are a number of other well-known and often readily accepted traditions about his life and ministry. . . . Put dramatically but without too much exaggeration: if the miracle tradition from Jesus' public ministry were to be rejected in toto as unhistorical, so should every other Gospel tradition about him."

[37]Wright stresses this even more than he stresses that the reconstitution of Israel is recurring, for "when Israel was restored, the whole creation would be restored" (*JVG* 193). Compare now, too, the major thrust of Greg K. Beale's "The Eschatological Conception of New Testament Theology," in *Eschatology in Bible and Theology: Evangelical Essays at the Dawn of a New Millennium,* ed. K. E. Brower and M. W. Elliott (Downers Grove, Ill.: InterVarsity Press, 1999), pp. 11-52.

[38]The last two sentences paraphrase and abbreviate Wright's own summary of the argument that spans all of chaps. 6-10.

[39]As esp. in Crossan, *Historical Jesus,* and Borg, *Jesus.*

[40]As, e.g., with Richard A. Horsley, *Jesus and the Spiral of Violence* (San Francisco: Harper & Row, 1987); Gerd Theissen, *The Shadow of the Galilean* (London: SCM Press; Philadelphia: Fortress, 1987).

[41]As, e.g., with Mack, *Myth of Innocence,* and Funk, *Honest to Jesus.*

[42]See now esp. N. T. Wright, *What Saint Paul Really Said: Was Paul of Tarsus the Real Founder of Christianity?* (Oxford: Lion; Grand Rapids, Mich.: Eerdmans, 1997).

[43]An observation, by the way, supporting historic or classic (i.e., nondispensational) premillennial eschatology, a perspective not nearly as popular or well understood in many circles as the various alternatives.

[44]Compare esp. George R. Beasley-Murray, *Jesus and the Last Days: The Interpretation of the Olivet Discourse* (Peabody, Mass.: Hendrickson, 1993); Beasley-Murray, *The Book of Revelation* (London: Marshall, Morgan & Scott, 1974). Dale C. Allison Jr. ("A Plea for Thoroughgoing Eschatology," *Journal of Biblical Literature* 113 [1994]: 651 n. 2) speaks of what I have in mind: "Herein I use 'end' to indicate not a literal termination (cf. Ps 102:25-26) but a transformation to an idyllic state in which God's will is done on earth as in heaven—in other words, an end to things as they are now. This state may be thought of either as a sort of millennial kingdom (cf. Rev 20:4; *4 Ezra* 7:27-31) or like the supramundane rabbinic 'world to come.' In either case its inauguration would be marked by extraordinary events—such as the ingathering of the twelve tribes and the establishment of a new or glorified temple—and changes in nature. Compare *Jubilees* 23; *4 Ezra* 7:25-27; *2 Baruch* 73; Papias in Irenaeus *Adv. haer.* 5.33.3-4. My own guess is that for Jesus, as for authors of 1 Enoch 6-36, 37-71; *Sibylline Oracles* 3; and *Psalms of Solomon* 17, the eschatological promises were to find their realization not in a completely new world but in a transformed world, an old world made new, in which the boundaries between heaven and earth would begin to disappear, in which evil would be defeated, and (perhaps) in which men and women would be 'like angels in heaven' (Mk 12:25)."

[45]Beginning with the very early texts of Paul, like those in 1 Thessalonians 4—5 or 2 Thessalonians 2, all of which allude to Jesus' apocalyptic language. See esp. David Wenham, *Paul: Follower of Jesus or Founder of Christianity?* (Grand Rapids, Mich., and Cambridge, U.K.: Eerdmans, 1995), pp. 305-19. Wright assures me in private correspondence that he does believe in a personal return of Jesus and believes that the rest of the New Testament developed this concept under the guidance of the Spirit. Given the ambiguities left unresolved in *JVG*, however, it would have been good for him to acknowledge this in the book too.

[46]Wright, *What Saint Paul Really Said*; Wright, *New Tasks for a Renewed Church* (London: Hodder & Stoughton, 1992); *Bringing the Church to the World* (Minneapolis: Bethany House, 1993).

[47]For elaboration cf. Blomberg, *Interpreting the Parables*, pp. 53-55.

[48]One of the clearest introductions to actantial analysis in biblical studies appears in Daniel Patte, *What Is Structural Exegesis?* (Philadelphia: Fortress, 1976), pp. 41-51.

[49]Robert Detweiler, "After the New Criticism: Contemporary Methods of Literary Interpretation," in *Orientation by Disorientation*, ed. Richard A. Spencer (Pittsburgh: Pickwick, 1980), p. 13; Vern Poythress, "Philosophical Roots of Phenomenological and Structuralist Literary Criticism," *Westminster Theological Journal* 41 (1978): 166.

[50]Sanders, *Jesus and Judaism*, pp. 200-209.

[51]Ibid, pp. 174-99; contra Joachim Jeremias, *New Testament Theology* (London: SCM Press; New York: Scribner's, 1971), pp. 108-13.

[52]Gerhard Lohfink, *Jesus and Community* (Philadelphia: Fortress, 1984).

[53]See, e.g., Meier, *Marginal Jew*, Crossan, *Historical Jesus* and Witherington, *Christology of Jesus.*

[54]Meier's second volume appeared in 1994, and at least one more is projected. Wright, of course, is developing an explicit alternative to the approach of Meier or Witherington, so we should not expect him to create the synthesis of the two methods.

[55]Richard Lischer, "The Sermon on the Mount as Radical Pastoral Care," *Interpretation* 41 (1987): 157-69; James L. Bailey, "Sermon on the Mount: Model for Community," *Concordia Theological Monthly* 20 (1993): 85-94. As an aside, Wright (*JVG* 287 n. 171) becomes the first historical Jesus scholar of recent times, of whom I am aware (besides myself), to approve of the rhetorical analysis of George A. Kennedy that suggests an original literary unity of the Sermon on the Mount; see George A. Kennedy, *New Testament Interpretation Through Rhetorical Criticism* (Chapel Hill: University of North Carolina Press, 1984), pp. 67-69. Compare Craig L. Blomberg, *The Historical Reliability of the Gospels* (Leicester, U.K.: Inter-Varsity Press; Downers Grove, Ill.: InterVarsity Press, 1987), p. 139.

[56]But cf. Walter Wink, "Jesus and the Nonviolent Struggle of our Time," *Louvain Studies* 18 (1993): 3-20.

[57]It is a pity that *JVG* and Richard B. Hays's *The Moral Vision of the New Testament: Community, Cross,*

New Creation (San Francisco: HarperSanFrancisco, 1996; Edinburgh: T & T Clark, 1997) were written apparently in complete independence of each other, esp. since Hays has been so well received and has an important discussion of pacifism that partially overlaps with and partially diverges from Wright (*JVG* 317-46).

[58]Thus, just as I fully endorse Wright's recognition of the central theme of the good Samaritan (Lk 10:25-37) as being about enemy love (*JVG* 305-7), I am not certain that one has to jettison the exemplary model of compassion or the implicit critique of professional religion that the other main characters of the passage embody. Wright hints at this (*JVG* 305). I have tried to make some more precise methodological suggestions about how to proceed in my book *Interpreting the Parables*: on the good Samaritan, see esp. pp. 229-33.

[59]For balanced surveys of the data, cf., e.g., Peter Toon, *Heaven and Hell: A Biblical and Theological Overview* (Nashville: Thomas Nelson, 1986); and Stephen H. Travis, *The Jesus Hope* (Leicester, U.K.: Inter-Varsity Press, 1974).

[60]Wright is here referring to Matthew's version of the discourse and to R. T. France's *The Gospel According to Matthew* (Leicester, U.K.: Inter-Varsity Press; Grand Rapids, Mich.: Eerdmans, 1985), p. 335. The two introductory questions appear in Matthew 24:3, leading France to subdivide the discourse into vv. 4-35 and vv. 36-51. Wright apparently assumes that his sociopolitical interpretation of parousia imagery in the first part of the sermon (which is all that he has discussed thus far in the book) excludes an interpretation that finds Jesus' personal return in any part of the sermon, but that does not necessarily follow. In fact vv. 29-31 should probably be taken with vv. 36-51 as referring to Jesus' second coming.

[61]Of recent literature in the never-ending flood of debate on the Son of Man, most helpful are I. Howard Marshall, "The Synoptic 'Son of Man' Sayings in the Light of Linguistic Study," in *To Tell the Mystery: Essays on New Testament Eschatology in Honor of Robert H. Gundry*, ed. Thomas E. Schmidt and Moisés Silva (Sheffield: JSOT, 1994), pp. 72-94; John J. Collins, "The Son of Man in First-Century Judaism," *New Testament Studies* 38 (1992): 448-66; Thomas B. Slater, "One Like a Son of Man in First-Century C.E. Judaism" *New Testament Studies* 41 (1995): 183-98.

[62]Cf. Darrell L. Bock's essay elsewhere in this volume.

[63]Rightly, Beasley-Murray, *Jesus and the Last Days*, p. 430; William L. Lane, *The Gospel According to Mark* (Grand Rapids, Mich.: Eerdmans, 1974), p. 476; D. A. Carson, "Matthew," in *The Expositor's Bible Commentary*, 12 vols., ed. Frank E. Gaebelein (Grand Rapids, Mich.: Zondervan, 1984), 8:505-6. That Jesus reapplies Old Testament language in what is not identified as an explicit quotation is of a piece with his redefinition of Son of Man (and other scriptural) imagery more generally and is no more difficult a problem for New Testament exegetes than, say, Paul's reversal of the direction of the action of Psalm 68:18 in Ephesians 4:8 (in what is an explicit quotation, also about Jesus' journeying to and from heaven).

[64]It also means that "these things" refer only to Mark 13:5-23 and par. Cf., e.g., C. E. B. Cranfield, *The Gospel According to St. Mark* (Cambridge: Cambridge University Press, 1977), p. 409; Robert H. Gundry, *Mark: A Commentary on His Apology for the Cross* (Grand Rapids, Mich.: Eerdmans, 1993), p. 746; W. D. Davies and Dale C. Allison Jr., *A Critical and Exegetical Commentary on the Gospel According to Saint Matthew*, International Critical Commentary, 3 vols. (Edinburgh: T & T Clark, 1997), 3:366-67 and n. 271.

[65]Classically, E. P. Sanders, *Paul and Palestinian Judaism: A Comparison of Patterns of Religion* (London: SCM Press; Philadelphia: Fortress, 1977); cf. James D. G. Dunn, in numerous works, again more commonly in the context of studying Paul, but see also *Jesus, Paul and the Law: Studies in Mark and Galatians* (London: SPCK; Louisville, Ky.: Westminster John Knox, 1990).

[66]For example, Sanders's rejection of the authenticity of most of the depictions of heated controversy and exchange between Jesus and the Jewish leaders, esp. during Jesus' Galilean ministry (*Jesus and Judaism*, pp. 270-93). See *JVG*, pp. 371-83. The double similarity and dissimilarity criterion again works well here (*JVG* 373-74). Wright's Jesus is also more radical vis-à-vis the Torah than Dunn's Jesus, even if for the most part only implicitly.

[67]For Sanders's views, see *Jesus and Judaism*, pp. 77-90.

[68] For example, in explaining the shorter form of Luke's Sermon on the Plain vis-à-vis Matthew's Sermon on the Mount. Cf., Darrell L. Bock, *Luke,* 2 vols. (Grand Rapids, Mich.: Baker, 1994), 1:556, 931-44, which is relatively distinctive among recent commentaries in this respect.

[69] Sanders, *Jesus and Judaism,* pp. 66-67.

[70] As these options unfold, however, they do not include viewing Jesus as merely a loving and harmless teacher. Although Wright may not intend an allusion here, one cannot help but think of the famous "trilemma" of liar, lunatic or Lord, made famous in the modern era by C. S. Lewis; see Lewis, *Mere Christianity* (London: Collins; New York: Macmillan, 1955), p. 52. The alliterative language was added and popularized by Josh McDowell, *Evidence That Demands a Verdict* (San Bernardino, Calif.: Here's Life, 1972), pp. 103-9. "Demonic, demented or divine" might fit the Gospel data even a little better.

[71] About the only quibble one might have with this material is that Wright in his discussion of Luke 12:4-7 and par. seems to introduce a false dichotomy of the kind he elsewhere eschews, as he remarks that "Israel's god is portrayed as the creator and sustainer, one who can be lovingly trusted in all circumstance, not the one who waits with a large stick to beat anyone who steps out of line" (*JVG* 455). Since Wright regularly notes elsewhere (see esp. *JVG* 182-86) that the God of both Old and New Testaments is a God of both love and judgment, it is wholly unclear as to why the one who numbers sparrows and hairs cannot also be the one (rather than Satan) who is to be feared. Cf., e.g., I. Howard Marshall, *The Gospel of Luke* (Exeter: Paternoster; Grand Rapids, Mich.: Eerdmans, 1978), pp. 513-14; Joel B. Green, *The Gospel of Luke* (Grand Rapids, Mich., and Cambridge, U.K.: Eerdmans, 1997), p. 482; Davies and Allison, *Matthew,* 2:206-7.

[72] A conclusion that the most methodologically convincing Third Questers are increasingly endorsing. Cf., e.g., James H. Charlesworth, *Jesus Within Judaism* (London: SPCK; New York: Doubleday, 1988); Meier, *Marginal Jew;* Markus Bockmuehl, *This Jesus: Martyr, Lord, Messiah* (Edinburgh: T & T Clark, 1994; Downers Grove, Ill.: InterVarsity Press, 1996).

[73] One recalls the shocking conclusion of the German Jewish rabbi Pinchas Lapide (*The Resurrection of Jesus* [Minneapolis: Augsburg, 1983; London: SPCK, 1984]) that the historical evidence made Jesus' resurrection probable, without in and of itself demonstrating his messiahship.

[74] Cf. esp. Seyoon Kim, *The Son of Man as the Son of God* (Tübingen: Mohr, 1983; Grand Rapids, Mich.: Eerdmans, 1985); Chrys C. Caragounis, *The Son of Man* (Tübingen: Mohr, 1986); Delbert Burkett, *The Son of Man in the Gospel of John* (Sheffield: JSOT, 1991).

[75] George B. Caird, *The Language and Imagery of the Bible* (London: Duckworth, 1980), p. 139. Contra, e.g., Geza Vermes, *Jesus the Jew* (London: Collins, 1973; Philadelphia: Fortress, 1974); Maurice Casey, *Son of Man: The Interpretation and Influence of Daniel 7* (London: SPCK, 1979); Barnabas Lindars, *Jesus Son of Man* (London: SPCK; Grand Rapids, Mich.: Eerdmans, 1983).

[76] Already toward the end of chapter eleven, he determines all the alternatives that scholars have put forward are so implausible that he concludes, "At this point, I suggest, a use might be found at last for the Enlightenment's scepticism about miracles, not to mention Ockham's razor" (*JVG* 522)!

[77] But Wright insists that "both parties knew he was not guilty of [revolution], or not in any straightforward sense" (*JVG* 544).

[78] Schweitzer, *Quest of the Historical Jesus,* pp. 387-97.

[79] On the question of the historicity of Jesus' passion predictions and related material, cf. esp. Hans F. Bayer, *Jesus' Predictions of Vindication and Resurrection* (Tübingen: Mohr, 1986), a rare instance of a work of which Wright betrays no knowledge. On Isaiah 52—53, Wright builds on the as yet largely unknown but extremely important study by Martin Hengel, "Zur Wirkungsgeschichte von Jes 53 in vorchristlicher Zeit," in *Der leidende Gottesknecht: Jeseja 53 und seine Wirkungsgeschichte,* ed. B. Janowski and P. Stuhlmacher (Tübingen: Mohr, 1996), pp. 47-87.

[80] Contra esp. John Dominic Crossan, *Who Killed Jesus? Exposing the Roots of Anti-Semitism in the Gospel Story of the Death of Jesus* (San Francisco: HarperSanFrancisco; London: HarperCollins, 1995).

[81] Compare I. Howard Marshall, "A New Understanding of the Present and the Future: Paul and

Eschatology," in *The Road from Damascus*, ed. Richard N. Longenecker (Grand Rapids, Mich., and Cambridge, U.K.: Eerdmans, 1997), p. 56: "It is vital to bear in mind that for all Jewish expectations the reign of the Messiah takes place on earth, whereas for the early Christians Jesus was no longer on earth. There has to be, therefore, a future Parousia to establish the kingdom on earth. This insight must have been developed at a very early stage, and our documents suggest that it was (Acts 3:21)." But if it appeared immediately after Jesus' resurrection, is it plausible to deny the concept to the earthly Jesus (the same kind of question Wright himself asks about messiahship)?

[82] Given Wright's discussion earlier (*JVG* 488) and here, it is strange that Thorsten Moritz's review of Wright in *European Journal of Theology* 6 (1997): 180, claims a treatment of the resurrection is missing.

[83] For more intentional apologetic along these same lines, see R. T. France, David Wenham and Craig L. Blomberg, eds., *Gospel Perspectives*, 6 vols. (Sheffield: JSOT, 1980-1986); Blomberg, *Historical Reliability*; and Michael J. Wilkins and J. P. Moreland, eds., *Jesus Under Fire* (Grand Rapids, Mich.: Zondervan, 1995).

[84] That is to say each remains in considerable discernible continuity with the major tenets that historic Christianity over the centuries has most commonly wished to affirm of the earthly Jesus, while at the same time generating creative and challenging alternatives to that tradition in numerous details not finally incompatible with it. This is quite different (and intended to be a compliment) from Crossan's accusation concerning Wright's "elegant fundamentalism"; see John Dominic Crossan, "What Victory? What God? A Review Debate with N. T. Wright on Jesus and the Victory of God," *Scottish Journal of Theology* 50 (1997): 351. To this Wright properly responds that he doubts whether "any actual fundamentalists will enjoy" his "historical reconstruction of Jesus" ("Doing Justice to Jesus: A Response to J. D. Crossan: 'What Victory? What God?'" *Scottish Journal of Theology* 50 [1997]: 366).

[85] Of course, we may distinguish between preunderstandings that bias one's study and applications to one's life that flow from one's study, but in reality all researchers work with a much more dialectical process, repeatedly oscillating between the two.

[86] For example, I suspect that almost every major strand of the Gospels' portraits of Jesus could be made to fit the double similarity and dissimilarity criterion, if for no other reasons than (1) our awareness of the considerable diversity of both pre-Christian Judaism and early Christianity and (2) the enormous gaps that still remain in our knowledge of antiquity more generally.

[87] The most detailed and hermeneutically sophisticated defense of these and related points is Anthony C. Thiselton, *New Horizons in Hermeneutics* (Grand Rapids, Mich.: Zondervan, 1992).

[88] I am also profoundly grateful to Wright for his detailed and careful response to a previous draft of this essay and for saving me from several embarrassing gaffes. On occasion I have reproduced portions of the actual wording of his letter to me when he was suggesting revisions, but I have used quotation marks only when citing his published works.

Chapter 3: The (W)Right Jesus

[1] Or, today, one could say between Robert W. Funk (*Honest to Jesus: Jesus for a New Millennium* [San Francisco: HarperSanFrancisco, 1996]) and Luke Timothy Johnson (*The Real Jesus: The Misguided Quest for the Historical Jesus and the Truth of the Traditional Gospels* [San Francisco: HarperSanFrancisco, 1996]).

[2] For Wright's thoughts on these matters see especially *JVG*, 8-11, 117-24, 137, 662.

[3] This has been true from the beginning; see Henk J. de Jonge, "The Loss of Faith in the Historicity of the Gospels: H. S. Reimarus (ca. 1750)," in *John and the Synoptics*, ed. A. Denaux, Bibliotheca ephemeridum theologicarum lovaniensium 51 (Leuven: Leuven University Press, 1992), pp. 409-21.

[4] For example, see the general sentiments and methodological comments of Robert W. Funk, Roy W. Hoover and the Jesus Seminar, *The Five Gospels: The Search for the Authentic Words of Jesus* (New York: Macmillan, 1993), pp. v-38.

[5]Wright follows Kenneth Bailey's remarkably balanced approach to this issue; see Bailey, "Informal Controlled Oral Tradition and the Synoptic Gospels," *Asia Journal of Theology* 5 (1991): 34-54.

[6]One model that has notorious problems in this regard is the "Cynic Jesus" hypothesis; for a survey and critique, see Paul R. Eddy, "Jesus as Diogenes? Reflections on the Cynic Jesus Thesis," *Journal of Biblical Literature* 115 (1996): 449-69.

[7]On the importance of such an endeavor see Bruce D. Chilton, "Jesus Within Judaism," in *Jesus in Context: Temple, Purity and Restoration* (Leiden: Brill, 1997), pp. 179-201.

[8]As opposed to the Jesus Seminar, which claims that one of the "seven pillars of scholarly wisdom" is that the burden of proof lies with those who argue for the authenticity of a text (see Funk, Hoover and Jesus Seminar, *Five Gospels*, pp. 4-5). Judging from the manner in which he makes authenticity decisions, Wright would disagree (e.g., *JVG* 303-4, 348-49, 512-19, 521-28, 648-50).

[9]Wright puts little stock in the extracanonical tradition, concluding, for example, that the *Gospel of Thomas* is both late and dependent upon the canonicals (*NTPG* 435-43). Thus, beyond occasional references, he makes very little use of them. It is worth noting that his reconstruction of Jesus relies primarily upon the Synoptics; the Fourth Gospel plays only a small role (see *JVG* xvi).

[10]For example, the following reviewers all express one degree or another regarding Wright's optimistic evaluation of the historical value of the canonical Gospels: John Dominic Crossan, "What Victory? What God? A Review Debate with N. T. Wright on *Jesus and the Victory of God*," *Scottish Journal of Theology* 50 (1997): 347-51; Anthony E. Harvey, review of *Jesus and the Victory of God* by N. T. Wright, *Theology* 100 (1997): 296; Clive Marsh, "Theological History? N. T. Wright's *Jesus and the Victory of God*," *Journal for the Study of the New Testament* 69 (1998): 80-81; and Geoffrey Turner, *Heythrop Journal* 38 (1997): 441.

[11]Others so encouraged include Hans Boersma, *Calvin Theological Journal* 32 (1997): 494; Robert H. Gundry, "Reconstructing Jesus," *Christianity Today*, April 27, 1998, p. 78.

[12]Here, Wright makes use of the categorization schema of Robert L. Webb; see Webb, *John the Baptizer and Prophet: A Socio-Historical Study*, Journal for the Study of the New Testament Supplement Series 62 (Sheffield: Sheffield Academic Press, 1991).

[13]Those who find room for the rubric "prophet" in their assessment of Jesus include Bruce D. Chilton and Craig A. Evans, John P. Meier, E. P. Sanders, Richard Horsley, Marcus Borg, Morna D. Hooker, William Telford, Adela Yarbro Collins, Gerd Theissen, R. David Kaylor, and Maurice Casey. The move away from Jesus as prophet within the Seminar is not surprising, given that the Cynic-sage thesis, with its largely Hellenized view of Jesus, holds sway over many of its members.

[14]For example, Ben Witherington III, *The Jesus Quest: The Third Search for the Jew of Nazareth* (Downers Grove, Ill: InterVarsity Press, 1995), pp. 186-87.

[15]From Gerd Theissen ("Itinerant Radicalism: The Tradition of Jesus Sayings from the Perspective of the Sociology of Literature," *Radical Religion* 2 [1975]: 84-93) to John P. Meier (*A Marginal Jew: Rethinking the Historical Jesus*, 2 vols. [New York and London: Doubleday, 1991-1994], 2:1040-41) to Crossan (*The Historical Jesus: The Life of a Mediterranean Jewish Peasant* [San Francisco: HarperSanFrancisco, 1991], 345-8), the consensus is Quest-wide. Arguments to the contrary are not convincing: e.g., see Frederick H. Borsch, "Jesus, the Wandering Preacher?" in *What About the New Testament? Essays in Honour of Christopher Evans*, ed. Morna D. Hooker and Colin Hickling (London: SCM Press, 1975), pp. 45-63.

[16]See Richard A. Horsley and John S. Hanson, *Bandits, Prophets and Messiahs: Popular Movements at the Time of Jesus* (San Francisco: Harper & Row, 1985), p. 257; Witherington, *Jesus Quest*, p. 150. On these two types see Horsley and Hanson, *Bandits*, pp. 160-89.

[17]"The designation 'prophet' is at least partially in the eye of the beholder, including the prophet himself" (Lester Grabbe, *Priests, Prophets, Diviners, Sages: A Socio-Historical Study of Religious Specialists in Ancient Israel* [Valley Forge: Trinity, 1995], p. 116).

[18]George B. Caird, *Jesus and the Jewish Nation* (London: Athlone, 1965); Caird, *The Language and Imagery of the Bible* (London: Duckworth, 1980).

[19] On the diversity within Jewish apocalyptic tradition, see Gabriele Boccaccini, "Jewish Apocalyptic Tradition: The Contribution of Italian Scholarship," in *Mysteries and Revelations: Apocalyptic Studies Since the Uppsala Colloquium,* ed. John J. Collins and James H. Charlesworth (Sheffield: JSOT, 1991), pp. 36-37.

[20] This is an interpretation of the Danielic (Dan 7) and Markan (Mk 13) "Son of Man" that Wright explicitly rejects (*JVG* 339-67). Edward Adams has challenged Wright at this point; see Adams, "Historical Crisis and Cosmic Crisis in Mark 13 and Lucan's Civil War," *Tyndale Bulletin* 48 (1997): 329-44. Wright has acknowledged such possibilities, but he concludes that such a view would be so "marginal" as to warrant little attention (*NTPG* 333). Even if Wright is correct, while this may be an appropriate conclusion for Jewish apocalyptic thought in general, when it comes to analyzing the views of one particular thinker (e.g., Jesus), the possibility that one is dealing with a "marginal" figure must be seriously entertained—all the more so when this figure has shown no hesitation in striking out on his own into other realms of creative marginality.

[21] Relatedly, why not an unprecedented cosmic event within the space-time world (such as the Son of Man's returning on a cloud) that is nonetheless "historical"? Unusual history, perhaps; history-making, certainly. But as "historical," one would think it would fit within the bounds of Wright's understanding of apocalyptic eschatology. Why should such possibilities be dismissed out of hand as "crass literalism" (*JVG* 361)?

[22] As John J. Collins notes with regard to the genre apocalypse, one consistently finds a "transcendent eschatology" that looks for ultimate solutions beyond the categories of ordinary history (*The Apocalyptic Imagination: An Introduction to the Jewish Matrix of Christianity* [New York: Crossroad, 1987], p. 9).

[23] See John Gray, *The Biblical Doctrine of the Reign of God* (Edinburgh: T & T Clark, 1979); Tryggve N. D. Mettinger, "Fighting the Powers of Chaos and Hell: Towards the Biblical Portrait of God," *Studia theologica* 39 (1985): 21-38; Tremper Longman III and Daniel G. Reid, *God Is a Warrior,* Studies in Old Testament Biblical Theology (Grand Rapids, Mich.: Zondervan, 1995).

[24] Maurice Casey, "Where Wright Is Wrong: A Critical Review of N. T. Wright's *Jesus and the Victory of God,*" *Journal for the Study of the New Testament* 69 (1998): 99-100; Harvey, review, p. 296.

[25] As demonstrated by Craig Evans; see his essay in this volume as well as his "Aspects of Exile and Restoration in the Proclamation of Jesus and the Gospels," in *Jesus in Context: Temple, Purity and Restoration* (Leiden: Brill, 1997), pp. 263-93.

[26] Rikki Watts notes that, in numerous apocalyptic texts of this period, "the exiles or captives are portrayed as being under Satan's power" (*Isaiah's New Exodus and Mark,* Wissenschaftliche Untersuchungen zum Neuen Testament 2/88 [Tübingen: Mohr-Siebeck, 1997] p. 148; cf. pp. 244, 248).

[27] The Jewish scholar Pinkhos Churgin argued this thesis earlier in the twentieth century. His best work in this area is available only in Hebrew; e.g., "The Period of the Second Temple: An Era of Exile," *Horeb* 8 (1944): 1-66. Among his more telling points is the fact of the stark absence, in the Old Testament, of a festival to mark the official end of the exile.

[28] As Craig Evans notes, as Roman sympathizers, the chief priests would hardly have made the temple a welcoming haven for anti-Roman revolutionaries ("Jesus and the 'Cave of Robbers': Towards a Jewish Context for the Temple Action," *Bulletin for Biblical Research* 3 [1993]: 108). See also Evans, "Jesus' Action in the Temple: Cleansing or Portent of Destruction?" *Catholic Biblical Quarterly* 51 (1989): 267-69; Robert H. Gundry, *Mark: A Commentary on His Apology for the Cross* (Grand Rapids, Mich.: Eerdmans, 1993), pp. 644-45.

[29] For example, *1 Enoch* 10:4; 54:4-5; 1QS 4; 1QM; 11QMelch 2:4-6; *Jubilees* 48; *Testament of Levi* 18:12; *Testament of Zebulon* 9:8; *Testament of Simeon* 6:6; *Testament of Dan* 5:10-13; *Assumption of Moses* 10:1, 3. Watts demonstrates that four common themes characterize many apocalyptic texts of that day: "A) the exiles or captives are portrayed as being under Satan's power, B) their deliverance is effected by a warrior figure, C) the whole is described in terms of God's reign and, D) is often expressed in ways reminiscent of the Isaianic day of salvation" (*Isaiah's New Exodus,* p. 148).

[30] See Gregory A. Boyd, *God at War: The Bible and Spiritual Conflict* (Downers Grove, Ill.: InterVarsity Press, 1997), chaps. 6-8.

[31] Watts, *Isaiah's New Exodus*, pp. 163-64, 180.

[32] See, e.g., Boyd, *God at War*, chaps. 6-8; James Kallas, *The Significance of the Synoptic Miracles* (Greenwich, Conn.: Seabury, 1961); Heinz Kruse, "Das Reich Satans," *Biblica* 58 (1977): 29-61; Graham H. Twelftree, *Jesus the Exorcist: A Contribution to the Study of the Historical Jesus* (Peabody, Mass.: Hendrickson, 1993), pp. 217-24; and Watts, *Isaiah's New Exodus*, pp. 137-82. In the light of Wright's methodology, many of the conclusions that Watts draws regarding "the Markan Jesus" could likely be drawn for the historical Jesus as well.

[33] I. Howard Marshall, "Uncomfortable Words: VI. 'Fear him who can destroy both the body and soul in hell' (Mt 10.28)," *Expository Times* 81 (1970): 276-80.

[34] Such enactments were patterned after the Old Testament prophets themselves. See W. D. Stacey, *Prophetic Drama in the Old Testament* (London: Epworth, 1990).

[35] Josephus *Antiquities of the Jews* 2097-9 (Theudas); *Antiquities* 18:85-7 (the Samaritan); *Antiquities* 20.169-72; *Jewish Wars* 2.261-3 (the Egyptian); *Antiquities* 20.168; *Jewish Wars* 2.258-60; 6.283-7; 7.437-41 (other unnamed prophetic types). For discussion see Jeffrey A. Trumbower, "The Historical Jesus and the Speech of Gamaliel (Acts 5.35-9)," *New Testament Studies* 39 (1993): 500-517; Horsley and Hanson, *Bandits*, pp. 171-72. On Jesus in the context of Jewish prophetic action more broadly see Morna D. Hooker, *The Signs of a Prophet: The Prophetic Actions of Jesus* (Harrisburg, Penn.: Trinity, 1997), pp. 1-16.

[36] For an impressive catalog see Hooker, *Signs of a Prophet*, pp. 35-54.

[37] Jesus' refusal at times to give a "sign" (Mt 16:1; Mk 8:11; Lk 11:16) is best understood as a refusal to provide self-authenticating miracles, "proofs" of his own authority; see *ibid*, pp. 17-34.

[38] Although Wright clearly asserts that he is not attempting to psychologize Jesus (*JVG* 480), some have wondered about the viability of such an endeavor (e.g., Marsh, "Theological History?" pp. 84-86).

[39] Wright here follows John's chronology (Jn 13:1; 18:28; 19:14).

[40] As Edward P. Meadors demonstrates with regard to these two strands of tradition in "Q" (*Jesus the Messianic Herald of Salvation* [Peabody, Mass.: Hendrickson, 1995], pp. 95-96).

[41] Others include Markus Bockmuehl, *This Jesus: Martyr, Lord, Messiah* (Downers Grove, Ill.: InterVarsity Press, 1994); Marinus de Jonge, *Jesus, the Servant-Messiah* (New Haven, Conn.: Yale University Press, 1991); Ben Witherington III, *The Christology of Jesus* (Minneapolis: Fortress, 1990).

[42] On such see Kim Huat Tan, *The Zion Traditions and the Aims of Jesus*, Society for New Testament Studies Monograph Series 91 (New York: Cambridge University Press, 1997). Those, like Crossan (*Who Killed Jesus? Exposing the Roots of Anti-Semitism in the Gospel Story of the Death of Jesus* [San Francisco: HarperSanFrancisco, 1995], p. 10), who generally see in the New Testament "prophecy historicized," as opposed to "history remembered," have yet to offer convincing evidence that such accounts originated in the minds of early Christians and not in the symbolic actions of Jesus. On this matter more broadly, see my "Response [to William L. Craig's 'John Dominic Crossan on the Resurrection of Jesus']," in *The Resurrection: An Inter-disciplinary Symposium on the Resurrection of Jesus*, ed. Stephen Davis, Daniel Kendall and Gerald O'Collins (New York: Oxford University Press, 1997), pp. 272-86.

[43] Hooker, *Signs of a Prophet*, pp. 43-44. Outside of one quotation, Mark seems generally oblivious to the Old Testament textual rootings of the episodes he narrates, while Matthew and John are aware of the connections. Against those who take such observations as fodder for messianic skepticism (e.g., Casey, "Where Wright Is Wrong," p. 101), Craig Evans's insights ("Jesus and Zechariah's Messianic Hope," paper presented at the annual conference of the Society of Biblical Literature, San Francisco, 1997) are suggestive; such evidence would also fit the thesis that historical remembrances of Jesus' symbolic acts were carried in the tradition only to be later explicitly reattached to the Old Testament Scriptures that gave birth to them in Jesus' own mind. See also Evans, "Aspects of Exile," pp. 292-93 n. 56.

[44] Against, e.g., Burton L. Mack, *A Myth of Innocence: Mark and Christian Origins* (Philadelphia: Fortress, 1988), pp. 273-75, 291-92. On its historicity see Gerd Theissen, "Die Tempelweissagung Jesu. Prophetie in Spannungsfeld von Stadt und Land," *Theologische Zeitschrift* 32 (1976): 144-58; Evans, "Jesus and the 'Cave of Robbers,' " pp. 94-100; Tan, *Zion Traditions*, pp. 159-64.

[45] On this split see Evans, "Jesus' Action." Others have come to a similar synthesis as well; see Ray-

mond E. Brown, *The Death of the Messiah: From Gethsemane to the Grave*, 2 vols. (New York: Doubleday, 1994), 1:455-60; Hooker, *Signs of a Prophet*, pp. 44-48.

[46]Beyond the general question of just what force a "symbolic cleansing or reform" would have (reform seems, almost by definition, to require more than mere symbolism), there is the consideration that, since Jesus was not arrested, it appears the incident took place in a limited space and time—hardly the type of event that suggests actual reform as the goal. The suggestion that Nehemiah 13:4-13 serves as analogy (Witherington, *Christology of Jesus*, p. 115) fails in that this incident represents an actual cleansing. See Tan, *Zion Traditions*, pp. 172-74.

[47]See Wright's ongoing dialogue with E. P. Sanders (*JVG* 247-58, 273, 370-83, 395-96, 413-26).

[48]Gundry, *Mark*, pp. 653-64.

[49]Against, e.g., Crossan, *Historical Jesus*, pp. 360-67. Brown (*Death of the Messiah*, 1:22) apparently counts it as "probable." See also Tan, *Zion Traditions*, pp. 198-200.

[50]Of related interest is Deborah Bleicher Carmichael's "David Daube on the Eucharist and the Passover Seder," *Journal for the Study of the New Testament* 42 (1991): 45-67. Here she mounts a defense for a messianic interpretation of the *afikoman* (the broken-off piece of unleavened bread in the Passover meal), wherein Jesus' identification with the bread would have been seen as a symbolic messianic claim.

[51]On the influence of the Isaianic new-exodus theme within Mark's Gospel (which, under Wright's methodological approach, can be viewed as a likely reflection of Jesus' own creative theological synthesis) see Watts, *Isaiah's New Exodus*, pp. 349-65.

[52]David Stacey, "The Lord's Supper as Prophetic Drama," in Morna D. Hooker, *The Signs of a Prophet: The Prophetic Actions of Jesus* (Harrisburg, Penn.: Trinity, 1997), pp. 80-95. While his skepticism regarding the historicity of the "cup" is unwarranted, Stacey's analysis (p. 92) of the bread as symbolizing the "founding of a new Israel" is insightful.

[53]See Tan, *Zion Traditions*, pp. 200-220.

[54]See Hooker, *Signs of a Prophet*, pp. 39, 48-54.

[55]Witherington, *Jesus Quest*, p. 223 (see p. 285 n. 117 for the connection to the Jesus-as-Israel thesis).

[56]Ibid, p. 230.

[57]H. Wheeler Robinson, *Corporate Personality in Ancient Israel*, rev. ed. (Philadelphia: Fortress, 1980); John Rogerson, "The Hebrew Conception of Corporate Personality: A Reexamination," *Journal of Theological Studies* 21 (1970): 1-16. These new studies include Perry Leon Stepp, *The Believer's Participation in the Death of Christ: "Corporate Identification" and a Study of Romans 6:1-14* (Lewiston, N.Y.: Mellen, 1996), pp. 1-37; Joel S. Kaminsky, *Corporate Responsibility in the Hebrew Bible*, Journal for the Study of the Old Testament Supplement Series 196 (Sheffield: Sheffield Academic Press, 1995).

[58]While willing to load more freight here than most, Wright is not alone in this general conclusion: see, e.g., J. Dupont, "L'origine de récit des tentations de Jésus au désert," *Revue biblique* 73 (1966): 30-76; Robert A. Guelich, *Mark 1—8:26*, Word Biblical Commentary (Dallas: Word, 1989), p. 37; Gundry, *Mark*, p. 62; John Nolland, *Luke 1—9:20* (Dallas: Word, 1990), p. 177.

[59]As Gundry ("Reconstructing Jesus," p. 78) has noted.

[60]For a helpful orientation to this new movement, see Jarl Fossum, "The New Religionsgeschichtliche Schule: The Quest for Jewish Christology," *Society of Biblical Literature Abstracts and Seminar Papers* (1991): 638-45.

[61]Larry W. Hurtado, "What Do We Mean by 'First-Century Jewish Monotheism'?" *Society of Biblical Literature Abstracts and Seminar Papers* (1993): 348-68.

[62]Just how early any precursors to the rabbinic "Two Powers" debate appeared is difficult to say. Alan Segal suggests that it can be traced at least into the first century (*Two Powers in Heaven: Early Rabbinic Reports About Christianity and Gnosticism*, Studies in Judaism in Late Antiquity 25 [New York: Brill, 1977]).

[63]See, e.g., Joel Marcus, *The Way of the Lord: Christological Exegesis of the Old Testament in the Gospel of Mark* (Louisville, Ky.: Westminster John Knox, 1992); Carl Judson Davis, *The Name and Way of the Lord: Old Testament Themes, New Testament Christology*, Journal for the Study of the New Testament

Supplement Series 129 (Sheffield: Sheffield Academic Press, 1996); Watts, *Isaiah's New Exodus*.

[64] At times, the themes and interpretations are virtual mirror images of Wright's: "The fearful trek of the befuddled, bedraggled little band of disciples is the return of Israel to Zion, and Jesus' suffering and death there are the prophesied apocalyptic victory of the divine warrior . . . [This redefined apocalyptic eschatology] hears in Jesus' cry of dereliction the triumph song of Yahweh's return to Zion, that paradoxically sees in his anguished, solitary death the long-awaited advent of the kingdom of God" (Marcus, *Way of the Lord*, p. 36). Wright simply takes the next step and traces the origination of this novel apocalyptic vision back to Jesus himself.

[65] For example, Mark 3:22-30; 4:35-41; 5:1-20; 6:45-52; Matthew 4:1-11 par.; Lk 4:1-13; Jn 12:31 in the context of the Old Testament "Yahweh as Warrior" tradition in general and certain Isaianic passages in particular (chaps. 40-66); see esp. Watts, *Isaiah's New Exodus*, pp. 137-69; Marcus, *Way of the Lord*, p. 23. Watts, for instance, notes the implications for an early high Christology of Mark's "apparent application of the Yahweh-Warrior motif to Jesus and his use of Isaiah and Malachi . . . both of which seem to deal with the very coming of Yahweh himself" (p. 388).

[66] Watts, *Isaiah's New Exodus*, p. 373; Marcus, *Way of the Lord*, pp. 31-37.

[67] Space does not allow a discussion of Wright's argument against the standard interpretive paradigm. While his reading does connect the parable to the journey narrative in an interesting and relevant manner, it seems to fail in other respects. Other Jewish parables may have tended to connect kings and masters with Yahweh. But especially on Wright's account, Jesus would be just the person to give such imagery a novel twist. And it seems he did. The man who is off to "receive a kingdom" does not fit the always-already king Yahweh as well as it does the in-messianic-process Jesus. That the ideal hearer is located at the end of the parable's time line, as Wright contends, is not at all clear. Finally, this reading is intimately connected with Wright's larger eschatological thesis, which, as previously noted, has its own problems. In short, there is no compelling reason to reject the standard interpretive paradigm for Wright's novel approach. Incidentally, a similar conclusion can be drawn for his reading of the so-called Little Apocalypse (Mk 13 and par.); see Gundry, *Mark*, pp. 785-86, where Borg's comparable views are addressed.

[68] That is, in the "calling" of the Twelve, Wright sees a "Jesus-as-Yahweh" connection, a symbolism that seems to suggest Jesus is other-than-Israel (*JVG* 645). Orthodox Christology has been forced to wrestle with a similar question for two millennia, and so, it seems, must Wright.

[69] N. T. Wright, "Theology, History and Jesus: A Response to Maurice Casey and Clive Marsh," *Journal for the Study of the New Testament* 69 (1998): 109; *JVG*, xv.

[70] One does not have to go as far as Wright does to find a view of apocalyptic thought or the apocalypse genre that provides a theological basis for such concerns in the evangelical community. See, e.g., Gale Z. Heide, "What Is New About the New Heaven and New Earth? A Theology of Creation from Revelation 21 and 2 Peter 3," *Journal of the Evangelical Theological Society* 40 (1997): 37-56.

[71] Wright himself (*JVG* 659) is quite aware of the problem.

[72] On the "inaugurated" view, see E. J. Epp, "Mediating Approaches to the Kingdom: Werner George Kümmel and George Eldon Ladd," in *The Kingdom of God in Twentieth-Century Interpretation*, ed. W. Willis (Peabody, Mass.: Hendrickson, 1987), pp. 35-52.

[73] If this final form of vindication—Jesus' exaltation to the throne of Yahweh—is to be realized in anything like the historical sense that would seem to be demanded by Wright's presentation of Jewish apocalyptic thought, it suggests the need for a historical resurrection. Wright's musings on this topic (*JVG* 487-88, 525, 658-59) are few and tantalizing. However, more recent work promises that a historical case for Jesus' resurrection will be forthcoming in a future volume; see N. T. Wright, "The Resurrection of the Son of God," *Stimulus* 4 (November 1996): 44-52; Wright, "Christian Origins and the Resurrection of Jesus: The Resurrection of Jesus as a Historical Problem," and "Early Traditions and the Origin of Christianity," *Sewanee Theological Review* 41 (1998): 107-40.

[74] In fact, this multiplex pattern is just what some scholars have argued is the case in Jesus' teaching; e.g., on the Little Apocalypse see Adams, "Historical Crisis"; Witherington, *Jesus Quest*, pp. 209-10.

Chapter 4: Reading & Overreading the Parables

[1] See Dale C. Allison Jr., "The Contemporary Quest for the Historical Jesus," *Irish Biblical Studies* 18 (1996): 174-94. This schema works best if one thinks only of German scholarship and of the period prior to the Third Quest, but it still leaves out of account people like Joachim Jeremias and Ethelbert Stauffer.

[2] See *JVG*, pp. 79, 86-89; and N. T. Wright, "Theology, History and Jesus: A Response to Maurice Casey and Clive Marsh," *Journal for the Study of the New Testament* 69 (1998): 106-7.

[3] See E. P. Sanders, *Jesus and Judaism* (Philadelphia: Fortress, 1985), and Ben F. Meyer, *The Aims of Jesus* (London: SCM Press, 1979).

[4] Wright had already offered an outline of his approach in an incisive and thoroughly convincing article in 1985. See N. T. Wright, "Jesus, Israel and the Cross," *Society of Biblical Literature 1985 Seminar Papers:* 75-95, an article that still merits attention.

[5] See Maurice Casey, "Where Wright Is Wrong: A Critical Review of N. T. Wright's Jesus and the Victory of God," *Journal for the Study of the New Testament* 69 (1998): 99-100.

[6] See Craig Evans, "Aspects of Exile and Restoration in the Proclamation of Jesus and the Gospels," in *Exile: Old Testament, Jewish and Christian Conceptions*, ed. James M. Scott (Leiden: Brill, 1997), pp. 299-328. Note the following: 2 Chronicles 29:9 LXX; Tobit 14:5; *Baruch* 2:6-15; 3:7; 2 Maccabees 2:5-8, 18; 1QM 1:2-3; CD 1:3-7; *Psalms of Solomon* 9:1-11; *Sibylline Oracles* 3:265-290; *Testament of Judah* 23; *Testament of Zebulon* 9:5-9; *Testament of Naphtali* 4:1-5; *4 Ezra* 1:31-52; 5:17-18, 28-30; 6:55-59; 10:7-24; 12:46-51; *2 Apocalypse of Baruch* 3:1-9; 67:1-9; 80:1-7; *Targum of Isaiah* 53:8. Obviously writings such as *2 Apocalypse of Baruch* and *4 Ezra* reflect the destruction of Jerusalem in 70 C.E., but they also evidence a Jewish pattern of thought with regard to exile.

[7] That is, they require the hearers to make a judgment on themselves.

[8] One would have expected *akrogōniaios* ("cornerstone") or at least *lithos* ("stone"), if reference were to the foundation of the temple. A distinction is consistently maintained in Jewish and Christian writings between *sûr*/petra ("rock") on the one hand and *'abn/lithos* ("stone") on the other, except for the parallelism in Isaiah 8:14 and references to this passage. However, I am in complete agreement with Wright's understanding of Jesus' temple action as an acted parable of judgment.

[9] For analysis of this parable see my book *The Parable of the Wicked Tenants* (Tübingen: Mohr-Siebeck, 1983) and my article "Recent Research on the Parable of the Wicked Tenants: An Assessment," *Bulletin for Biblical Research* 8 (1998): 187-216.

[10] Apparently Wright would see the parables of the wedding feast and banquet as variations on the same theme rather than as the same parable rendered in divergent ways.

[11] Other aspects of the interpretation of the parable of the seed growing secretly are unclear and unconvincing. Wright says that the seed also sleeps and rises, for which I see no basis. As others have done, he suggests overtones of resurrection and that the description of the seed portrays how "god" raises the dead in the inauguration of the kingdom, that is, in a hidden way. I see no basis for such a conclusion.

[12] If the parable is a reusing of such a controlling narrative, it has stripped the narrative and changed its subject.

[13] A point Wright makes himself (*JVG* 645). On *JVG* 233-34, Wright says the sowings do not describe a chronological sequence but rather different results from simultaneous sowings. Yet, on *JVG* 236, he states the previous sowings represent the unfruitful work of the prophets. It would be better to say the different results encountered with Jesus' preaching correspond to or mirror the rejection of Isaiah and other prophets throughout Israel's history. On *JVG* 237, Wright suggests those who look and do not see refers to the Romans, Herod and zealous Jews, but these are not the people "outside." The words from Isaiah 6:9 are applied to all those who do not respond to the message, and, of course, Jesus' audience is made up of Jewish people in general.

[14] Especially given his reference to E. P. Sanders's sarcastic comment about those who think Jesus was spinning parables that can be unraveled only by twentieth-century literary analysis (*JVG* 173 n. 115).

[15] Compare *JVG* 302, 404.

[16]The basis of this interpretation is that in most parables kings/masters and subjects/servants stand for God and Israel or its leaders/prophets (*JVG* 634). Basically this is true, but it cannot be assumed. Further, the key question with a parable is how the analogy functions, not what allegorical correspondences exist.

[17]See *JVG* 305. Wright's discussion of the parable of the good Samaritan as a redefining of the covenant boundary of Israel is quite helpful.

[18]Is it Satan who can destroy both body and soul in hell (Mt 10:28 par. Lk 12:4-5), as Wright suggests (*JVG* 454-55), or is it God?

[19]No doubt, Wright would argue that some or all these texts are about judgment on Israel, but I do not find that argument convincing.

[20]Obviously the nuance of *ekdikēsis* in Luke 21:22 is different from its nuance in the parable. It is used positively of vindication in the parable but negatively of destruction in 21:22.

[21]John Nolland, *Luke 9:21—18:34*, Word Biblical Commentary (Dallas: Word Books, 1993), p. 871.

[22]Other parables of a master returning (such as in Lk 12:35-48) are understood as referring primarily to the fate of Jesus and Jerusalem (*JVG* 635, 640-64).

[23]C. H. Dodd, *The Parables of the Kingdom*, rev. ed. (London: Nisbet, 1936), pp. 175-94.

[24]Wright does not think two separate stories have been conflated (*JVG* 633).

[25]Wright states that New Testament treatments of the second coming do not suggest condemnation of some within the church, but numerous passages do focus on judgment of those who think they are followers: e.g., Matthew 7:22; 25:31-46; 2 Corinthians 5:10.

[26]Wright unjustly translates the present *aphietai* in Matthew 23:38 as if it were a perfect ("your house has been abandoned") and understands it in reference to God's prior abandoning of the temple rather than to future abandonment or destruction (*JVG* 184, cf. *JVG* 456). This renders meaningless the words "you will not see me until you say."

[27]Obviously the Gospel of John emphasizes these themes repeatedly.

[28]Luke Timothy Johnson argues—somewhat similarly to Wright—that Luke does not seek to refute the eschatological excitement but to confirm it and demonstrate that Jesus is king (cf. Lk 19:38). See Johnson, "The Lukan Kingship Parable (Lk 19:11-27)," *Novum Testamentum* 24 (1982): 139-59. I do not find his attempt convincing.

Chapter 5: Jesus & the Continuing Exile of Israel

[1]See the collection in James M. Scott, ed., *Exile: Old Testament, Jewish and Christian Conceptions* (Leiden: Brill, 1997). Also see D. J. Verseput, "The Davidic Messiah and Matthew's Jewish Christianity," *Society of Biblical Literature Abstracts and Seminar Papers* 34 (1995): 102-16. According to Verseput, the exile "remained for many an unfinished story" (p. 104). Finally, see also Daniel G. Reid, "Jesus: New Exodus, New Conquest," in Tremper Longman III and Daniel G. Reid, *God Is a Warrior*, Studies in Old Testament Biblical Theology (Grand Rapids, Mich.: Zondervan, 1995), pp. 91-118.

[2]See Clive Marsh, "Theological History? N. T. Wright's *Jesus and the Victory of God*," and Maurice Casey, "Where Wright Is Wrong: A Critical Review of N. T. Wright's *Jesus and the Victory of God*," *Journal for the Study of the New Testament* 69 (1998): 77-94, 95-103. N. T. Wright responds in his "Theology, History and Jesus: A Response to Maurice Casey and Clive Marsh," *Journal for the Study of the New Testament* 69 (1998): 105-12.

[3]Casey, "Where Wright Is Wrong," p. 99.

[4]In his reply ("Theology, History and Jesus," p. 111), N. T. Wright explains, "I, like many other contemporary students of first-century Judaism, was using 'exile' as a shorthand to mean 'the time of desolation' begun by the Babylonian destruction. 'Exile' in this sense is a *period of history* with certain characteristic features, not a mere geographical reference." Wright goes on to cite with approval a comment by M. A. Knibb: "[Many believed that] Israel remained in a state of exile long after the return in the last decades of the sixth century" (*The Qumran Community* [Cambridge: Cambridge University Press, 1987], p. 20).

[5]Translation, with some modifications, from Louis H. Feldman, *Josephus IX*, Loeb Classical Library

(London: Heinemann; Cambridge: Harvard University Press, 1965), pp. 441, 443.

[6]Translation, with some modifications, from H. St. J. Thackeray, *Josephus II*, Loeb Classical Library 203 (London: Heinemann; Cambridge: Harvard University Press, 1927), pp. 423, 425.

[7]Translation, with some modifications, from Feldman, *Josephus IX*, pp. 479, 481.

[8]E. Schürer, *The History of the Jewish People in the Age of Jesus Christ*, ed. Geza Vermes, F. Millar and M. Black, 4 vols. (Edinburgh: T & T Clark, 1973-1987), 1:605-6.

[9]See P. W. Skehan and A. A. Di Lella, *The Wisdom of Ben Sira*, Anchor Bible 39 (New York: Doubleday, 1987), pp. 421-22.

[10]The Hebrew 4QTobit (4Q200) reads, "because you are banished among them" (6 i 8).

[11]See F. Zimmermann, *The Book of Tobit* (New York: Harper, 1958), p. 112. D. Flusser ("Psalms, Hymns and Prayers," in *Jewish Writings of the Second Temple Period*, ed. M. E. Stone, Compendia Rerum Iudaicarum ad Novum Testamentum 2.2 [Assen: Van Gorcum; Philadelphia: Fortress, 1984], pp. 551-71, esp. p. 556) has identified Tobit 13 as an eschatological psalm.

[12]Zimmermann, *Book of Tobit*, p. 113; G. W. E. Nickelsburg, "Tobit," in *Harper's Bible Commentary*, ed. J. L. Mays (San Francisco: Harper & Row, 1988), p. 792: "Tobit is thoroughly exilic in its viewpoint, and return to the land of Israel and Jerusalem is a consummation devoutly to be awaited."

[13]See C. A. Moore, *Daniel, Esther and Jeremiah: The Additions*, Anchor Bible 44 (New York: Doubleday, 1977), pp. 257-58, 291.

[14]O. H. Steck, *Das apokryphe Baruchbuch: Studien zu Rezeption und Konzentration 'kanonischer' Überlieferung* (Göttingen: Vandenhoeck & Ruprecht, 1993), p. 267. Baruch appears to be a composite work, parts of which are quite pessimistic.

[15]Jonathan A. Goldstein, "How the Authors of 1 and 2 Maccabees Treated the 'Messianic' Promises," in *Judaisms and Their Messiahs at the Turn of the Christian Era*, ed. Jacob Neusner et al. (Cambridge: Cambridge University Press, 1987), pp. 69-96, esp. pp. 81-85.

[16]Translations from M. O. Wise, E. M. Cook and M. G. Abegg Jr., *The Dead Sea Scrolls: A New Translation* (San Francisco: HarperCollins, 1996), pp. 56, 121, 151.

[17]Translations from Wise, Cook and Abegg, *Dead Sea Scrolls*, pp. 411-12.

[18]Paul Garnet, *Salvation and Atonement in the Qumran Scrolls*, Wissenschaftliche Untersuchungen zum Neuen Testament 2/3 (Tübingen: Mohr-Siebeck, 1977). Garnet speaks of an "exilic motif" in the Qumran Scrolls.

[19]H. G. M. Williamson comments that "the final consummation is by no means yet reached" (*Ezra-Nehemiah*, Word Biblical Commentary 16 [Dallas: Word, 1985], p. 136).

[20]Translation from E. Isaac, "1 (Ethiopic Apocalypse of) Enoch," in *The Old Testament Pseudepigrapha*, ed. James H. Charlesworth, 2 vols. (New York: Doubleday, 1983-1985), 1:69.

[21]Translation from J. Priest, "Testament of Moses," in *The Old Testament Pseudepigrapha*, ed. James H. Charlesworth, 2 vols. (New York: Doubleday, 1983-1985), 1:929.

[22]Translation from A. F. J. Klijn, "2 (Syriac Apocalypse of) Baruch," in *The Old Testament Pseudepigrapha*, ed. James H. Charlesworth, 2 vols. (New York: Doubleday, 1983-1985), 1:644.

[23]See J. Tromp, *The Assumption of Moses: A Critical Edition with Commentary*, Studia in Veteris Testamenti pseudepigrapha 10 (Leiden: Brill, 1993), p. 225.

[24]This expectation helps us understand the prophetic frenzy that gripped the inhabitants of Jerusalem when the army of Titus surrounded the city in 69 C.E. According to Josephus, many "prophets" spoke of imminent salvation.

[25]C. A. Moore rightly observes that "Assyria's destruction in 14:15 represented a partial solution to Israel's problem and, more importantly, augured well for the ideal solution: the end of the Diaspora and the reestablishment of Jerusalem and its Temple" (*Tobit*, Anchor Bible 40A [Garden City: Doubleday, 1996], pp. 295-96). W. Soll comes to a similar interpretation, when he says that it is "in these last chapters that the prospect of an end to the exile is held out" ("Misfortune and Exile in Tobit: The Juncture of a Fairy Tale Source and Deuteronomic Theology," *Catholic Biblical Quarterly* 51 [1989]: 230).

[26]As rendered by Jonathan A. Goldstein, *II Maccabees*, Anchor Bible 41A (Garden City: Doubleday, 1983), p. 187; Goldstein, "How the Authors of 1 and 2 Maccabees," p. 83. Goldstein restores *apodōsei*,

which he believes has dropped out. Without the restoration, the text reads: *ho de theos ho sōsas ton panta laon autou kai apodous tēn kleronomian pasin kai to basileion kai to hierateuma kai ton hagiasmon* ("God who has saved his entire people and has restored to us all the heritage, the kingdom, the priesthood, and the sanctification"). The problem with the unemended text is that the sentence lacks a verb. Goldstein's restoration could well be correct.

[27] R. H. Charles understands the gathering of the "destroyed" sheep as an allusion to the resurrection of the righteous ("Book of Enoch," in *The Apocrypha and Pseudepigrapha of the Old Testament*, ed. R. H. Charles, 2 vols. [Oxford: Clarendon Press, 1913], 1:260).

[28] Translation from R. B. Wright, "Psalms of Solomon," in *The Old Testament Pseudepigrapha*, ed. James H. Charlesworth, 2 vols. (New York: Doubleday, 1983-1985), 2:660-62, 665, 667, 669.

[29] Translation from Klijn, "2 (Syriac Apocalypse of) Baruch," p. 648.

[30] See Bruce D. Chilton, *The Isaiah Targum*, The Aramaic Bible 11 (Wilmington: Glazier, 1987), pp. xx-xxviii.

[31] Translation from ibid., p. 54.

[32] See Bruce D. Chilton, *The Glory of Israel: The Theology and Provenience of the Isaiah Targum*, Journal for the Study of the Old Testament Supplement Series 23 (Sheffield: JSOT, 1982), pp. 97, 110-11.

[33] For further echoes and allusions, see C. H. Dodd, *According to the Scriptures: The Sub-Structure of New Testament Theology* (London: Nisbet, 1952), pp. 92-94; see also Chilton, *Glory of Israel*, p. 90.

[34] For further discussion of the exile theme in the Isaiah Targum, see the essay by Bruce D. Chilton, "Salvific Exile in the Isaiah Targum," in *Exile*, ed. J. M. Scott (Leider: Brill, 1997).

[35] Translation from F. H. Colson, *Philo VIII*, Loeb Classical Library 341 (London: Heinemann; Cambridge: Harvard University Press, 1939), pp. 417-21.

[36] For a very preliminary assessment, see Paul Garnet, "Jesus and the Exilic Soteriology," in *Studia Biblica 1978, II: Papers on the Gospels (Sixth International Congress on Biblical Studies, Oxford, 1978)*, ed. E. A. Livingstone, Journal for the Study of the New Testament Supplement Series 2 (Sheffield: JSOT, 1980), pp. 111-14.

[37] For arguments supporting authenticity, see Ben F. Meyer, *The Aims of Jesus* (London: SCM Press, 1979), pp. 172-73; E. P. Sanders, *Jesus and Judaism* (London: SCM Press; Philadelphia: Fortress, 1985), pp. 98-106; Sanders, *The Historical Figure of Jesus* (London: Penguin, 1993), pp. 184-87; *JVG* 299-301. The criterion of dissimilarity in this case applies to the discontinuity between Jesus' use of the symbol "twelve" and its later use by the early church. There is, however, important continuity between Jesus and Jewish eschatological hopes of his time. This sort of continuity does not, *pace* many scholars of the New Quest and the Jesus Seminar, tell against the authenticity of tradition credited to Jesus.

[38] Sanders, *Jesus and Judaism*, p. 98.

[39] On the authenticity of this saying, see Meyer, *Aims of Jesus*, pp. 167-68, 297-98 n. 129.

[40] As is argued in Dale C. Allison Jr. and W. D. Davies, *The Gospel According to Saint Matthew*, International Critical Commentary, 2 vols. (Edinburgh: T & T Clark, 1991), 2:551.

[41] See T. C. Vriezen, *An Outline of Old Testament Theology* (Oxford: Basil Blackwell, 1958), p. 350.

[42] See Jeffrey A. Trumbower, "The Historical Jesus and the Speech of Gamaliel (Acts 5.35-9)," *New Testament Studies* 39 (1993): 500-517.

[43] Translation from Wise, Cook and Abegg, *Dead Sea Scrolls*, p. 176.

[44] Translation, with some modification, from H. St. J. Thackeray, *Josephus III*, Loeb Classical Library 210 (London: Heinemann; Cambridge: Harvard University Press, 1928), pp. 459-61.

[45] Both Matthew 21:13 and Luke 19:46 omit "for all the nations." Having been destroyed, the temple can hardly serve as a place of prayer for the nations. Also, would not the church be the place of prayer for the nations? For these reasons the later Evangelists modified Mark's longer but older version. The improbability that the early church would have invented a saying about the temple as the place of prayer for Gentiles strongly supports the authenticity of the saying. Sanders dismisses the saying because it compromises his problematical theory that Jesus' demonstration in the temple precincts was not critical or judgmental (*Jesus and Judaism*, pp. 66-67). For studies that defend the saying as

authentic, see Craig A. Evans, "Jesus' Action in the Temple: Cleansing or Portent of Destruction?" *Catholic Biblical Quarterly* 51 (1989): 237-70; Evans, "Jesus' Action in the Temple and Evidence of Corruption in the First-Century Temple," *Society of Biblical Literature Abstracts and Seminar Papers* 28 (1989): 522-39; Evans, "Jesus and the 'Cave of Robbers': Towards a Jewish Context for the Temple Action," *Bulletin for Biblical Research* 3 (1993): 93-110.

[46]See *JVG* 418-19; Craig A. Evans, "From 'House of Prayer' to 'Cave of Robbers': Jesus' Prophetic Criticism of the Temple Establishment," in *The Quest for Context and Meaning: Studies in Biblical Intertextuality in Honor of James A. Sanders*, ed. Craig A. Evans and S. Talmon, Biblical Interpretation Series 28 (Leiden: Brill, 1997), pp. 417-42.

[47]The appearance of *ta ethnē* in Jesus' allusion to Isaiah hardly constitutes evidence against authenticity (*pace* Anthony E. Harvey, *Jesus and the Constraints of History* [London: Duckworth, 1982], p. 132).

[48]The text is taken from A. Sperber, *The Bible in Aramaic*, 5 vols. (Leiden: Brill, 1959-1973), 3:112-13; J. F. Stenning, *The Targum of Isaiah* (Oxford: Clarendon, 1949). The English translation is based on Chilton, *Isaiah Targum*, p. 109.

[49]In *The Temple of Jesus: His Sacrificial Program Within a Cultural History of Sacrifice* (University Park: Pennsylvania State University Press, 1992), Bruce D. Chilton has made a compelling case that Jesus' demonstration in the temple precincts was largely motivated out of concerns for purity. Although not disputing his conclusions, I do think that concerns over perceptions of injustice and of callous disregard for the poor and the defenseless—whom the temple establishment is to protect, not exploit (cf. Deut 14:29; 26:12-13; Ps 68:5; Jer 7:6)—played an important part.

[50]Translation from K. J. Cathcart and R. P. Gordon, *The Targum of the Minor Prophets*, The Aramaic Bible 14 (Wilmington: Glazier, 1989), pp. 187-88.

[51]See Sanders, *Jesus and Judaism*, pp. 106-8; *JVG* 248-49.

[52]Joseph A. Fitzmyer, *The Gospel According to Luke X—XXIV*, Anchor Bible 28A (Garden City: Doubleday, 1985), p. 852.

[53]See *ibid*, p. 1034; Meyer, *Aims of Jesus*, p. 207-8.

[54]Fitzmyer, *Gospel According to Luke X—XXIV*, pp. 1254-55.

[55]The Danielic dimension in Jesus' ministry is most readily seen in the ubiquitous epithet "Son of Man." Jesus alludes to this figure, who, according to Daniel 7:14, is given "dominion [Aramaic *sltn*]/authority [LXX *exousia*] and glory and kingdom." He appeals to the authority of this human figure in forgiving sins (Mk 2:10) and with respect to his activities on the sabbath (Mk 2:28). The promise that the disciples will sit on thrones judging the twelve tribes of Israel (Mt 19:28 par. Lk 22:30) echoes Daniel 7:9, which describes "thrones" being set up, as well as Daniel 7:14, which promises the Son of Man "glory." Jesus' asseveration that "the Son of Man came not to be served but to serve" (Mk 10:45) appears to be a deliberate reversal of Daniel 7:14, which says that "all peoples, nations, and languages should serve him [the Son of Man]." Jesus' reply to Caiaphas, "You will see the Son of Man seated at the right hand of Power, and 'coming with the clouds of heaven'" (Mk 14:62), alludes to Daniel 7:13. Daniel's understanding of kingdom, both human and divine, is instructive for understanding Jesus and his predilection for referring to himself as the Son of Man. According to Daniel, God is the giver of kingdoms. He gives the kingdom to the Babylonian king (Dan 2:36-38; 5:18) and, after taking it away, returns it (Dan 4:36). Likewise, God gives the kingdom to the Son of Man (Dan 7:13-14) and to the "holy ones of the Most High" (Dan 7:27). Indeed, God gives the kingdom to whomsoever he will (Dan 4:32). In reference to God, Daniel frequently says "his kingdom [*mlkwth*]" (Dan 3:33 [Eng. 4:3]; 4:31 [Eng. 4:34]; 6:27 [Eng. 6:26]; 7:27). In the first three passages it is the pagan king who confesses that God's kingdom is eternal (in contrast to their own). Jesus' reference to himself as Son of Man, his proclamation of the kingdom of God and his claims to authority reflect the language of Daniel.

[56]Jesus' entry into the city, mounted on an ass (Mk 11:1-11), in all probability was consciously patterned after Solomon and the prophecy of Zechariah 9:9 The obscure description of Jesus' refusal to permit anyone to carry a vessel through the temple (Mk 11:16) seems to reflect in some way Zechariah 14:20-21. On the night of his arrest Jesus foretells his disciples' defection, paraphrasing Zechariah 13:7: "I will strike the shepherd, and the sheep will be scattered" (Mk 14:27). Jesus' reference to the

"little flock" in Luke 12:32 and his description of the people of Israel as "sheep without a shepherd" (Mk 6:34) probably allude to the sheep and shepherd imagery of Zechariah (cf. 11:11; 13:7). Jesus' saying about faith that can move mountains may allude to Zechariah 14:4. The language of Zechariah 11:6 may have contributed to Jesus' anticipation of arrest and martyrdom and the language he used to express it (Mk 9:31). The saying about the Son of Man's coming accompanied by his angels (Mt 25:31) may echo the words of Zechariah 14:5 (esp. "Then the LORD my God will come, and all the holy ones with him").

[57] Jesus' proclamation and understanding of the "gospel" (*euaggelion*, which is derived from *b'śrâ*) are rooted in Isaiah 40:9 ("Get you up to a high mountain, O Zion, herald of good tidings; lift up your voice with strength, O Jerusalem, herald of good tidings"), Isaiah 52:7 ("How beautiful upon the mountains are the feet of the messenger who announces peace") and Isaiah 61:1-2 ("The spirit of the Lord GOD is upon me, because the LORD has anointed me; he has sent me to bring good news to the oppressed"). His miracles were probably understood in terms of Isaiah 35:5-6 ("the eyes of the blind shall be opened") and Isaiah 61:1-2 ("to bind up the brokenhearted, . . . recovery of sight to the blind"), as seen in the reply to the messengers of the Baptist (cf. Mt 11:4-5 par. Lk 7:22). The Servant imagery also probably played a role in Jesus' understanding, though to what extent is much debated (see discussion above and accompanying note).

[58] See my essay, "From Gospel to Gospel: The Function of Isaiah in the New Testament," in *Writing and Reading the Scroll of Isaiah: Studies of an Interpretive Tradition*, ed. C. C. Broyles and Craig A. Evans, Vetus Testamentum, Supplements 70.2, Formation and Interpretation of Old Testament Literature 1.2 (Leiden: Brill, 1997), pp. 651-91, esp. pp. 667-74.

Chapter 6: The Trial & Death of Jesus

[1] Special thanks goes to Tim Morgan, whose feedback helped to nuance certain points. Also special appreciation goes to N. T. Wright, who carefully suffered through interacting with earlier drafts over e-mail. His feedback was most helpful in making sure I appreciated what he was and was not saying.

[2] These consist of his reply (using John the Baptist) about his authority, the cursing of the fig tree, the casting the mountain into the sea remark, the parable of the wicked tenants, the remarks about tribute to Caesar and the question about David's son being David's Lord.

[3] Perhaps the best summation of Wright's view here is his statement that among the traditions Jesus evokes are included "the somewhat more nebulous but still important traditions which spoke of a human figure sharing the divine throne" (*JVG* 651). Later in comparing his view to traditional statements of Gospel Christology he says, " 'Awareness of vocation' is by no means the same thing as Jesus having the sort of 'supernatural' awareness of himself, of Israel's god, and the relation between the two of them, such as is often envisaged by those who, concerned to maintain a 'high' christology, place it within an eighteenth-century context of implicit Deism where one can maintain Jesus' 'divinity' only by holding some form of docetism. Jesus did not, in other words, 'know that he was God' in the same way that one knows one is male or female, hungry or thirsty, or that one ate an orange an hour ago. His 'knowledge' was of a more risky, but perhaps more significant, sort: like knowing one is loved. One cannot 'prove' it except by living it. . . . Forget the 'titles' of Jesus, at least for a moment; forget the pseudo-orthodox attempts to make Jesus of Nazareth conscious of being the second person of the Trinity; forget the arid reductionism that is the mirror-image of that unthinking would-be orthodoxy" (*JVG* 652-53).

[4] Ben F. Meyer, *Critical Realism and the New Testament*, Pittsburgh Theological Monograph Series 17 (Allison Park, Penn.: Pickwick, 1989), p. 167.

[5] See also J. Klausner, *From Jesus to Paul* (New York: Macmillan, 1943), pp. 4, 439-41, 514-15.

[6] George B. Caird, *The Language and Imagery of the Bible* (London: Duckworth, 1980), pp. 243-71.

[7] On this scroll see O. Betz, "Probleme des Prozesses Jesu," *Aufstieg und Niedergang der römischen Welt* II.25.1 (1982): 606-8; Betz, "The Temple Scroll and the Trial of Jesus," *Southwestern Journal of Theology* 30 (1988): 5-8; Betz, "Jesus and the Temple Scroll," in *Jesus and the Dead Sea Scrolls*, ed. James H. Charlesworth (New York: Doubleday, 1992), pp. 79-83. The following translation follows that of

Betz in "Jesus and the Temple Scroll," p. 81. I have a more focused discussion on this historical background and whether a text like this can be used to discuss general Jewish practice in Darrell L. Bock, "Crucifixion, Qumran, and the Jewish Interrogation of Jesus," *Literary Studies on Luke-Acts: Essays in Honor of Joseph B. Tyson* (Macon, Ga.: Mercer University Press, 1998).

[8] For discussion on the age of this prayer and a rendering of its key versions, see Emil Schürer, *The History of the Jewish People in the Age of Jesus Christ,* ed. Geza Vermes, Fergus Millar and Matthew Black, rev. ed. (Edinburgh: T & T Clark, 1979), 2:454-63.

[9] R. J. McKelvey, *The New Temple: The Church in the New Testament,* Oxford Theological Monographs (Oxford: Oxford University Press, 1969), pp. 17-22. He argues that the benediction cited above is pre-70 C.E.

[10] I have in mind here his associations, his handling of sabbath issues, his prophetic challenges to the faith and his claims with regard to the forgiveness of sin. It should be noted that these disputes involving sin and the sabbath were no minor irritant. Their presence made it more imperative that the temple action not be ignored.

[11] I have in mind his remarks on *JVG* 627-29, where the Jewish traditions about a second power in heaven raise the questions about whether a "second god" could be foreseen for a unique victorious figure within the scope of the monotheistic claims of Judaism. Acknowledging that "second god" might be saying too much, Wright correctly notes exaltation that uses Daniel 7 and Ezekiel 1 as models of an enthronement scene are certainly possible for Jesus. Later in his discussion (*JVG* 642-44) he adds the influence of Psalm 110:1 to this motif (*JVG* 551). This has recently proved to be a fertile area of study for Christology; works like that by Larry W. Hurtado (*One God, One Lord: Early Christian Devotion and Ancient Jewish Monotheism* [Philadelphia: Fortress Press, 1988]) have tried to explore how this background can help us understand the Christology of the early church.

[12] This topic is the subject of my monograph *Blasphemy and Exaltation in Judaism and the Final Examination of Jesus,* Wissenschaftliche Unterrsuchungen zum Neuen Testament 2/106 (Tübingen: Mohr Siebeck, 1998). A summary of its argument can be found in my "Key Jewish Texts on Blasphemy and Exaltation and the Jewish Examination of Jesus," *Society of Biblical Literature Abstract and Seminar Papers* (1997): 115-60.

[13] One caveat concerning definition must be made here. If "end of exile" simply means, for Wright, dealing once and for all with sin by all that Jesus does and, as a result, equals access to restoration, then it functions in a highly metaphorical sense and can perhaps be affirmed. My question regarding the metaphor critiqued here is not what Wright wants to affirm through it but whether other imagery from Judaism might be a better, or perhaps clearer, choice. The response to Wright up until now has suggested that many do not get this point, much less accept it. I know I did not after having read through the book several times. I believe the confusion may emerge with the sheer scope of what Wright wishes to cover by the image. I want to ask questions like, can restoration (with YHWH's return to Zion) and return from exile (understood metaphorically, nongeographically and thus as an image presented in a fresh, now varied light as Wright seems to understand it [*JVG* 428-38]) be distinguished? My sense is that perhaps restoration of the people or the end of any judgment against the people equals the restored images to which he appeals. Included here are the restored people, restored land (spiritually, not literally), redefined family, redefined Torah and rebuilt temple. But there still remain those images of regathering, which also reflect in Judaism the end-of-exile imagery and which are seemingly explicitly saved for some future events like the "regeneration" (Mt 19:28) or the gathering from the corners of the earth or the four winds (Mt 24:31; Mt 25:32). These events look as if they come later, and they function in parables that look to a decisive judgment of sorting out the nations, which makes one suspect that a failure to distinguish here has produced confusion in the discussion. Such a judgment seems more compelling when the events before these images speak of unprecedented tribulation in the suffering that comes, or of the shortening of days to limit the suffering or of the gospel that goes out into all the world before this day. In other words, the language of the eschatological discourse seems to look beyond 70 C.E.

[14] Although Wright sees the concept of a descending Jesus as hard to accept (and even derides it with sarcasm), it is no more difficult than the idea of his ascent, which seems to be anticipated by his

remarks at the trial!

[15] I know I read this text differently than does Wright, but I do not have time to develop this argument. It falls outside the scope of Wright's current volume anyway. For a defense of a future at least for ethnic Israel argued for from this text, see C. E. B. Cranfield, *The Epistle to the Romans*, International Critical Commentary, 2 vols. (Edinburgh: T & T Clark, 1979), 2:448.

Chapter 7: Jesus & the Victory of Apocalyptic

[1] Some ancients, however, seemingly could take riding on the clouds literally; see e.g., *b. Sanhedrin* 98a and the other texts cited by Geza Vermes, *Jesus the Jew* (London: Collins, 1973), pp. 186-88.

[2] Wright's position is closely akin to that of George B. Caird, *The Language and Imagery of the Bible* (London: Duckworth, 1980), and Wright cites Caird often.

[3] Wright says that, according to Albert Schweitzer, "the Jews of the first century expected the physical world to be brought to an end" (*NTPG* 284). He cites two of Schweitzer's books—*The Quest of the Historical Jesus: A Critical Study of Its Progress from Reimarus to Wrede* (New York: Macmillan, 1961) and *The Mysticism of Paul the Apostle* (New York: Seabury, 1968)—but gives no page numbers.

[4] Rudolf Bultmann, *Theology of the New Testament*, 2 vols. (New York: Charles Scribner's Sons, 1951), 1:4.

[5] This, for what it is worth, has always been my own understanding. See my article "A Millennial Kingdom in the Teaching of Jesus?" *Irish Biblical Studies* 7 (1985): 46-52.

[6] Johannes Weiss, *Jesus' Proclamation of the Kingdom of God* (Philadelphia: Fortress, 1971): 101-5.

[7] E. P. Sanders, "Jesus: His Religious 'Type,'" *Reflections* 87 (1992): 7; cf. *NTPG*, pp. 332-33.

[8] Matthew 5:18 (although I very much doubt this comes from Jesus) and Mark 13:31 (the origin of this is uncertain) do, on their face, speak of heaven and earth passing away.

[9] See Q 13:28-29 and 22:28-30. I have discussed the former in Dale C. Allison Jr., *The Jesus Tradition in Q* (Valley Forge, Penn.: Trinity Press International, 1997), pp. 176-91. On the latter see W. D. Davies and Dale C. Allison Jr., *A Critical and Exegetical Commentary on the Gospel According to Matthew*, International Critical Commentary, 3 vols. (Edinburgh: T & T Clark, 1997) 3:55-58.

[10] So Q 13:28-29, on which see again Allison, *Jesus Tradition in Q*, pp. 176-91.

[11] So Mark 12:18-27. For the authenticity of this see J.–G. Mudiso Mbâ Mundla, *Jesus und die Führer Israels: Studien zu den sog. Jerusalemer Streitgesprächen*, Neutestamentliche Abhandlungen 17 (Münster: Aschendorff, 1984), pp. 71-109, and O. Schwankl, *Die Sadduzäerfrage (Mk 12.18-27 parr.): Eine exegetisch-theologische Studie zur Auferstehungserwartung*, Bonner biblische Beiträge 66 (Frankfurt am Main: Athenäum, 1987), pp. 466-587.

[12] Compare Wright: "There is, I suggest, no good evidence to suggest anything so extraordinary as the view which Schweitzer and his followers espoused. As good creational monotheists, mainline Jews were not hoping to escape from the present universe into some Platonic realm of eternal bliss enjoyed by disembodied souls after the end of the space-time universe. If they died in the fight for the restoration of Israel, they hoped not to 'go to heaven,' or at least not permanently, but to be raised to new bodies when the kingdom came, since they would of course need new bodies to enjoy the very much this-worldly shalom, peace and prosperity that was in store" (*NTPG* 286). Do these words leave an accurate impression of Schweitzer? On the one hand, Schweitzer never clarifies, in his book on Jesus, what exactly he means by "the supra-mundane phase of the eschatological drama" (*Quest of the Historical Jesus*, p. 371); and on the other, he plainly holds that Jesus anticipated resurrection (e.g., *Quest of the Historical Jesus*, pp. 345, 346 n. 1). One can, moreover, make some reasonable inferences about what Schweitzer thought about Jews and Jesus from what he says about Paul. According to Schweitzer, the apostle expected in the near future not the end of the world but a messianic kingdom, a "Paradise upon the earth" that will see nature "pass through a transformation" (*Mysticism of Paul*, p. 66). Schweitzer also affirms that "eternal blessedness is thought of by Paul not as a purely spiritual existence, but as an existence in the condition incident on the bodily resurrection." Schweitzer's argument presupposes that Paul's ideas on these matters were taken over from Jewish apocalyptic, and Schweitzer gives us no reason to think that Jesus' expectations were any different.

[13] C. H. Dodd asks whether we must assume that apocalyptic writers "always intended their visions of the end, unlike their visions of coming events within history, to be taken with the strictest literal-

ness, or does a consciously symbolic element still persist?" He goes on: "It is at least open to the reader to take the traditional apocalyptic imagery as a series of symbols standing for realities which the human mind cannot directly apprehend, and as such capable of various interpretation and re-interpretation as the lessons of history or a deepening understanding of the ways of God demand" (*The Parables of the Kingdom*, rev. ed. [New York: Charles Scribner's Sons, 1961], p. 81). Caird's debt to Dodd appears, among other places, in *Language and Imagery*, pp. 252-54. Here we read that Dodd "rescued New Testament scholarship from the cul-de-sac into which Weiss and Schweitzer had directed it."

[14] Although even here one may understand "the moon [shall be turned] to blood" to be a poetic way of prophesying a literal darkness (cf. the preceding line—"the sun shall be turned to darkness").

[15] But here we should keep in mind there are clear markers in Daniel that the beasts are metaphors: (a) 7:17 says "these four great beasts are four kings," (b) the beasts are not real beasts (the lion and the leopard have wings) and (c) the prophecy is a "vision" in a "dream."

[16] Jean Daniélou, *The Theology of Jewish Christianity* (London: Darton, Longman & Todd, 1964), pp. 377-404.

[17] See also George R. Beasley-Murray, *Jesus and the Last Days: The Interpretation of the Olivet Discourse* (Peabody, Mass.: Hendrickson, 1993), 423-27.

[18] In the *Apocalypse of Abraham* 30—31 the end-time woes are ten plagues reminiscent of the plagues upon Egypt—distress through want; the burning of cities; destruction of cattle through pestilence, starvation, earthquake and sword; hail and snow; animal attacks; famine and pestilence; sword and flight in terror; thunder and earthquakes. Here the natural world falls apart right before Israel is saved and the wicked punished.

[19] Josephus *Jewish Wars* 6.288-300: a star, a comet, a light at midnight around the temple altar, a cow giving birth to a lamb, the opening of its own accord of the eastern gate of the inner court of the temple, armies in the clouds, a voice in the temple. According to Wright, "Sometimes, no doubt, extraordinary natural phenomena were both expected, witnessed and interpreted within a grid of belief which enabled some to see them as signs and portents. No doubt eclipses, earth-quakes, meteorites and other natural phenomenon were regarded as part of the way in which strange socio-political events announced themselves" (*NTPG* 285). I agree, although "sometimes" leaves a false impression; and Wright's admission does not obviously fall in line with his metaphor-ical treatment of Mark 13.

[20] The distance between ancient and modern conceptions of stars also comes to mind while reading Wright's nonliteral interpretation of the *Testament of Moses* 10:1-10 (*NTPG* 304-6). When one reckons with the prevalence of belief in literal astral immortality among ancients, including Jews, much is to be said for the possibility that looking down from the heights upon the earth should be taken at face value.

[21] Dale C. Allison Jr., *The End of the Ages Has Come: An Early Interpretation of the Passion and Resurrec-tion of Jesus* (Philadelphia: Fortress, 1985), p. 89; cf. *4 Ezra* 3:18-19 and *b. Zebaḥim* 116a.

[22] "On the morning of the third day there was thunder and lightning, as well as a thick cloud on the mountain, and a blast of a trumpet so loud that all the people who were in the camp trembled . . . Now Mount Sinai was wrapped in smoke, because the LORD had descended upon it in fire; the smoke went up like the smoke of a kiln, while the whole mountain shook violently."

[23] I quote from the edition of Carl R. Holladay, *Fragments from Hellenistic Jewish Authors, Volume III: Aristobulus,* Texts and Translations 39/PS 13 (Atlanta: Scholars Press, 1995), pp. 142-47.

[24] Compare the variant of this passage of Aristobulus preserved by Clement of Alexandria *Stromateis* 63.32.

[25] Although I cannot discuss the issue here, I also recant my earlier assumption that the similar accounts of the giving of the law in *4 Ezra* 3:18-19 and *b Zebaḥim* 116a should be given nonliteral interpretations. I am now unsure.

[26] See on this Peder Borgen, *Philo of Alexandria: An Exegete for His Time,* Supplement to Novum Tes-tamentum 86 (Leiden: Brill, 1997), pp. 262-64.

[27] Philo also took the prophecy of the return of the lost tribes quite literally (*De Praemiis et Poenis*

164ff.).

[28] Wright does not discuss 1 Thessalonians 4:13-18 when interpreting Mark 13. One expects that the passage will be treated in a later volume.

[29] For example, John Lightfoot, *Horae Hebraicae et Talmudicae* (Oxford: Oxford University Press, 1859), 3:442-43. R. T. France argues that Mark 13:1-31 is about the destruction of Jerusalem within Jesus' generation while Mark 13:32ff. is about the second coming and last judgment (*Jesus and the Old Testament* [London: Tyndale, 1971], pp. 227-39).

[30] See Lars Hartman, *Prophecy Interpreted: The Formation of Some Jewish Apocalyptic Texts and of the Eschatological Discourse Mark 13 Par.* Coniectanea Biblica Neotestamentica 1 (Uppsala: Gleerup, 1966).

[31] See further Maurice Casey, *Son of Man: The Interpretation and Influence of Daniel 7* (London: SPCK, 1979) 172-77.

[32] See Allan J McNicol, *Jesus' Directions for the Future: A Source and Redaction-History Study of the Use of the Eschatological Traditions in Paul and in the Synoptic Accounts of Jesus' Last Eschatological Discourse*, New Gospel Studies 9 (Macon, Ga.: Mercer, 1996).

[33] "The day of the Lord will come like a thief," and it is the day in which the heavens will be kindled and dissolved.

[34] Those who are not ready for Jesus' coming like a thief are contrasted with those who will wear white robes and be found in the book of life when Jesus confesses them before his Father and the angels.

[35] I here presuppose the two-source theory.

[36] It would be tendentious to hold that the coming in Matthew 24:36ff is different from the coming in 24:30. Moreover, although I cannot argue the point here, it seems to me that Matthew's formulation in 24:3 ("when will this be, and what will be the sign of your coming and of the end of the age?") as well as the material Matthew added to Mark 13 (e.g., Mt 24:25) shows us that the First Evangelist read Jesus' eschatological discourse as having to do primarily with the last things and only secondarily with the destruction of Jerusalem and its temple.

[37] This is strongly suggested by *NTPG* 285: if Jews and early Christians were deceived in their eschatological expectations, then "we know that they were crucially wrong about something they put at the centre of their worldview, and must therefore either abandon any attempt to take them seriously or must construct a hermeneutic which will somehow enable us to salvage something from the wreckage." But in *JVG* (342) Wright seemingly denies that his reading is apologetically grounded.

[38] See Robert W. Balch, John Domitrovich, Barbara Lynn Mahnke and Vanessa Morrison, "Fifteen Years of Failed Prophecy: Coping with Cognitive Dissonance in a Baha'i Sect," in *Millennium, Messiahs and Mayhem: Contemporary Apocalyptic Movements*, ed. Thomas Robbins and Susan J. Palmer (New York and London: Routledge, 1997), pp. 78-79.

[39] We should grant him this, because he insists that apocalyptic language has a concrete (if not literal) referent. For example, the coming of the Son of Man on the clouds refers to a concrete event (Jerusalem's fall) but is not to be understood literally.

[40] E Zürcher, " 'Prince Moonlight': Messianism and Eschatology in Early Medieval Chinese Buddhism," *T'oung Pao* 68 (1982): 1-59.

[41] James Mooney, *The Ghost Dance: Religion and the Sioux Outbreak of 1890*, ed. Anthony F. Wallace (Chicago: University of Chicago Press, 1965).

[42] Peter Worsley, *The Trumpet Shall Sound: A Study of "Cargo" Cults in Melanesia*, new, aug. ed. (New York: Schocken, 1968), p. 154.

[43] Lawrence Sullivan, *Icanchu's Drum: An Orientation to Meaning in South American Religions* (New York: Macmillan, 1988), p. 675. For illustrations from South America, see pp. 560, 562-63.

[44] Wright does not tell us what he thinks of these texts. Note that 1QH 11(3):29-32 teaches the same thing (cf. Hippolytus *Refutation of All Heresies* 27), and for related rabbinic texts see Strack-Billerbeck 3:842-47.

[45] See Caird, *Language and Imagery*, pp. 256-57.

[46] For example, *1 Enoch* 1-16; *Liber Antiquitatum Biblicarum* 3:9-10; *LAE* 49:3; *2 Peter* 3:6-7; *2 Enoch* 70:10.

[47]Wright would no doubt agree; he speaks of the consummation as the final outworking of the Christ event. But I would claim that more texts have to do with this consummation than he thinks (e.g., Mk 13) and that the New Testament's note of fulfillment is distorted when removed from what has traditionally been understood by the word *Naherwartung*.

Chapter 8: Victory over Violence

[1]See Robert W. Funk, R. W. Hoover and the Jesus Seminar, *The Five Gospels: The Search for the Authentic Words of Jesus* (New York: Macmillan, 1993). For Wright's incisive account of recent Jesus research, see *JVG* 28-82.

[2]Readers acquainted with my analysis of New Testament ethics in Richard B. Hays, *The Moral Vision of the New Testament: Community, Cross, New Creation* (San Francisco: HarperSanFrancisco, 1996) will recognize immediately the affinity between Wright's approach and mine.

[3]For example, in Josephus *Jewish Wars* 2.411-16, the Pharisees join with the chief priests in expressing indignation against Eleazar and his supporters for "provoking the arms of the Romans and courting war with them"; they try to persuade Eleazar's partisans to allow the Romans to offer sacrifice in the temple.

[4]See, e.g., Richard B. Hays, *Echoes of Scripture in the Letters of Paul* (New Haven, Conn., and London: Yale University Press, 1989).

[5]Hays, *Moral Vision*, pp. 407-43.

[6]Ibid., p. 167.

[7]Ibid., pp. 298-306.

Chapter 9: Reality, Symbol & History

[1]Alister E. McGrath, *Iustitia Dei: A History of the Christian Doctrine of Justification*. 2 vols. (Cambridge: Cambridge University Press, 1986); McGrath, "Justification," in *Dictionary of Paul and His Letters*, ed. Gerald F. Hawthorne, Ralph P. Martin and Daniel G. Reid (Downers Grove, Ill.: InterVarsity Press, 1993), pp. 517-23.

[2]George M. Marsden, *Reforming Fundamentalism: Fuller Seminary and the New Evangelicalism* (Grand Rapids, Mich.: Eerdmans, 1987); Alister E. McGrath, *Evangelicalism and the Future of Christianity* (Downers Grove, Ill.: InterVarsity Press, 1995); McGrath, *A Passion for Truth: The Intellectual Coherence of Evangelicalism* (Downers Grove, Ill.: InterVarsity Press, 1996).

[3]Mark Noll, *The Scandal of the Evangelical Mind* (Grand Rapids, Mich: Eerdmans, 1994).

[4]Alister E. McGrath, *J. I. Packer: A Biography* (Grand Rapids, Mich.: Baker, 1997), pp. 248-55.

[5]See Anthony C. Thiselton, *Interpreting God and the Postmodern Self: On Meaning, Manipulation and Power* (Edinburgh: T & T Clark, 1995); Rowan Williams, " 'Religious Realism': On Not Quite Agreeing with Don Cupitt," *Modern Theology* 1 (1994): 3-24.

[6]Don Cupitt, *Only Human* (London: SCM Press, 1985), p. 9.

[7]William P. Alston, *A Realist Conception of Truth* (Ithaca, N.Y.: Cornell University Press, 1996).

[8]Mark P. Achtemeier, "The Truth of Tradition: Critical Realism in the Thought of Alasdair MacIntyre and T. F. Torrance," *Scottish Journal of Theology* 47 (1994): 355-374; John D. Morrison, "Heidegger, Correspondence Truth and the Realist Theology of Thomas Forsyth Torrance," *Evangelical Quarterly* 59 (1997): 139-55; Thomas F. Torrance, *Reality and Scientific Theology: Theology and Science at the Frontiers of Knowledge* (Edinburgh: Scottish Academic Press, 1985); Torrance, "Realism and Openness in Scientific Inquiry," *Zygon* 23 (1988): 159-69.

[9]John Milbank, *Theology and Social Theory: Beyond Secular Reason* (Oxford: Blackwell, 1993).

[10]Ian G. Barbour, *Myths, Models and Paradigms: A Comparative Study in Science and Religion* (New York: Harper & Row, 1974), pp. 29-70.

[11]Wentzel van Huyssteen, *Theology and the Justification of Faith: Constructing Theories in Systematic Theology* (Grand Rapids, Mich: Eerdmans, 1989), pp. 143-97.

[12]Jonathan Bennett, *Kant's Dialectic* (Cambridge: Cambridge University Press, 1974), pp. 52-59.

[13]Michael Levin, "Realisms," *Synthese* 85 (1990): 115-38.

[14]Richard Boyd, "The Current Status of Scientific Realism," in *Scientific Realism*, ed. Jarrett Leplin

(Berkeley: University of California Press, 1984), pp. 41-82.

[15] Nicholas Rescher, *Scientific Realism: A Critical Appraisal* (Dordrecht: D. Reidel, 1987).

[16] Alasdair MacIntyre, *Whose Justice? Which Rationality?* (London: Duckworth, 1988), p. 334.

[17] Ibid., p. 6.

[18] L. Gregory Jones, "Alasdair MacIntyre on Narrative, Community and the Moral Life," *Modern Theology* 4 (1987): 53-69.

[19] Brad J. Kellenberg, "Unstuck from Yale: Theological Method After Lindbeck," *Scottish Journal of Theology* 50 (1997): 191-218; Alister E. McGrath, "An Evangelical Evaluation of Postliberalism," in *The Nature of Confession: Evangelicals and Postliberals in Conversation*, ed. T. R. Philips and D. L. Okholm (Downers Grove, Ill.: InterVarsity Press, 1996), pp. 23-44; Miroslav Volf, "Theology, Meaning and Power: A Conversation with George Lindbeck on Theology and the Nature of Christian Difference," in *The Nature of Confession: Evangelicals and Postliberals in Conversation*, ed. T. R. Philips and D. L. Okholm (Downers Grove, Ill.: InterVarsity Press, 1996), pp. 45-66.

[20] Torrance, *Reality and Scientific Theology*, pp. 98-130.

[21] Milbank, *Theology and Social Theory*, p. 389.

[22] N. T. Wright, *The Climax of the Covenant: Christ and the Law in Pauline Theology* (Edinburgh: T & T Clark, 1991).

[23] Ibid., p. 151.

[24] Ibid., p. 147.

[25] Ibid., p. 141.

[26] Ibid., pp. 150-51.

[27] See, for example, Robert H. Gundry, "Grace, Works and Staying Saved in Paul," *Biblica* 66 (1985): 1-38.

[28] Wright, *Climax of the Covenant*, 144-45.

[29] Ibid., p. 150.

[30] E. P. Sanders, *Paul and Palestinian Judaism: A Comparison of Patterns of Religion* (Philadelphia: Fortress Press, 1977).

[31] Wayne Grudem, *Systematic Theology: An Introduction to Biblical Doctrine* (Grand Rapids, Mich: Zondervan, 1994), pp. 730-31.

[32] Wright, *Climax of the Covenant*, p. 156.

[33] Carl Andersen and Gunter Klein, eds., *Theologia crucis, Signum crucis: Festschrift für Erich Dinkler* (Tübingen: Mohr-Siebeck, 1979); Erich Dinkler, *Im Zeichen des Kreuzes: Aufsätze* (Berlin: de Gruyter, 1992).

[34] Wright, *Climax of the Covenant*, p. 138.

Chapter 10: Methodological Naturalism in Historical Biblical Scholarship

[1] For a succinct characterization of Ernst Troeltsch's type of view, see his essay "Historiography," in *Encyclopedia of Religion and Ethics*, ed. James Hastings (New York: Charles Scribner's Sons, 1922). F. H. Bradley's views can be found in his book *The Presuppositions of Critical History* (1874; reprint, ed. Lionel Rubinoff, Chicago: Quadrangle Books, 1968). Van A. Harvey's development and articulation of a Troeltschian view is found in his book *Historian and the Believer: The Morality of Historical Knowledge and Christian Belief* (1966; reprint, with a new introduction, Urbana: University of Illinois Press, 1996). All quotations from Harvey will be taken from this edition.

[2] See, for example, Harvey, *Historian and the Believer*, p. 5: "The problem was not, as many theologians then believed, that the biblical critics emerged from their libraries with results disturbing to believers, but that the method itself, which led to those results, was based on assumptions quite irreconcilable with traditional belief."

[3] Ibid., pp. 186-87.

[4] For more on all of these principles, along with detailed criticisms, see chapter eight of C. Stephen Evans, *The Historical Christ and the Jesus of Faith* (Oxford: Oxford University Press, 1996).

[5] This is because "a positive judgment that a miracle has taken place is always a philosophical or theological judgment. Of its nature it goes beyond any judgment that a historian operating precisely as a historian can make" (John P. Meier, *A Marginal Jew: Rethinking the Historical Jesus*, 2 vols. [New

York: Doubleday, 1991-1994], 2:514).

[6]Meier, *Marginal Jew*, 1:1-2.

[7]Luke Timothy Johnson, *Journal of Biblical Literature* 117 (1998): 169.

[8]See W. V. Quine and J. S. Ullian, *The Web of Belief*, 2d ed. (New York: Random House, 1978).

[9]It is worth noting here that Wright, correctly in my opinion, does not see such an epistemology as leading to an "antirealist" or purely pragmatist view of truth; rather he assumes that the holistic dimension of theory confirmation is consistent with a "critical realist" position in which it is possible for us to make progress toward a true understanding of the way things really are.

[10]Thomas Aquinas, *Summa Contra Gentiles* I6.4, trans. Anton C. Pegis (Garden City, N.Y.: Doubleday, 1955), p. 73.

[11]For a fuller discussion of this question, see chapter seven of Evans, *Historical Christ*.

[12]See John Dominic Crossan, *The Historical Jesus: The Life of a Mediterranean Jewish Peasant* (San Francisco: HarperSanFrancisco, 1991), pp. 305-10.

[13]See chapter seven of Evans, *Historical Christ*, for arguments for this claim.

Chapter 11: A Historiographical Response to Wright's Jesus

[1]N. T. Wright, *What Saint Paul Really Said: Was Paul of Tarsus the Real Founder of Christianity?* (Grand Rapids, Mich: Eerdmans, 1997).

[2]J. P. Meier, *A Marginal Jew: Rethinking the Historical Jesus*, 2 vols. (New York: Doubleday, 1991-1994); Wright's index lists only six references to Meier's massive project (*JVG* 55, 84, 147, 395, 615, 631).

[3]B. F. Meyer, *The Aims of Jesus* (London: SCM Press, 1979).

[4]A. Schweitzer, *The Quest of the Historical Jesus: A Critical Study of Its Progress from Reimarus to Wrede* (1906; London: A & C Black, 1954); Schweitzer, *The Mystery of the Kingdom of God* (1901; London: A & C Black, 1925).

[5]Especially E. P. Sanders, *Jesus and Judaism* (Philadelphia: Fortress, 1985), and Sanders, *The Historical Figure of Jesus* (London: Penguin, 1993).

[6]See R. W. Funk, *Honest to Jesus: Jesus for a New Millennium* (San Francisco: HarperSanFrancisco, 1996), pp. 181-89.

[7]For my discussion of these points, see Luke Timothy Johnson, *The Real Jesus: The Misguided Quest for the Historical Jesus and the Truth of the Traditional Gospels* (San Francisco: HarperSanFrancisco, 1996), pp. 1-58.

[8]Ibid., pp. 81-104.

[9]Johnson, *Journal of Biblical Literature* 113 (1994): 536-38.

[10]David Hackett Fischer, *Historians' Fallacies: Toward a Logic of Historical Thought* (New York: Harper & Row, 1970).

[11]See ibid., p. 87, for more on the aesthetic fallacy; see ibid., p. 104, for more on the fallacy of statistical sampling. It is amusing, apropos the Jesus Seminar, to note that in 1970 Fischer parodies the "fallacy of prevalent proof" by imagining a group of scholars settling a historical problem by "resorting to a vote" (ibid., p. 52)!

[12]See ibid., pp. 276-77, for more on black-and-white fallacy; see ibid., pp. 9-12, for more on the fallacy of the false dichotomy.

[13]See ibid., pp. 49-51, for the "fallacy of circular proof."

[14]See Rudolf Bultmann, "History of Salvation and History," in *Existence and Faith: Shorter Writings of Rudolf Bultmann*, ed. S. M. Ogden (Cleveland: World Publishing, 1960), pp. 226-40.

[15]See Fischer, *Historians' Fallacies*, p. 265.

[16]Ibid., pp. 201-3.

[17]Jacob Neusner, *From Politics to Piety* (Englewood Cliffs, N.J.: Prentice-Hall, 1973).

[18]Our sources here are mishnaic and talmudic, and the disputes they describe are halachic rather than political or eschatological.

[19]Fischer, *Historians' Fallacies*, pp. 209-13.

[20]Ibid., p. 287.

[21]Wayne A. Meeks, *The Prophet-King: Moses Traditions and the Johannine Christology,* Supplement to Novum Testamentum 14 (Leiden: Brill, 1967).

[22]For discussion and bibliography, see Luke Timothy Johnson, "Luke-Acts," *The Anchor Bible Dictionary,* ed D. N. Freedman (New York: Doubleday, 1992), 4:403-420.

[23]See Luke Timothy Johnson, "Which Paul?" *First Things* 80 (1998): 58-60.

[24]Wright speaks of Jesus' "regarding" his ministry as in some way unique (*JVG* 163) and as in continuity with the great prophets (*JVG* 167). Jesus "envisaged his own work," and he "really did believe" he was inaugurating the kingdom (*JVG* 197). Jesus "expects" a great event within a generation or two (*JVG* 207). "Jesus' understanding of his own vocation belonged closely with an implicit understanding of his own self" (*JVG* 222). Jesus "regarded himself" as Messiah (*JVG* 489), and so forth.

Chapter 12: An Appreciative Disagreement

[1]Marcus J. Borg and N. T. Wright, *The Meaning of Jesus: Two Visions* (San Francisco: HarperSanFrancisco, 1999). Eight topics are treated in chapters written by each of us: method, public activity, death, resurrection, Christology, birth, second coming and the meaning of Jesus for Christians today.

[2]John Dominic Crossan, *Who Killed Jesus?* (San Francisco: HarperSanFrancisco, 1995).

[3]Wright argues that " 'you will see the Son of man seated at the right hand of the Power,' and 'coming with the clouds of heaven'" in Mark 14:62 does not refer to the second coming but to Jesus' vindication by God (*JVG* 642-44). Here I agree with a number of the contributors to this volume: I think this language in the total context of Mark (especially 13:24-30) is more plausibly understood as a reference to the second coming. However, I do not think it goes back to Jesus. I do not think Jesus spoke of his own second coming but that the community after Easter did.

[4]See chapter eight of Borg and Wright, *Meaning of Jesus.*

[5]See ibid., pp. 81-82, 146-47.

[6]See ibid., pp. 137-42.

[7]N. T. Wright, *The Climax of the Covenant: Christ and the Law in Pauline Theology* (Minneapolis: Fortress, 1992).

[8]E. P. Sanders, *Jesus and Judaism* (Philadelphia: Fortress, 1985); Sanders, *The Historical Figure of Jesus* (London: Penguin, 1993); Dale C. Allison Jr., *Jesus of Nazareth: Millenarian Prophet* (Minneapolis: Fortress, 1998). See also Bart Ehrman, *Jesus: Apocalyptic Prophet of the New Age* (New York: Oxford University Press, 1999).

[9]For a compact treatment of how I see these matters, see Borg and Wright, *Meaning of Jesus,* pp. 130-35.

[10]1 Cor 15:44-46. See Borg and Wright, *Meaning of Jesus,* p. 120.

Chapter 13: In Grateful Dialogue

[1]Ernst Käsemann, *Perspectives on Paul* (London: SCM Press, 1971), p. 60.

[2]Luke Timothy Johnson's attempt to say that my Jesus is more "simple" than the Synoptics' "more complex" one and that therefore I simply invented a "Jesus" out of thin air, claiming that the Synoptists got it wrong, is all the more bizarre when coupled with his concluding statement that I have merely developed "one of the aspects of the theology of the Synoptic tradition." When I study Jesus' motivation and aims, in particular, I am precisely not attributing to Jesus things I do not find in the Synoptic tradition; I am elucidating, in their first-century context (as opposed, often enough, to oversimplified devotional or scholarly ones), the things that I do find there. I suppose I should be glad that someone found my 662-page treatment of Jesus "simple." That is not what most people have said.

[3]See also Dale C. Allison Jr., *Jesus of Nazareth: Millenarian Prophet* (Minneapolis: Fortress, 1998), pp. 167-69. I shall return to the substantive issue below.

[4]Marcus J. Borg and N. T. Wright, *The Meaning of Jesus: Two Visions* (San Francisco: HarperSanFrancisco, 1999), pp. 15-27. I am amused, by the way, by Stephen Evans's speculations about what might be helpful for me to think "as a clergyman." I wonder how many Episcopal priests he actually

knows?

[5]P. L. Gardiner, "History, History of the Philosophy Of," in *The Oxford Companion to Philosophy*, ed. Ted Honderich (Oxford: Oxford University Press, 1995), p. 363. R. G. Collingwood's classic exposition was *The Idea of History* (Oxford: Oxford University Press, 1946).

[6]See, above all, Ben F. Meyer, *The Aims of Jesus* (London: SCM Press, 1979); also Meyer, *Critical Realism and the New Testament*, Princeton Theological Monograph Series 17 (Allison Park, Penn.: Pickwick, 1989), and Meyer, *Reality and Illusion in New Testament Scholarship* (Collegeville, Minn.: The Liturgical Press, 1994). Compared with these works, much New Testament scholarship remains philosophically naive.

[7]An obvious example would be the meaning of repentance: see *JVG* 246-58.

[8]T. O'Loughlin, *Saint Patrick: The Man and His Works* (London: Triangle, 1999), p. 4-5.

[9]For an explanation of why I use lower case for "god," see *NTPG* xiv-xv.

[10]Martin Goodman, *The Ruling Class of Judea: The Origins of the Jewish Revolt Against Rome, A.D. 66-70* (Cambridge: Cambridge University Press, 1987). See *NTPG* 178-79. My reservations about Goodman's overall thesis do not mean that we should completely discount such involvement.

[11]See details in *NTPG* 181-203, esp. pp. 189-96.

[12]Josephus *Jewish Wars* 6.312-15. See the full discussion of this passage, and of the reasons why (against Craig A. Evans [p. 94 in the present volume] and others) it is unlikely to be referring to Numbers 24:17-19, in *NTPG* 312-14. On calendrical calculations by different Jews of the period, see R. T. Beckwith, *Calendar and Chronology, Jewish and Christian: Biblical, Intertestamental and Patristic Studies*, Arbeiten zur Geschichte des antiken Judentums und des Urchristentums 33 (Leiden: Brill, 1996).

[13]Daniel 9:2; cf. Jeremiah 25:11-12; 29:10; 2 Chronicles 36:21; Ezra 1:1.

[14]Ezra 9:6-9; Nehemiah 9:36-37.

[15]Compare, e.g., the historical/eschatological scheme in 4QMMT, section C, where Deuteronomy 30 provides the basis for a reading of Scripture in which the monarchy under David and Solomon represented the original blessing, the exile following Zedekiah represented the curse (which was continuing to the time of writing) and the blessing following the curse was expected imminently. The curse of Deuteronomy 30 was, of course, exile (Deut 28:36, 49-68; 29:21-28; summed up in 30:4); and the blessing that followed the curse was therefore return from exile (Deut 30:5).

[16]I first stated this, with a fair amount of accompanying annotation, in *NTPG* 268-72. I amplified it in *JVG* xvii-xviii (not noticed in Craig Evans's list), and I developed it throughout that volume, not least, e.g., pp. 126-27, 203-4, 248-50. Much fuller discussions are found in various readily available secondary sources, to which I (and Evans) refer, notably James M. Scott, ed., *Exile: Old Testament, Jewish and Christian Conceptions*, Journal for the Study of Judaism in the Persian, Hellenistic and Roman Period Supplement Series 56 (Leiden: Brill, 1997).

[17]Richard B. Hays, *First Corinthians*, Interpretation (Louisville, Ky.: Westminster John Knox, 1997). See too Hays, "The Conversion of the Imagination: Scripture and Eschatology in 1 Corinthians," *New Testament Studies* (forthcoming).

[18]See Darrell L Bock, p. 309 n. 13. The fact that Bock can ask the questions the way he does shows that he still has not understood what I am saying—the fault for which, presumably, still lies with me. However, to argue from what we now know has and has not happened in fulfillment of prophecy, back to what Second Temple Jews, and Jesus among them, believed was happening in their own days, is straightforwardly illegitimate.

[19]As is rightly seen by Paul R. Eddy, p. 45, with helpful notes.

[20]On double similarity and dissimilarity see *JVG* 131-33. I am glad that several essayists saw the point and approved of it.

[21]Bock rightly questions the view of some—that my proposal is "a denial of eschatology or apocalyptic" (p. 119). Allison, though normally careful in his usage, reveals where the problem lies when he says that 2 Peter 3 and Revelation 3 give the simile of the thief in the night "an eschatological sense"— meaning an "end-of-the-world" sense, which I am taken to deny. Craig Evans does something similar (p. 98) when he contrasts "eschatological judgment" with "temporal destruction and exile."

[22]This discussion relates, too, to the debate between myself and John Dominic Crossan in *Scottish Journal of Theology* 50 (1997), some small parts of which I here repeat; it also relates to the debate between myself and Borg (see Borg and Wright, *Meaning of Jesus*).

[23]The word *concrete* is interesting in itself. We today may think of it as referring literally to the compound regularly used in building and so on; hence, we may think of it as referring metaphorically, as in the last sentence, to solid physical entities as opposed to abstract ones. But its original meaning, from the Latin *concrescere*, had to do with the putting together of solids, so that the meaning "physical, nonabstract" is the more literal meaning and the meaning "the substance used in building" the more metaphorical.

[24]Note this revealing sentence: "The darkness is richly symbolic, but presumably Mark nonetheless thought it historical, not metaphorical" (p. 132). Likewise "that in itself does not imply those signs are metaphors as opposed to literal events that are symbolic" (p. 132). Allison has, it seems, taken fright at the word *metaphor*, perhaps because of (what seems to me) its misuse in some other current scholarship, a misuse I have been careful to avoid. I fully share his insistence, which, in more accurate terminology, is that *concrete* events can carry *spiritual* meaning—a meaning that can then be brought out by referring to them through *metaphor*. The question is: which sentences refer to which concrete events? And how do we decide when a stock expression is intended literally and when it is intended metaphorically? At this point mere assertion will not do. On p. 312 n. 39, Allison suddenly notes the distinction between *literal* and *concrete*, but he has not allowed it to penetrate the rest of the discussion.

[25]Allison (pp. 135-36) seems to think that *metaphor* and *spiritualization* are closely allied. There are, sadly, some colleagues in the discipline who perpetuate this muddle, but I plead not guilty to the charge.

[26]See, too, Borg and Wright, *Meaning of Jesus*, chap. 14.

[27]For example, Blomberg, p. 33.

[28]Allison's argument on pp. 134-35 is remarkably specious: (a) Jewish apocalyptic is about the last judgment, (b) Mark 13 is like Jewish apocalyptic, therefore (c) Mark 13 is about the last judgment; but (d) the last judgment hasn't happened yet, therefore (e) the events referred to in Mark 13 haven't happened yet. One could prove anything with logic like this. Blomberg (p. 33) suggests that I simply assert, rather than argue, that Mark 13 is all about the fall of Jerusalem, citing *JVG* 346 n. 105; but that statement was merely proleptic. The argument is provided in the detail of the twenty pages that follow. Conservative apologists wishing to retain a "second coming" reading of Mark 13 must face this embarrassing question: why did Mark get it wrong in 13:1-23?

[29]Dale C. Allison, *The End of the Ages Has Come: An Early Interpretation of the Passion and Resurrection of Jesus* (Philadelphia: Fortress, 1985).

[30]This is an aside in response to Johnson.

[31]I cannot see, however, that this has anything to do with the (to me) rather strange sequence of events that Blomberg offers under the rubric of "the option that seems most likely to reflect prevailing Jewish beliefs" (p. 28). One reason why I do not address his "option" is because it is nowhere even mentioned in the Gospels or, so far as I can see, in the Jewish texts. Blomberg's suggestion that "the parousia" is hinted at in Jewish literature (p. 32) seems to me very strange, taking the phrase to mean what he clearly intends; where in Jewish literature do we find any notion of a messiah going to heaven and returning to earth?

[32]Klyne Snodgrass is generously anxious to credit me with believing that Jesus spoke of the ultimate future, though I am not sure that my discussion of the parable of the Good Samaritan (*JVG* 304-7) proves the point. Nor do I think that "a good deal of Jesus' message focuses on *end* judgment" (p. 63, emphasis original) except in the sense that from Jesus' point of view Calvary, Easter and 70 C.E. are all "end judgment." I do think that passages like Matthew 22:29-32/Mark 12:24-27/Luke 20:34-38 speak of the ultimate future; Matthew 19:28 does too (though it would be a bold critic who built anything solid about Jesus' own view on that text); and a line runs across from Matthew 19:28, of course, to Matthew 25:31, which, by introducing the climactic section of that chapter, could be thought to imply the same meaning for the earlier sections as well, not to mention for the

previous chapter. Once again we are in the familiar critical cleft stick. Were I to build anything on this foundation, I would be mocked by some for reading Matthew's theology back into the mind of Jesus. Were I to omit it (which I admit I all but did in *JVG*), I would be castigated for thinking that Jesus could have meant something other than Matthew meant.

[33]Compare esp. *JVG* 524-25. I did not there stress the resurrection as one aspect of Jesus' expected vindication, partly because the texts I was discussing did not refer to it directly; but I did stress that his expectation of vindication "included"—that is, was not exhausted by—what we with hindsight think of as the events of 70 C.E. In the light of several of the essays, I now want to stress that I include Jesus' resurrection as the chief among the "vindicating" events. It was seen thus by the early church.

[34]This is my answer to the careful questioning of Eddy (pp. 59-60). The "not yet" aspects of Jesus' own vision are not entirely fulfilled by the events of Calvary, Easter and 70 C.E.; and yet from Jesus' point of view the entire fulfillment must have appeared in a more or less undifferentiated future. Or are we to credit Jesus with preternatural knowledge on the one subject about which he confessed ignorance?

[35]Colossians 1:24; 2:14-15.

[36]So Eddy, p. 47; Allison, pp. 140-41; Hays, p. 155.

[37]This (the conviction of the early church) was what I was reporting at *JVG* 322. The early church knew as well as we do that in another sense that "victory remains agonizingly incomplete" (Allison, p. 141). Romans 8:31-39 holds the two in typical tension—a tension that contemporary interpreters seem all too unwilling even to acknowledge, let alone grapple with.

[38]N. T. Wright, *The Lord and His Prayer* (London: SPCK; Grand Rapids, Mich.: Eerdmans, 1996). This and my other books of edited sermons from the same publishers (*Following Jesus* [1994]; *The Crown and the Fire* [1995]; *For All God's Worth* [1997]; *The Way of the Lord* [1999]), together with my new book, *The Millennium Myth* (Louisville, Ky.: Westminster John Knox; London: SPCK, 1999), all address Hays's proper question about the way in which my realized (I would prefer "inaugurated") eschatology enhances the internal tension of the theodicy question.

[39]This is in partial response to the worthwhile questions of Eddy, pp. 46, 52.

[40]Similar comments could be made about Snodgrass's questioning of my analysis of Jesus' challenge to repentance. It is not the case that national zeal was, as it were, a particular sort of sin to which Jesus was especially opposed; it summed up for him Israel's failure to be the light of the world.

[41]Blomberg, pp. 35-36, is a notable exception here.

[42]See particularly Wright, *Crown and the Fire*, chap. 1.

Chapter 14: From (Wright's) Jesus to (the Church's) Christ

[1]Parts of this essay first appeared in the paper "The Son of Man: Messiah or Lord?" delivered at the Trinity Summit, Dunwoodie, New York, Easter 1998.

[2]See Thomas F. Torrance, *The Trinitarian Faith: The Evangelical Theology of the Ancient Catholic Church* (Edinburgh: T & T Clark, 1988). Obviously, this statement is currently under assault by those who belong to the "re-newed, new Quest" (to use N. T. Wright's categories). Jesus is imaged as a noneschatological, non-Jewish Hellenistic wisdom teacher. The church's divinization of Jesus was only one, and a most unfortunate one at that, way of construing the tradition about Jesus (see below). Seen in this light, Wright's proposal is either quite radical or a bit old-fashioned—or both.

[3]The evidence for the divinity of Jesus should not be limited to the use of *theos* as a way to refer to Jesus, although that evidence is significant (on which see Murray J. Harris, *Jesus as God: The New Testament Use of* Theos *in Reference to Jesus* [Grand Rapids, Mich.: Eerdmans, 1992]). For a full listing of the evidence and discussion, see Richard Bauckham, "Jesus, Worship of," *Anchor Bible Dictionary*, ed. David Noel Freedman, 6 vols. (New York: Doubleday, 1992), 3:812-19.

[4]Romans 8:11; 15:15-16, 30-32; 1 Corinthians 8:4-6; 12:4-6; 2 Corinthians 1:21-22; 13:13; Galatians 4:6; Ephesians 4:4-6 So, e.g., A. W. Wainwright, *Trinity and the New Testament* (London: SPCK, 1963). To argue in this fashion is to cast your lot with those who think orthodoxy preceded

heresy (and not the other way round). See Arland J. Hultgren, *The Rise of Normative Christianity* (Minneapolis: Fortress, 1994).

[5]For the evidence, see Larry W. Hurtado, "The Binitarian Shape of Early Christian Worship," in *The Jewish Roots of Christological Monotheism: Papers from the St. Andrews Conference on the Historical Origins of the Veneration of Jesus*, ed. Carey C. Newman et al., Journal for the Study of Judaism in the Persian, Hellenistic and Roman Period Supplement Series (Leiden: Brill, 1999).

[6]J. C. O'Neill, *Who Did Jesus Think He Was?* (Leiden: Brill, 1995).

[7]Margaret Barker, *The Great Angel: A Study of Israel's Second God* (London: SPCK, 1992).

[8]Margaret Barker, "The High Priest," in *The Jewish Roots of Christological Monotheism: Papers from the St. Andrews Conference on the Historical Origins of the Veneration of Jesus*, ed. Carey C. Newman et al., Journal for the Study of Judaism in the Persian, Hellenistic and Roman Period Supplement Series (Leiden: Brill, 1999).

[9]Martin Hengel, "The Song About Christ in Earliest Worship," in *Studies in Early Christology* (Edinburgh: T & T Clark, 1995), pp. 227-91.

[10]Larry W. Hurtado, *One God, One Lord: Early Christian Devotion and Ancient Jewish Monotheism*, 2d ed. (Edinburgh: T & T Clark, 1999), pp. 114-24.

[11]James D. G. Dunn, *The Partings of the Ways: Between Christianity and Judaism and Their Significance for the Character of Christianity* (London: SCM Press, 1991).

[12]P. M. Casey, *From Jewish Prophet to Gentile God: The Origins and Development of New Testament Christology* (Louisville, Ky.: Westminster John Knox, 1991). See also Paula Fredriksen, *From Jesus to Christ: The Origins of the New Testament Images of Jesus* (New Haven, Conn.: Yale University Press, 1988). The positions of Casey and Fredriksen owe themselves ultimately to Wilhelm Bousset, *Kyrios Christos* (1913; Nashville: Abingdon, 1970). See *JVG* 118.

[13]James M. Robinson and Helmut Koester, *Trajectories Through Early Christianity* (Philadelphia: Fortress, 1971).

[14]Nils A. Dahl, "The Crucified Messiah," in *Jesus the Christ*, ed. D. Juel (Minneapolis: Fortress, 1991), pp. 27-47.